GATEWAY TO THE GREAT BOOKS

GATEWAY
TO THE
GREAT BOOKS

Gateway
to the
Great Books

ROBERT M. HUTCHINS, MORTIMER J. ADLER
Editors in Chief

CLIFTON FADIMAN
Associate Editor

---

1 12873

INTRODUCTION

SYNTOPICAL GUIDE

Encyclopædia Britannica, Inc.

WILLIAM BENTON
Publisher

Chicago, London, Toronto, Geneva, Sydney, Tokyo, Manila

Note on Texts and Text Illustrations

The spelling and punctuation of certain texts in this set have
been changed in accordance with modern British and American usage.
Translations and transliterations added by the editors
are enclosed in brackets.
Text illustrations in Volumes 8 and 9 have been revised
and adapted to show modern equipment.

Portraits of authors in Volumes 2 through 10
are by Fred Steffen of Chicago

Contents
of Volume 1

A Letter
to the Reader

Dear Reader:

The offerings we present to you here are intended to lead you on, to fortify you, to encourage you, to seduce you into the habit of reading, and in particular into the habit of reading *Great Books of the Western World.*

A reader who has read, or is in the midst of reading, *Great Books of the Western World* will find an attractive, instructive, entertaining interlude or supplement in *Gateway to the Great Books.*

I would conclude my letter here if I did not know, from painful experience garnered over forty years, what you will be told by your well-meaning friends. The Hutchins Poll shows they will say, "Too hard," "No time," "Too dull," "What good is it?" Since Mr. Adler and I have not the slightest interest in manufacturing furniture to decorate your living room, and still less in building up your social prestige by handing you, as it were, a poor man's Harvard diploma to hang on the wall, I must trespass on your patience a little longer to expose the absurdity of the popular answers to which I have referred. Of course, I do not attribute them to you. If you were so unintelligent as to share such views, you would not be holding this book in your hand; you would not have bothered to open it. No, what I am trying to do is to protect you from the slings and arrows of your outrageous neighbors.

I think I understand your neighbors very well, though it has taken me some time to do so. (My difficulty with them is they are products

1

of the modern age; and I was brought up half a century ago.) Now
we have the Fun Society, molded and supported by Technology,
Affluence, and Advertising. The question now is not, "Are you doing
anything worthwhile, anything interesting or important?" The question is, "Are you having any fun?" With all the gadgets, the aim of
which is to provide comfort or amusement, and all the affluence that
has made it possible to buy them, and all the advertising that urges
us to do so, fun has become something bought with money, supplied
by gadgets, and endorsed by advertising. If we aren't doing something that involves these elements and meets these requirements, we
can't be having any fun.

Reading, which does not involve these elements or meet these
requirements, therefore cannot be any fun; and the sight of a person
reading must be dispiriting to a dedicated member of the Fun
Society. If the person reading appears to be enjoying himself, the
conclusion must be that he is putting on an act or that he is some sort
of vestigial remains from a soon-to-be-forgotten era. A comic book
may perhaps be forgiven him, or, in a pinch, a bad Western, though
a Western on television would obviously be more fun because it
would be less trouble.

Today two objects consume our time: work and distraction. The
same forces that have reduced the work of most men have increased
their distractions. These distractions have now got to such a point
that in addition to reorienting the culture and our attitude toward
life they have made it almost impossible for us to keep our minds on
anything for more than half an hour. The uninterrupted half hour is
a rare occurrence. But the important thing is that keeping the mind
on something for more than half an hour is an effort, and, if we are
making an effort, we are not having any fun. Fun is identified with
distraction—and the absence of any strain on the mind, or even on
the body. The popularity of spectator sports, where thousands of
people sit more or less inert and watch a few exhaust, or even kill,
themselves in gladiatorial combat, shows we are not much more
disposed to get fun from physical than from mental exertion.

It must be admitted that reading is an effort. And it seems likely
that it will be more and more of an effort, and hence more and more
unpopular, with more and more people. In 1962 the Superintendent
of Schools in New York City announced that 10,000 pupils in the
seventh grade in New York were four years or more behind in reading. This is reminiscent of a recent report to UNESCO showing that

in 65 countries the number of illiterates is increasing because the annual increase in the population in these countries exceeds the increase in the number of pupils in school. The New York figures make the news from UNESCO look even gloomier, for those figures suggest that even if pupils go to school they may not learn to read.

Perhaps I ought to tell you I am not against fun. My quarrel is not with fun but with the current conception of it and of its role among the aims of life. My quarrel with the current conception of fun involves me in a quarrel about what it means to be human, what a human society is, and what is good for—or even interesting to—a human being and a human society. I am afraid I shall also have to make a few remarks about current conceptions of education and of leisure. But I know this is a letter and not a philosophical treatise, and I shall try to make what I have to say on these topics as short, simple, and clear as the subjects will permit.

The trouble with fun is that it is boring. It is simply not possible to spend more than a certain number of hours, days, weeks, or years having fun. And when the fatigued funster looks back over what he has done, he can only sigh and recognize, too late, his stupidity.

Why is this so? Why must it be so? It is because of the kind of animals people are. It is against nature for a man to devote himself to occupations little different from those which might be enjoyed by a pig, a pigeon, or even a whale. When we read in the article on Learning in the *Encyclopædia Britannica*, "Chimpanzees make fewer mistakes in performing when they are reinforced with bananas than when reinforced with lettuce, according to the observations of O. Tinklepaugh," we say, "What of it?" We are not talking about chimpanzees but about men, who may be indifferent, at any given time, both to bananas and to lettuce. Man is distinguished from the other animals by his mind, and the infinite capacity and variety thereof. As nobody can deny fun is important to man, so nobody can expect a uniform diet of fun (or bananas, or lettuce) to satisfy him.

Recreation, play, or fun *is* important. The reduction of drudgery and the opportunity for rest and relaxation it affords are among the greatest of the blessings technology has conferred on modern man. In my lifetime, the working week has been cut by a third and the working life has been shortened at both ends by the prohibition of child labor, the prolongation of education, and the provisions for retirement. *But* the time thus set free has been transferred, with almost mathematical exactitude, to the television set. Hence Walter Reuther, the most thoughtful labor leader in the country, hinted the other day he did not like to negotiate for shorter hours. Mr. Reuther intimated that if bowling and televiewing were what the members of the United Automobile Workers were going to do with their free time, they might be better off working.

I hope I am not presuming too much when I say you want to lead a human life. Well, if you do, you have to cope with the resounding pronouncement with which Aristotle begins his *Metaphysics:* "All men by nature desire to know." Aristotle was not so foolish as to mean by this that men want to know the most recent "facts" discovered or invented by scientists or newspaper reporters or the lady next door. What Aristotle meant was that all men want to understand. Understanding is an activity of the mind, and it demands an effort of the mind.

I suppose the next question is whether the effort is worthwhile. If you carry on the kind of dialogue that Mr. Adler recommends you carry on with the authors of these books, you will find the effort will vary from author to author, from work to work. But it will be an effort all the same. Perhaps you will ask, in the contemporary lingo, whether you can have any fun in the process.

It depends on what you mean by fun. John Keats says:

> Much have I travell'd in the realms of gold,
> And many goodly states and kingdoms seen;
> Round many western islands have I been
> Which bards in fealty to Apollo hold.

> Oft of one wide expanse had I been told
> That deep-brow'd Homer ruled as his demesne:
> Yet did I never breathe its pure serene
> Till I heard Chapman speak out loud and bold.

Then Keats tells us how he felt on reading Chapman's translation of Homer.

> Then felt I like some watcher of the skies
> When a new planet swims into his ken;
> Or like stout Cortez, when with eagle eyes
> He stared at the Pacific—and all his men
> Look'd at each other with a wild surmise—
> Silent, upon a peak in Darien.

Did he have fun? Of course he did, in any respectable, human definition of the word. The greatest human fun is that of discovery. Discovery is a synonym for learning.

Discovery, or learning, may come through casual contact, through conversation, or even through television. What the discoverer discovers is the world of the person who discovers it to him. Chapman helped Keats discover the world of Homer. So the philosopher Scott Buchanan talks about learning as the discovery of possible worlds.

The disadvantage of being illiterate is that all possible worlds are closed except those which can be seen or heard. And even those worlds may not be fully intelligible, because pictures and speech are likely to be full of references to writings past and present.

The most enduring human pleasure is the discovery (and, I may add, the rediscovery) of possible worlds. It is delightful; and it is not very hard. Effort is required, but not much. As the Plan of Graded Reading shows, nothing in this set is above the capacity of a freshman or sophomore in college, and there are about fifty selections recommended for readers thirteen or fourteen years old. Here I say nothing of past epochs, of the way in which medieval school boys and the Founding Fathers of the United States used to gobble up the classics. Perhaps those days are gone forever. The Plan of Graded Reading is based upon the known and demonstrated abilities of young Americans today, with all the distractions of our time and all the insufficiencies of contemporary education upon their heads.

I hope you won't be too slavish about the Plan of Graded Reading. My advice is, reach in anywhere. If what you look at doesn't interest you, put it down and try something else. Everything in this set will interest you sooner or later. I recommend browsing as the best method of locating the possible world you want first to explore.

This recommendation is based on my own experience. I have to admit that as a boy I lived at a time so different from this one that my experience may be of no value to you. I am literally antediluvian: I lived before the Flood, the flood brought on by Technology, Affluence, and Advertising.

In those far-off days, ownership of an automobile showed you were rich, and not merely that you had a job at the time when the dealer persuaded you to sign the note. In my home town there was only one boy whose father had one. He was of a race apart. This was before radio, before television, almost before the movies, and not long after the phonograph and the telephone. (I never make a long-distance call now without looking over my shoulder to see whether somebody is watching, because I was brought up to believe it was a sinful extravagance. As the first John D. Rockefeller used to say to his children, "A two-cent stamp is enough.") We had nowhere to go and no way to get there. Cleveland, which was thirty miles away, was as inaccessible to us as the other side of the moon is today (except to the Russians). If there had been any way to get to Cleveland, and if we had been able to pay the fare, we would not have been able to pay for the amusements that Cleveland must have offered.

We had been granted the precious gift of poverty. Of course, we didn't know we were poor because everybody was in the same situation, except the boy whose father owned the automobile. Because we were poor, we had to resort to "fun" that didn't cost much.

I was fortunate: my father was a minister and a professor. There were books all over the house. Then there was the public library. Then there was the small and miscellaneous collection on a few shelves in the Men's Building of Oberlin College.

I read them all, all the books in the house, all the books in the library, all the books in the Men's Building. At least that's the way it seems to me now. Until I went into the Army at 18, I did very little but read; and one of the hardships of Army life was the difficulty of continuing to do so. As a substitute I took to memorizing long stretches of *Faust* in German on guard duty in Italy. If there had been an Un-American Activities Committee then, they would doubtless have brought me to trial as an enemy agent.

Why do I recite these poignant passages from my autobiography? I want to show that in a remote hamlet in northeastern Ohio fifty years ago it was possible, under conditions that would now be regarded as primitive, to explore Mr. Buchanan's possible worlds— and to have a marvelous time doing it.

I will not claim my method was the best, or even that I had one. I read whatever came next. I read all of G. A. Henty, all of Horatio Alger, all of Oliver Optic, all of Ralph Henry Barbour, I even read all of the Little Colonel series, which was written for girls. I read it for the same reason the climber gave for climbing Mt. Everest: it was there.

But I also read all of Mark Twain, all of Dickens, all of Scott, and all of Thackeray. My father read all the Bible to us at morning prayers. Gradually I came to have some understanding of the difference between a good book and a poor one.

I got off on this Salute to Myself by starting to talk about browsing. But this may be just a personal peculiarity, such as Ronald Firbank attributes to a character in one of his novels: " 'Well, somewhere in me, far down,' Miss Dawkins declared, 'I don't mind admitting, there's a field with cows browsing.' " Those of you who are not like Miss Dawkins and me will want to adhere more strictly to the Plan of Graded Reading.

I suppose you will have to anyway because of the lamentable circumstances of your lives. You are distracted. You have all this technology, affluence, and advertising on your hands. This means that you must make every minute count. Mr. Adler and I have tried to do a certain amount of your browsing for you.

We have also tried to spare you one rather regrettable aspect of my experience. I have to admit that I absorbed large chunks of very inferior nourishment. When the mess sergeant said to the private who kept demanding more coffee, "You like coffee, don't you?" the private replied, "Yes. That's why I'm willing to go through so much hot water to get some." Mr. Adler and I have tried to spare you the necessity of going through the hot water. In our judgment everything in this set is worth consuming. In the world of the Little Colonel series, all about that dear little girl and her Old Kentucky Home, there was not much coffee—and far too much sugar—to the gallon.

This leads me to tell you one thing about reading that editors don't usually admit, at least not in public. Reading can be boring. Why did I abandon the likes of Horatio Alger and Oliver Optic? Because they weren't saying anything important about anything important. After you once got the idea that there were Bad Guys and Good Guys and that, in spite of apparently insuperable obstacles placed in their path by the Bad Guys, the Good Guys would ultimately get rich or go to the White House, there was nothing more to learn. The only thing that keeps reading from being boring is learning, the discovery of possible worlds.

It is of course possible to make learning boring. What has given learning a bad name is textbooks. This is not ordinarily the fault of the writers or publishers. There is a widespread impression that knowledge is facts. If education is the acquisition of knowledge, it must consist of the memorization of facts. Therefore textbooks must consist largely of lists of facts to be memorized. Add to this that examinations, which are often tests of the facts memorized, hang over the heads of teachers, pupils, and textbook writers alike, and you will understand that it is almost inevitable that textbooks must be boring.

Whatever claims can be made for textbooks, nobody ever ventured to suggest that they were inspiring. They are said to be accurate, or complete, or up-to-date. But the most flamboyant publisher will seldom go so far as to assert that they are interesting. Xenophon and Prescott are better than any Western, and no more difficult to read. We learn through reading Xenophon and Prescott what a great historian can do to a mass of dead facts.

We can almost say that what has given learning a bad name is our educational system. That's where most of us pick up our notions about learning. In the educational system, for reasons of economy, we have to do our learning in groups. Now, as everybody knows, the principal difference between pupils is the difference between the fast and the slow. The slow are not necessarily inferior to the fast, though they are often spoken of as though they were second-class citizens. The fast may, in fact, turn out to be flashes in the pan. But we are not concerned here with the merits of these two groups: we are interested only in the fact that they exist and that their existence causes the boredom almost universally incidental to the processes of education. The fast must be bored because they are too quick for the others. The slow must feel frustrated, which can be very boring, too.

There is an easy remedy for this unfortunate situation, but it is not one that has gained general acceptance. It is a simple matter to have everybody proceed at his own pace, taking the examinations whenever he is ready for them. Perhaps the new "teaching machines," most of which are not machines at all but simply books facilitating independent study, will help popularize the notion that the student should go at the rate suitable to him, no matter what the average rate of the class may be. At present the idea of proceeding at one's own pace appears to make little headway because of the prevalent view that the object of education is not intellectual development but social adjustment. It is generally thought undesirable for a young person to get out of his age group. If he is quicker than the others, he must stay behind until they catch up. If he is slower, he must go on anyway, and slow down the progress of the others.

The curse of facts, combined with the curse of adjustment, makes learning boring. I am told that the ideal of adjustment is losing its grip. If so, perhaps, we may some day understand the role of facts in education. Clearly facts are not knowledge. We do not have knowledge until we have organization. A possible world is an organization of ideas and facts. The facts are made intelligible only through the organization. A telephone book is knowledge only in the most limited sense. Such sense as it has it acquires through its alphabetical organization.

A good many years ago the President of Columbia University and the President of the American Statistical Association announced simultaneously, but independently, that so many new facts were being discovered that it would be necessary to prolong adolescence at least until age 45 in order to pour them all into the students. These scholars would have been nearer the mark if they had said that so many new facts were being discovered that it was useless for the layman to try to learn them. What the citizen, not the specialist, has to do is to formulate some general ideas into which any new facts that may be discovered can fit. The question for the citizen is not, what are the latest discoveries in science? In order to answer that question he would have to devote all his time to the scientific journals, of which there are now 36,000. The question for the citizen is, how do I understand the latest scientific discoveries? He can answer this question if he understands what science is about and what the leading ideas in it are.

When I was going to school, I do not remember hearing any teacher say what any subject was about. In general, I was taught to get some facts into my head so that I could pass an examination and go on to the next course. I never quite understood why I was supposed to take the courses I took rather than some other courses. All I knew was that they were required for graduation, or for my major, or as prerequisite to something else.

Some subjects are at first sight less attractive than others, because they employ languages that are special and sometimes repulsive. With these subjects, browsing will get you nowhere. Here the Plan of Graded Reading is indispensable.

You have probably heard of the young lady who asked the clerk in a bookstore whether he had any recent translations of Shakespeare. Her mistake is even more likely to be made by someone who faces mathematics and its special language for the first time. When

I was a boy, my father happened to remark to me that he hadn't liked arithmetic when he was my age. I had to make it a matter of filial devotion not to like it either. The result is that I have been permitted to glory in the possession of an "unmathematical mind." I know now, when it is too late, that, if I had been given some faint glimpse of what mathematics was about, my father's example, powerful as it was, could not have prevented me from understanding the fascination of mathematics.

In other words, I needed a proper introduction. Precisely that, a seductive introduction, is provided by the little masterpieces in this set of books. The world of mathematics and science becomes intelligible, and then exciting, when presented by the great men who in these papers transmit their own excitement to the uninitiated.

Tyndall, Einstein, Fabre, Haldane, and Hogben are no ordinary teachers, and it is no disparagement of ordinary teachers to say so. Even extraordinary teachers in schools and colleges have obligations and undergo pressures from which the writers in this set are free. Our writers can speak directly to your condition, at your leisure, in the order in which you want to know.

This is the Age of Obsolescence. An education that aims to transmit current information and inculcate current practices is bound to fail because current information and practices are obsolescent. We are committed to the highest possible rate of technological change. It now takes less time to go round the world than it took the Founding Fathers to go from New York to Philadelphia. And the world we go round looks entirely different from the way it looked only twenty years ago. Pity the poor atlas maker, who has to slip a few new countries into his book just as it is going to press and who knows that even then it will be out of date long before it appears. We are committed to change, and we are equipped to produce it. As everybody knows, 90 per cent of the scientists and research workers who ever lived are alive today.

Under these conditions, what is a "practical" education, an education that is in any sense useful? We can begin by saying what kind of education is in every sense useless. A totally useless education is one that aims to transmit current information and inculcate current practices. A useful education, on the other hand, is one that leads to understanding. With understanding the youth of today can face the unknown tomorrow feeling some confidence that no matter what shape it takes he will be able to cope with it.

If I were to try to sum up in four words my advice to the younger generation, I would say, "Get ready for anything." By this I mean, don't get ready for any specific thing, to be done in a specific way, at a specific time and place. Don't, for example, devote yourself to getting ready to make steam turbines in Columbus, Ohio, in 1969. It is most unlikely that anybody will be making steam turbines in Columbus in 1969. There is some evidence that nobody will be making them anywhere. One of the two plants that manufacture them has just closed. (I use this moving illustration because a friend of mine did exactly what I advise against doing: he spent two years in the Cornell Engineering School getting ready to make steam turbines in Columbus. He never saw a steam turbine for the rest of his life.)

The world has always been changing. But the rate of change, and our commitment to the highest possible rate, are entirely new. The Minister of Education in Russia told the publisher of these books that there was no use trying to say what would happen in the future. He said the changes that would take place in the next five years would be greater than those which had occurred from the time of the Pharaohs to the present day. Perhaps the Minister should have said ten years, or twenty-five, but the precise time span doesn't make much difference. Whatever the precise time span is, it will be short.

There is one element of super-novelty in this novel outlook. This is the appearance of machines that can "think." We are used to machines that are substitutes for brawn. It's going to take us some time to get accustomed to machines that are substitutes for brains. But that is what computers are, in the sense that they do work that was done not by the hands but by the minds of men. The rough-and-ready miner has long since been replaced by vast, complicated machinery. Now the office worker is fated to follow the miner. And even what is known as "middle management" will sooner or later follow the clerks. The service trades are being automated as manufacturing has been. Automatic elevators have thrown 40,000 elevator operators out of work in New York City alone. At last reports R. H. Macy & Co. was experimenting with an electronic salesgirl. Sooner or later she (or it) will appear.

These developments, which are taking place before our eyes, have the most serious consequences for education. In the first place, they prove the case against the popular conception of "practical" education. Training for a trade or vocation, going through in school the routines one expects to go through in earning a living, has been ineffective in the face of the relatively mild changes that we have seen in the last half century. The obsolescence of techniques, and even of whole industries, and the high mobility of our population (15,000,000 Americans move every year) have long since convinced educators who took the trouble to consider the matter objectively that training with a view to earning a living in a certain place in a certain way is a waste of time. It is worse: it may unfit the pupil to earn his living in that vocation because the techniques he learns will be out of date by the time he has a chance to use them. The present rate of technological change leaves no room for argument on this point.

In the second place, we now face for the first time in human history the probability that work is not going to occupy the major portion of the time and attention of the individual. Even if the educational system were able to prepare people for work, it would not be wise for it to make the attempt, because education should prepare people for those activities which will occupy the bulk of their time and attention. The aim of education must now be to prepare people to make intelligent use of their free time.

This is an enormous task. We can't say that we are making intelligent use of the free time we have now. The latest reports from the labor front, where one would think this question would be much agitated, suggest that all that our people want to do with their free time is to get another job—moonlighting is the most popular of all the ways of using up vacant hours—or, as I have pointed out already, to watch television. In some labor circles, we are told, "culture" is regarded as something "continental," meaning European and un-American.

If Aristotle was correct in saying that all men by nature desire to know, then we must assume that the ball game, the television set, and the beer can will eventually cease to convey the full meaning of the American Dream. For the first time in human history, I say, we are all of us going to have the chance to lead human lives, to make the most of ourselves, and to make the most of our communities, too. Man is distinguished from the brute creation by his mind. Human communities are distinguished from those of gregarious animals, like wolves and bees, by their *deliberate* pursuit of the common good.

In this new world, formal, institutional education must therefore become preparation for a life of learning. The life of learning, conducted on behalf of the development of the individual and of his community, has always been the ideal of what was called the "leisure class." Now we are all going to have the chance to pursue that ideal if we will.

The habit is the thing. Abandoning all illusions about social adjustment and vocational preparation as the aims of education, we have to begin in childhood to discover the delights of the mind and the rewards of the life of the mind. The object of formal, institutional education must be to develop the habits that promote and sustain the life of the mind.

An educational system so conceived and so dedicated will be supported by this set of books; and, pending the development of such an educational system, this set of books and *Great Books of the Western World* can do a good deal of the job. Through this set of books, the habit of reading, which is indispensable to the discovery of possible worlds, can be almost painlessly acquired. Through Great Books the exploration begun here can be carried to whatever distance, height, or depth you desire.

The two sets of books are complementary. Each is an introduction to the other, for those who have read the longer works in Great Books will want to read the shorter in this set. Many of the Gateway authors are comparable in stature to those in Great Books. The choice of the Gateway authors is based in part on their having shorter works to represent them at their best: in Great Books only great, major works appear. Among the authors in this set who had to be excluded from Great Books are Ibsen, Shaw, Einstein, Emerson, Cicero, Dickens, Molière, Malthus, Russell, Whitehead, Epicurus, Mark Twain, Lucian, Lyell, Dewey, Schopenhauer, Voltaire, Thoreau, and de Tocqueville. With the publication of Gateway, we are satisfied that few if any of the first-rank authors in western civilization are missing from the two sets combined.

Most of the works in Gateway are readable and enjoyable by an ordinary sixteen-year-old. They are, every one of them, in considerable measure understandable the first time they are read. In another sense, every one of these books is too hard for any sixty-year-old. They are too hard because the subject with which they deal—man and his universe—is too hard for man to understand. But magnificent writing takes us by the hand and leads us on.

So the many references to Shakespeare in Gateway whet our

appetite for the complete works of Shakespeare in *Great Books of the Western World*. So, too, Melville's *Billy Budd* moves us to read his masterpiece, *Moby Dick*. Darwin's *Autobiography* in this collection turns us toward *The Origin of Species*, which revolutionized man's understanding of his beginnings.

Among the authors of *Great Books of the Western World* to whom we are introduced in this set, and the masters who make the introductions, are Homer (Matthew Arnold), Herodotus (J. B. Bury), Thomas Aquinas (Henry Adams), Dante (T. S. Eliot), Montaigne (Sainte-Beuve and Emerson), Machiavelli (Thomas Babington Macaulay), Shakespeare (Samuel Johnson), Newton (Voltaire, Einstein and Infeld), Locke (Voltaire), Swift (Hazlitt), and Faraday (Tyndall).

Authors in this set whose major works appear in *Great Books of the Western World* are Plutarch, Tacitus, Dante, Galileo, Bacon, Hume, Swift, Rousseau, Kant, Mill, Faraday, Melville, Darwin, Tolstoy, and William James.

This set is the Gateway. As you go through it, and upward and onward thereafter, we say "Bon voyage."

And, we venture to add, "Have fun!"

Robert M. Hutchins

Santa Barbara, California
September, 1963

Introduction

I

The Ways–and Whys–of Reading

Great Books and the Gateway to Them

The works in this set are outstanding creations of the human mind, but they are not of the same order as the works included in *Great Books of the Western World.* They consist of short stories, plays, essays, scientific papers, speeches, or letters; and in some cases they are relatively short selections from much larger works. In contrast, *Great Books of the Western World* contains whole books or extensive collections of books.

The works in that set not only have a certain magnitude, but they also occupy a unique place in the formation and development of Western culture. Each of them represents a primary, original, and fundamental contribution to man's understanding of the universe and of himself. It has been said of them that they are books which never have to be written again, that they are inexhaustibly rereadable, that they are always contemporary, and that they are at once the most intelligible books (because so lucidly written) and the most rewarding to understand (because they deal with the most important and profound subjects). It has also been said of them that they are the repository and reservoir of the relatively small number of great ideas which man has forged in his efforts to understand the world and his place in it; and that they are over everyone's head all of the time, which gives them the inexhaustible power to elevate all of us who will make the effort to lift our minds by reaching up to the ideas they contain.

These things can be said of few books, and the few books of which they can be truly said are truly great books, the only great books. The works included in *Gateway to the Great Books* not only lack the magnitude of the great books; they also have less seminal power. Nevertheless, they do have some of the special attributes which distinguish the great books. Some of the things which have been said of the great books can also be said of them.

The works in this set are, each of them, masterpieces of the imagination or intellect of man. Many of them are modern, even recent; some were written in ages past; but they are all forever contemporary. In whatever time or place we live, they speak to us of our own condition. Like the great books, they are readable again and again, with renewed pleasure and added profit. And like the great books, they throw light on as well as draw light from the great ideas. They, too, have the power to lift our minds up to new levels of enjoyment, new levels of insight, new levels of understanding. They have that power by virtue of holding out more to understand than most of us can manage to understand in a first reading. And if we make the effort to understand more in subsequent readings, they sustain such effort by the intellectual excitement they afford us—the excitement and the challenge of coming to closer grips with the great mysteries of nature and human nature, the order of the universe and the course of human history.

Like the great books in these respects, the selections included in this set are entitled to be regarded as proper companions to the greatest works of the human mind. That, however, does not fully describe the function they are intended to perform. They are more than just companion pieces. We have another and what seems to us a more important reason for associating the contents of these volumes with the contents of *Great Books of the Western World*.

Because this set consists of much shorter works and, on the whole, of things somewhat easier to read, we think that the reading of the selections here included will effectively serve as an induction into the reading of the great books. That is why we have called this set a *gateway* to the great books. The reader who opens his mind to all, or even to some, of the works in this set, has opened the gates for himself and is on the high road to the world of ideas and the lifetime of learning which the great books, and only the great books, make accessible to him.

Their relative shortness is one reason, but not the only reason, why the selections included in this set are easier to read than the great books. Other things being equal, shorter works tend for the most part to be more manageable to young readers as well as to older ones who have not yet fully developed the skills and habits of the constant reader. In addition, these short works are more readily understandable. They tend to deal with easier and more familiar subjects.

More than half of the contents of this set consists of stories and plays, essays, speeches, and letters. Good writing of this kind almost has to be about things and experiences and feelings which are familiar to every human being; and when the writing is of a high order of excellence, as it is in the case of all the selections here included, it deals with the familiar aspects of life in a way that is at once lively and illuminating. The reader is quickly entertained and, to the extent that he is entertained (which means that his attention is held with delight), he reads—and learns.

While the political, scientific, and philosophical readings in *Gateway to the Great Books* must be read with more conscious effort to attend to what they try to teach us, they nevertheless remain easier than the basic political, scientific, and philosophical treatises in *Great Books of the Western World*. In part, this is due to their brevity; in part, it must be also said that what they try to teach us is more readily grasped.

All the works included in this set are comprehensible to any adult, young or old, who will give them the measure of attention which they require. That requirement is easy to fulfill, and can be fulfilled with pleasure, precisely because all these works have the quality of entertainment. Entertaining books invite and sustain our attention, delighting us at the same time that they profit us. The pleasure and profit that the reader derives from this set of books should—and, the editors think, will—help him to develop the habits and improve the skills which should make the great books easier for him to read, some at the same time, some later.

Kinds of Reading Matter

Different kinds of reading matter call for different kinds of reading. A reader must, first of all, decide what type of reading matter he has in his hand; and he must then read it accordingly. Every piece of reading matter that comes before our eyes is not equally worth reading; nor do all make equal claims on our attention. All do not deserve from us the same devotion to the task of considering what the writer has in mind—what he is trying to teach us or to make us feel.

A telephone book, an air-line timetable, or a manual for operating a washing machine may be useful or even indispensable reading, requiring attention to certain details; but they certainly do not deserve sustained study or devoted consideration. Most periodicals that come our way do not deserve more than passing attention. And what is called "light reading" is no different from most television programs or motion pictures which succeed only if they give us the relaxation that we seek from them. Whatever use or value these things may have for us, they are seldom worth reading twice, and none of them is worth reading over and over again.

The great books, and the smaller masterpieces that constitute a gateway to them, exert a whole series of claims upon us that other kinds of reading seldom make. They have treasures to yield, and they will not yield their treasures without our digging. They will not give something to us unless we give something to them. Such works command our interest, our humility, and our fidelity. They have much to teach us—if we want to learn.

These are the things which are most worth reading for the first time, precisely because we will find, on that first reading, that they deserve to be read over and over again. It might almost be said that a book which is not worth rereading one or more times is not really worth reading carefully in the first place. Like the great books, the works in this set are not idle-hour affairs, mere time passers like picture magazines. None of them is a sedative compounded of paper and ink. Every one of them calls for and deserves active, as contrasted with merely passive, reading on our part.

Young people—and older ones—who in ages past had access to only a few books in a lifetime knew how to read them without being told. We all know to what good use young Abraham Lincoln, by the light of the log fire, put the Bible, Euclid, Blackstone, Bunyan, and a few other books. He, and others like him, read not only with eyes wide open but also with a mind fully awake—awake because it was intensely active in an effort to get, by reading, everything that the writer had to offer.

We need to remind ourselves of this bygone situation in which a book was a lifelong treasure, to be read again and again. Deluged as we are with a welter of printed words, we tend to devaluate all writing, to look at every book on the shelf as the counterpart of every other, and to weigh volumes instead of words. The proliferation of printing, on the one hand a blessing, has had, on the other, a tendency to debase (or, in any case, homogenize) our attitude toward reading.

What was true centuries ago is still true: there are great books and masterpieces of writing which can entertain us while they enlighten us; there are merely useful books or printed materials which we go to only for specific facts or instruction; there are trivial books which, like the average detective story, amuse us briefly or help us pass the time, and then disappear forever from mind and memory; and there is trash, like many magazine, paper-back, or even hard-cover romances which actually dull our taste for better things. Of these, only the first constitute the readables which deserve our effort to keep as wide awake as possible while reading. We can do that only by reading as actively as possible.

How does one do that? The answer is easier to give than to apply, but anyone who wants to get the most out of the things that are most worth reading can do what is required, if he applies his will to the task. And the more he is willing to do what is required, the easier he will find it to do.

What is required of the reader who wishes to be wakeful and active in the process of reading is simply the asking of questions. He must ask questions while he reads—questions which he himself must try to answer in the course of reading. Any questions? No. The art of reading a book or piece of writing consists in asking the right questions in the right order. They are as follows: (1) What is this piece of writing about? What is its leading theme or main point? What is it trying to say? (2) How does it say what it is trying to say? How does the writer get his central point across? How does he tell his story or argue for his conclusion to produce the effect in us that he is aiming at? (3) Is it true—factually or poetically—in whole or part? Has he won our assent or sympathy? And if not, what reasons do we have for disagreeing with or rejecting his view of things? (4) What of it? What meaning does it have for us in the shape of opinions or attitudes that we are led to form for ourselves as the result of reading this piece?

These four questions underlie and motivate all the specific things that we have to do in order to read well what is worth reading well. We shall state these more specific recommendations presently; but first it is necessary to observe the difference between fiction and non-fiction as objects of our active attention in reading; and, among nonfiction works, the difference between writings in the field of history and politics, writings in the sphere of natural science and mathematics, and writings in the realm of philosophy.

The Four Colors

In the binding of *Great Books of the Western World,* four different colors, based on traditional academic insignia for the various arts and sciences, are used to signify four types of subject matter to be found in the great books. Yellow in the binding signifies works of the imagination—epic and dramatic poetry, novels, and essays. Blue in the binding signifies biographies and histories, treatises in politics, economics, and jurisprudence. Green in the binding signifies major contributions to the fields of mathematics and the natural sciences. Red in the binding signifies the great works in philosophy and theology.

The writings included in *Gateway to the Great Books* are similarly ordered. A patch of color on the spine of each volume indicates the character of the works contained therein. Volumes 2, 3, 4, and 5, identified by a patch of yellow, contain works of the imagination. Fiction, in the form of short stories or excerpts from novels, is to be found in Volumes 2 and 3; and, in Volume 4, in the form of plays. Critical essays, largely concerned with the world of imaginative writing and writers, are to be found in Volume 5. Identified by a patch of blue, Volumes 6 and 7 contain writings about man and society, in the form of biographies and histories, letters and speeches, political documents and political treatises, together with works on a variety of related subjects such as education, war and peace, population growth, money, taxes, and trade. Then in Volumes 8 and 9, identified by a patch of green, we have scientific and mathematical papers: the scientific papers cover the range of the natural sciences —astronomy, physics, chemistry, biology, and psychology—and include as well writings about science and about scientists; the mathematical papers are largely about the nature, methods, uses, and study of mathematics, though there are also some discussions of specific mathematical notions and applications. Finally, Volume 10, identified by a patch of red, contains philosophical essays, concerned with the life of reason, aspects of nature, and with ways of thinking and living.

Gateway to the Great Books is divided into these four kinds of writing for good and sufficient reason. We have but to consider the subject matter of the various courses that we take in high school and college—no matter what their titles—to realize that most of them of importance fall into one or another of these four categories. Nor is there any mystery about it: all writing may be thus partitioned because the resulting parts represent four aspects of ourselves as we use words to communicate what we know, think, feel, or intend.

First, we are all storytellers, listeners to stories, and critics of the stories we hear. Imaginative literature, represented by Volumes 2–5 of this set, is native to the life of every human being.

Second, as free men and citizens, we have always had the responsibility, now heavier than ever before, to deal with the social and political problems which are considered in Volumes 6 and 7. We are called upon to examine ourselves in the light of man's past and future. These are illuminated by the historical and biographical writings contained in Volumes 6 and 7.

Third, the most distinctive characteristics of our modern world are the product of inventions and technology which are, in turn, the product of scientific discovery and mathematical theory, the two inseparable subjects dealt with in Volumes 8 and 9. Some understanding of these fields is essential if we wish to feel at home in the rapidly changing environment of the twentieth century.

Finally, every man and woman who has ever lived has asked himself, from childhood and youth on, What am I? How should I think? What is the meaning of life? How should I live? These are some, if not all, of the philosophical questions which men of wisdom, in every age, have considered and tried to answer. Such considerations appear in Volume 10 of *Gateway to the Great Books*.

To say that these are four different kinds of writing—writings about four different kinds of subjects—is not enough. They represent four different kinds of thinking, too. And they reflect four different aspects of our one human nature. They are four in one, at once different and the same. Since these four kinds of writings all spring from the mind of man, and since that is a unity, so in the end all thought is unified.

The mind is not four separate compartments. No single thought is unrelated to any other. Our ideas, beliefs, sentiments, and fancies do not exist in isolation, to be collected artificially and arbitrarily. Neither is a set of volumes representing all the major aspects of human thought and feeling an aggregation of snippets. For all its diversification of content, *Gateway to the Great Books* has an underlying unity—the unity of the human mind itself.

Most of the writers in this set, though they lived at different times and had special interests and abilities, are talking to each other across the centuries. Like the authors of the great books, they are engaged in a continuing conversation. They are talking to each other through the walls that seem to separate the physicist from the novelist, the philosopher from the historian; for all are involved in a common adventure—the unending exploration of man, of his mind and imagination, of his earth-home, and of the illimitable cosmos of which he is, though a small part, by far the most interesting member. He who reads and rereads all the selections in this whole set— and that may take a long time—will in the end gain a vision of this common adventure and sense the unity which underlies the whole.

But in the beginning, as the reader threads his way among the many different strands here woven together, he would be well advised to observe the differences in the four kinds of writing included in this set. They have to be read differently. Each of them has to be approached with a special attitude, a particular frame of mind. Confusion and bewilderment would result from our addressing a poet as if he were a mathematician, a philosopher as if he were a historian, or a historian as if he were a scientist. So, too, we would tend to confuse and bewilder ourselves if we failed to distinguish between fiction and nonfiction, or between philosophy and science, history and mathematics, and read them as if they were all the same.

These different kinds of writing require different kinds of reading on our part, because to read them well—with an active mind—we must ask different sorts of questions as we read. Unless we know what to look for (and how to look for it) in each kind of reading that we do, we shall demand of fiction knowledge it cannot give us, ascribe to history values it does not have, ask science for opinions that lie wholly outside its scope, and expect philosophy to produce a mode of proof that is impossible for it to achieve.

Some Rules of Reading

So basic are the differences among various kinds of writing that it is almost impossible to formulate rules of reading which are general enough to apply to every kind of writing in the same way. But there is one rule which takes account of this very fact; for it recommends that we pay attention, first of all, to the character of the writing before us. Is it fiction or nonfiction? And if the latter, what sort of expository writing is it—criticism, history, political theory, social commentary, mathematics, science, or philosophy?

There is one other rule which applies to every piece of writing, in so far as it has the excellence that is common to all pieces of writing that are works of art, whether they are imaginative or expository writing. A work of art has unity. The reader must apprehend this unity. It may be the unity of a story or of a play, or the unity of a historical narrative, a scientific theory, a mathematical analysis, a philosophical argument. But whatever it is, it can be stated simply as a kind of summary of what the whole work or piece of writing is about. The reader should make the effort to say what the whole is about in a few sentences. When he has done this, he has answered for himself the first of the four questions which should be asked about anything worth reading actively and with a mind fully awake.[1] Since a work of art is a complex unity, a whole consisting of parts, the reader should also try to say what the major parts of the work are and how they are ordered to one another and to the whole.

The rules to which we now turn apply most readily to nonfiction (expository writing of all sorts), though, as we shall presently see, corresponding rules can be stated for guidance in the reading of imaginative literature.

The writer of an expository work is usually engaged in solving a problem or a set of problems. Hence the reader, in dealing with such works as wholes, should try to summarize the problems which the author set before himself and tried to solve. What are they? How are they related to one another? Knowing the author's problems is necessary to any understanding of the answers he tries to give and to the judgment we make of his success or failure in giving them.

Examining a piece of writing as a whole and as an orderly arrange-

---

[1] See p. 19 above for an enumeration of the four questions.

ment of parts is only one approach to it. It constitutes one way of reading a book or anything less than a book which has artistic unity. A second approach involves attention to the language of the author, with concern not only for his use of words and the manner in which he expresses his meaning, but also for the verbal formulation of his opinions and the reasons that he has for holding them. Here the reader should do a number of things, in successive steps, each a way of trying to get at the thought of the writer by penetrating through his language to his mind.

He should, first of all, try to come to terms with the author, that is, try to discover the basic terms which express the author's central notions or ideas. This can be done only by noting his words carefully and discovering the five or ten (rarely more than twenty) which constitute his special vocabulary. Finding such words or phrases will lead the reader to the writer's basic terms. Thus, for example, a careful reader of Calhoun's "The Concurrent Majority" from *A Disquisition on Government* (Volume 7) can come to terms with Calhoun only by discovering what he means by such words or phrases as "constitution," "numerical majority," "concurrent majority," "interposition," "nullification," and "veto."

A term is a word used unambiguously. It is a word tied down to a special meaning which does not change within the context of a particular piece of writing. We come to terms with an author by noting the one or more meanings with which he uses the words in his own special vocabulary. Good writers are usually helpful, indicating explicitly by verbal qualifications, such as quotation marks, underlining, or parenthetical explanations, that a word is now being used in one sense and now in another; but even the best writers frequently depend upon the context to provide such qualifications. This requires the reader to do the work of interpretation which is involved in coming to terms.

Language is a difficult and imperfect medium. For the transmission of thought or knowledge, there must be communication, which can occur only when writer and reader have a common understanding of the words which pass from one to the other. Terms made by the one and discovered by the other produce communication.

Coming to terms underlies all the subsequent acts of interpretation on the part of the reader. Terms are the building blocks of propositions, and propositions are put together in arguments. The next two steps in the process of interpretation concern the author's propositions and his arguments—represented on the printed page by sentences and paragraphs, just as terms are represented there by words and phrases.

The reader should try to find out what the author is affirming and denying—what his bedrock assertions are. To do this, he must spot the crucial sentences in the text, the sentences in which the author expresses the opinions which are central in his mind. Most of the sentences in a piece of writing are not crucial. Only a few set forth the propositions which the author is undertaking to defend. Spotting these is not enough. The reader must know what they mean.

There are two simple ways in which we can test our understanding of the crucial sentences in an author's work. First, can we say precisely in our own words what the author is saying in his; that is, can we extract the author's meaning from his words by translating it into another form of speech? Second, can we think of examples that clearly illustrate the author's meaning or apply it to concrete experiences?

The third step of interpretative reading requires us to look for and find the key paragraphs which express the writer's basic arguments in support of the opinions that he wishes to persuade us to accept. An argument is a sequence of propositions, having a beginning in principles and an end in conclusions. It may be simple, or it may be complex, having simpler arguments as parts. Sometimes the writer will put his whole argument down in one place in the form of a summary paragraph; but more frequently the reader must piece together the parts of the argument by connecting sentences, or parts of paragraphs, which are on different pages.

The first of the suggested approaches to reading a book or piece of writing is analytical: it dissects a whole work into its parts and relates the parts. The second is interpretative: it attempts to construe what a writer means from what he says. There is a third approach, which should follow and complement the other two. It is critical.

Here the task is to judge a piece of writing in terms of the truth and falsity of its basic propositions, both its principles and its conclusions, in terms of the cogency or soundness of its arguments, and in terms of the adequacy or completeness of its analysis. It is at this stage or in this phase of reading that the reader must decide whether he agrees or disagrees with the writer, or determine the extent of his agreement or disagreement. In doing this, he should be governed by a number of rules or maxims.

The first is that the reader should neither agree nor disagree with an author until he is sure that he understands what the author is saying. To agree with what you do not understand is inane; to disagree in the absence of understanding is impertinent. Many readers start to disagree with what they are reading almost at once—before they have performed the tasks of analysis and interpretation which should always precede that of criticism. In effect, they are saying to an author: "I don't know what you are talking about, but I think you are wrong." It would be just as silly for them to say "right" as it is for them to say "wrong." In either case, they are expressing prejudices rather than undertaking genuine criticism, which must be based on understanding.

This rule calls for patience and humility on the reader's part. If he is reading anything worth reading—anything which has the power to instruct him and elevate his mind—he should be loath to judge it too soon, for it would be rash to presume that he has so quickly attained an adequate understanding of it. If he suspects that he has fallen short in his understanding, he should always blame himself rather than the author. Not only is that the proper attitude if the author is worth reading at all; but, in addition, such an attitude may keep the reader's mind on the task of interpretation. There is always time for criticism after that is well done.

A second maxim by which we should be guided can be stated thus: there is no point in winning an argument if we know, or even suspect, that we are wrong. This is an important rule of intellectual behavior in face-to-face discussions—one, unfortunately, which is frequently violated. It is even more important in the very special one-way conversation that a good reader carries on with an author. The author is not there to defend himself. Disagreement with an author demands the utmost in intellectual decency on the part of the reader.

A third closely related maxim recommends to the reader that he should not undertake criticism unless he is as willing to agree as to disagree—unless he is prepared to agree intelligently as well as to disagree intelligently. In either case, the critical reader should be able to give reasons for the position that he takes.

The reasons for disagreement can be roughly grouped under four headings. We may disagree (1) because we think that the author is uninformed on some essential point that is relevant to his conclusions; or (2) because we think that he is uninformed about some equally essential consideration, which would alter the course of his argument if he were aware of it; or (3) because we think that he has committed some fallacy or error in reasoning; or (4) because we think that his analysis, however sound in its bases and its reasoning, is incomplete. In every one of these instances, we are under an obligation to be able to prove the charge that we are making. Men and their works are finite and fallible, every last one; but a writer of eminence is ordinarily more competent in his field than the reader, upon whom, therefore, the heavy burden of proof is imposed.

The foregoing rules, as already pointed out, apply primarily to expository writing rather than to imaginative literature—fiction in the form of novels, short stories, or plays. Nevertheless, they do suggest analogous recommendations for the reader to follow in reading fiction. As terms, propositions, and arguments are the elements involved in the interpretative approach to expository writing, so the cast of characters, their actions and passions, their thought and speech, the sequence of events, and the plot together with its subplots are the things with which the reader must concern himself in interpreting a work of fiction. As factual truth and logical cogency are central considerations in the criticism of expository writing, so a narrative's verisimilitude or credibility (its poetic truth) and its unity, clarity, and coherence (its artistic beauty) are important objects of criticism in the case of fiction.

It is possible to offer a few other recommendations that are especially appropriate to imaginative literature, and applicable to the varied assortment of stories and plays in Volumes 2, 3, and 4.

In every piece of fiction to be found there, the subject matter of the writer is men and women. But he approaches this subject matter in a way that is quite different from that employed by the historian, the psychologist, or the moral philosopher, all of whom are concerned with human character and conduct, too. The imaginative writer approaches this subject matter indirectly and, in a sense, subjectively.

He sees men and women partially, in terms of his own limited temperament, his own overriding passions, and also in terms of their willingness, as it were, to subject themselves to the particular pattern or frame that he has in mind. Dickens, in *The Pickwick Papers,* and Mark Twain, in *The Man That Corrupted Hadleyburg,* are placed side by side in Volume 2. But in other ways they are far apart. To sense the distance separating them, the reader need only ask this simple question after he has read these two stories: Which seems to *like* mankind more? He will then become aware that these two storytellers hold different views of mankind—each his own partial view with its own partial truth.

To read fiction with pleasure, the reader must abandon himself for the moment to the writer's partial vision. As he reads more and more imaginative literature, he will begin, almost unconsciously, to obtain new insights from each of them.

Finally, it may be helpful to point out a few differences between imaginative and expository literature, from the point of view of what is involved in reading them carefully and well.

A story must be apprehended as a whole, whereas an expository treatise can be read in parts. One cannot read enough of a story, short of the whole, "to get the idea"; but one can read a portion of a scientific or philosophical work and yet learn something of what the author is driving at.

An expository work may require us to read other works by the same or different authors in order to understand it fully, but a story requires the reading of nothing outside itself. It stands entirely by itself. It presents a whole world—for us to experience and enjoy.

The ultimate unity of an expository work, especially in the fields of political theory, natural science, mathematics and philosophy, lies in a problem or a set of related problems to be solved. The unity of a narrative lies in its plot.

There is a fundamental difference in the use of language by imaginative and expository writers. In exposition, the aim of a good writer is to avoid ambiguity by a literal or precise use of words. Imaginative writers often seek to utilize ambiguity and they do this by recourse to metaphor and simile and other figures of speech. The use of language moves in one direction when its ultimate aim is to accord with fact, and in another when its ultimate aim is to give wings to fancy.

And, lastly, the difference between imaginative literature and expository writing calls for different types of criticism on the reader's part. Aristotle pointed out that "the standard of correctness is not the same in poetry and politics," which we can generalize by saying that the soundness of a fictional narrative is not to be judged in the same way as the soundness of a scientific or philosophical exposition. In the latter, the standard is objective truth; in the former, internal plausibility. To be true in its own way, fiction need not portray the world as it actually is. Its truth is not that of simple factual realism or representation. Its truth depends upon an internal necessity and probability. Characters and action must fit together to make the narrative a likely story. However fanciful the story may be, it has the ring of truth if it is believable as we read it—if we can feel at home in the world that the imaginative writer has created for us.

The differences that we have pointed out between imaginative and expository writing should not be allowed to obscure the fact that there are mixed works—works which somehow participate in the qualities of both types. One example of this will suffice. Historical narratives are, in a way, mixtures of poetic and scientific or philosophical writing. They offer us knowledge or information about the past, gained by methodical investigation or research, but that knowledge or information comes to us in the form of a story, with a sequence of events, a cast of characters, and a plot. Hence histories must be read in both ways. They must be judged by the standard of objective truth—truth of fact—and also by the standard of internal plausibility—truth of fiction.

Some Further Suggestions to the Reader

One way of putting into practice the rules of reading outlined in the preceding pages is to read with a pencil in hand—to mark the pages being read, without scruples about damaging the volume. Marking a book is not an act of mutilation, but one of love. Of course, no one should mark a book that is not his. But the books that a man buys, he is at liberty to mark or write in as he reads.

Buying a book is only a prelude to owning it. To own a book involves more than paying for it and putting it on the shelf in one's home. Full ownership comes only to those who have made the books they have bought part of themselves—by absorbing and digesting them. The well-marked pages of a much handled volume constitute one of the surest indications that this has taken place.

Too many persons make the mistake of substituting economic possession or physical proprietorship for intellectual ownership.

They substitute a sense of power over the physical book for a genuine grasp of its contents. Having a fine library does not prove that its legal owner has a mind enriched by books. It proves only that he was rich enough to buy them. If a man has a handsome collection of volumes on his shelves—unread, untouched—you know that he regards books as part of the furnishing of his home. But if his books, many or few, are dog-eared and dilapidated, shaken and loosened by continual use, marked and scribbled in from cover to cover, then you know that he has come into the full ownership of his books.

Why is marking a book so important a part of reading it? It helps to keep you awake while reading—not merely conscious, but mentally alert. And since reading, if it is an active process, involves thinking, and thinking tends to express itself in words, spoken or written, writing in the book enables the reader to express his thoughts while reading. Marking a book thus turns the reader into a writer, engaged, as it were, in a conversation with the author.

There are many ways of marking a book intelligently and fruitfully. As one discovers the terms, propositions, and arguments in an expository work, one can mark them by underlining or by asterisks, vertical lines, or arrows in the margin. Key words or phrases can be circled; the successive steps of an argument can be numbered in the margin. Imaginative works can be similarly treated: underlining or marginal notations can be used to mark significant developments in character, crucial turns in plot, or revelations of insight by the author himself. In addition, one should not hesitate to use the margin, or the top or bottom of the page, to record questions that the text arouses in one's mind, or to jot down one's own comments about the significance of what is being read.

The margins of a book, or the space between its lines, may not afford enough room to record the thoughts of an intensive reader. In that case, he should read with a scratch-pad in hand. The sheets of paper on which the notations have been made can then be inserted into the book at appropriate places.

The person who marks a book cannot read it as quickly as one who reads it passively or merely flips its pages inattentively. Far from being an objection to marking books, this fact constitutes one of the strongest recommendations for doing it. It is a widely prevalent fallacy that speed of reading is a measure of intelligence. There is no right speed for intelligent reading. Some things should be read quickly and effortlessly, some should be read slowly and even laboriously. The sign of intelligence in reading is the ability to read different things differently according to their worth. With regard to the great books, or with regard to the selections in this set, the point is not to see how many of them you can get through, but rather to see how many can get through you—how many you can make your own.

Most things worth reading carefully are likely to present some difficulties to the reader on a first reading. These difficulties tend to slow us up. But we should never allow them to stop us in our tracks. The reader who bogs down completely because he cannot fully understand some statement or reference in the course of his reading fails to recognize that no one can be expected to achieve complete understanding of a significant work on the first go at it. A first reading is bound to be a relatively superficial one, as compared with the reading in greater and greater depth that can be done when one rereads the same work later.

The reader who realizes this should adopt the following rule in reading worth-while materials for the first time. The rule is simply to read the work through without stopping to puzzle out the things one does not fully understand on that first reading. Failure to clear all the hurdles should not lead one to give up the race. The things which may be stumbling blocks on the first reading can be surmounted on later readings, but only if they are not allowed to become insuperable obstacles that prevent the first reading from being completed.

The first reader should pay attention to what he can understand, and not be stopped by what he does not immediately grasp. He should go right on reading past the point where he has difficulties in understanding, and he will soon come again to paragraphs and pages that he readily understands. He should read the work through, undeterred by paragraphs, arguments, names, references, and allusions that escape him. If he lets himself get tripped up by any of these stumbling blocks, if he gets stalled by them, he is lost. In most cases, he would not have been able to puzzle the thing out by sticking to it. He will have a much better chance of understanding it on a second reading, but that requires him to have read the work *through* at least once.

Reading it through the first time, however superficially, breaks the crust of the book or work in hand. It enables the reader to get the feel or general sense of what he is reading, and some grasp, however incomplete, of what it is all about. It is necessary for him to get some grasp of the whole before he can see the parts in their true perspective—or, sometimes, in any perspective at all.

Most of us were taught in school to pay attention to the things we did not understand. We were told to go to a dictionary when we met with an unfamiliar word. We were told to go to an encyclopedia or some other reference work when we were confronted with allusions or statements we did not understand. We were told to consult footnotes, scholarly commentaries, or other secondary sources in order to get help. Unfortunately, we never received worse advice.

The tremendous pleasure that comes from reading Shakespeare was spoiled for generations of high school students who were forced to go through *Julius Caesar* or *Macbeth* scene by scene, to look up all the words new to them in a glossary, and to study all the scholarly footnotes. As a result, they never read a play of Shakespeare's. By the time they got to the end of it, they had forgotten the beginning and lost sight of the whole. Instead of being forced to take this pedantic approach, they should have been encouraged to read the play through at one sitting and discuss what they got out of that first quick reading. Only then, if at all, would they have been ready to study the play carefully, and closely, because they would have understood enough of it to be able to learn more.

What is true of reading a play by Shakespeare applies with equal force to all the works included in this set, both the fiction and the nonfiction. What a first reader of these works will understand by reading each of them *through*—even if it is only 50 per cent or less—will help him to make the additional effort later to go back to the difficult places which he wisely passed over on the first reading. Even if he does not go back, understanding 50 per cent of something really worth reading is much better than not understanding it at all, which will certainly be the case if he allows himself to be stopped by the first difficult passage he comes to.

There are some technical books—usually written by professors for professors, and in the jargon of the trade—which are not only difficult for a first reader, but impossible for the nonprofessional to understand by any means. Such books are difficult because they are written in a way that is not intended for the person of ordinary background and training. In contrast, the great books, and to a lesser extent the masterpieces included in this set, are difficult for a quite different reason.

It is not because the author has not tried to make himself clear to the ordinary reader. It is not because the author is not a good writer. The difficulty, where it exists, lies in the subject matters being treated and in the ideas being conveyed. Precisely because the authors of *Great Books of the Western World* and the writers represented in *Gateway to the Great Books* have a mastery of these difficult subject matters or ideas, do they have the power to deal with them as simply and clearly as possible. Hence they make such material as easy as it can be made for the reader.

No major subject of human interest, nor any basic idea, need be a closed book to the ordinary man. On every one of them, there exist great books or masterpieces of writing which afford enlightenment to anyone who will make the effort to read them. However difficult the subject matter being treated or the idea being expounded, these writings help the ordinary and inexpert reader to make some headway in understanding if he will only follow the rule of cracking a tough nut by applying pressure at the softest spot. That, in other words, is the rule of paying maximum attention to what you do understand, and not being deterred by what you fail to understand, on the first reading of these works.

A Word about What Follows

The succeeding sections of this introductory essay will attempt to acquaint the reader with the four types of subject matter which are represented in *Gateway to the Great Books*. Section II will discuss the works of the imagination that are included in Volumes 2–5; Section III, the writings about man and society that are included in Volumes 6 and 7; Section IV, the works in natural science and in mathematics that are included in Volumes 8 and 9; and Section V, the philosophical writings that are included in Volume 10.

Each of these sections will try to provide a general framework in which the writings indicated above can be read. Illustrative materials from *Great Books of the Western World*, as well as references to particular selections in *Gateway to the Great Books*, will be utilized to bring the reader face to face with the ideas and themes appropriate to each kind of writing, and to fill him in on the basic background in each field. In addition, reference will be made from time to time to the *Syntopicon*, which, under the title of *The Great Ideas*, comprises Volumes 2 and 3 in *Great Books of the*

Western World. The quotations from the *Syntopicon* are drawn from the introductions which open its chapters, 102 in all, one on each of the great ideas.[2]

A word should be said about the style of the references that will appear in parentheses in the pages to follow.

Where the reference is to a passage in *Great Books of the Western World*, it is indicated by the letters GBWW, followed by the number of the volume in that set, and the citation of the particular page or pages on which the passage occurs. Sometimes these page numbers are accompanied by letters, *e.g.*, 129a, or 321b-c. These letters indicate sections of the page. In volumes of GBWW which are printed in a single column, "a" and "b" refer to the upper and lower halves of the page. In volumes which are printed in two columns, "a" and "b" refer to the upper and lower halves of the left column, "c" and "d" to the upper and lower halves of the right column.

Where references are made to authors or works included in this set, they will be accompanied simply by a parenthetical citation of the number of the appropriate volume in *Gateway to the Great Books*.

And where reference is made to the *Syntopicon*, the reference will be to either Volume 2 or Volume 3 in GBWW, and to the appropriate pages in that volume.

---

[2] The reader who wishes to acquaint himself with the 102 great ideas will find them listed on the rear endpapers of each volume of *Great Books of the Western World*. He can also find the list of authors included in that set by examining the front endpapers of any volume. If he does that, he will discover that some of the authors included in *Great Books of the Western World* are also represented, by other and somewhat easier works, in *Gateway to the Great Books*.

II

The Imagination of Man

What Is Imagination?

"Tell me a story," says the child, and the storyteller begins. In an instant, the world of common reality is left behind, and a new reality —more captivating, more intense, more real—catches up the listener on the wings of imagination.

We never, as long as we live, stop saying, "Tell me a story." Our hunger is never satisfied; the more we read, the more we want to read; and the richer the feast, the hungrier we grow. For the master of creative imagination evokes the creativity in all of us, makes us all shareholders in the treasure that literature brings to life. The story —in prose or poetry, in art or music—is the magic of every man's life. By comparison, the most staggering achievements of science and industry and statesmanship seem to some people bodiless and cold.

Charles Darwin writes in his *Descent of Man* that, while reason is the greatest of all human faculties, "The *Imagination* is one of the highest prerogatives of man. By this faculty he unites former images and ideas . . . and thus creates brilliant and novel results. . . . The value of the products of our imagination depends . . . to a certain extent on our power of voluntarily combining them. As dogs, cats, horses, and probably all the higher animals, even birds have vivid dreams . . . we must admit that they possess some power of imagination. There must be something special, which causes dogs to howl in the night, and especially during moonlight, in that remarkable and melancholy manner called baying" (GBWW, Vol. 49, p. 292a-b).

What is the imagination, which produces both the howling of a dog and Mozart's *Magic Flute,* the dream of a cat and Dante's *Divine Comedy?* Psychologists ancient and modern agree with Darwin that it is common to man and at least the higher brutes, and that it is peculiarly linked with memory. In Chapter 56 of the *Syntopicon* on MEMORY AND IMAGINATION (GBWW, Vol. 3, pp. 133–157), we learn that the two powers "depend upon sense-perception or upon previous experience. Except for illusions of memory, we do not remember objects we have never perceived or events in our own life, such as emotions and desires, that we have not experienced. The imagination is not limited in the same way by prior experience, for we can imagine things we have never perceived and may never be able to."

How is this possible, when our imagination depends upon sense-perception or upon previous experience? We do not know, except that we have both the involuntary instinct (as in dreams) and the voluntary power of *combining.* "Even when imagination outruns perception," the *Syntopicon* continues, "it draws upon experience for the materials it uses in its constructions. It is possible to imagine a golden mountain or a purple cow, though no such object has ever presented itself to perception. But, as Hume suggests, the possibility of combining a familiar color and a familiar shape depends upon the availability of the separate images to be combined."

The *Syntopicon* quotes Hume—some of whose shorter works we read in Volumes 5 and 7 of this set—as saying, "When we think of a golden mountain, we only join two consistent ideas, *gold* and *mountain,* with which we were formerly acquainted. . . . All this creative power of the mind amounts to no more than the faculty of compounding, transposing, augmenting, or diminishing the materials afforded us by the senses and experience." A congenitally color-blind man who lived entirely in a world of grays would not be able to imagine a golden mountain or a purple cow, though he might be able to imagine other things as unreal as these.

The object imagined, then, need not be located in the past like the object remembered, though the former depends upon the memory of the objects combined to produce it. But the imagined object need not have any definite location in time and space. It need have no actual existence. It may be a mere possibility, unlike the kind of object which cannot be known without being known to exist; it is a *figment* or construction. Having seen horses, we do not imagine a horse; we remember it. Having seen both horses and birds, we cannot remember a winged horse, but we have all imagined one. Memory preserves those things which are no longer present or no longer exist. Imagination evokes those things which have never existed, and, maybe, never will.

". . . in which he dwells delighted."

Consider for a moment what memory and imagination mean to our human experience and our civilization. "Without them," says the *Syntopicon,* "man would live in a confined and narrow present, lacking past and future, restricted to what happens to be actual out of the almost infinite possibilities of being." But what imagination means to the life of each of us is perhaps best stated by a master of the art. In *The Lantern-Bearers* (Vol. 7), Robert Louis Stevenson asserts that, "Justice is not done to the versatility and the un-plumbed childishness of man's imagination. . . . His life from without may seem but a rude mound of mud; there will be some golden chamber at the heart of it, in which he dwells delighted. . . ."

To the poet Shelley the imagination is the key to all goodness: "The great secret of morals is love; or a going out of our own nature, and an identification of ourselves with the beautiful which exists in thought, action, or person, not our own. A man, to be greatly good, must imagine intensely and comprehensively: he must put himself in the place of another and of many others; the pains and pleasures of his species must become his own. The great instrument of moral good is the imagination . . . We want the creative faculty to imagine that which we know; we want the generous impulse to act that which we imagine; we want the poetry of life . . ." (*A Defence of Poetry,* Vol. 5).

Let us recall the shipwrecked sailor in Stephen Crane's *The Open Boat* (Vol. 3). Doomed, as he thought, in a tiny lifeboat which could not make land, he suddenly remembered a poem of his child-hood that began, "A soldier of the Legion lay dying in Algiers," and only now, for the first time, understood it; for the first time he felt sorry for that soldier now that he himself "lay dying." His own mortal experience brought that soldier before him. What Shelley insists upon is that all men, so few of whom have such an experience, use their imaginations to put themselves "in the place of another and of many others."

This is what poetry—the traditional term for what we call "fiction" —does for us. The poet's imagination takes us into the heart of another, of a man, a place, an event, and in doing so moves and lifts us. Volumes 2, 3, and 4 of *Gateway to the Great Books* are a collection of masterpieces of the imagination, Volume 5 a collection of the great critical and imaginative essays which enlighten our appreciation and enjoyment of what we read.

We emphasize appreciation and enjoyment, in addition to understanding, because the test of an imaginative work is its beauty. The French expression for such works, both stories and essays, is *belles-lettres;* literally untranslatable, it would have to be rendered something like "beautiful knowledge." But the test of knowledge is truth, not beauty; does this mean that poetry is false? And—if it is—how can it possibly serve us? We say that a person has "let his imagination run away with him" when we don't believe him. What then, if fiction or poetry be untrue, can it profit us?

The apparent contradiction has never been more clearly resolved than in Aristotle's little treatise *On Poetics* (GBWW, Vol. 9, pp. 681–699). "The poet's function," he says, "is to describe, not the thing that has happened, but a kind of thing that might happen, *i.e.*, what is possible. . . . The distinction between historian and poet is not in the one writing prose and the other verse—you might put the work of Herodotus into verse, and it would still be a species of history; it consists really in this, that the one describes the thing that has been, and the other a kind of thing that might be. Hence poetry is something more philosophic and of graver import than history, since its statements are of the nature rather of universals, whereas those of history are singulars. By a universal statement I mean one as to what such or such a kind of man will probably or necessarily say or do—which is the aim of poetry, though it affixes proper names to the characters; by a singular statement, one as to what, say, Alcibiades did or had done to him" (*ibid.*, p. 686a-b).

". . . a kind of thing that might happen"—this is poetry, fiction, the work of the imagination. Not the actual here and now, or yesterday, or in 1776, nor *this* man, John Smith of 1332 State Street, Philadelphia; but the possible, today, tomorrow, yesterday, here or anywhere, as it might happen to such and such a *kind* of man. And in so far as we see ourselves as such a kind of man, and those we know as this or that kind, we are moved emotionally, to sympathy, to pity, forgiveness, love, noble deeds and impulses (and, conversely, to fear and hate and cruelty and ignoble deeds and impulses). But what moves us—through its beauty—is the universal truth of the tale; in it we recognize ourselves or others. It is the possible, and the possible cannot be false.

Thomas De Quincey calls imaginative works "the literature of power" as opposed to the literature of knowledge. The function of the latter is to teach us, of the former to move us. In his *Literature of Knowledge and Literature of Power* (Vol. 5), he asks, "What do you learn from *Paradise Lost?* Nothing at all. What do you learn from a cookery-book? Something new." What we owe the immortal author of the first, he goes on, is power—the materialization of our own latent capacity to move and be moved. "Were it not that human sensibilities are ventilated and continually called out into exercise by the great phenomena . . . of literature . . . it is certain that, like any animal power or muscular energy falling into disuse, all such sensibilities would gradually droop and dwindle. It is in relation to these great moral capacities of man that the literature of power, as contradistinguished from that of knowledge, lives and has its field of action." He points out that the Psalmist asks the Lord to give him not understanding, but an "understanding heart."

After attending a theater for the first time as a child, Charles Lamb tells us that he "knew nothing, understood nothing, discriminated nothing. I felt all, loved all, wondered all—*Was nourished, I could not tell how*" (*My First Play*, Vol. 5). What had happened to him?—The play had brought his heart into contact with those peculiar sources of joy which, in the cultivation of the intellect alone tend, according to psychologist William James, to dry up and leave us "stone-blind . . . to life's more elementary . . . goods" (*On a Certain Blindness in Human Beings*, Vol. 7). Literature, says Stevenson in *The Lantern-Bearers*, moves us with "something like the emotions of life . . . Not only love, and the fields, and the bright face of danger but sacrifice and death and unmerited suffering humbly supported touch in us the vein of the poetic. We love to think of them, we long to try them, we are humbly hopeful that we may prove heroes also."

This is what the great works of the imagination do to us, and their effect is not without its dangers. The human heart is at once the best and worst of our blessings. So readily and so mysteriously moved, and in turn moving us to the great actions of life, its power may carry us to beatitude or perdition—depending on the goal to which it is moved and the means we choose to reach the goal.

This is where criticism comes in. The critic or essayist is part "poet" and part "historian." His art comprehends the imagination and analyzes its output. He may deal (as De Quincey and others do in Vol. 5) with specific works or forms of literature, or (like Bacon) with man himself. In either case, he examines and instructs or admonishes. Like the preacher, he wants to direct and deepen our view of beauty; like the scientist, he inquires into the truth of that view.

What Makes a Book Good?

The great issue here is the existence or nonexistence of standards of criticism. Can we say of a literary work that it is "good" or "bad," or "true or false," as we can of a pot or a pan—or a mathematical formula? And, if we can, with what degree of certainty? Can we say that it is "good" or "bad" only here and now, for our time or for our place; or can we criticize it in universal terms of time and place? And, if we can, what are the standards by which we do it, and how are they arrived at? What—or who—is the ultimate authority?

In Volume 5 of *Gateway to the Great Books* Sainte-Beuve looks at the history of criticism and reminds us that "the greatest names to be seen at the beginning of literatures are those which disturb and run counter to certain fixed ideas of what is beautiful and appropriate in poetry. For example, is Shakespeare a classic? Yes, now, for England and the world; but in the time of Pope he was not considered so. Pope and his friends were the only pre-eminent classics; directly after their death they seemed so forever. At the present time they are still classics, as they deserve to be, but they are only of the second order, and are forever subordinated and relegated to their rightful place by him who has again come to his own on the height of the horizon" (*What Is a Classic?*).

We are all familiar with the famous aphorisms, the Latin *de gustibus non est disputandum* ("there is no disputing about tastes") and the French *chacun á son goût* ("each to his taste"). But Hume (*Of the Standard of Taste,* Vol. 5) is willing to say that there *is* a way to measure literature: ". . . strong sense, united to delicate sentiment, improved by practice, perfected by comparison, and cleared of all prejudice, can alone entitle critics to this valuable character; and the joint verdict of such, wherever they are to be found, is the true standard of taste and beauty."

But the difficulties are at once apparent: How do we determine "strong sense"? How do we define "delicate sentiment"? How does a man, that creature of prejudice, clear himself of all prejudice? What if the verdict of such men is not joint at all, but divided?

While different forms of literature are to be criticized differently —see Schopenhauer's essays *On Style* and *On Some Forms of Literature* (Vol. 5)—we can generally accept the traditional view that the unity and completeness of an imaginative work—plus the harmony of its construction—serve as criteria under the experienced examination of the critic. To these there may be added the usually paired criteria of universality and durability applicable to all works of the mind. But many critics take the position that artistic taste has no absolute validity but is relative to the conditions under which it is produced or "consumed." Among them are the Marxists, who maintain that *all* values are determined by the economic form of the society.

In his essay on Montaigne (Vol. 5), Sainte-Beuve says, "He was like Socrates, who did not consider himself a citizen of one city but of the world . . . he embraced the universality of countries and of ages . . . To get away from the present state of feeling, to restore lucidity and proportion to our judgments, let us read every evening a page of Montaigne." [Montaigne's collected essays constitute Vol. 25 of *Great Books of the Western World*.] But the relativists would say that "there ain't no such animal" as this man who embraces countries and ages, that Socrates reflected the master-slave civilization of ancient Athens and that Montaigne reflected the feudal society of sixteenth-century France.

The issue is, in all probability, never to be resolved, for it involves the ultimate mystery of human nature we call the heart. And of all disputes that go on endlessly, that of taste in art is the most complicated, for art is man's modification of nature. Were the materials to form themselves into a finished work, like a mountain or a sea, our view of their beauty might be more dispassionate. As it is, they bear the touch and the genius of man, and the problem of reflexivity, which besets ethics and politics, also bedevils art: Man is judging himself and his own handiwork, and his passions, from which his view of the nonhuman may be free, are inextricably interwoven with his judgment.

T. S. Eliot argues (*Tradition and the Individual Talent*, Vol. 5) that "criticism is as inevitable as breathing," but a much dimmer view of it is taken by the author of the most humorous of all *Great*

Books of the Western World, Laurence Sterne, in his novel, *Tristram Shandy* (Vol. 36, p. 288b): "Of all the cants . . . in this canting world . . . the cant of criticism is the most tormenting . . . I would go fifty miles on foot . . . to kiss the hand of that man whose generous heart will give up the reins of his imagination into his author's hands—be pleased he knows not why, and cares not wherefore." But the serious Eliot is obviously right when he says that we are all critics, good or bad.

The purpose of our reading the great critics is, then, to become better critics ourselves; not merely to distinguish better between good and bad writing, and thus improve our own, but also to get the most pleasure out of everything we read, adding new dimensions to our own imagination. Criticism is the expressed response of the mind *and* the emotions of the critic to a work of art. It tends to awaken in us the sensibilities of which De Quincey speaks, to build Stevenson's golden chamber at the heart of the "rude mound of mud" of our lives, to lead us to brighter enjoyment. Coleridge was a kind of walking essay to William Hazlitt, who rhapsodizes on the effect of their conversations on him: "I was at that time dumb, inarticulate, helpless, like a worm by the wayside, crushed, bleeding, lifeless; but now . . . my ideas float on winged words" (*My First Acquaintance with Poets,* Vol. 5).

On the Perilous Edge

In the weird scenes at the close of Goethe's masterpiece, Faust, in extreme old age, still bound by the sale of his soul to the Devil, envisions a people living behind a dike. On the other side of the dike the raging waters gnaw away at the wall and the community lives on the alert in constant danger and constant trial. And the savant who has now seen and done everything—with Mephistopheles for escort and councilor—sees "wisdom's final fruit" in the spectacle of the constantly imperiled city:

> Of freedom and of life he only is deserving
> Who every day must conquer them anew
> (*Faust,* in GBWW, Vol. 47, p. 281b).

So dream we all of conquering anew every day, the waters, the mountains, the heavens, far countries and topless towers; would-be heroes all of us. But like Walter Mitty, we dream; and the waking life of most of us (of nearly all of us) is a round of routine which, as

Bacon says, denies the satisfaction to the mind of man "in those points wherein the nature of things doth deny it, the world being in proportion inferior to the soul; by reason whereof there is, agreeable to the spirit of man, a more ample greatness, a more exact goodness, and a more absolute variety [in reading fiction] than can be found in the nature of things" (*Advancement of Learning,* in GBWW, Vol. 30, p. 38d).

We are nearly all of us shut-ins of a sort, rich and poor and in between, city man and even country man, bound to the commonplace affairs of the workaday world. Adventurers we would be—for man's is an adventurous nature—but the four walls of home and work and family confine us all our lives. This is the common fate, and always was. The frontiersmen are the few, and the new frontiersmen confront the redskins from their rocking chairs. So we read about daredevils going to the bottom of the sea, the center of the earth, the top of the sky. We are all ground-floor cosmonauts, air-conditioned explorers, nineteenth-hole champions, careening over the trackless freeways with wings on our radiator caps and fins on our fenders, to pull up safely into the company parking lot and punch the giant time clock right on the nose. We have our splendid adventures second hand; have them we must, "the world being in proportion inferior to the soul."

Of all the adventurers who ever were—or were ever imagined—two of the world's favorites are Homer's Odysseus (Ulysses) and Daniel Defoe's Robinson Crusoe. Homer and Defoe lived thousands of years apart, but *The Odyssey* and *Robinson Crusoe* continue to fascinate the old and the young in every language and in every land. They are the all-time best-selling adventure stories. *The Odyssey* (along with *The Iliad*) constitutes Volume 4 of *Great Books of the Western World,* and sections of Crusoe's classic (in spite of everyone's having read it as a child) have their place (in Vol. 2 of this set) in the living library of every young and old adult.

Ulysses was a divinely descended king, Crusoe a common sailor boy. Their adventures were in some ways radically different: Ulysses had his men and his ships, and wherever he went his life was thronged with companions lovely or terrible, human or divine; Crusoe, shipwrecked on a desert island, lived without the sound of human voice or the sight of human face until his "man Friday" came and relieved the solitude in which he faced and mastered fate. But the two figures are essentially more alike than different: In

Dante's *Divine Comedy* (GBWW, Vol. 21, p. 39a) the shade of Ulysses bemoans the fact that neither fondness for his small son nor piety for his father nor the love of his wife had been able to overcome "the ardor which I had to become experienced of the world" —an ardor which delayed his return home from the Trojan War by ten years. And Crusoe, cursing his restlessness and curiosity as "the general plague of mankind," says that half of men's miseries flow from their "not being satisfied with the station wherein God and Nature hath placed them."

Ulysses deliberately sought out every challenge that man or god could muster, and Crusoe, all alone, tamed primeval nature to his civilized wants. Such heroes, increasing their stature to giant size, vicariously increase the size of those who read of their exploits. Men ourselves, we say, "mind you, a mere man did this." Crusoe's ingenious devices for carving a home for himself out of next to nothing have their echo in the do-it-yourself kit with which we moderns construct or repair an implement we could have bought cheaper at the store; we are all Crusoes and Ulysseses and our small adventures spring from their great. "Neither in the theoretic nor in the practical sphere," says William James (*Principles of Psychology,* in GBWW, Vol. 53, p. 826b), "do we care for, or go for help to, those who have no head for risks, or sense for living on the perilous edge. . . . We draw new life from the heroic example."

The sedate philosopher John Stuart Mill tells us in the opening chapters of his *Autobiography* (Vol. 6) how the young Crusoe enriched his own sheltered childhood in which raw adventure had no place. So all of us, sheltered from the most primitive trials of life, are enriched by the youngster who would not and could not be kept to a way of life calculated for "peace and plenty . . . moderation, quietness," the way in which "men went silently and smoothly through the world, and comfortably out of it. . . ." Like him, we all rebel against the smooth, silent way, but he, unlike us, was pushed on by fate, "born," he says, "to be my own destroyer."

The Adventure of Comedy

The heroism of all adventure stories is essentially comic: It is read for delight, and its pervasive character is the happy ending. It *pleases* us. But where the adventurer increases our own stature vicariously, the comic victim (even while we are laughing at him) reduces it. "This, too," we say again, "is a mere man, like me," and thus Marcus Aurelius, in his *Meditations* (GBWW, Vol. 12, p. 302d), finds comedy useful in "reminding men to beware of insolence." It enables man (says Melville in *Moby Dick*, in GBWW, Vol. 48, p. 168a), to take "this whole universe for a vast practical joke . . . at nobody's expense but his own."

But it has a much higher aim, according to Schiller (*On Simple and Sentimental Poetry*, Vol. 5); it enables man to liberate himself "from the influence of violent passions, and taking a calm and lucid survey of all that surrounds him, and also of his own being, and of seeing everywhere occurrence rather than fate or hazard, and ultimately rather smiling at the absurdities than shedding tears and feeling anger at sight of the wickedness of man."

This certainly sounds as if comedy has a purpose beyond mere entertainment, though perhaps we should consider these the *effects* of comedy rather than its *aim*. Still, comedy may be a way of communicating a deadly serious message. Works like Dickens' *The Pickwick Papers* (Vol. 2) involve a sharp—if often hilarious— critique of the deplorable social situation in England in the nineteenth century. Sheridan's *The School for Scandal* and Molière's *The Misanthrope* and *The Doctor in Spite of Himself* (all three plays in Vol. 4) are "drawing-room comedies" in which we are seen saying and doing the opposite of what we feel. The comedy of manners (such as those just mentioned) more often than not involves the traditionally and universally amusing, but none the less real, "battle of the sexes," with the helpless woman winning.

The characters in comedy do not bleed when they are pricked— their suffering is usually mere embarrassment—and the authors are making fun. But in making fun of man's foibles they are nevertheless *arguing*. They seem to have no purpose, no message, no moral, but Sainte-Beuve, in his *What Is a Classic?* (Vol. 5) reminds us that Goethe said that Molière "is so great that he astonishes us afresh every time we read him." The king of critics (as Sainte-Beuve calls him) would hardly have spoken thus of a writer whose power was limited to making us laugh. The fact is that when we reject every sermon, every plea, and every scientific proof, and cling obstinately to our prejudices, comedy may still reach us where the other forms of discourse fail.

It is at this point that comedy gives rise to its most purposeful— and often savage—form in what is known as satire. The writer is a satirist, says Schiller (*On Simple and Sentimental Poetry*, Vol. 5), "when he takes as subject the distance at which things are from nature, and the contrast between reality and the ideal . . . he may place earnestness and passion, or jests and levity, according as he takes pleasure in the domain of the will or in that of the understanding. In the former case it is avenging and pathetic satire; in the second case it is sportive, humorous, and mirthful satire. . . . In satire the real as imperfection is opposed to the ideal, considered as the highest reality." But of *all* satire we may certainly say that it has a purpose, and that its purpose, unlike that of pure comedy, is never nebulous or concealed.

Voltaire's little satire, *Micromégas* (Vol. 2), for instance, brings a gigantic visitor to earth from the stars to inspect and make mock of the tiny dwellers on our tiny planet. The device of size to take us down a peg is, of course, also used by Jonathan Swift in the greatest of all satires, *Gulliver's Travels* (GBWW, Vol. 36). Nothing so well illustrates the saying that "there is no such thing as a children's book" as does *Gulliver's Travels*. Beloved of youngsters the world over, it says infinitely more to the world of adults than it does to children.

But where Voltaire in his disillusionment is "sportive, humorous," Swift, in his, is "avenging and pathetic." We have only to turn to Volume 7 and read the great Irishman's *A Modest Proposal for Preventing the Children of Ireland from Being a Burden to Their Parents or Country* to see how satire can be the agonized cry of a great heart against man's inhumanity to man. Hazlitt (*On Swift*, Vol. 5) says of this "children's" writer that "the ludicrous in Swift arises out of his keen sense of impropriety, his soreness and impatience of the least absurdity. He separates, with a severe and caustic air, truth from falsehood. . . . His better genius was his spleen. It was the biting acrimony of his temper that sharpened his other faculties."

Which is the more effective, gentle or sharp satire? In the latter category we find Shaw's *The Man of Destiny* (Vol. 4), which, like Aristophanes' renowned *Lysistrata* (GBWW, Vol. 5, pp. 583–599), is a theater piece mirthfully satirizing the most terrible of all man's activities, war. Here men are seen deluding themselves with grandiose aims and purposes, justifying their most monstrous behavior by the highest ideals. "When [an Englishman] wants a thing," says Shaw, "he never tells himself that he wants it. He waits patiently until there comes into his mind, no one knows how, a burning conviction that it is his moral and religious duty to conquer those who possess the thing he wants." In both Shaw and Aristophanes, the heart of the satire is the victory of "helpless" woman over both warriors and war.

Satire may play an effective role in all works of social criticism, even in the construction of literary utopias—imaginary places where people live under ideal conditions. The most famous utopias (included in *Great Books of the Western World*) are Plato's *Republic* (Vol. 7), founded on virtue; St. Augustine's *The City of God* (Vol. 18), founded on the Christian faith; and Francis Bacon's *New Atlantis* (Vol. 30), founded on science. But Machiavelli, that hardest-boiled of all hard-boiled realists, is scornful of such depictions of "republics and principalities which in fact have never been known or seen, because how one lives is so far distant from how one ought to live, that he who neglects what is done for what ought to be done, sooner effects his ruin than his preservation" (*The Prince*, in GBWW, Vol. 23, p. 22b).

This dim view of the confection of ideal commonwealths whose inhabitants exist under perfect conditions inspired one great utopian reformer to produce his plan in the form of a satire. This is Samuel Butler's *Erewhon* (Vol. 2 of this set). *Erewhon*—an anagram of "nowhere"—is borrowed directly from the word "utopia," compounded from the Greek οὐ, not, and τόπος, a place. Butler uses the device of holding a mirror to our institutions so that we see them in reverse: In Erewhon, disease, misfortune, debt, and poverty are treated as crimes against society and are punished. But what *we* call crimes are treated as diseases—as, indeed, many modern psychologists think they are—and are treated as such by men trained in "soul-craft" (we would say "psychiatry") called "straighteners" (our "therapists").

The reason for satire is plain: Whoever is moved to criticize man and his ways has to choose between a direct and a devious approach to his audience. The satirist chooses the latter, in the hope that, by entertaining them the while, he can circumvent the resistance they ordinarily display to criticism. He tries to "kid" them into facing their defects, where the moralist or preacher tries to compel them to face them. The literature of social protest tries to compel men, to shock them into awareness. As *belles-lettres* it is rarely successful, but in Henrik Ibsen it reaches its artistic peak. In *An Enemy of the*

People (Vol. 4) we see man on his feet fighting social evil. He is beaten but he is never stupid, as he is in satire, or ridiculous, as he is in comedy.

The Society—and the Man

In social protest we always see a minority pitted against what John Stuart Mill calls "the tyranny of the majority." (See *On Liberty,* in GBWW, Vol. 43, p. 269b-c.) "The strongest man in the world," says the heroic (some would say bullheaded) Dr. Stockmann in Ibsen's classic, "is he who stands most alone," echoing Walt Whitman's words in his *Preface to Leaves of Grass* (Vol. 5): "take off your hat to nothing known or unknown, or to any man or number of men." Standing alone against the commercial cupidity of the whole community—including the government and the press—Ibsen's honest physician is destroyed, but in his destruction we read his triumph. He has triumphed over the materialism of a civilization which teaches a man, says Matthew Arnold in his *Sweetness and Light* (Vol. 5), "to value himself not on what he *is* . . . but on the number of the railroads he has constructed, or the bigness of the tabernacle he has built."

What a man is brings us to the heart of literature and to the heart of life: the individual. Social criticism focuses on society and, in so far as it treats of the Dr. Stockmanns, portrays the worth and nobility of human nature in, if not the many, then at least the few. It shows us a man daring alone, the adventurer. So, too, comedy, though it mocks our professions and our professional humbug (the law, in Dickens' "A Full and Faithful Report of the Memorable Trial of Bardell against Pickwick," from *The Pickwick Papers,* Vol. 2; medicine in Molière's *The Doctor in Spite of Himself,* Vol. 4; philosophy, in Voltaire's *Micromégas,* Vol. 2). Deflating our pretenses and exposing our hypocrisies, comedy and light satire still say to us: "Man knows better, is better, than he says or does"; thus puffing us up (even as adventure does) while it lets the straw out of the stuffed shirt front. But the somber—and universal—adventure of every individual's life is still to be dealt with.

Kipling's *Mowgli's Brothers* (Vol. 2) and Balzac's *A Passion in the Desert* (Vol. 3) show man confronting the world of beasts and pitting himself against the arid waste. Conrad's *Youth* (Vol. 2), Crane's *The Open Boat* (Vol. 3), Victor Hugo's dreadful "The

Battle with the Cannon" (Vol. 2) use the ferocious sea as the adversary. So, of course, does Homer's *Odyssey* and many another classic, including Melville's incomparable story of the hunt for the white whale (*Moby Dick*, in GBWW, Vol. 48). But the ferocity of the struggle with "nature in the raw" is child's play compared with the struggle with man in the raw—the struggle of man with himself. "Consider," says Melville (*ibid.*, pp. 204b-205a), "the subtleness of the sea; how its most dreaded creatures glide under water . . . treacherously hidden beneath the loveliest tints of azure. . . . Consider . . . the universal cannibalism of the sea; all whose creatures prey upon each other, carrying on eternal war since the world began. Consider all this; and then turn to this green, gentle, and most docile earth; consider them both, the sea and the land; and do you not find a strange analogy to something in yourself? For as this appalling ocean surrounds the verdant land, so in the soul of man there lies one insular Tahiti, full of peace and joy, but encompassed by all the horrors of the half-known life. God keep thee! Push not off from that isle, thou canst never return!"

Many are the masterpieces of literature that deal with man's soul "pushing off" from some peaceful Tahiti, to which he tries ever to return without the power to make land again. Physically he may never have ventured beyond his home town, but pride and ambition and greed and lust cut him loose from his moorings and launch him upon the treacherous waters of violence or deceit or injustice. The two sides of his nature—the docile earth and the subtle sea—tear him to pieces. "If each . . . could but be housed in separate identities," says Stevenson in his most famous short story, *The Strange Case of Dr. Jekyll and Mr. Hyde* (Vol. 2), "life would be relieved of all that was unbearable." Alas, both are housed in each of us. But our misfortune is also our freedom, for, as Hegel says, in his *Philosophy of Right* (GBWW, Vol. 46, p. 130b), "It is only man who is good, and he is good only because he can also be evil." Only man is free.

Or is he? Plato thought that no man "voluntarily does evil and dishonourable actions" (*Protagoras*, in GBWW, Vol. 7, p. 56b), and Aristotle insisted that "every wicked man is ignorant of what he ought to do and what he ought to abstain from, and it is by reason of error of this kind that men become unjust . . ." (*Nicomachean Ethics*, in GBWW, Vol. 9, p. 356c); and so the great debate over good and evil begins. In the masterpieces of the imagination we see the struggle *within man* imperishably illustrated. In Volumes 2 and 3 of this set, Poe's *The Tell-Tale Heart*, George Eliot's *The Lifted Veil*, Hawthorne's *Rappaccini's Daughter* take us into the awful mystery of ourselves; and stories of a less somber character, like Mark Twain's *The Man That Corrupted Hadleyburg*, portray human nature as a poor thing and man as ignoble.

In Tolstoy's *The Death of Ivan Ilyitch* (Vol. 3), man's suffering consists of his self-deception; as soon as he realizes (too late to repair it) that his life was lived wrong, his salvation begins. So, too, old Maurya, in Synge's *Riders to the Sea* (Vol. 4), when her last son is lost beneath the waves, is strengthened by the realization that life can do no more to her. Henry James discovers this insight in children who suffer in an atmosphere of adult exploitation (*The Pupil*, Vol. 3). But the dawn of true consciousness is less often the theme of the great storytellers than is the bewilderment that overtakes men when they see things go wrong.

Bunin's *The Gentleman from San Francisco* (Vol. 3) can only mutter, "This is dreadful." The characters in Chekhov's *The Cherry Orchard* (Vol. 4)—an invariable hit when it is revived on the modern stage—refuse to look at their desperation and go to the end of the road in an attitude of complete unreality. But Akaky in Gogol's wonderful story of *The Overcoat* (Vol. 2) has accepted loneliness, insignificance, and poverty, and the incident that brightens his wretched existence just before he is crushed is enough to sustain him to the end. More often we see suffering—suffering locked within the heart of an individual—as the consequence of man's being trapped by social bonds that he *might* have burst, as in the haunting account of Frank Ashurst in Galsworthy's *The Apple-Tree* (Vol. 3), in Sir Walter Scott's *The Two Drovers* (Vol. 2), and in Isak Dinesen's *Sorrow-Acre* (Vol. 3).

Opposing "necessity" and the persistent theme of fate among the ancients is the doctrine of moral freedom under the servitude of God, notably illustrated by Tolstoy's *What Men Live By* and *The Three Hermits* (both in Vol. 3). In the former strange story the angel sent to live with the shoemaker has come to earth to learn the truth about men. He learns that men live by their love for each other, and not by caring for themselves. This is likewise the motive of the French master Flaubert, in whose *Legend of St. Julian the Hospitaller* (Vol. 3) a man who has lived a life of violence and accidentally kills his parents becomes a beggar in penitence and achieves salvation by absolute charity. The power of faith reaches its heights here, as it does in Tolstoy's hermits, who simply cannot learn the outward forms of prayer the mighty bishop tries to teach them.

The ultimate human adventure is tragedy, and so is the ultimate achievement in storytelling. Each of the greatest tragedies of literature weaves a web of action around a man or woman who plays the role of the tragic hero; a role so universal in its appeal that the spectator is filled, as Aristotle says, with pity and fear (*On Poetics,* in GBWW, Vol. 9, pp. 686c-688c); pity for the character which, without being really wicked, suffers the worst of punishments, fear lest what befalls an Oedipus or a Macbeth, mighty kings, might all the more easily befall ourselves.

Why do we read of such macabre matters? Why do we *enjoy* reading of them—enjoy them more than we enjoy light comedy or dazzling adventure? Aristotle says in his famous analysis (*ibid.*) that the spectacle serves as a catharsis, evoking and purging us of our most dreadful emotions. The passions of comedy are small, of tragedy great; and thus the relief we obtain from comedy is less than that which we find in tragedy. "It is difficult," says Shelley, "to define pleasure in its highest sense; the definition involving a number of apparent paradoxes. . . . Sorrow, terror, anguish, despair itself are often the chosen expressions of an approximation to the highest good. Our sympathy in tragic fiction depends on this principle; tragedy delights by affording a shadow of that pleasure which exists in pain" (*A Defence of Poetry,* Vol. 5).

In *Gateway to the Great Books* we encounter tragedy in many of the stories in Volumes 2 and 3, in Scott's *The Two Drovers,* in Dinesen's *Sorrow-Acre,* above all in Herman Melville's *Billy Budd.* Is young Billy wrongly condemned to die? Was he actually innocent? His commander, who judged him and sent him to his death, never knew; nor do we, though there is no mystery (in the ordinary sense) about the events that lead to the climax. Is Billy the tragic hero, or is Captain Vere? Whose plight is the worse? Who suffers the more? Which of the two is wrong, or right? We may read *Billy Budd* many times and still ask ourselves these questions; *this* is the nature of tragedy.

Instead of saying that truth is stranger than fiction, we may say, after reading these masterpieces, that fiction is as strange as truth, and that the best fiction is closer to truth than the commonplace events we encounter every day of our lives. Closer to truth, so to say, than truth itself, for it speaks to us of the worlds within us that the white light of day rarely or never illuminates. Everything that *can* happen—for good or ill—is buried within us and directs our dreams, our desires, our ambitions, our choices with its unseen hand. The masters of imagination, entertaining us the while, bring us always nearer to the possession of the "understanding heart" which the Psalmist besought of God.

III
Man and Society

Neither a Beast nor a God

Men have always lived in society; man is a social animal. True, there have been occasional hermits or "solitaries," whether by their own intent or, like Robinson Crusoe, accidentally, but they have come *out of* the society to which men generally belong. Being by nature a member of a community, the individual does not, and normally cannot, set up standards of thought or conduct for himself without reference to others. Human history is the history of individuals whose lives mold, and are molded by, the community.

Nor is it a mere relationship, like that of a citizen and his government, or even that of a husband and wife, a relationship of independent entities which may be broken leaving each of them intact. It is integral, and the view of the Greeks that he who lives outside society is not a man, but "a beast or a god," is a basic assumption of many political theorists. For them, living in society is indispensable to living humanly. Individual morality and politics (in the highest sense of the word) are inseparable, for the moral man is, among other things, just, and justice is the bond of men in communities.

History, then, is the account of that unique society compounded of sameness (in that men, like the bees, are invariably social) and differences (in that men form a variety of societies, public and private, and in constantly changing forms). *Gateway to the Great Books* includes the shorter works of some of the greatest historians of the ages, *Great Books of the Western World* the long masterpieces beginning with Herodotus, "the father of history," who tells us that he has written his account of the Persian War "in the hope of thereby preserving from decay the remembrance of what men have done . . ." (*History*, in GBWW, Vol. 6, p. 1a).

Is this all that history can do? No, says Hume, in his *Of the Study of History* (Vol. 7); it also "amuses the fancy . . . improves the understanding . . . strengthens virtue."

But isn't it also the key to the future? Here is where historians—and we with them—get into deep water. If only men would, like the bees, do tomorrow what they did yesterday, history would be an infallible guide and solve our problems for us. But will men do tomorrow what they did yesterday? The second great ancient historian, Thucydides, seemed to think so; at the opening of his marvelous account of the long war between Athens and Sparta—which ended in the ruin of both—he says he will be content if his book be judged useful "by those inquirers who desire an exact knowledge of the past as an aid to the interpretation of the future, which in the course of human things must resemble if it does not reflect it . . ." (*The History of the Peloponnesian War,* in GBWW, Vol. 6, p. 354c-d).

"Peoples and governments never have learned anything from history, or acted on principles deduced from it," says the great German philosopher of history, G. W. F. Hegel. "Each period is involved in such peculiar circumstances, exhibits a condition of things so strictly idiosyncratic, that its conduct must be regulated by considerations connected with itself, and itself alone" (*The Philosophy of History,* in GBWW, Vol. 46, p. 155c).

But surely there are situations in our own day which, as Thucydides says, resemble the past? No doubt. But so, too, each individual confronts personal situations which at least resemble those the preceding generation confronted, and we know how hard it is for parents to persuade their children, on the basis of their own experience, to a course of action or a way of life. The fact seems to be that man is so variable a creature, so strong-willed and individualistic, that he must learn, if at all, from his own experience alone.

The Road We Have Traveled

If history cannot prophesy the future, it should at least be able to show us the road we have traveled thus far; we ought then to be able to say something, however unsurely, about the next stages in the journey. But even here we appear to be asking more of Clio—the mythological muse of history—than she can tell us. The ancients thought of history as a kind of cycle, or a repetitious round which men mistook for change. But when science and technology began to alleviate the hardships of human life, the idea of historical progress was born. Toward the close of the eighteenth century Gibbon concluded his study of ancient Rome with "the pleasing conclusion that every age of the world has increased and still increases the real wealth, the happiness, the knowledge, and perhaps the virtue, of the human race" (*The Decline and Fall of the Roman Empire*, in GBWW, Vol. 40, p. 634c).

Far from having caught (or from having been caught by) this pleasing conclusion, Rousseau at the same time reached the un-pleasing conclusion that "Man is born free; and everywhere he is in chains" (*The Social Contract*, in GBWW, Vol. 38, p. 387b). His "noble savage" was better, and better off, than modern man. A century later a leading exponent of the doctrine of progress an-swered Rousseau: "To believe," said Darwin in 1859, "that man was aboriginally civilized and then suffered utter degradation in so many regions, is to take a pitiably low view of human nature. It is apparently a truer and more cheerful view that progress has been much more general than retrogression; that man has risen, though by slow and interrupted steps, from a lowly condition to the highest standard as yet attained by him in knowledge, morals and religion" (*The Descent of Man*, in GBWW, Vol. 49, p. 330a-c).

These same three traditional readings of human history—the cyclical, the progressive, and the retrogressive—appear in many of the great writers in *Gateway to the Great Books*. Of the three views, the cyclical is, in modern times, least often taken. Tacitus (as might be expected of an ancient historian) sees no great change in things; he tells us how the Romans led the conquered Britains "step by step . . . to things which dispose to vice . . . All this in their ignorance they called civilization, when it was but a part of their servitude" (*The Life of Gnaeus Julius Agricola*, Vol. 6). But Guizot, in nine-teenth-century France, is convinced that "all the great develop-ments of the internal man have turned to the profit of society; all the great developments of the social state to the profit of individual man" ("Civilization," Vol. 6). On the eve of the twentieth century Ruskin's *An Idealist's Arraignment of the Age* (Vol. 7) attacks this optimistic attitude (especially as it springs from scientific progress) with consummate eloquence—and scorn.

Can we say, then, that there is a science of history? Again we have no agreement of historians or philosophers of history. Karl Marx of course believes that there is, or at least that there are dis-coverable laws that flow from history, that "the economic formation of society is . . . a process of natural history . . ." (*Capital*, in

GBWW, Vol. 50, p. 7c). Hume in his *Enquiry Concerning Human Understanding* (GBWW, Vol. 35, p. 479c) agrees that history is a collection of "experiments, by which the politician or moral philosopher fixes the principles of his science," but William James seems to reflect the overwhelming majority of thinkers on the subject when he calls it folly "to speak of the 'laws of history' as of something inevitable, which science has only to discover . . ." (*Great Men and Their Environment*, Vol. 7).

One of the central difficulties is assessment of the role played by the "great man" in history. The extent to which man has freedom to act in the drama of history has long been debated. Some say he is governed completely by necessity, while some, according to the *Syntopicon*, say the "motions of men are directed by laws which leave [men] free to work out a destiny which is determined by, rather than determines, the human spirit" (GBWW, Vol. 2, p. 717b).

William James believes that the *opportunity* and the *man* are inseparable: "The relation of the visible environment to the great man is in the main exactly what it is to the 'variation' in the Darwinian philosophy. It chiefly adopts or rejects, preserves or destroys, in short *selects* him. And whenever it adopts and preserves the great man, it becomes modified by his influence in an entirely original and peculiar way. He acts as a ferment, and changes its constitution . . ." (*Great Men and Their Environment*, Vol. 7).

But, says James, "Not every 'man' fits every 'hour.' . . . A given genius may come either too early or too late." This, says Carlyle in *The Hero as King* (Vol. 6), was the fate of Cromwell; he was too great for his time. "One man, in the course of fifteen hundred years; and this was his welcome. He had adherents by the hundred or the ten; opponents by the million. Had England rallied all round him —why, then, England might have been a Christian land! As it is, vulpine knowingness sits yet at its hopeless problem, 'Given a world of Knaves, to educe an Honesty from their united action'; how cumbrous a problem."

Thoreau's *A Plea for Captain John Brown* (Vol. 6) compares the fanatical hero of the Abolition movement with Cromwell, his little band of men with Cromwell's troops, and his speeches with Cromwell's, closing his plea by quoting from Brown himself: " 'I think, my friends, you are guilty of a great wrong against God and humanity, and it would be perfectly right for anyone to interfere with you so far as to free those you willfully and wickedly hold. . . . I pity the poor in bondage that have none to help them; that is why I am here; not to gratify any personal animosity, revenge, or vindictive spirit. It is my sympathy with the oppressed and the wronged, that are as good as you, and as precious in the sight of God.'" John Brown may also have been too great for his time—but his time came soon after him.

The influence of a great man may lie, after all, with his distant heirs far removed from the age in which he lives. So Walt Whitman, in his *Death of Abraham Lincoln* (Vol. 6), finds that "the final use of the greatest men of a nation is, after all, not with reference to their deeds in themselves, or their direct bearing on their times or lands. The final use of a heroic-eminent life—especially of a heroic-eminent death—is its indirect filtering into the nation and the race, and to give, often at many removes, but unerringly, age after age, color and fiber to the personalism of the youth and maturity of that age, and of mankind."

The Way to Write History

The schoolboy definition of history as "what happened next" suggests that nothing in the world would be easier to write. But serious consideration of the problem reveals that just the opposite is the case. The first issue is the relationship of the historian in time and place to the events with which he deals. He may write of events in which he participated personally. (An example in Vol. 6 of this set is Xenophon's famous "March to the Sea," from *The Persian Expedition*. Here the author relates the movements of the Greek army, a portion of which he commanded, and his account has a real ring of authenticity.) Or he may write of his own times, using the evidence of eyewitnesses, if possible, or as near to eyewitnesses as he can obtain. (The letter of Pliny the Younger to Tacitus in Vol. 6, describing the eruption of Vesuvius, is a case in point. The letter tells of the death of his uncle, Pliny the Elder, at Pompey during the eruption, and ends by saying, "I have faithfully related to you what I was either an eye-witness of myself or received immediately after the accident happened, and before there was time to vary the truth.")

More often, the historian would find his material through both means, *i.e.*, his own experience, and through the experience of others who had left some record of it. The great early historians,

Herodotus, Thucydides, and Tacitus, used this technique. The work of Tacitus on Agricola in this set (Vol. 6) is an example. Julius Agricola was Tacitus' father-in-law, and many of the details of his life were certainly known personally to Tacitus. It is obvious, however, that much of the material he presents on the Roman general's life must also have come from other sources.

Finally, the historian may write wholly of the past, and one view (the great historians of antiquity notwithstanding) is that the loss involved in doing so is more than compensated by the detachment of the scholar. True, the flesh-and-blood vividness of personal knowledge has to be sacrificed, but the history gains both impartiality and depth by the writer's distance from the passions of the occasion, the time, and the place. Prescott's "The Land of Montezuma" (Vol. 6) is such a history, relating the approach of Cortez and his men to the rich and lush heartland of Montezuma, the Aztec ruler. It is clear that Prescott has done immense research to bring us the picture of the reckless daring of the tiny band of Spaniards, as well as Montezuma's fear and paralysis as the Spaniards approach his capital.

History, says Lucian, "is nothing from beginning to end but a long narrative" (*The Way to Write History*, Vol. 6). But the story of history is restricted because it depends on facts, and the historian must balance his role as a storyteller with his role as an investigator. If he concentrates only on facts, his history is deadly dull. If he concentrates on story, he may be tempted to sacrifice truth to entertainment. And there is no doubt in Lucian's mind that the historian's first duty is truth: "The historian's one task is to tell the thing as it happened."

A contrary view is presented by the great historian Macaulay, in his essay on Machiavelli (Vol. 7). "The best portraits," says Macaulay, "are perhaps those in which there is a slight mixture of caricature, and we are not certain that the best histories are not those in which a little of the exaggeration of fictitious narrative is judiciously employed. Something is lost in accuracy; but much is gained in effect. The fainter lines are neglected; but the great characteristic features are imprinted on the mind for ever."

J. B. Bury goes so far as to claim that Herodotus was more of an epic poet than a historian: "He had a wonderful flair for a good story . . . It is fortunate for literature that he was not too critical; if his criticism had been more penetrating and less naive, he could not have been a second Homer" (*Herodotus*, Vol. 6). "The classical histories," says Macaulay, "may almost be called romances founded in fact." If they were *purely* factual, they would have had few readers. And though popularity should be sacrificed to truth, we have only to reflect for a moment to realize that it is impossible to write a factual history that tells the truth. The facts themselves are *in fact* hearsay; do we know that "Columbus discovered America" when and where and how we say he did? Indeed we do not. We have it from participants, to be sure, but do we know (or do we simply assume) that they were telling the truth, or that any one of them actually *saw* the events he describes? Historical facts turn out to be slippery; in general they are based on a consensus of individual reports, any or all of which may be false.

But the difficulty is greater than this. The truth of an event includes the feelings and the spirit of the participants and the onlookers; indeed, these nonfactual ingredients are often the most significant in any historical recital. Consider, for example, the Nazi invasion of Poland on September 1, 1939, which followed a number of clashes on the border between the two countries. Hitler was clearly the aggressor on that day and subsequently, but he and his followers claimed that the Poles had attacked them and that they were defending their country. The *truth* not only includes, but includes above all else, the real attitude and intentions of the German and Polish leaders and the sentiments of the two peoples, and such definitive things are so close to impossible to know (even if there are written records purporting to reveal them) that they probably will be argued by historians to the end of time.

The Way to Read History

The writer of history cannot present *only* the facts—or *all* the facts. He has to weigh and judge them. As the *Syntopicon* puts it (GBWW, Vol. 2, pp. 711–718), the historian "tries to make credible statements about particular past events. He makes an explicit effort to weigh the evidence himself or, as Herodotus so frequently does, to submit conflicting testimony to the reader's own judgment. 'Such is the account which the Persians give of these matters,' he writes, 'but the Phoenicians vary from the Persian statements'; . . . or 'such is the truth of this matter; I have also heard another account which I do not at all believe'; or again, 'thus far I have spoken of Egypt from my own observation, relating what I myself saw, the ideas that I formed, and the results of my own researches. What follows rests on accounts given me by the Egyptians, which I shall now repeat, adding thereto some particulars which fell under my own notice.' "

The historian is human (or shall we say "only human"). His judgment and interpretation of the relevance or irrelevance of the materials that come under his eye, of the weight to assign to Document A or Witness B, are the judgment and interpretation of a man, not a god. We should suppose that he ought to be dispassionate in his approach, a neutral. But what man is dispassionate or neutral? What man lives today, or ever has, or ever will, who meets the requirements established for the historian by Lucian?— ". . . fearless, incorruptible, independent, a believer in frankness and veracity; one that will call a spade a spade, make no concession to likes and dislikes, nor spare any man for pity or respect or propriety; an impartial judge, kind to all, but too kind to none; a literary cosmopolite with neither suzerain nor king, never heeding what this or that man may think, but setting down the thing that befell" (*The Way to Write History*, Vol. 6).

"Setting down the thing that befell"—as if history were an almanac, and an endless almanac at that! "Clearly," the *Syntopicon* says, "the historians have different criteria of relevance in determining the selection and rejection of materials and different principles of interpretation in assigning the causes which explain what happened. These differences are reflected in the way each historian constructs from the facts a grand story, conceives the line of its plot and the characterization of its chief actors." The writer of history is not an Olympian—or even a Martian. He is a citizen of one nation or another, conditioned, like all of us, by the values and habits of his time and place. Above all, he is an individual human being, with human biases. He is a man dealing with the actions of men, and his view of historical actions can hardly help but reflect his views of human action in general.

The best he—and we—can hope for is his consciousness of his biases. If he is unconscious of them, he can do nothing to correct them; if he is conscious of them, he can submit his judgment and interpretation to colleagues who, if not unbiased, are at least blessed with biases contrary to his own. He may even warn the reader against himself, but perhaps that is too much to hope, of the historian or of any man. Bury, finding in Herodotus a strong bias for the

Athenians in the only history we have of the earth-shaking Persian War, says that "it was the work of a historian who cannot help being partial; it was not the work of a partisan who becomes a historian for the sake of his cause" (*Herodotus*, Vol. 6).

Perhaps no historian can help being partial; in which case what Bury said of Herodotus may be said of every great historian and of all great history. Bertrand Russell long ago urged that a country's history used for study in the schools should be written by citizens of other countries than that in which it is studied, and in an age like ours, deluged on all sides by government propaganda, the student of history, present or past, has got to read sharply, if not suspiciously. His consciousness of the forms which human bias takes—including his own—is imperative. The study of the great historians and philosophers of history in *Gateway to the Great Books* (and then in *Great Books of the Western World*) will serve him in the development of that consciousness so crucial to a realistic apprehension and a balanced appraisal of the modern world.

The Domain of Liberty

Much of human history—and certainly its most stirring episodes —involves the struggle for human liberty. But the meaning of liberty is itself controversial, and always has been; more so today, perhaps, than ever before, in spite of the fact that the greatest thinkers of every age have argued it. One point should be kept in mind: individual liberty and national independence must never be confused. Though the American Revolution was fought both for human liberty and national independence, it was not fought for the latter alone, as indeed, many colonial revolutions, or uprisings against the oppression of a foreign power, have been. An *independent* government may exist without human liberty.

Individual liberty is the domain of *man's* freedom, not society's. What it is, how much of it there should be, and why, are questions that raise a host of other questions. And the questions it raises take us always more deeply into all of the great ideas dealing with man. What is man? What is God? What is the will? The soul? What is fate? Necessity? Law? Justice? Equality? Slavery? Government? The State? Society? Happiness? Pursuing these ideas through the set of *Great Books of the Western World*—the passages dealing with them are all indexed under these terms in the *Syntopicon*—we are sooner or later drawn to almost every one of the other great ideas. And nowhere is the dispute among thinkers hotter than it is in connection with this one concept, liberty.

Most of the works in Volumes 6 and 7 of *Gateway to the Great Books* deal with liberty, as do many of the writings in the other volumes. The collection in Volume 6 entitled *Great Documents* is as good a starting point as any for the reader's study. Proceeding from *The English Bill of Rights* (1689) to the *Universal Declaration of Human Rights* in 1948, we may trace the development of the theory of liberty in the past two and a half centuries since John Locke, the English philosopher whose essay *Concerning Civil Government* (GBWW, Vol. 35, pp. 25–81) promulgates the doctrine that man has a natural right to "life, health, liberty [and] possessions"—a phrase which the authors of the American *Declaration of Independence* borrowed and amended to read, "life, liberty, and the pursuit of happiness" (Vol. 6).

The liberties of Englishmen are held in the 1689 document to rest mainly with the sovereignty of Parliament against the king. Their statement, expanded through the successive documents in Volume 6, culminates in the United Nations' statement of the rights of man as man. In addition to the general rights asserted by the earlier documents, it asserts the individual's freedom of residence and movement, both within his own country and for the purpose of leaving his own or any other country (*and* to return to his own country). It asserts the freedom of association—and the freedom *not* to associate. It maintains the universal right to work, free choice of employment, the right to form and join trade unions, "just and favorable conditions of work," protection against unemployment, social security, education, and a "standard of living adequate for the health and well-being of [every individual] and of his family."

Can these be said to be rights in any strict sense? Who is to guarantee them? Government? And if not government, who? And how is, for example, a "standard of living adequate for health and well-being" to be guaranteed by government (or any other power) in the underdeveloped and overpopulated societies in which most people live on or over the brink of starvation?

We may note that these "rights" are not only a spelling-out of the political liberties implied in the older documents but include economic conditions which the older documents do not touch; conditions which, in fact, cannot be guaranteed in the same way as political liberty. What the *Declaration* reveals is the growing power in the world of the doctrine, so boisterously maintained by the Communists, but also embraced by the hungry of the new nations of Africa and Asia, that economic "rights" take precedence over the political. The *Universal Declaration of Human Rights* must, indeed, be considered in the context of the divided world in which we live. Like its predecessors—including *The Declaration of Independence*—it may be taken to be a statement of an ideal rather than a statutory or contractual commitment.

The *Declaration* was adopted by the United Nations by a 48-0 vote, with several abstentions, including those of the Communist countries in which such liberties as assembly, association, employment, and travel are rigidly restricted, and in which the *Declaration's* "freedom of opinion and expression" range from curtailment to nonexistence. But it is clear in any case that the extension of the basic political liberties is only a sentiment in behalf of a vision of what might be, since most, if not all, governments outside the Communist bloc (including the United States) maintain the policy of refusing passports to certain of their citizens. Indeed, it cannot be gainsaid that no society now exists, or ever has, in which all the rights of the *Declaration* are fully protected.

What does appear as we peruse the historic statements of liberty is the development of the modern idea that it includes self-government as one of its essentials. Beginning with the assertion in *The English Bill of Rights* that "the pretended power of suspending of laws, or the execution of laws, by regal authority, without consent of parliament, is illegal," the doctrine of self-government reaches its full flower two and a half centuries later in the United Nations *Declaration:* "Everyone has the right to take part in the Government of his country, directly or through freely chosen representatives. . . . The will of the people shall be the basis of the authority of government; this shall be expressed in periodic and genuine elections which shall be by universal and equal suffrage."

How is the sovereignty of the people to be exercised? "By representative government," wrote James Mill, in his *Essay on Government* a century and a half ago. "For though the people, who cannot exercise the powers of government themselves, must entrust them to some one individual or set of individuals, and such individuals will infallibly have the strongest motives to make bad use of them, it is possible that checks may be found sufficient to prevent them." But only a generation later his still more renowned son, John Stuart Mill, is worrying whether checks, not on the government but on the people themselves, may be found: "In a representative body actually deliberating, the minority must of course be overruled; and in an equal democracy . . . the majority of the people, through their representatives, will outvote and prevail over the minority and their representatives. But does it follow that the minority should have no representatives at all?" (*Representative Government*, in GBWW, Vol. 43, p. 370c.)

This concern over the "tyranny of the majority" is also found in de Tocqueville's study of the United States in the early nineteenth century. He concludes that "the advantage of democracy [over aristocracy] is not, as has sometimes been asserted, that it protects the interests of the whole community, but simply that it protects those of the majority" ("Observations on American Life and Government," Vol. 6).

Thus we encounter in America, prior to the Civil War, the doctrine of "the concurrent majority" in John C. Calhoun's essay by that name (Vol. 7). Calhoun, representing the minority view of the slaveholders, argues that the majority-elected government may be kept from oppressing the minority by "dividing and distributing the powers of government," and giving "to each division or interest, through its appropriate organ, either a concurrent voice in making and executing the laws or a veto on their execution." An adaptation of this "state's rights" principle may be seen in the *Charter of the United Nations*, in which the veto by any one permanent member of the Security Council blocks action.

But then it is plain that the society does not have one indivisible government but is a federation of sovereign powers. This scheme may indeed protect minorities against the majority in a democratic society, but will it hold the society together? Here is the central issue in the United Nations, as it was in the League of Nations. Here was the issue of the American Civil War, as it is today in the conflict between the central and the state governments in the United States on the issue of racial integration. The twin dangers—of too much power or too little, of dictatorship or anarchy—are argued throughout the Federalist Papers written by Hamilton, Madison, and Jay in support of the new American *Constitution* after the War of Independence (GBWW, Vol. 43).

With absolute majority rule, what guarantee of rights can there ever be? Representative democracy established the rights of all against a tyrannical government; how are the rights of the minority to be maintained against the majority? The minority may be 49.99+% of the electorate—in which event it is hard for the majority to oppress it—or it may be a very small percentage of numerically helpless dissenters. Or it may be a single individual, asserting the rights of the individual against society. This figure we see among the heroes and martyrs of history, beginning with Christ and Socrates. Their "rights" are crushed. But can we expect *any* form of social organization to allow one individual to hamstring its activities?

This is the hard question to which Henry David Thoreau addresses himself in his powerful essay, *Civil Disobedience* (Vol. 6). Thoreau refused to pay his taxes because a portion of them supported the Mexican War and slavery in the United States. He was sent to prison and released when his friend Emerson (whose essay on Thoreau we read in Vol. 6), paid his taxes for him. Thoreau, seeing the one individual at the mercy of the majority, asks if democracy as we know it is "the last improvement possible in government? Is it not possible to take a step further toward recognizing and organizing the rights of man? There will never be a really free and enlightened state until the state comes to recognize the individual as a higher and independent power."

But can there be such a State? Would it still be a State? Would it not instantly dissolve into anarchy? Washington in his *Farewell Address* (Vol. 6) says that until the *Constitution* is changed it is "sacredly obligatory upon all." Abraham Lincoln, taking the oath as President in the dreadful year 1860, asserts in his *First Inaugural Address* (Vol. 6) that "it will be much safer for all, both in official and private stations, to conform to, and abide by, all those acts which stand unrepealed, than to violate any of them. . . ." But John Brown claimed that he had a more sacred obligation than the *Constitution* and the laws, an obligation to free the slaves; and as Thoreau defends the abolitionist (*A Plea for Captain John Brown,* Vol. 6), so Carlyle, in *The Hero as King* (Vol. 6), defends the words of Oliver Cromwell against the scandal they produced: "If the King should meet me in battle, I would kill the King."

Land of the Free—and Equal

The state so consecrated to human liberty that it long stood on the brink of anarchy—and the one and only state ever so established —was the United States of America. Elsewhere the rights of man have been won piecemeal: the tree of liberty was watered by the blood of millions, from the time of the slave revolutions like that of Spartacus in Rome (Plutarch, *Lives*, in GBWW, Vol. 14, pp. 442a– 444a, 508c-d). In America, it was planted by the men who founded the new nation and nurtured by the waves of the oppressed of Europe who swarmed to her open shores.

The United States is the case history of a human community hewn out of the wilderness to serve as a laboratory for utopianism then and thereafter. The American experiment staggered mankind and triggered all the revolutions that followed it. And it is a relatively new revolution and a new history, its beginnings voluminously recorded by capable writers and keen observers; a historian's paradise. A geographical paradise, too: a "vast tract of continent," as George Washington said, "comprehending all the various soils and climates of the world, and abounding with all the necessaries and conveniences of life." An Eden, with an indigenous population so small and scattered as to be routed by what, in military terms, were merely skirmishes.

An empty paradise, in effect, into which poured all the national and racial stocks of the earth in a process of self-selection. Only those came who wanted to start life anew, build "new heavens and a new earth," in the words of Christopher Columbus taken from the Book of Isaiah. "Here," says the American chronicler Crèvecoeur, "individuals of all nations are melted into a new race of men, whose labours and posterity will one day cause great changes in the world" ("The Making of Americans," Vol. 6). None of the nations of the earth had been (or has up to now been) populated by peoples so diverse in background as America; nor of any other nation, past or present, may it be said that its people were there because they wanted to be there *and went there*.

In *Gateway to the Great Books*, we read the works of many Americans and commentators on America. Among the former are its greatest men of letters, Hawthorne, Emerson, Thoreau, Mark Twain, Melville, Poe, Whitman, James; among the latter such European geniuses as de Tocqueville, whose "Observations on American Life and Government" (Vol. 6) should be studied by every American interested to know his own country as only a stranger can study a country and know it. The America that fascinated de Tocqueville in the 1830's fascinates us today, with its people and their manners and attitudes brilliantly delineated, their accomplishments, their short-comings, and their perils both seen and unseen in their utopian form of government and the spirit of their society.

Urged by a variety of motives—high and low—the dissatisfied came pouring into the new land. Crèvecoeur, who saw them come, found that in the new land: "Everything has tended to regenerate them; new laws, a new mode of living, a new social system; here they are become men: in Europe they were as so many useless plants, wanting vegetative mold, and refreshing showers; they withered, and were mowed down by want, hunger, and war; but now by the power of transplantation, like all other plants they have taken root and flourished!" ("The Making of Americans," Vol. 6.) There was room for everybody, and room for everybody to go on and up. The "new world," it was called; it was the old dream at long last come true, and it uncoiled the springs in the hearts of men "within half an hour after landing at New York," as Henry Adams said ("The United States in 1800," Vol. 6).

They were the "laboring poor" of Europe, who were suddenly numbered as free and independent citizens, for the first time in history the equal of every other man. There was all the work they wanted, and no unemployment, and they had only to work and save for a few years to become independent farmers and tradesmen. They came to think of themselves as individuals, and to be moved by individual self-interest to get ahead and always further ahead. Under their suddenly animated hands the economy sprang to life, and the sanctity of private property, the right to acquire it in free competition, to improve it, to dispose of it as one wished, grew at the center of the American faith, a doctrine shared enthusiastically by statesmen as different from one another as Thomas Jefferson and Herbert Hoover.

The rich open country afforded men good land cheap and even free—men whose ancestors had from time immemorial slaved on other men's land in Europe. Freedom of speech and press and assembly and worship created a society in which, as de Tocqueville noted, everyone talked politics all the time and everyone joined associations of every kind. And freedom to exercise one's talents and ambitions released in these new men and women a materialism pent up for generations; people whose parents had starved to death dreamed of seeing their children rich. And that, too, came to pass.

But at the heart of the phenomenon lay something other than the love of freedom, said de Tocqueville: "I think that democratic communities have a natural taste for freedom; left to themselves, they will seek it, cherish it, and view any privation of it with regret. But for equality, their passion is ardent, insatiable, incessant, invincible: they call for equality in freedom; and if they cannot obtain that, they still call for equality in slavery. They will endure poverty, servitude, barbarism, but they will not endure aristocracy" ("Observations on American Life and Government," Vol. 7).

The passion for equality was fortified by the country's freedom from the militarism which had formed the base of all European caste and class. The puny thirteen American colonies had repulsed the British Empire; behind the moat of the two oceans they could not be successfully attacked. Maintaining that a militia would be enough to defend the new country, Washington in his *Farewell Address* (Vol. 6) warned against "those overgrown military establishments which under any form of government are inauspicious to liberty, and which are to be regarded as particularly hostile to republican liberty"; an echo of the assertion in the great *Virginia Declaration of Rights* (Vol. 6) that "standing armies, in time of peace, should be avoided as dangerous to liberty."

Believing, according to Adams, that "in the long run interest, not violence, would rule the world, and that the United States must depend for safety and success on the interests they could create, [the early Americans] were tempted to look upon war and preparations for war as the worst of blunders; for they were sure that every dollar capitalized in industry was a means of overthrowing their enemies more effective than a thousand dollars spent on frigates or standing armies. The success of the American system was, from this point of view, a question of economy. If they could relieve themselves from debts, taxes, armies, and government interference with industry, they must succeed in outstripping Europe in economy of production; and Americans were even then partly aware that if their machine were not so weakened by these economies as to break down in the working, it must of necessity break down every rival" ("The United States in 1800," Vol. 6).

We may say now that these men were optimists; but they had

reason to be. Everything—except history—was propitious to their experiment. Above all, they believed in it—and not just the eminent leaders but the millions and more millions who came to participate in it. They believed that it was, in Jefferson's words, "the world's best hope" (*First Inaugural Address*, Vol. 6); in Washington's, "a most conspicuous theater, which seems to be peculiarly designated by Providence for the display of human greatness and felicity" (*Circular Letter to the Governors of All the States on Disbanding the Army*, Vol. 6). And Adams observed that European travelers in this early America "noticed that everywhere, in the White House at Washington and in log cabins beyond the Alleghenies, except for a few Federalists, every American, from Jefferson and Gallatin down to the poorest squatter, seemed to nourish an idea that he was doing what he could to overthrow the tyranny which the past had fastened on the human mind."

The Shadow of War

In the 1830's Alexis de Tocqueville wrote the following remarkable words: "There are, at the present time, two great nations in the world which seem to tend towards the same end, although they started from different points: I allude to the Russians and the Americans. . . . Their starting point is different and their courses are not the same; yet each of them seems to be marked out by the will of Heaven to sway the destinies of half the globe" ("Observations on American Life and Government," Vol. 6).

What de Tocqueville did not predict—nor did anyone else—was that the hostility of Russia and America would one day threaten the extinction of the human race. There was little his imagination failed to grasp, but its grasp did not reach to the scientific development in which weapons, which in his time measured their carrying power in yards, would carry their deadly message for thousands of miles across oceans and continents.

On the contrary, he appeared to see a prospect for world peace in the fact that "the nations seem to be advancing to unity. Our means of intellectual intercourse unite the most remote parts of the earth; and it is impossible for men to remain strangers to each other, or to be ignorant of the events which are taking place in any corner of the globe." If this was true in 1835, how much truer it is today! Never has the world been so close to unification as now; never before could unification be imagined on an other than utopian basis. But this so nearly unified world is more bitterly divided than it has ever been, and everywhere men speak nowadays not of peace and unity but of aggression and war.

"Certain attitudes toward war between states seem to recur in every century," according to the *Syntopicon's* introduction to the subject of WAR AND PEACE (GBWW, Vol. 3, p. 1010 *et seq.*). "In the face of the ever-present fact of war, men deplore its folly or find some benefit to compensate for its devastation. But throughout most of the tradition, those who see only suffering, no less than those who celebrate the martial spirit, seem to accept the necessity of war. Good or bad, or a mixture of the glorious and the horrible, war seems, to most of those who write about it, an inevitable thing—as ineradicable as disease and death for the living body, as inescapable as tragedy. Only in recent times has the inevitability of war been questioned, and the possibility of lasting peace proposed."

If war between individuals can be controlled by the establishment of the civil commonwealth, why cannot the war of state against state be placed under a world organization of law and order? Must we say that the nation-state is the ultimate development of human society? Is an association beyond it impossible to man? Or is it a stage in social progress, requiring decades or centuries before men will subordinate national interests and customs to those of the world unified by technology?

In *Gateway to the Great Books* there are several selections which bear on this question. Clausewitz, in his *What Is War?* (Vol. 7) represents the viewpoint of war's inevitability. To him, it is a natural part of the political intercourse between nations; for no moral force exists apart from the conception of a state and law. "We have to think of war not as an independent thing, but as a political instrument. . . . We see," he says, "that war is not merely a political act but a real political instrument, a continuation of political intercourse, a carrying out of the same by other means. . . . for the political design is the object, while war is the means, and the means can never be thought of apart from the object." He sees human intelligence concerned only with the question of when to use war, not with its elimination.

Malthus is an unhappier apologist for war. In his essay, "The Principle of Population," in Volume 7, he expounds his theory that "the power of population is indefinitely greater than the power in the earth to produce subsistence for man," and that war is one of the means by which this imbalance is corrected. Even so, he noted that "the commission of war is vice, and the effect of it misery," but adds: "To prevent the recurrence of misery, is, alas! beyond the power of man."

But there have always been men—more today than ever before —who have refused to concede that the misery of war is beyond man's power to prevent. And the commonwealth *within which* peace prevails has long since suggested to poets and philosophers (and more recently to many "practical" men) that a commonwealth of the whole earth is the solution. The argument for world government as a means to world peace was first made by Dante himself in the thirteenth century in his "On World Government," in Volume 7 of this set. "Wherever there can be contention," he wrote, "there judgment should exist. . . . Between any two governments, neither of which is in any way subordinate to the other, contention can arise. . . . Therefore there should be judication between them. And since neither can know the affairs of the other, not being subordinated (for among equals there is no authority), there must be a third and wider power which can rule both within its own jurisdiction.

"This third power is either the world government or it is not. If it is, we have reached our conclusion; if it is not, it must in turn have its equal outside its jurisdiction, and then it will need a third party as judge, and so ad infinitum, which is impossible. So we must arrive at a first and supreme judge for whom all contentions are judiciable either directly or indirectly. . . . Therefore, world government is necessary for the world."

He realized that the obstacles were formidable: "O race of men, how many storms and misfortunes must thou endure, and how many shipwrecks, because thou, beast of many heads, strugglest in many directions! Thou art sick at heart and sick in mind, both theoretical and practical! No irrefutable arguments appeal to thy theoretical reason, and no amount of experience to thy practical intelligence, and even thine emotions are not moved by the sweet, divine persuasiveness which sounds to thee from the trumpet of the Holy Spirit."

Centuries later Immanuel Kant, in his *Perpetual Peace* (Vol. 7), found that nature's "mechanical march evidently announces the grand aim of producing among men, against their intention, harmony from the very bosom of their discords." Here he refers to the fact that man's warlike nature has forced him to submit to coercive laws in his own self-interest, and not as a matter of morality, resulting in societies and states. But perpetual peace requires "moral politicians," he says, reminding us of the immortal dictum of Socrates that only when kings are philosophers and philosophers kings will society know surcease.

As to the form the future world organization would take, Kant thinks that "The public right ought to be founded upon a federation of free states." The *ideal* would be "a society of nations" which would "submit themselves to coercive laws," but as this is a practical impossibility, "there can only be substituted, to the positive idea of an universal republic (if all is not to be lost) the negative supplement of a permanent alliance . . ."; in short, a federation, not a union.

The Issue of Our Time

And this—federation or union—is the heart of the issue. Rousseau, in his *A Lasting Peace through the Federation of Europe* (Vol. 7), in the eighteenth century proposed a European *federation* (since, he said, Europe was already homogenous because of geography, trade and commerce, habit and custom, and religion), but it was actually a federal *union*, with a legislative body with power to pass binding laws, a coercive force to enforce laws and prohibitions, and the power to prevent the withdrawal of any member. But he concluded gloomily that such an organization could never be established except by a revolution. "That being so," he says, "which of us would dare to say whether the League of Europe is a thing more to be desired or feared? It would perhaps do more harm in a moment than it would guard against for ages."

If the problem of conflicting sovereignties is to be resolved, all conflicts which arise between states must be submitted to a higher power for arbitration, and, as in civil society, this power must have the force to ensure that its decisions are obeyed. An *indissoluble* community requires a government superior to any or all of its components. This was the issue of the American Civil War, and before that, the heart of the greatest of the great debates in American history—whether to adopt the *Constitution* in place of the unworkable *Articles of Confederation.*

In the *Charter of the United Nations* (Vol. 6), the preamble states that the people are "determined to save succeeding generations from the scourge of war. . . ." But Chapter I, Article 2, Paragraph 1, asserts that "the Organization is based on the principle of the sovereign equality of all its Members"—just as were the ill-fated American *Articles of Confederation*. And after establishing the all-powerful Security Council, Paragraph 3 of Article 27 provides, in effect, that any permanent member may prevent action by the Security Council by casting a negative vote—the power of veto. And the veto is coupled with a still broader assertion of national sovereignty, which provides that "nothing contained in the present Charter shall authorize the United Nations to intervene in matters which are essentially within the domestic jurisdiction of any state or shall require the Members to submit such matters to settlement under the present Charter" (Chap. I, Art. 2, Par. 7).

But these are the same guarantees of sovereignty which, as "state's rights," had wrecked the confederation of American states after the Revolution. Similar guarantees of national sovereignty undid the League of Nations. Germany quit the League in 1935, just as South Carolina had seceded from the American Union in 1860—both of them on the principle of sovereignty which forbade interference in their domestic affairs or organizational action without their consent. Can we say that a community from which a member resigns when he is charged with an offense is a true community?

Like the League, and like every federation of sovereigns before it, the United Nations was destined to great achievements *in matters on which the sovereign members could agree*. The United Nations could, and did, and still does, prevent or end "small wars," and, in so doing, earned the gratitude of all mankind. The only war it cannot prevent is the big one on the verge of which the world seems to have teetered since 1948. None of the heads of the three great powers (Britain, the U.S.A., and the U.S.S.R., who agreed to the veto at Yalta in 1945) nor, in all probability, their peoples, were able to move beyond Hegel's conception of the nation-state as "the absolute power on earth" (*The Philosophy of Right,* in GBWW, Vol. 46, p. 108d).

Like war, chattel slavery was for thousands of years regarded as part of the order of the universe. An Aristotle thought it was natural (*Politics,* in GBWW, Vol. 9, p. 448c); a John Locke accepted it as a concomitant of conquest (*Concerning Civil Government,* in GBWW, Vol. 35, p. 43d); a Thomas Jefferson wrote *The Declaration of Independence* (Vol. 6) without denouncing it. But it was destroyed at last, partly, to be sure, by machinery that was cheaper even than slaves, but partly by the slowly evolving moral and religious sentiment of mankind. The combination of man's self-interest and morality may do away with war—before war does away with man.

The issue is man himself. What is he? What is the nature and limit of his freedom, his will, his passions? Can he change or be changed, and in turn change the character of human society? These are the ultimate questions that have to be answered. By science? Or by philosophy?

IV

Science and Mathematics

Product and Process

Every day, every hour, every minute, modern man feels the accelerating impact of science on his life. Science has a hand in nearly everything which affects him—his food, clothing, shelter, job, amusements, and cultural pursuits. The very air he breathes has been changed by the combustion engine and by nuclear fission. His whole environment is constantly being altered.

Should we not, then, try to understand science? Why? Why should we not be content, rather, simply to read the instructions on the outside of the package, and forget about the ideas, the techniques, and the processes that went into the making of the product? Are not the findings, after all, the only things that need concern us? We read a poem written two thousand years ago because it still has something to tell us. But science is progressive and rapidly outdated; why read about ideas that have been superseded by two thousand years, or even two years? And if science is a mystery story, why not just read the last page?

But the last page has not yet been written, the mystery is still not solved. Perhaps it will never be; and if it is, it may turn out that the clues were in the first chapter. And in all the chapters, from the first to the latest, there is the story of one of the most important activities of man: his struggle to comprehend his universe.

Man is the question-asking animal, and his first questions begin with the world he sees around him, the "world of science." He wonders, and his wonder will not let him rest. He feels that he is growing when he is inquiring and investigating and only when he is inquiring and investigating. He wants to know—and always to push beyond the known. He is a "natural-born" frontiersman. Let him discover a new world, and he pushes on to a new planet, a new universe. To ask is to be excited. To be excited is to live.

True, this curiosity is not evenly distributed among all men. All of us possess it in insatiable quantity at birth. Unfortunately, most of us lose it, or stifle it, as we grow older. A few men and women retain it, and are activated by it, all their lives. They become the persistently, professionally curious whose curiosity changes the world. This is the fraternity to which the great scientists—like the great poets and philosophers—belong.

The rest of us need not be content with only the end product of science. We may all know the why and the how. True, the terminology of science and technology is "another language," but it is a language which we can comprehend, above all when we tackle the original masterpieces—the exposition of the fundamental discoveries upon which the highly technical applications are all based. And our comprehension is facilitated by the fact that many such works are expounding theories which, once strange and spectacular, have long since become familiar to us.

It is in the presentation of a new concept that the scientist is most precise, clear, and simple. He is not, at this point, speaking to specialists and technicians—they will come later—and he is not talking shop with his colleagues. At the great turning points in the advance of science there is no inside group waiting to receive the word in language that only it can understand. Here the scientist comes closest to speaking to everyone; it is here that he is most eloquent and lucid.

A scientific theory is like a shelter against chaos. It is designed to hold in some sort of order the known facts of the universe. New facts require a little juggling of the old, the addition of a new wing or second story; some sections may have to be torn down and rebuilt. Increasingly inadequate, the structure stands, representing a world view, a comfort to man who cannot rest until he perceives that nature has a pattern.

Then, one day, there is a crisis. The foundation begins to crumble. A hypothesis that has been brought in to "save the appearances" has become an embarrassment, and is now a skeleton in the closet. But most pressing of all, new knowledge has been acquired that does not fit in anywhere. It is time for a move.

Rescuing materials that will be useful in building anew, the scientist starts all over again to build a shelter; never entirely from scratch, for he always manages to salvage something, often a great deal. It is in the salvaged material that the continuity of science exists. There are no complete breaks in the story. There are dormant periods, blind alleys, revolutions, and crises, but no breaks.

Sometimes the new structure can be built only because the framework had been created decades, or even centuries, before by mathematicians, who, pursuing mathematical knowledge for its own sake, foresaw no possible applications of their formulas to science. The idea of conics was for more than 1500 years a purely intellectual exercise. Euclid, Archimedes, and Apollonius investigated the mathematical properties of these curves, which were not then known in nature. Then, early in the 17th century, when Kepler discovered that planets move in elliptical orbits, the language in which to express his theory was found in conics.

The story of science could be told in a series of such crises. "There are no eternal theories in science," Albert Einstein and Leopold Infeld write in "The Rise and Decline of Classical Physics" (Vol. 8). "It always happens that some of the facts predicted by a theory are disproved by experiment. Every theory has its period of gradual development and triumph, after which it may experience a rapid decline. . . . Nearly every great advance in science arises from a crisis in the old theory, through an endeavor to find a way out of the difficulties created. We must examine old ideas, old theories, although they belong to the past, for this is the only way to understand the importance of the new ones and the extent of their validity."

The establishment and development in the seventeenth century of classical physics, to which Einstein and Infeld refer, represented just such a crisis—a break with the past. It began, as so often happens, with a revolution, the "Copernican revolution." The new structure was imposing, and the architects were giants. Copernicus, Galileo, Kepler, and Newton outlined the material framework for the world in which man lived from the second half of the seventeenth century to the end of the nineteenth.

The Greek astronomer Ptolemy was a great synthesizer of knowledge, and his sytem of the world also represented a break with the past. Before Ptolemy, astronomy consisted largely of a mass of more or less unconnected observations of the movements of the heavenly bodies. Ptolemy's theory imposed a unity upon these masses of data and was adequate to the phenomena then observable. The shift from Ptolemy, who believed that the earth was the center of the universe, to Copernicus, who offered the simpler hypothesis that the sun was at the center, and therefore that the earth was only a small part of a vast cosmic arrangement, was a shock to the imagination. The trust that man placed in his senses seemed to be undermined; things were not as they appeared to be. Still worse, the belief that the universe had been created especially for man seemed to be shaken by the new theory.

Sigmund Freud characterizes this change as the first "great outrage" upon humanity's "naïve self-love . . . when it realized that our earth was not the centre of the universe, but only a tiny speck in a world-system of a magnitude hardly conceivable; this is associated in our minds with the name of Copernicus . . ." (*A General Introduction to Psycho-Analysis,* in GBWW, Vol. 54, p. 562c-d). This "outrage" expressed itself in the form of fear and resistance. Sometimes it grew so strong and so bitter that it burst forth as outright persecution. Galileo was a brilliant scientist, whose monumental contributons in the fields of astronomy and physics had kept the Copernican revolution surging ever forward. His investigations were so disturbing that he was finally accused of defying religious authority.

Tommaso Campanella, in his seventeenth-century defense of Galileo, described the objections to Galileo in the following manner: "Holy Scripture counsels us to 'seek nothing higher, nor attempt to know more than it is necessary to know'; that we 'leap not over the bounds which the fathers set'; and that 'the diligent searcher of majesty is overcome by vain-glory.' Galileo disregards this counsel, subjects the heavens to his invention, and constructs the whole fabric of the world according to his pleasure. Cato rightly taught us to 'leave secret things to God, and to permit Heaven to inquire concerning them; for he who is mortal should concern himself with mortal things'" ("Arguments for and against Galileo," Vol. 8). But to Galileo, subjecting the heavens to the "spyglass" he had invented, it seemed "a matter of no small importance to have ended the dispute about the milky way by making its nature manifest to the very senses as well as to the intellect" (*The Starry Messenger,* Vol. 8).

"To Venture Forth"

The human spirit is resilient, and gains courage from knowledge. Though Pascal says that he is frightened when he sees himself "engulfed in the infinite immensity of spaces of which I am ignorant and which know me not," he also writes: "It is not from space that I must seek my dignity, but from the government of my thought. I shall have no more if I possess worlds. By space the universe encompasses and swallows me up like an atom; by thought I comprehend the world" (*Pensées*, in GBWW, Vol. 33, p. 211a; p. 234a). Mankind slowly learned to accept the continuing questioning of science, even when it produced profoundly disquieting and bewildering results.

Having once and for all been thrown out of the center of the universe, man lost a throne, but achieved mobility. The modern conception of man, located somewhere between the edge of infinity in one direction and the nucleus of the atom in the other, is presented pictorially in *Cosmic View*, by Kees Boeke (Vol. 8). The ability to measure man in space is scientific and modern; the insight that bridges distances and dispels the terror of immensity is philosophical and ancient. Centuries ago, Marcus Aurelius wrote: "Whether the universe is a concourse of atoms, or nature is a system, let this first be established, that I am a part of the whole which is governed by nature . . ." (*Meditations*, in GBWW, Vol. 12, p. 297a).

Modern scientists claim the "right to venture forth in the world of ideas [as well as] to extend . . . horizons in the physical universe" (*Beyond the Googol*, Vol. 9). This right has been won. And the world of ideas includes such once "dangerous" concepts as the idea of the end of the world. But nowadays, even such a prediction of ultimate natural catastrophe arouses no condemnation and produces no martyrs of science. It is neither delivered, nor received, with terror or anguish. Arthur Eddington, for instance, sees the universe as inexorably running down, with no possibility of its being wound up again to repeat the cycle. So be it, he says. He would rather "that the universe should accomplish some great scheme of evolution and, having achieved whatever may be achieved, lapse back into chaotic changelessness, than that its purpose should be banalised by continual repetition. I am an Evolutionist, not a Multiplicationist" (*The Running-Down of the Universe*, Vol. 8).

Modern scientific theory is flexible, making no claim to being the last word, or even, except provisionally, the right word. Modern science says: This is the way we describe things—today. Copernicus upset a world that had been saying: This is the way things are—forever. The world that he upset was the world that had been ruled by the thought of Aristotle for over 1,500 years.

Since the beginning of the seventeenth century, almost every scientific advance has had to begin with a refutation of some Aristotelian doctrine. Why is Aristotle now regarded as having long imposed a barrier to scientific progress? Is it because, as the *Syntopicon* suggests, he relied too strongly on his senses? "Just as Ptolemy's astronomy conforms to what we see as we look at the heavens, so Aristotle's physics represents a too simple conformity with everyday sense-experience. We observe fire rising and stones falling. Mix earth, air, and water in a closed container, and air bubbles will rise to the top, while the particles of earth will sink to the bottom. To cover a multitude of similar observations, Aristotle develops the theory of the natural motions and places of the four terrestrial elements—earth, air, fire, and water. Since bodies move naturally only to attain their proper places, the great body which is the earth, already at the bottom of all things, need not move at all. Being in its proper place, it is by nature stationary" (GBWW, Vol. 2, p. 92b).

The fate that Aristotle suffered at the hands of his successors, who took his tentative conclusions as a rounded body of complete knowledge rather than as incentives to inquiry and further discovery, indicates that science is the making of knowledge, and not knowledge as such. And in the making of knowledge, modern science uses two tools that Aristotle did not use—experiment and mathematics.

Experiment and Observation

While the scientific method employs both experiment and observation, it is clear that not all branches of science are experimental. As the *Syntopicon* points out: "It is not always possible for the scientist to perform experiments, as, for example, in astronomy, where the phenomena can be methodically observed and exactly recorded, but cannot be manipulated or controlled. Among the great books of natural science, the biological writings of Hippocrates, Aristotle, Galen, and Darwin, the astronomical works of Ptolemy, Copernicus, Kepler, and Newton, and the clinical studies of Freud are examples of scientific works which are more or less empirical, but not experimental" (GBWW, Vol. 2, p. 474b).

Due, however, to the great strides made by physics and chemistry from the middle of the nineteenth century, experiment has gained so much prestige that it has been hailed by some as the only method of obtaining knowledge of any kind, scientific or otherwise. Furthermore, it has been said that questions which cannot be answered by scientific methods are not only unanswerable: they should not even be asked.

In *The Great Conversation* (in GBWW, Vol. 1), we find a discussion of the question whether the scientific method can be extended beyond the natural sciences. "Consider, for example, statements about God's existence or the immortality of the soul. These are answers to questions that cannot be answered—one way or the other—by the experimental method. If that is the only method by which probable and verifiable knowledge is attainable, we are debarred from having knowledge about God's existence or the immortality of the soul. If modern man, accepting the view that he can claim to know only what can be demonstrated by experiment or verified by empirical research, still wishes to believe in these things, he must acknowledge that he does so by religious faith or by the exercise of his will to believe; and he must be prepared to be regarded in certain quarters as hopelessly superstitious."

The author of *The Great Conversation* goes on to consider what is meant by the scientific method. "If all that is meant is that a scientist is honest and careful and precise, and that he weighs all the evidence with discrimination before he pronounces judgment, then we can agree that the scientific method is the only method of reaching and testing the truth in any field." But, he adds, these methods have been used by historians, philosophers, and theologians since the beginning of time, and it is misleading to name after science a method used in so many fields.

Does the scientific method mean the observing and collecting of facts? Though facts are indispensable, they are not sufficient. "To solve a problem it is necessary to think. It is necessary to think even to decide what facts to collect. Even the experimental scientist cannot avoid being a liberal artist, and the best of them, as the great books show, are men of imagination and of theory as well as patient observers of particular facts."

Whatever is meant by scientific method, the writer continues, "the issue remains whether the method associated with experimental science, as that has developed in modern times, is the only method of seeking the truth about what really exists or about what men and societies should do" (GBWW, Vol. 1, pp. 33–37 *passim*).

Questions raised by the experimental method are not confined to its use outside of natural science. There is also a feeling that even within certain branches of science, it is no longer sufficient unto itself. This is the attitude of Max Planck, one of the giants of contemporary physics. (He is the "father" of quantum mechanics.) "Scientists," says Planck, "have learned that the starting point of their investigations does not lie solely in the perceptions of the senses, and that science cannot exist without some small portion of metaphysics. Modern physics impresses us particularly with the truth of the old doctrine which teaches that there are realities existing apart from our sense perceptions, and that there are problems and conflicts where these realities are of greater value for us than the richest treasures of the world of experience" (*The Universe in the Light of Modern Physics,* reprinted in *The Great Ideas Today 1962,* p. 521).

All through the great books, we find examples of man's efforts to seek the truth about the world and himself, and the boundary line between the scientific and the nonscientific method is not always clear. Consider, for instance, the collecting of facts. Since facts are beyond number, and since the man of science must make a judgment when he decides *which* facts to consider, on what basis does he make his judgment? It is the aesthetic sensibility that chooses, says Henri Poincaré. "It may be surprising to see emotional sensibility invoked *à propos* of mathematical demonstrations which, it would seem, can interest only the intellect. This would be to forget the feeling of mathematical beauty, of the harmony of numbers and forms, of geometric elegance. This is a true esthetic feeling that all real mathematicians know, and surely it belongs to emotional sensibility" (*Mathematical Creation,* Vol. 9).

Considering the application of mathematics to science, Campbell touches on the same point when he says that "relations which appeal to the sense of the mathematician by their neatness and simplicity are found to be important in the external world of experiment. . . . The expert mathematician has a sense about symbols, as symbols; he looks at a page covered with what, to anyone else, are unintelligible scrawls of ink, and he immediately realizes whether the argument expressed by them is such as is likely to satisfy his sense of form; whether the argument will be 'neat' and the results 'pretty.'" The author believes that "the only way to understand what Einstein did is to look at the symbols in which his theory must ultimately be expressed and to realize that it was reasons of symbolic form, and such reasons alone, which led him to arrange the symbols in the way he did and in no other" (*Numerical Laws and the Use of Mathematics in Science*, Vol. 9).

The same application of mathematical order and neatness to data resulted in the discovery of another important piece of scientific knowledge—the periodic law of the chemical elements ("The Genesis of a Law of Nature," Vol. 8). Is the man of science, then, for all his devotion to cold, hard facts, essentially an artist? Where do the patterns lie from which he constructs his model of reality? In nature, or in his mind?

Whose Footprint?

The interplay between the mind and the universe—which governs which?—may be a subject for the philosopher, but the scientist also has his philosophical moods. Tobias Dantzig (selections from his work are in Vol. 9 of this set) asks, "Has the universe an existence *per se* or does it exist only in the mind of man?" Giving a tentative answer to the age-old dilemma, he continues: "To the man of science, the acceptance of the one hypothesis or the other is not at all a question of 'to be or not to be'; for from the standpoint of logic either hypothesis is tenable, and from the standpoint of experience neither is demonstrable. So the choice will forever remain a matter of expediency and convenience. The man of science will act *as if* this world were an absolute whole controlled by laws independent of his own thoughts or acts; but whenever he discovers a law of striking simplicity or one of sweeping universality or one which points to a perfect harmony in the cosmos, he will be wise to wonder what role his mind has played in the discovery, and whether the beautiful image he sees in the pool of eternity reveals the nature of this eternity, or is but a reflection of his own mind" (*Number, The Language of Science*, 4th ed., The Macmillan Co., 1954, p. 233).

A. S. Eddington said, in *Space, Time and Gravitation* (Cambridge University Press, 1959 edition, p. 201), "We have found a strange foot-print on the shores of the unknown. We have devised profound theories, one after another, to account for its origin. At last, we have succeeded in reconstructing the creature that made the foot-print. And Lo! it is our own."

The question of the actual existence of the objects of scientific inquiry is nowhere more puzzling than in the field of mathematics.

Do mathematical truths reside in the external world, or are they man-made inventions? The answers reflect the dual role that mathematics plays—appearing sometimes as servant of science, sometimes as queen in her own right.

To Bertrand Russell, mathematics is independent of man, and her true role is that of queen. "To those who inquire as to the purpose of mathematics, the usual answer will be that it facilitates the making of machines, the travelling from place to place, and the victory over foreign nations, whether in war or commerce." Russell regards these ends of doubtful value, and adds: "As respects those pursuits which contribute only remotely, by providing the mechanism of life, it is well to be reminded that not the mere fact of living is to be desired, but the art of living in the contemplation of great things. . . . Mathematics, rightly viewed, possesses not only truth, but supreme beauty—a beauty cold and austere, like that of sculpture, without appeal to any part of our weaker nature, without the gorgeous trappings of painting or music, yet sublimely pure, and capable of a stern perfection such as only the greatest art can show. . . . The contemplation of what is non-human, the discovery that our minds are capable of dealing with material not created by them, above all, the realization that beauty belongs to the outer world as to the inner are the chief means of overcoming the terrible sense of impotence, of weakness, of exile amid hostile powers . . ." (*The Study of Mathematics*, Vol. 9).

But it is about mathematics as the servant of science that Lancelot Hogben writes when he says that mathematics is a language, a *size* language, developed in response to man's material needs: "Plato's exaltation of mathematics as an august and mysterious ritual had its roots in dark superstitions which troubled, and fanciful puerilities which entranced, people who were living through the childhood of civilization, when even the cleverest people could not clearly distinguish the difference between saying that 13 is a 'prime' number and saying that 13 is an unlucky number. His influence on education has spread a veil of mystery over mathematics and helped to preserve the queer freemasonry of the Pythagorean brotherhoods, whose members were put to death for revealing mathematical secrets now printed in school-books" (*Mathematics, the Mirror of Civilization*, Vol. 9).

It was from the "queer freemasonry" of the Pythagorean teachers that Plato derived the so-called "Platonic bodies," the five regular polyhedra that have equal sides and equal angles. The teachings of the Pythagoreans, who held that numbers have a real and separate existence, may seem fanciful now, but fancies have often been of value to science. It was from consideration of the "Platonic bodies" that Kepler developed the first unitary scheme of the universe (*Epitome of Copernican Astronomy*, in GBWW, Vol. 16, pp. 851b–872b).

In addition to having a reality apart from man, mathematics had, for Plato, "something in them which is necessary and cannot be set aside," something of "divine necessity." Plato believed that the necessities of knowledge which are divine and not human are "those of which he who has no use nor any knowledge at all cannot be a God, or demi-god, or hero to mankind, or able to take any serious thought or charge of them. And very unlike a divine man would he be, who is unable to count one, two, three, or to distinguish odd and even numbers . . ." (*Laws*, in GBWW, Vol. 7, p. 728b-c).

An opposing view about the nature of mathematics is presented by Henri Poincaré. With the development of non-Euclidean geometrics, it seems reasonable to ask which geometry is true. But the question is without meaning, says Poincaré. "Geometry is not true, it is advantageous." But does not one geometry come closest to being true? "One geometry cannot be more true than another; it can only be *more convenient*" (*Space*, Vol. 9). But this seems to say that the mathematician builds a habitation for himself rather than (as the Platonists believe) finds one eternally standing.

Such questions may be unanswerable, but even unanswerable questions serve as beacons. We cannot, for instance, know the *why* of things, says Claude Bernard. Absolute knowledge of the very essence of phenomena will always remain beyond our reach. "When we know that friction and that chemical action produce electricity, we are still ignorant of the primary nature of electricity." But, he continues, the search is not unfruitful. If a man of science carries experimental analysis far enough, he will see that though he is ignorant of the cause of the phenomenon, he will become its master. "The instrument at work is unknown, but [he] can use it" (*Experimental Considerations Common to Living Things and Inorganic Bodies*, Vol. 8).

Man's reluctance to believe that the universe may be without plan is centuries old. "Either it is a well-arranged universe or a chaos huddled together," admitted Marcus Aurelius. "But," he asked, "can a certain order subsist in thee, and disorder in the All?" (*Meditations*, in GBWW, Vol. 12, p. 266a). The persistence of the question indicates that, although much of modern science is directed toward controlling man's environment, scientific inquiry is based, at least partly, on man's desire to know what he himself is.

Evicted Again

Displacement from the center of the universe was only the first disruption of man's concept of his place in the scheme of nature. According to Freud, "The second was when biological research robbed man of his peculiar privilege of having been specially created, and relegated him to a descent from the animal world, implying an ineradicable animal nature to him: this transvaluation has been accomplished in our own time upon the instigation of Charles Darwin . . ." (*A General Introduction to Psycho-Analysis*, in GBWW, Vol. 54, p. 562c-d).

No scientific theory has ever extended so rapidly into every field of human endeavor as the theory of evolution. The substance of the theory is expounded in Volume 49 of *Great Books of the Western World;* the story of the author is told in Darwin's *Autobiography* in Volume 8 of *Gateway to the Great Books.* The influence of the theory continues to manifest itself in history, biology, sociology, medicine, geology, psychology, and other fields of study.

The raging controversies aroused by Darwin's theory of evolution in no way diminished scientific activity. In such fields as chemistry, anatomy, paleontology, and geology, the probing continued. The combined effect of all these areas of investigation was to present an ever-changing, sometimes radically-changing, picture, not only of the physical world, but of the very nature of life itself—and man's attitudes changed with that picture and are still changing. It is claimed, for example, that the discovery of DNA requires an entirely new conception of life.

The work of Friedrich Wöhler (*On the Artificial Production of Urea*, Vol. 8) had already weakened the arguments of the vitalists, who, dating from Aristotle, explained the nature of life as being due to a vital force peculiar to living organisms. Claude Bernard (*Experimental Considerations Common to Living Things and Inorganic Bodies*, Vol. 8) developed the theory that chemical laws are valid for living organisms. Comparative anatomy, the beginnings of which are found in the works of Aristotle and Galen, was used by Thomas H. Huxley to bolster the theory of man's kinship to the animals (*On the Relations of Man to the Lower Animals*, Vol. 8). And although the mechanism of heredity was unknown in Darwin's day, statistical methods had been devised and applied in such works on the subject as Francis Galton's "The Classification of Human Ability," from *Hereditary Genius* (Vol. 8).

Charles Lyell, who deeply influenced Darwin's whole thought and work, had suggested that natural forces still at work could account for the present structure of the earth. His glimpses into the past, revealed by the study of fossils, contributed to biological researches on which were based the concept of evolution ("Geological Evolution," Vol. 8). To Huxley, geology opened a book, whose authority could not be impeached. "There is a writing upon the wall of cliffs at Cromer, and whoso runs may read it," he says (*On a Piece of Chalk*, Vol. 8). For Huxley the writings pointed toward a connection between the physical changes of the world and the changes in its living inhabitants.

From the time of Galileo, many men have held that the worth of a science or a philosophy could be estimated by the degree to which it could be presented under mathematical formulas. David Hume, the eighteenth-century philosopher, went so far as to say, at the end of *An Enquiry Concerning Human Understanding:* "If we take in our hand any volume; of divinity or school metaphysics, for instance; let us ask, *Does it contain any abstract reasoning concerning quantity or number?* No. *Does it contain any experimental reasoning concerning matter of fact and existence?* No. Commit it then to the flames: for it can contain nothing but sophistry and illusion" (GBWW, Vol. 35, p. 509d).

Yet in the nineteenth century it was the nonmathematical geologists and biologists who framed most precisely the questions: What is man? What is his past and what is his future? If he is part of the animal world, does he differ from animals in having a soul? Does the doctrine of the survival of the fittest apply to human institutions? Does evolution necessarily mean progress? A large part of the essay on MAN in the *Syntopicon* is devoted to the questions that arise when man is considered in connection with the idea of evolution. The chapters on SOUL, EVOLUTION, PROGRESS, and NATURE are relevant too.

The study of man is an ancient one, and is the only study in which the knower and known are one. It may be that this unique relationship poses insoluble problems, and that the quest for knowledge will forever travel in a circle. But the *Syntopicon* says that the "ultimate questions which man asks about himself are partly answered by the very fact of their being asked. The answer may be that man is the measure of all things; that he is sufficient unto himself or at least sufficient for the station he occupies and the part he plays in the structure of the universe. The answer may be that man is not a god overlooking the rest of nature, or even at home in the environment of time and space, but rather that he is a finite and dependent creature aware of his insufficiency, a lonely wanderer seeking something greater than himself and this whole world. Whatever answer is given, man's asking what sort of thing he is, whence he comes, and whither he is destined symbolizes the two strains in human nature—man's knowledge and his ignorance, man's greatness and his misery" (GBWW, Vol. 3, p. 10c-d).

The whole structure of science is now so vast that no one person can hope to comprehend it. The scientist tends to specialize more and more intensely *within* a field—and to flounder as helplessly as any layman when he moves outside it. But the original thinking that characterized the early "greats" of science is still to be found in our time. Such thinking—in contrast to the work of the specialist or technician—inevitably leads the scientist to the ultimate questions about the universe. At the center of these questions stands man. What is man and what is the purpose of life? Once we ask *these* questions, we enter into the realm of philosophy.

V

Philosophy

Questions without Answers?

How ought we to live? Or is there an "ought"? Is there in fact a good (or right) way of life, and where are we to look for the knowledge of it? Is it demonstrable knowledge, like that of mathematics? Are we bound in reason to accept it as we are the findings of the scientists based on controlled experimentation and observation? If so, why don't we all cleave to its truth as we do to the physicist's or the engineer's? If not, are we to conclude that the realm of living is only a matter of speculation, in which one man's opinion is as good as another's and knowledge does not exist at all?

A true science (as we use the term today) does not tell us that we ought to do anything. Its business is to tell us what is, not what should be or should be done. The engineer does not tell us whether we ought to build a bridge. He says, "If you want to build a bridge, I can tell you how," and if we say, "But should we build a bridge rather than a school or a school rather than a hospital?" he says, "That's not for me to say. I'm only an engineer." So, too, the physician. He may tell us to stop smoking if we want to live longer, but when we say we'd rather smoke than live longer, he shrugs his shoulders and says, "That's up to you. I'm only a physician."

Who is there who is not only an engineer, or a physician, or a man who can answer all the questions but the hard ones? Who can help us make moral choices and political decisions? If there is a science of living, there should be a scientist whose "field" is just that, who can tell us what life is and what the right way to live is. If there is an applied science (or art) of living, there should be, not just a Doctor of Medicine, but a Doctor of Life, who can tell us with doctoral authority not how to live longer but how to live well. If there is a science or art of human life, it would certainly be the queen of all the sciences and merit the concentration of every young (and old) man and woman.

We sometimes speak of "a philosophy of life," as if philosophy is that science. But is it in fact a science, or even an art derived (like all the other arts) from the conclusions of science? Where are its laboratories in which rigorous experimentation is carried on by highly trained specialists under rigidly controlled conditions? Where are its proofs, to which every reasonable person must yield? Where are its experts, whose judgments are made on certain and indisputable knowledge? Or is it a science in a different sense? Or is it something else entirely?

These are the questions to which the selections in Volume 10 of *Gateway to the Great Books* lead us. Nor need we read very far before we discover that there are two disciplines which claim to have the knowledge—as surely as science has knowledge—of the way men ought to live: philosophy and theology. Neither need we read very far before we discover that not the least of the difficulties both of them have in maintaining their claims is their frequent and bitter opposition (in modern times) to each other. In his famous *History of Western Philosophy*, philosopher-mathematician Bertrand Russell (whom we read on mathematics in Vol. 9 of this set) tries to define the fields and their opposition and their problems thus:

"Philosophy . . . is something intermediate between theology and science. Like theology, it consists of speculations on matters as to which definite knowledge has, so far, been unascertainable; but like science, it appeals to human reason rather than to authority, whether that of tradition or that of revelation. All *definite* knowledge —so I should contend—belongs to science; all *dogma* as to what surpasses definite knowledge belongs to theology. But between theology and science there is a No Man's Land, exposed to attack from both sides; this No Man's Land is philosophy.

"Almost all the questions of most interest to speculative minds are such as science cannot answer, and the confident answers of theologians no longer seem so convincing as they did in former centuries. Is the world divided into mind and matter, and, if so, what is mind and what is matter? Is mind subject to matter, or is it possessed of independent powers? Has the universe any unity or purpose? Is it evolving towards some goal? Are there really laws of nature, or do we believe in them only because of our innate love of order? Is man what he seems to the astronomer, a tiny lump of impure carbon and water impotently crawling on a small and unimportant planet? Or is he what he appears to Hamlet? Is he perhaps both at once? Is there a way of living that is noble and another that is base, or are all ways of living merely futile?" (*A History of Western Philosophy*, Simon and Schuster, 1945, p. xiii.)

To such questions, as Russell says, no answers can be found in the laboratory. Where can they be found? Whose business is the answering of them? If they are unanswerable—unanswerable by science, theology, and philosophy—are we not in a fine fix indeed? What boots it to be able to answer the lesser questions of the physical and biological worlds if we cannot answer the greater?

Immanuel Kant, at the opening of his famous *Critique of Pure Reason*, maintains that we have no choice: the questions bedevil us, and we cannot dodge them. "Human reason," he says, "is called upon to consider questions, which it cannot decline, as they are presented by its own nature, but which it cannot answer, as they transcend every faculty of the mind" (GBWW, Vol. 42, p. 1a). Thus, as the *Syntopicon* notes in the Introduction to Chapter 66: "Socrates speaks of philosophy as the love of wisdom, implying thereby its pursuit rather than its attainment. A man would not be called a scientist in a particular field—mathematics, let us say—unless he actually had some mathematical knowledge; but a man who is not actually wise can be called a philosopher by virtue of his effort to become wise" (GBWW, Vol. 3, p. 342d). What kind of learning is this that is a form of *love*? What is this pursuit of the unattainable?

Thunderbolts of the Gods

It is through the dialogues of Plato that we come to know the "father" of philosophy, the incomparable Socrates. Socrates, though he always denied that he had any knowledge, when he was on trial for his life warned the judges of Athens that they should not offer him acquittal on the condition that he cease to inquire and speculate. To such an offer, he says, he would have to reply, "Men of Athens, I honour and love you; but I shall obey God rather than you, and while I have life and strength I shall never cease from the practice and teaching of philosophy, exhorting any one whom I meet and saying to him after my manner: You, my friend,—a citizen of the great and mighty and wise city of Athens,—are you not ashamed of heaping up the greatest amount of money and honour and reputation, and caring so little about wisdom and truth and the greatest improvement of the soul, which you never regard or heed at all?" (*Apology*, in GBWW, Vol. 7, p. 206b-c). He seems to believe that philosophy is useful, nay, indispensable to life, and as he defends himself in court he makes one of the most celebrated assertions in history: "The unexamined life is not worth living."

Socrates speaks of "god" and the "soul," but we must remember that he was a pagan who, at his trial, steadfastly denied that he disbelieved in the gods of the state. We must also remember that "soul" to the Greeks was a metaphysical, not a theological concept; it was simply the essence of a living thing, that which, when we are alive, makes us what we are. When it leaves a man, he is no longer a man but the mere shell of a man.

The first great pagans did not separate philosophy from the mysticism of religion. But in the Roman philosopher Lucretius we have the lineal forerunner of the modern religious skeptic, agnostic, or atheist, who, like Russell, wants to save man from "fairy tales" by a philosophy which has no help from the scientist's laboratory and has no certainty of its own. The materialism of Lucretius, says Santayana in his essay on him (Vol. 10), "carries with it no commandments and no advice. It merely describes the world . . ." but Lucretius himself believes that he provides a remedy for the deepest of human ills by "freeing the mind from the close bondage of religion."

The philosophy of Lucretius is known as Epicureanism because it followed the thinking of the Greek Epicurus. Lucretius saw (as the *Syntopicon* puts it) that men feared the thunderbolts of the gods, their intervention in the course of nature and human affairs, and the punishments of afterlife in the pagan religion. Before Epicurus taught the mortality of the soul and the atomic character of all things —including the mind and its thinking—"human life" says Lucretius, "lay foully prostrate upon earth crushed down under the weight of religion . . . This . . . darkness of mind must be dispelled . . . by the aspect and law of nature" (*On the Nature of Things*, in GBWW, Vol. 12, pp. 1d, 15d, 31b).

We read in the *Syntopicon* (GBWW, Vol. 3, p. 344a-c): "Except for Lucretius, the triumph of philosophy over religion does not seem to be central to ancient conceptions of philosophy's contribution to the mind and life of man. In the pagan world, religious belief is either combined with philosophy to constitute the worship of the gods, which seems to be Plato's views in the *Laws;* or it represents the superstitions of the ignorant as opposed to the sophistication of the educated. Gibbon [in his *Decline and Fall of the Roman Empire* (GBWW, Vols. 40–41)] describes the rift between religion and philosophy not as a matter of intellectual controversy, but as a division of society into classes lacking or having the benefits of education— or, what is the same in the ancient world, instruction in philosophy.

"But in the medieval world, the distinction between philosophy and religion seems to be essential to the consideration of the nature and value of philosophy. The importance of the distinction appears alike in the great books of the Christian tradition and in the great writings of the Mohammedan and Jewish cultures—in Augustine and Aquinas, Avicenna, Averroës, and Maimonides—though the problem of philosophy's relation to religion and theology may be quite differently solved by each. In all three religious communities secular learning and sacred doctrine are set apart by their origin— the one from the efforts of human reason, the other from the word of God as revealed to the faithful. Even when it is held in highest esteem as the best achievement of secular learning, philosophy is for the most part regarded as inferior to the teachings of religion."

The reason is obvious: the medieval culture of Europe was unified by religious faith. Before the Dark Ages fell upon Europe a great burst of light appeared in the person of Augustine (whose *Confessions* and *City of God* we read in Vol. 18 of *Great Books of the Western World*). The next volume in *Great Books of the Western World* is written eight hundred years later—the formidable *Summa Theologica* of Thomas Aquinas. In the interval between them, and until the renaissance of classical learning long after Aquinas, philosophy (like all other manifestations of the ancient Mediterranean civilization) was preserved by the Church and by churchmen. St. Augustine is one of the Fathers of the Christian Church, St. Thomas the "holy doctor" and his *Summa* the thirteenth-century capstone of the Middle Ages.

No one denies that these two towering figures were great philosophers; nor that they were first of all men of religious faith.

In Augustine's view (according to the *Syntopicon*) philosophy "can . . . be dispensed with in all the major concerns of knowledge, love, or action. But Augustine does not argue that it should therefore be discarded. 'If those who are called philosophers,' he says, 'and especially the Platonists, have said aught that is true and in harmony with our faith, we are not only not to shrink from it, but to claim it for our own use from those who have unlawful possession of it,' even as the spoils of the Egyptians belong to the Jews."

The *Syntopicon* continues: "Though Augustine and Aquinas conceive the relation of faith and reason differently, they seem to share a conception of philosophy as the handmaiden of theology when faith seeks understanding. For Aquinas this does not appear to imply lack of dignity or even the loss of a certain autonomy on the part of philosophy. On the contrary, so highly does he regard the demonstrations of Aristotle, whom he calls 'the philosopher,' that he opens the *Summa Theologica* with the question `Whether, besides the philosophical sciences, any further doctrine is required.'

"He answers that 'it was necessary for the salvation of man that certain truths which exceed human reason should be made known to him by divine revelation. Even as regards those truths about God which human reason can investigate, it was necessary that man be taught by a divine revelation. For the truth about God, such as reason can know it, would only be known by a few, and that after a long time, and with the admixture of many errors; whereas man's whole salvation, which is in God, depends upon the knowledge of this truth . . .'" (GBWW, Vol. 3, pp. 344d–345b).

Two Kinds of Theology

Thus the need of the "sacred science," theology. But here it is necessary to make the classical division of theology itself—a division which the modern skeptics deny or, more often, ignore. Theology has two branches—the dogmatic and the natural. Dogma is based upon the revelation of the Scriptures. God does not argue with Moses, or try to prove the validity of the Ten Commandments; he says, "Thou shalt" and "Thou shalt not"; he is laying down the Law. So, too, Christ's ever-repeated phrase, "*I say unto you . . .*" is the voice of authority which neither reasons nor appeals to reason (however "reasonable" or "unreasonable" the commandments may be). Moses and Christ are not philosophers.

Dogmatic theology is the explication of the articles of faith; it belongs wholly to religion proper, and draws upon reason only to reach conclusions from premises established by the Word of God. But natural theology rests wholly upon reason. It may serve faith; in any case, reason must reach the same conclusions as faith (though it may not reach so far) if faith is taken to be true; in the religious view, faith and the *power* of reason both proceed from God, Who, being perfect, is without falsehood or contradiction. But the problems of natural theology are in no sense whatever dogmatic. They are independent of religion, and they are studied and argued by men of all religions and of none.

Whoever wants to see natural theology in operation should open the *Summa Theologica* to page 12d (GBWW, Vol. 19) and study the short passage which begins with the celebrated words, *"I answer that,* the existence of God can be proved in five ways." The famous "five proofs" are all of them drawn from reason alone, and, indeed, they draw most heavily upon the thinking of the great Greek pagan, Aristotle. They are not all of them easy to comprehend at every point —far from it—and some of them are subject of philosophical attack. But in no respect does any one of them at any step rely upon revelation or faith. And Henry Adams, in his essay on Aquinas (Vol. 10), expounding on the great struggle between theology and science, points out that "the quality that rouses most surprise in Thomism is its astonishingly scientific method."

As philosophy attacks theology, so science attacks philosophy; and on the same ground, namely, that it cannot demonstrate its procedures or verify its conclusions in the way that the natural sciences do. The phrase "armchair philosophy" makes the point; without the laboratory and its controlled experimentation and demonstration *in action* no knowledge is really binding upon the reason, and no claim to knowledge can be validated. The ancient and medieval scientists called themselves philosophers, but the giants of modern science—beginning with Galileo, Newton, Huygens, and, in the eighteenth century, Lavoisier and Fourier—made the distinction of calling their work "experimental philosophy."

"In this phrase," according to the *Syntopicon* (GBWW, Vol. 3, p. 346b–347a), "lies the root of the distinction between philosophy and science as that distinction is generally understood by writers since the eighteenth century. The word 'experimental' applied to philosophy signifies a radical difference in the method of inquiry and even in the objects to be investigated, for certain objects can be known only by experimental or empirical research. Kant appears to be the first (in the great books at least) to make a sharp separation between the investigation of either nature or mind by what he calls 'empirical' as opposed to 'rational' methods. He still uses the name 'science' for both sorts of investigation, but he appears to restrict 'philosophy' to the latter—the pure, the *a priori*, the rational sciences.

"Kant's innovations in vocabulary plainly announce the separation of philosophy from mathematics and experimental science, which is only intimated by earlier modern writers. . . . The final step is taken in the nineteenth century when the word 'science' is restricted to mathematics and to such knowledge of nature, man, and society as can be obtained by the methods of experimental or empirical research. William James, for example, stresses the fact that he is trying to expound psychology as one of the natural sciences, and to that end he tries to separate the problems which are capable of empirical investigation from those which belong to philosophical speculation. For Freud that separation is an accomplished fact, and one which leaves to philosophy no problem that can be solved by science.

"According to Freud, 'it is inadmissable to declare that science is one field of human intellectual activity, and that religion and philosophy are others, at least as valuable, and that science has no business to interfere with the other two.' On the contrary, Freud thinks it is right for scientific research to look 'on the whole field of human activity as its own,' and to criticize the unscientific formulations of philosophy. The trouble with philosophy is that 'it behaves itself as if it were a science . . . but it parts company with science, in that it clings to the illusion that it can produce a complete and coherent picture of the universe.' It is this illusion which science continually punctures, since, in Freud's opinion, 'that picture must needs fall to pieces with every new advance in our knowledge.' "

It is questionable whether the nineteenth-century scientist who said that he "never saw a soul in a test tube" would accept either James' psychology or Freud's psychoanalysis as science; but it is clear that he would accept neither theology *nor* philosophy. So, too, the atheist of our own time, observing, as did the Soviet cosmonaut Titov, that he "saw no God or angels" during his orbits of the earth may find himself drawn all the way back to the outright materialism of the ancient Roman Lucretius, who, though his view of the world was not as sophisticated as the modern physicist's, believed that the universe and everything in it could be explained by the constitution and motion of atoms. The denial of the existence in man—or anywhere else—of the *immaterial* leads ineluctably to the denial not only of the Greek or Christian ideas of soul, but also of the concept of the existence of mind apart from brain cells and central nervous system.

Mind Looks at Itself

The age-old effort of man to comprehend the mind and catch it "red-handed" in the act of thinking has resulted in some of the most penetrating inquiry of both philosophers and, in modern times, psychologists. In his *Principles of Human Knowledge* (GBWW, Vol. 35, p. 405c), the eighteenth-century English philosopher Berkeley staunchly refuses to concede that there is *any* question that the mind cannot answer. "I am inclined to think," he says, "that the far greater part . . . of those difficulties which have . . . blocked up the way to knowledge, are entirely owing to ourselves—that we have first raised a dust and then complain we cannot see." But Berkeley's optimism has not been justified—at least not yet. We are still asking, two hundred years later, what the mind is and how it works.

Modern psychology, particularly in America, though it may not have advanced the inquiry, has produced an approach to it that had not previously been emphasized, in either ancient or modern Europe. "The Americans," the *Encyclopædia Britannica* says, "were bound to be practical and functional, to see mind in terms of its use for the survival of the organism in the struggle of the race for existence and in the social competition of the individual for success." Hence in the United States, at the end of the nineteenth century, there emerged a functional—or "is-for"—view of the human mind.

This view, which first appears in William James's *Principles of Psychology* (GBWW, Vol. 53) is the basis of pragmatism, the philosophy which appears in his writings (in Vols. 7 and 10 of this set). But its most famous exponent is the late John Dewey, whose influence on American philosophy was almost as great as his "progressive" influence in education.

Dewey does not ask what the mind *is;* he asks what it is *for*. Thinking, he asserts, is a process that appears in response to one's need to make a more adequate adjustment to the environment. It is aimed at straightening out tangles in the achievement of goals. Man wants something, and the activity of the mind is directed at getting it. The value of thinking lies in the fact that it makes action possible. "There is," says Dewey ("The Process of Thought," Vol. 10), "a challenge to understanding only when there is either a desired consequence for which means have to be found by inquiry, or things . . . are presented under conditions where reflection is required to see what consequences can be effected by their use."

It is man's desire to get what he wants that underlies philosophy and all philosophical systems, says James: "Pretend what we may, the whole man within us is at work when we form our philosophical opinions. Intellect, will, taste, and passion cooperate just as they do in practical affairs; and lucky it is if the passion be not something as petty as a love of personal conquest over the philosopher across the way. . . . It is almost incredible," he goes on to say, "that men who are themselves working philosophers should pretend that any philosophy can be, or ever has been, constructed without the help of personal preference, belief, or divination. How have they succeeded in so stultifying their sense for the living facts of human nature as not to perceive that every philosopher, or man of science either, whose initiative counts for anything in the evolution of thought, has taken his stand on a sort of dumb conviction that the truth must lie in one direction rather than another . . . ?" (*The Sentiment of Rationality*, Vol. 10).

This view that intellectual objectivity is impossible would be familiar to the great philosophers of earlier times and equally to the natural scientists of our own day. A nuclear physicist might object to being told that he has "taken his stand on a sort of dumb conviction." Yet there is a sense in which philosophy long ago posited something analogous to the "dumb conviction" as the indispensable first step in thinking, and that is in regard to first principles. First principles, or statements of ultimate ends, are classically the starting points of all thought. And from Aristotle's argument that first principles are apprehended intuitively to Mill's assertion that no first principle can be proved, philosophers ancient and modern have maintained that these foundations of reasoning are not to be discovered by the reasoning process.

Whence, then, come first principles? What is meant by "intuition," a term commonly held in contempt? Is it the same in all men, or different from society to society (or even from individual to individual)? Traditionally philosophy has taken the view that it proceeds from *natural law*—not to be confused with the laws which govern the physical universe. Natural law (which theology also recognizes) is thought to be inherent in the mind of every man. Man—any man anywhere—has but to consult his reason to discover, at once, or intuitively, the principles of the natural law and the ends to which life is directed. The natural law is what every man is, so to say, born knowing.

Is it sufficient without human law? No; human law is required in society to explicate it, to spell out the natural law in terms of the varied and complicated circumstances of society. Is it sufficient without faith? The believer would say No, in so far as we are directed to an end beyond nature, but natural theology would say that it is sufficient for this life.

When the authors of *The Declaration of Independence* speak of "the separate and equal station to which the laws of nature . . . entitle" a people (Vol. 6), they are referring to the natural law, not to the "laws of nature" by which the physical universe seems to operate. What is the relation between these laws of nature and the natural law? Ralph Waldo Emerson's essay on *Nature*—perhaps his most famous piece of work—is published in Volume 10 of this set. In it Emerson sees man and everything he is and does to be a part of nature. "If," he says, "we consider how much we are nature's, we need not be superstitious about towns, as if that terrific or benefic force did not find us there also, and fashion cities. Nature, who made the mason, made the house. . . . A man does not tie his shoe without recognizing laws which bind the farthest regions of nature. . . ." J. S. Mill, in his essay by the same name (also in Volume 10), disagrees. Nature is reckless. Nature is cruel. Nature is the enemy, frustrating man's best efforts, and to follow it would be irrational, wasteful, and immoral. Almost everything that makes life endurable is the work of man's art; nature must be rejected as the measure of right and good because "the course of natural phenomena being replete with everything which when committed by human beings is most worthy of abhorrence, anyone who endeavoured in his actions to imitate the natural course of things would be universally seen and acknowledged to be the wickedest of men."

Rx: Consult the Heart

But what man has created with his arts—above all, with those arts we nowadays call science—he fears will destroy him. And even if it does not destroy him, he feels himself being engulfed by it. The urge to "get away from it all" overwhelms every sensitive man from time to time. William James, commenting on the "modern mechanico-physical philosophy of which we are all so proud, because it includes the nebular cosmogony, the kinetic theory of heat and gases, etc., etc.," laments that, "The sentimental facts and relations are butchered at a blow" (*Principles of Psychology*, in GBWW, Vol. 53, p. 883a). And he adds: "Science can tell us what exists; but to compare the *worths*, both of what exists and what does not exist, we must consult not science, but what Pascal calls our heart. Science herself consults her heart when she lays it down that the infinite ascertainment of fact and correction of false belief are the supreme goods for man" (*The Will to Believe*, Vol. 10 in this set).

But where—and what—is this "heart" that we must consult instead of science when we ask about the worth of things? Is it philosophy? Religion? What? It is easy to speak of the heart, and James shows us that even the man of science finds *his* first principle there; but to bring the mind to bear upon it, even to locate it intellectually, is less easy. If the laws of nature (which science investigates in order to achieve its mastery of nature) do not disclose the "heart" to us, what does? Is it the anciently accepted—and more often rejected today—natural law which reason reveals to him "who will but consult it"? Is the nature of man something entirely other than the nature of the physical universe? Is the secret of life locked up in it beyond the power of anything more scientific than intuition?

In his *Ethics of Belief* (Vol. 10), W. K. Clifford refuses to accept these indemonstrables. He is not satisfied with James's "heart," and he protests that, "It is wrong in all cases to believe on insufficient evidence; and where it is presumption to doubt and to investigate, there it is worse than presumption to believe." He says "It [belief] is desecrated when given to unproved and unquestioned statements, for the solace and private pleasure of the believer; to add a tinsel splendour to the plain straight road of our life and display a bright mirage beyond it; or even to drown the common sorrows of our kind by a self-deception which allows them not only to cast down, but also to degrade us."

But how are we to live, when the things we are able to know on "sufficient evidence" are inadequate to our happiness? Whither shall we turn to meet our needs in this life?

Philosophy has always called man back to himself, to the study and knowledge of his own nature; and to the law of life which he discovers there. Noting that "all men plume themselves on the improvement of society, and no man improves," Emerson, in his passionate essay on *Self-Reliance* (Vol. 10) summons the individual to "learn to detect and watch that gleam of light which flashes across his mind from within . . ." He who does—and he only—will be a man. But to be a man, Emerson insists, is to be a nonconformist to society: "To be great is to be misunderstood."

There is something of the ancient Stoic philosophy in this acceptance of self even if it means rejection by the world. Plutarch (*Contentment*, Vol. 10) points out that whatever may happen to a man is largely beyond his control; but how he reacts to what happens to him is within his own power: "Fortune can infect a man with sickness, take his money away, malign him to his countrymen or a tyrant; but she cannot make a good and virile and high-spirited man a poltroon or mean-spirited or ignoble or envious." And the most stoical of all the Stoics, Epictetus, declares that, "You can be unconquerable if you enter into no combat in which it is not in your own power to conquer" (*The Enchiridion*, Vol. 10).

Is this the way to live—or is it the counsel of escape from the challenge of life? Epicurus, in his *Letter to Menoeceus* (Vol. 10), reveals how close to Stoicism is the Epicurean doctrine that pleasure is the end of life. For pleasure here involves, above all, one's freeing oneself from desire for external things: "Independence of desire we think a great good—not that we may at all times enjoy but a few things, but that, if we do not possess many, we may enjoy the few in the genuine persuasion that those have the sweetest pleasure in luxury who least need it, and that all that is natural is easy to be obtained, but that which is superfluous is hard."

Here the serenity which Plutarch counsels seems to be the ultimate goal and the key to successful living. Philosophy appears in its role of consolation and solace which Clifford disdains, enabling us to accept life rather, perhaps, than to live. But Santayana, in his essay on Goethe (Vol. 10), finds another moral entirely in *Faust:* "To live, to live just as we do, that—if we could only realize it—is the purpose and the crown of living." So, too, Walter Pater in "The Art of Life" (Vol. 10): "Not the fruit of experience, but experience itself, is the end. . . . To burn always with this hard, gemlike flame, to maintain this ecstasy, is success in life." The service of philosophy to the human spirit, he adds, "is to rouse, to startle it to a life of constant and eager observation."

However philosophy may serve the human spirit—or whether it serves it at all—the fact is that we are all philosophers. Our philosophy may be good or bad, profound or nonsensical, useful or useless, but we cannot help asking the questions *it* asks: What and who am I? What is life for and how should I live it? What is right and what is wrong? What are my rights and duties toward others? What is happiness, and how is it to be pursued, obtained, and secured? In a word, we all philosophize, and philosophy, unlike the so-called "exact" sciences, deals with all the commonplace problems of everyone's life. In this sense every good book we read, every painting, every sunset, every symphony is philosophical: It says something to us about the questions we cannot help asking.

We are all philosophers and, it may be, theologians. We may not know it; we may not like it; we may call ourselves agnostics (know-nothings) or atheists (disbelievers); but whether we affirm or deny God's existence, or say that we simply don't know, we are saying something about a theological subject. Willingly or unwillingly, wittingly or unwittingly, we are moving in the realm of natural theology. Are we all dogmatists, too? Believers? The atheist *believes* that there is no God. The motorist driving at high speed *believes* that he won't have a blowout. The scientist *believes* that it is good to know.

But there are things we none of us know "for sure," and other things we cannot know at all. The future is hidden from us, and prediction and prophecy fail. We plan—and catastrophe (or a stroke of good fortune) smashes our plan to smithereens. Today's sixteen-year-old is old enough to know how radically different the world is today from what we thought it would be, *intended* it to be, at, say, the end of the Second World War. And it would be a reckless man indeed who was ready to say today that he *knew* what the world will be like a year from now.

Of Youth and Age

Amid the uncertainties of life, this much is certain: Whoever lives long enough will grow old. This too: Whoever grows old will first grow older. And this: Whoever lives to sixty or seventy will be old much longer than he was young.

What follows from this succession of obvious certainties is the common-sense conclusion that we should prepare ourselves for all of life, and not just for that part that passes fastest.

It is not *impossible* to form new mental habits in middle life, or even in old age; but it is an achievement of note, an exception. On the other hand, we all know of men whose mental powers, developed in youth, were more acute than ever in their eighties and even in their nineties—from Sophocles in the fourth century b.c. to Justice Oliver Wendell Holmes in our own time. Sophocles must have been ninety, when, according to Cicero in his *On Old Age* (Vol. 10), "his sons brought him into court to get a judicial decision depriving him of the management of his property on the ground of weak intellect. . . . Thereupon the old poet is said to have read to the judges the play he had on hand and had just composed—*Oedipus Coloneus* [*Oedipus at Colonus*, GBWW, Vol. 5, pp. 114–130]—and to have asked them whether they thought that the work of a man of weak intellect. After the reading he was acquitted by the jury."

What we all want is a satisfying life. Assuming a modest economic sufficiency, he who is happy (or as happy as one may be expected to be in this life) is everywhere esteemed rich, and he who is unhappy poor. Nor have the philosophers dismissed wealth, power, or fame as the condition of human happiness simply because these goods are unworthy, but, rather, because they are achieved and lost by chance, because they depend on others for their achievement and loss, and because, like the pleasures of the moment, they are transient.

When, then, we think of happiness over a whole life and ask ourselves what course we should take in youth that will be most likely to produce it, the wisdom of the ages commends to us the path of Socrates, who in his old age was sent to his death by an Athens whose chief glory he is today. While his trial, imprisonment, and execution are set forth in those three magic dialogues of Plato, the *Apology*, the *Crito*, and the *Phaedo* (GBWW, Vol. 7, pp. 200–251), another of his contemporaries, Xenophon, tells us ("The Character of Socrates," Vol. 6) of a conversation the great philosopher held with his friend Hermogenes just before the trial:

"When Meletus had actually formulated his indictment," Hermogenes told Xenophon, "Socrates talked freely in my presence, but made no reference to the case. I told him that he ought to be thinking about his defence. His first remark was, 'Don't you think that I have been preparing for it all my life?' And when I asked him how, he said that he had been constantly occupied in the consideration of right and wrong, and in doing what was right and avoiding what was wrong, which he regarded as the best preparation for a defence. Then I said, 'Don't you see, Socrates, that the juries in our courts are apt to be misled by argument, so that they often put the innocent to death, and acquit the guilty?' 'Ah, yes, Hermogenes,' he answered, 'but when I did try to think out my defence to the jury, the deity at once resisted.' 'Strange words,' said I; and he, 'Do you think it strange, if it seems better to God that I die now? Don't you see that to this day I never would acknowledge that any man had lived a better or a pleasanter life than I? For they live best, I think, who strive best to become as good as possible: and the pleasant life is theirs who are conscious that they are growing in goodness.'"

There may be those who think that Socrates was wrong—or who live as if they did—but there are few who want to argue the point with him. Most of us, rather, as we grow older, spend our time putting the blame on others—or on bad luck—for our failure to live as he did and enjoy as pleasant a life. But the abiding pleasure of a whole life is not entirely in our stars, but in ourselves. There is no one so persistently ridden by misfortune that he has not had the occasion, again and again, to choose freely this fork in the road or that one, to resist or to yield, to say "Yes" or "No" and affect his own fate accordingly.

To most men the last years of life are, says Cicero in his *On Old Age* (Vol. 10), "so hateful that they declare themselves under a weight heavier than Aetna." He points out the contradiction that old age is something "to which all wish to attain, and at which all grumble when attained," and examines the contradiction in the form of a dialogue, the most beautiful ever written on the subject, between the great Marcus Cato as an old man and two of his younger friends who come to inquire what the end of life is like. Jonathan Swift, in his *Resolutions when I Come to Be Old* (Vol. 7), means "Not to be peevish, or morose, or suspicious" but at the end of his resolutions indicates that he is likely to be all of them.

Cicero, however, does not find Cato unhappy. The great Roman's secret of happiness in old age is simply that men "keep their minds active and fully employed," thus retaining the power of their intellects. Reminding his young friends that the aged Solon grew old "daily learning something new," he asks them which of the two they would rather have given to them—the bodily strength of Milo, who stepped into the Olympics carrying a live ox on his shoulders, or intellectual strength like that of Pythagoras.

Of Death

There is one more certainty in life—the absolute of all absolutes—and that is death. This one certainty overrides our lives from the first time we have seen a sparrow, or a worm, that doesn't move no matter how we prod it. But we do not know what it is to die—nor do we know if we shall know even at the moment of death—nor what it is to be dead. What little we know of death is physiological: the dust returneth to dust. For the rest, we believe. We are, we must be, dogmatists, however we try to escape.

And death colors our view of life—and more than colors it. It forms it. It lies at the very center of all our philosophy. It tells us some of the answers to some of the hardest questions philosophy asks. It tells us—as Sir Thomas Browne says—of our "vanity, feeding the wind, and folly." In his deathless dissertation on death ("Immortality," from *Urn-Burial,* Vol. 10), this seventeenth-century doctor-philosopher-theologian celebrates the futility of monuments and of man's every effort to be great, in life no less than in memory. Those who would build themselves monuments would be well advised to live according to the precepts of philosophy: Had the builders of their own mausoleums "made as good provisions for their names as they have done for their relics, they had not so grossly erred in the art of perpetuation. . . . Happy are they whom privacy makes innocent, who deal so with men in this world that they are not afraid to meet them in the next, who, when they die, make no commotion among the dead."

Browne's notable essay will ring strange in youthful ears. It is a classic contribution to the literature of melancholy, and youth is more properly addicted to mirth, adventure, success, and the stars. So philosophy is hard to "sell" to young people; but it is young people above all who have the courage to confront it, and to be undismayed by the questions that are hardest to answer. The key to philosophy is nothing more than this: Since every child philosophizes, youth is not a moment too soon to enter the company of the great philosophers and partake of the banquet they spread before us.

VI

The Endless Journey

In the *Republic*, Plato outlines an ideal system of education. Here is the timetable: up until the age of twenty, music and gymnastics, for the development of a useful body and sharpened sensibilities; between twenty and thirty, the liberal arts, grammar, rhetoric, logic, and especially mathematics, for the training of a disciplined mind, a mind skilled in the operations of learning and thinking; between thirty and fifty, a period devoted to the world's work, engagement in the various activities of civic life, experience of the pains and frustrations of practical problems, personal and public; and then, finally, at fifty, return to the academy for ten years of the study of philosophy. Then—and only then—is a man fit to govern the state!

Plato's scheme is as Utopian now as it was in his day. It nevertheless makes the point that there is no way to rush maturity; understanding in its deepest sense, of things both theoretical and practical, requires the long, hard experience that the years alone provide.

To say that a young man or woman is intellectually mature is only to say that the mind well-disciplined and self-disciplined is as perfect an instrument for operating on the materials of thought as it ever will be. But the materials are not yet available, nor can they be made available, by theoretical procedures or by imitations of real life.

The problems that confront older persons are more complex than those of youth; and the consequences of their decisions are more far-reaching. The young adult can choose wrongly and rectify his error; his life is ahead of him. The middle-aged adult has a harder time rectifying his errors and "starting over," for too much of his life is behind him; the price has risen; and others are profoundly affected by his failures and successes.

There is something poignant about understanding; the deeper it sinks itself into our lives the sadder we are, thinking of the good use we might have made of it had we had it earlier. Poignant, too, is the effort of the old to impress their understanding on the young, for the young are unable to comprehend it; intellectually, yes; emotionally, no. Adventure beckons us when we are young, reflection upon adventure enlightens us later on. Without the adventure, human progress would be impossible; without the reflection it might be disastrous.

The thinking of great writers does more than elevate our own. It throws a light on our own experiences and our own lives that inspires us. What we learn, as experience and reflection accumulate, is to examine ourselves; and it is with self-examination that the way to wisdom is hewn. Wisdom does not come packaged nor does other men's wisdom attach itself to us uninvited. Neither do we put it on all at once like a suit of clothes. Rather it grows as we grow, organically. The cross-examination to which the great books submit us has a friendly, not a punitive, purpose: to lead us to cross-examine ourselves and to test our own thinking.

This is education. And in this sense it may be said without qualification that only adults can become educated. The young man or woman fresh from school or college does not know that he does not know. How could he? Has he not spent ten or fifteen years doing nothing but learning? Has he not had the benefit of the best schools, the best teachers—even, for argument's sake, the best books? If there were anything important to teach him, would not a first-class school system have found it out "by this time"? The older person cannot resist smiling—nor can the young man himself ten or twenty years afterward.

Here is the paradox of our existence. The soil which education requires—maturity—is never ready for it. To be mature is to have finished growth; a mature apple is a ripe apple. Its maturity lasts, so to say, for a moment. Before that moment it was green; after that moment it begins to die. When does a human being reach that perfect and evanescent state of his development?

The mature man is one, strictly, who has as nearly as possible become ripe, his adult potentialities fully developed. But some men are cut off at eighty or ninety by physical death while they are still maturing. The growth of a Sophocles or a Holmes, who are still at work when the end comes, is far from finished when death interrupts it. The man who stops growing intellectually and spiritually at thirty or forty is as mature as he will ever be, however long he lives. But he has not really grown up, for he is satisfied with less than he might have. We spend our adult lives, then, approaching maturity. We never reach it. Strictly speaking, the mature man has never existed.

"It is better," says John Stuart Mill, "to be a human being dissatisfied than a pig satisfied . . . And if the fool, or the pig, are of a different opinion, it is because they only know their own side of the question. The other party to the comparison knows both sides."

It may be objected, Mill goes on, "that many who begin with youthful enthusiasm for everything noble, as they advance in years sink into indolence and selfishness. But I do not believe that those who undergo this very common change, voluntarily choose the lower description of pleasures in preference to the higher. I believe that before they devote themselves exclusively to the one, they have already become incapable of the other. Capacity for the nobler feelings is in most natures a very tender plant, easily killed, not only by hostile influences, but by mere want of sustenance; and in the majority of young persons it speedily dies away if the occupations to which their position in life has devoted them, and the society into which it has thrown them, are not favourable to keeping that higher capacity in exercise" (*Utilitarianism*, in GBWW, Vol. 43, p. 449c-d). The dissatisfied man, in other words, is the one who is continuously maturing. He has embarked on a journey without an end.

We never fully grow up, but we must continue to try to. The earlier the habit of reading good books is formed, the sooner it becomes habitual. It enables us even in youth, and all the more so as we go on in years, to be at home in the world of clear thinking and exalted imagination. A schooled and skilled people is a free people in the fullest sense only when it is a thinking people. The societies of the West, America above all, are not distinctively contemplative; they are societies of great action whose triumphs of discovery, invention, and production have changed the face of the earth. Now they must turn, not to the moon, but to themselves, to make of life a rich experience and of the world a livable place. If anything is clear to us today, it is that the rising generation will have to think, and to think hard and straight.

Neither the random romping of a child, nor the porcine satisfaction of a pig, nor yet the dreadful monotony of an empty adulthood will serve ourselves or the family of man. What will serve both is the constant employment of our highest faculties, at once assuaging and aggravating the divine discontent of the thinker. So far may human happiness extend over the whole of a long life. This set is published with the faith that all human beings, of whatever age, can achieve that happiness, and in the hope that they will.

Syntopical Guide

As its name implies, this guide to the contents of *Gateway to the Great Books* is based on the *Syntopicon*, which comprises Volumes 2 and 3 of *Great Books of the Western World*.

The *Syntopicon* serves the reader of the Great Books in a number of ways. It contains 102 essays introducing the reader to the great ideas as these are discussed in the Great Books. It contains lists of additional readings on each of the 102 great ideas. It provides the reader with useful bibliographical information. But what it does principally is to enable him, on any subject of special interest, to read *in* the Great Books in a way that relates what various authors have to say on that subject. This mode of reading is quite different from reading a single book *through*. Without the *Syntopicon*, it would be impossible for the individual to do this kind of syntopical reading, for unless he had already read through the whole set, not once, but many times, he could not even begin to assemble all the related passages in the Great Books on a particular topic.

The Syntopical Guide to *Gateway to the Great Books* is a similar device, enabling the reader to do another kind of syntopical reading. For any particular selection in this set which happens to interest the individual reader, the Syntopical Guide directs him to other related selections in Gateway; it recommends the reading of related sections or passages in *Great Books of the Western World;* and it relates all these selections in Gateway and passages in Great Books to the great ideas, or, more strictly, to certain topics under the great ideas which happen to be major themes in the particular selection with which the reader began.

The Syntopical Guide thus provides directions for reading *in* this set of books before one has read the whole set *through*. It does more than that for the person who also has *Great Books of the Western*

World on his shelves. It helps him to go from each selection in Gateway to the most germane of related passages in Great Books.

Anyone who examines the Syntopical Guide will quickly see why this set is a gateway to the great books; anyone who uses the Syntopical Guide will have opened the gates for himself. It is the key—and one that is quite easy to turn.

In Section I of the Introduction, on ways of reading, some rules are recommended. It is there suggested that the active reading of a work requires us to ask—and try to answer—four questions about it: (1) What is the piece about? What is it trying to say? (2) How does it say what it is trying to say? (3) Is it true in whole or part? What reasons do we have for disagreeing with it? (4) What of it? What meaning does it have for us? (See page 19, above.) In addition, a whole series of rules are proposed for reading any piece of literature, whether narrative or expository, in a number of ways—analytically, interpretatively, and critically. (See pp. 23-29, above.) All these rules or recommendations serve the reader well when his aim is to read one book or one piece of writing as thoroughly as possible—*but by itself and in isolation from other books or pieces of writing.* The good reader, however, usually has one further question in mind, a question which goes beyond the four questions proposed in the Introduction. He asks himself how the particular piece that he is reading is related to other pieces of writing. Or, to put the question another way, he wants to know what other pieces of writing deal with the same general themes—themes which are central in the piece he is reading now.

The Syntopical Guide answers this question for him, at least so far as two large sets of books are concerned, comprising in all more than six hundred works. The rules proposed earlier give the reader guidance on how to read a single work, whereas the Syntopical Guide shows him how to read not just one but two large collections of works.

To do this, the Syntopical Guide has been organized in the following manner. It lists in alphabetical order each of the authors who has one or more writings in Gateway. It thus provides an alphabetical index, by authors' names, to the contents of this set. (The endpapers, to be found in each volume of the set, indicate the contents of the several volumes by listing the names of the authors in the order in which they appear in that volume.)

The authors' names constitute what we shall call the main entries in the Syntopical Guide. There are 133 of them. The operative units of the Guide are more numerous, for they are constituted by the one or more works of each author included in this set.

For example, in the case of Charles Darwin, one selection—his *Autobiography*—constitutes the syntopical unit. In the case of Ralph Waldo Emerson, there are four such units, *i.e.*, one for each of the four of his essays included in this set: *Thoreau, Nature, Self-Reliance,* and *Montaigne; or, the Skeptic.* In the case of David Hume, there also happen to be four units, but one of these units comprises three essays which are grouped together because they all deal with the same general themes; thus here the four syntopical units are as follows: (1) *Of the Standard of Taste;* (2) *Of Refinement in the Arts;* (3) *Of Money, Of the Balance of Trade,* and *Of Taxes;* (4) *Of the Study of History.* Wherever two or more selections, whether singly or grouped, constitute distinct syntopical units under a main entry (*i.e.*, a particular author), the units are placed in an order that corresponds to the order in which the several selections appear in the volumes of this set.

So much for the over-all structure of the Syntopical Guide—its 133 main entries (one for each author) and the one or more syntopical units under each of these. Now let us turn to the structure of the syntopical units, of which there are 214. Each of these is divided into three principal parts. The first part carries the heading SUGGESTED READINGS IN THE *Syntopicon;* the second part, the heading RELATED AUTHORS AND WORKS IN *Great Books of the Western World;* the third part, the heading RELATED AUTHORS AND WORKS IN *Gateway to the Great Books.* In certain instances, there is a fourth heading, which usually consists of a reference to other works by the author in question when these are included in *Great Books of the Western World.* For example, in the case of Darwin, this fourth heading reads "For other works by Darwin in *Great Books of the Western World,* see Vol. 49." And when a selection in Gateway deals with an author in Great Books, this fourth heading refers to the works of the latter. For example, in the case of Macaulay's essay on Machiavelli, the fourth heading reads "For Machiavelli's *The Prince* in *Great Books of the Western World,* see Vol. 23, pages 3–37."

The fourth heading needs no further explanation, but something more must be said about the three principal headings of each syntopical unit. Let us take these up in the order in which they occur.

(1) SUGGESTED READINGS IN THE *Syntopicon*. Here the subordinate entries consist of the names of one or more of the great ideas, concerning each of which there is a separate chapter in the *Syntopicon*. The great ideas referred to are listed in the alphabetical order in which they appear in the *Syntopicon*. In every case, the reference to a great idea is followed by the citation of the volume and pages in the *Syntopicon* where that great idea is treated.

For example, an entry may read as follows: "CUSTOM AND CONVENTION, Vol. 2, pages 268–285." This sends the reader to Volume 2 in *Great Books of the Western World*, where on pages 268–285 he will find the whole chapter on CUSTOM AND CONVENTION. Or the entry may read as follows: "WISDOM, Vol. 3, pages 1102–1117." This sends the reader to Volume 3 in *Great Books of the Western World* and to the pages where he will find the chapter on WISDOM.

The opening section in each chapter of the *Syntopicon* consists of an essay on the great idea that is the subject of that chapter, giving an account of its meanings, its development, and the major issues or problems that have been discussed. *It is strongly recommended to the user of the Syntopical Guide who also owns a* Syntopicon *that he read the essays on whatever ideas are cited under the first heading in the syntopical unit with which he happens to be dealing.*

In most cases, but not always, the citation of a chapter in the *Syntopicon* is followed by reference to one or more topics that are especially of interest to the reader in connection with the work in Gateway under consideration. For example, in the case of Darwin's *Autobiography*, the user of the Syntopical Guide will find a reference that runs as follows:

EVOLUTION, Vol. 2, pages 451–467, especially
> Topic 5: The theory of evolution: the origin of new species from a common ancestry

He will also find a reference which involves two or more topics, as follows:

SCIENCE, Vol. 3, pages 682–705, especially
> Topic 2*b*: The comparison of science with poetry and history
> Topic 5*a*: The role of experience: observation and experiment

The one or more topics referred to in each case will be found in that section of a *Syntopicon* chapter which is called *"OUTLINE OF TOPICS."* This always immediately follows the essay with which the chapter opens. It in turn is immediately followed by a section called *"REFERENCES."* Here the owner of the *Syntopicon* will again find the particular topics to which he has been referred, but now under each topic are listed references to the relevant passages in *Great Books of the Western World.* Hence he can look up for himself passages in Great Books that are related to the selection in Gateway in which he happens to be interested; and he can do this in the light of the topic under which these passages are assembled.

The reader of Gateway who does not own a *Syntopicon* cannot, of course, make the aforementioned use of these references to the great ideas and topics under them; but he should not therefore dismiss them entirely. They have considerable significance for him, inasmuch as they indicate the principal themes or subjects being discussed or treated in the Gateway selection under consideration. In addition, they control the content of the next two parts of the syntopical unit with which he is working. The related authors or works in *Great Books of the Western World* or in *Gateway to the Great Books* are related to the Gateway selection under consideration precisely because they are relevant to the same general themes or subjects—those indicated by the ideas and topics cited under the first principal heading of each syntopical unit.

(2) RELATED AUTHORS AND WORKS IN *Great Books of the Western World.* Here the subordinate entries consist of references to authors in the Great Books set, listed in the order in which they appear in that set, according to volume number and pages. In addition to giving the number of the volume in which the author appears, the reference always gives the title of the work by the author who is being referred to. Sometimes the whole work is cited, but more frequently the reference is to a relatively short passage or series of passages. Where the work as a whole is cited, the reference is simply to the page numbers; but where a short passage is cited, the reference will sometimes give the part of the work from which it is taken as well as the page numbers. The following examples represent five different typical styles of reference:

(i) Shakespeare, Vol. 26, *Romeo and Juliet,* pages 285–319
    (which is a reference to the whole play)

(ii) Plato, Vol. 7, *Apology*, pages 208–209
(which is a reference to a short passage in this dialogue)

(iii) Aristotle, Vol. 9, *Ethics*, Bk. IV, Chaps. 2–4, pages 368–372
(which is also a reference to a short passage, but this time one that cites the part of Aristotle's *Ethics* from which the passage is taken as well as the pages in Vol. 9 of *Great Books of the Western World* where the passage can be found)

(iv) Kant, Vol. 42, *Critique of Pure Reason*, pages 32–36, 41–44
(which is like the reference to Plato above, except that it cites more than one passage in Kant's work, for which it gives simply the page numbers)

(v) Lucretius, Vol. 12, *On the Nature of Things*, Bk. I, pages 8–12; Bk. II, pages 24–26
(which is like the reference to Aristotle above, except that it cites more than one passage in Lucretius' work, for which it gives not only the page numbers but also the part of the work from which it is taken)

(3) RELATED AUTHORS AND WORKS IN *Gateway to the Great Books.* Here the subordinate entries consist of references to authors in the Gateway set, listed in alphabetical order—the order in which they appear in the Syntopical Guide. As contrasted with the references above to related authors in the Great Books set, most of which cite relatively short passages rather than whole works, the references to related authors in the Gateway set always cite the whole selection as it appears in Gateway; and the reference always gives the number of the volume in Gateway and the pages where that selection occurs. One example will suffice to explain all the entries under the third principal heading of any syntopical unit: "Darwin, *Autobiography*, Vol. 8, pages 47–93" sends the reader to Volume 8 in this set and to pages 47–93 where he will find Darwin's *Autobiography*.

The reader of Gateway who also owns Great Books will be able to make use of the references given under the first and second headings. For him, the second heading supplements the first in the following fashion.

The references given under the second heading recommend works or passages in the Great Books set which, in the judgment of the editors, are most germane to the selection in Gateway under consideration; *i.e.*, they are works or passages which are most relevant to the ideas or topics treated in that Gateway selection. Under the first heading, those same ideas or topics are cited. If the reader, by making use of the Syntopicon, were to look up all the passages in the Great Books cited under the ideas and topics mentioned, he would have undertaken the fullest possible exploration of related passages, and he would necessarily have found passages varying widely in degree of relevance, not just the ones that are most germane.

Thus the entries under the first heading provide the reader with a way of making the fullest possible exploration of related passages in the Great Books set, whereas the entries under the second heading enable him to confine himself to the most relevant of related passages, selected by the editors. The latter entries are clearly not meant to be exhaustive. The reader who wishes to make a more exhaustive exploration of related passages in Great Books can do so by using the *Syntopicon* with the guidance of the entries under the first heading.

So much for the reader who owns both sets. We have already pointed out the significance of the first heading for the reader who has only *Gateway to the Great Books* (see page 113, above). For such a reader, the second heading has only the minimum utility of calling to his attention, for later study, related authors and works in Great Books. So far as his further syntopical reading is concerned, it is the entries under the third heading which are of maximum utility for him at once; for, by using them, he can turn from the selection in Gateway that he is reading to other related selections in this set.

A syntopical reading of the contents of Gateway is, of course, not the only way to read this set. Another way, which many readers may prefer, is suggested elsewhere—dipping in here and there, according to one's individual taste or fancy (see page 5, above). There is still another way of reading the materials here contained: Start with the easiest or most readable selections and go on, in progressive stages of reading, to more and more difficult ones.

For those who wish to proceed in this latter fashion, the Plan of Graded Reading (set forth in Appendix A, which follows the Syntopical Guide) lists the selections in Gateway in an order that roughly corresponds to ascending grades of difficulty. This Plan enables the individual to pursue an organized course of readings in this set.

It differs from the Syntopical Guide in that it recommends the reading of whole works, one after another, *without regard* to their special relevance to one another (though the Plan does group the readings in Gateway according to the type of literature to which they belong); whereas, in contrast, the Syntopical Guide recommends the reading of related works *without regard* to their level of difficulty. But in another respect the Plan of Graded Reading resembles the Syntopical Guide—at least for readers who own *Great Books of the Western World* as well as *Gateway to the Great Books;* for just as the Syntopical Guide serves as a bridge from one set to the other, so in its own way does the Plan of Graded Reading. The Plan, at each level of difficulty, lists not only selections from Gateway but also selections from Great Books of comparable difficulty. (See the explanatory note which accompanies the Plan of Graded Reading, pp. 350–353, below.) Thus the Plan of Graded Reading, like the Syntopical Guide, gives reality to the title of this set, by showing the reader how he can use it, if he will, as a gateway to the great books.

HENRY ADAMS, 1838–1918

"The United States in 1800"
from *History of the United States of America*
Vol. 6, pages 322–359

SUGGESTED READINGS IN THE *Syntopicon*

DEMOCRACY, Vol. 2, pages 303–322, especially
  Topic 2: The derogation of democracy: the anarchic tendency
    of freedom and equality
LABOR, Vol. 2, pages 921–940, especially
  Topic 7f: The relation of economic to political freedom:
    economic democracy
LIBERTY, Vol. 2, pages 991–1012, especially
  Topic 6a: The historical significance of freedom: stages
    in the realization of freedom; the beginning and end
    of the historical process
PROGRESS, Vol. 3, pages 437–453, especially
  Topic 1: The idea of progress in the philosophy of history
  Topic 6: Intellectual or cultural progress: its sources
    and impediments
STATE, Vol. 3, pages 826–865, especially
  Topic 4: The physical foundations of society: the geographical
    and biological conditions of the state

Topic 9a: Commerce and trade between states: commercial rivalries and trade agreements; free trade and tariffs

WEALTH, Vol. 3, pages 1038–1070, especially

Topic 3: The production of wealth in the political community

RELATED AUTHORS AND WORKS IN *Great Books of the Western World*

Plato, Vol. 7, *Republic*, Bk. VIII, pages 408–414
Smith, Vol. 39, *Wealth of Nations*, Bk. IV, Chap. I, pages 182–192
Articles of Confederation, Vol. 43, pages 5–9
Hamilton, Madison, Jay, Vol. 43, *Federalist*, Nos. 13–14, pages 59–62
Hegel, Vol. 46, *Philosophy of Right*, Third Part, pages 110–114; *Philosophy of History*, Fourth Part, pages 348–369, especially pages 360–369

RELATED AUTHORS AND WORKS IN *Gateway to the Great Books*

Calhoun, "Concurrent Majority," Vol. 7, pages 276–290
Crèvecoeur, "Making of Americans," Vol. 6, pages 546–559
Franklin, *Proposals Relating to the Education of Youth in Pennsylvania*, Vol. 6, pages 536–542
Great Documents, *Virginia Declaration of Rights*, Vol. 6, pages 415–417; *Declaration of Independence*, pages 418–421
Guizot, "Civilization," Vol. 6, pages 302–317
Jefferson, *First Inaugural Address*, Vol. 6, pages 518–521
Lincoln, *Address at Cooper Institute*, Vol. 6, pages 737–746
Tocqueville, "Observations on American Life and Government," Vol. 6, pages 564–690
Washington, *Farewell Address*, Vol. 6, pages 484–497

St. Thomas Aquinas

Vol. 10, pages 422–450

SUGGESTED READINGS IN THE *Syntopicon*

GOD, Vol. 2, pages 543–604, especially

Topic 2b: The evidences and proofs of God's existence
Topic 5a: God as first and as exemplar cause: the relation of divine to natural causation
Topic 5g: God's will: divine choice

MIND, Vol. 3, pages 171–203, especially

Topic 2a: The immateriality of mind: mind as an immaterial principle, a spiritual substance, or as an incorporeal power functioning without a bodily organ

WILL, Vol. 3, pages 1071–1101, especially

Topic 4a: The relation of the divine will and intellect

ADAMS, St. Thomas Aquinas
continued

Topic 6*b*: The distinction between the will's freedom
of exercise and the will's freedom of choice

RELATED AUTHORS AND WORKS IN *Great Books of the Western World*

Aquinas, Vol. 19, *Summa Theologica*, First Part, Q 1–11, pages 3–50
Dante, Vol. 21, *Divine Comedy*, Paradise, Canto I, pages 106–107;
    Cantos X–XII, pages 121–125; Canto XXXIII, pages 156–157
Montaigne, Vol. 25, *Apology for Raimond de Sebonde*, pages
    208–294
Descartes, Vol. 31, *Meditation III*, pages 81–89
Spinoza, Vol. 31, *Ethics*, Part I, pages 355–372
Pascal, Vol. 33, *Pensées*, Sect. IV, pages 217–218; Sect. VII, page
    256; Sect. VIII, page 272
Locke, Vol. 35, *Essay Concerning Human Understanding*, Bk. II,
    Chap. XXI, pages 180–181; Chap. XXIII, pages 205–212
Hume, Vol. 35, *Enquiry Concerning Human Understanding*,
    Sect. XI, pages 497–503
Freud, Vol. 54, *New Introductory Lectures on Psycho-Analysis*,
    Lecture 35, pages 873–884

RELATED AUTHORS AND WORKS IN *Gateway to the Great Books*

Clifford, *Ethics of Belief*, Vol. 10, pages 16–36
Eliot, T. S., *Dante*, Vol. 5, pages 371–403
Emerson, *Nature*, Vol. 10, pages 512–524
Flaubert, *Legend of St. Julian the Hospitaller*, Vol. 3, pages
    371–392
Mill, J. S., *Nature*, Vol. 10, pages 477–508
Singer, *Spinoza of Market Street*, Vol. 3, pages 466–480
Tolstoy, *Three Hermits*, Vol. 3, pages 700–706

For Aquinas' *Summa Theologica* in *Great Books of the Western World*,
see Vols. 19–20

SHERWOOD ANDERSON, 1876–1941

I'm a Fool
Vol. 2, pages 511–520

SUGGESTED READINGS IN THE *Syntopicon*

CUSTOM AND CONVENTION, Vol. 2, pages 268–285, especially
    Topic 5*b*: The effect of custom on the training and character
    of men

Topic 7d: The influence of custom on the liberty
of the individual
DESIRE, Vol. 2, pages 323–344, especially
Topic 2b: The objects of desire: the good and the pleasant
Topic 2c: Desire as a cause of action: motivation or purpose;
voluntariness
HAPPINESS, Vol. 2, pages 684–710, especially
Topic 2b(5): The importance of friendship and love
for happiness
TRUTH, Vol. 3, pages 915–938, especially
Topic 8c: Truth in relation to love and friendship: the pleasant
and the unpleasant truth

RELATED AUTHORS AND WORKS IN *Great Books of the Western World*

Plato, Vol. 7, *Symposium,* pages 161–162
Montaigne, Vol. 25, *Of Giving the Lie,* pages 322–324
Shakespeare, Vol. 26, *Much Ado About Nothing,* pages 503–531;
As You Like It, pages 597–626
Pascal, Vol. 33, *Pensées,* Sect. II, pages 191–192
Melville, Vol. 48, *Moby Dick,* Chap. 10, pages 36–39

RELATED AUTHORS AND WORKS IN *Gateway to the Great Books*

Anonymous, *Aucassin and Nicolette,* Vol. 2, pages 523–551
Apuleius, "Cupid and Psyche," Vol. 3, pages 197–212
Balzac, *Passion in the Desert,* Vol. 3, pages 436–447
Bunin, *Gentleman from San Francisco,* Vol. 3, pages 102–123
Conrad, *Youth,* Vol. 2, pages 210–236
Dostoevsky, *White Nights,* Vol. 3, pages 276–319
Eliot, G., *Lifted Veil,* Vol. 3, pages 157–193
Galsworthy, *Apple-Tree,* Vol. 3, pages 323–367
Plutarch, *Of Bashfulness,* Vol. 7, pages 97–109
Turgenev, *First Love,* Vol. 3, pages 217–271

ANONYMOUS, *c.* early 13th century

Aucassin and Nicolette
Vol. 2, pages 523–551

SUGGESTED READINGS IN THE *Syntopicon*

ETERNITY, Vol. 2, pages 437–450, especially
Topic 4d: The eternity of Heaven and Hell: everlasting life
and death

ANONYMOUS, *Aucassin and Nicolette*
continued

Topic 5: The knowledge and imagery of eternity

LOVE, Vol. 2, pages 1051–1082, especially

Topic 1e: The intensity and power of love: its increase
or decrease; its constructive or destructive force

Topic 2c: Romantic, chivalric, and courtly love: the idealization
and supremacy of the beloved

POETRY, Vol. 3, pages 400–419, especially

Topic 1: The nature of poetry: its distinction from other arts

Topic 6a: The expression of emotion in poetry

Topic 7d: Spectacle and song in drama

RELATED AUTHORS AND WORKS IN *Great Books of the Western World*

Plotinus, Vol. 17, *Third Ennead*, Seventh Tractate, pages 120–123

Dante, Vol. 21, *Divine Comedy*, Paradise, Canto II, page 109
and *passim*

Chaucer, Vol. 22, *Troilus and Cressida*, Bk. II, page 41
and *passim*

Shakespeare, Vol. 26, *Romeo and Juliet*, pages 285–319

Milton, Vol. 32, *Psalm LXXXVII*, page 88; *Paradise Lost*, Bk. III,
pages 141–150

RELATED AUTHORS AND WORKS IN *Gateway to the Great Books*

Anderson, *I'm a Fool*, Vol. 2, pages 511–520

Apuleius, "Cupid and Psyche," Vol. 3, pages 197–212

Bacon, *Of Love*, Vol. 10, pages 351–352

Bunin, *Gentleman from San Francisco*, Vol. 3, pages 120–123

Chekhov, *Darling*, Vol. 3, pages 452–462; *Cherry Orchard*, Vol. 4,
pages 249–294

Dostoevsky, *White Nights*, Vol. 3, pages 276–319

Flaubert, *Legend of St. Julian the Hospitaller*, Vol. 3, pages
371–392

Galsworthy, *Apple-Tree*, Vol. 3, pages 323–367

Hawthorne, *Rappaccini's Daughter*, Vol. 3, pages 128–152

Hazlitt, *On the Feeling of Immortality in Youth*, Vol. 10, pages
565–570

Schiller, *On Simple and Sentimental Poetry*, Vol. 5, pages
155–211

Turgenev, *First Love*, Vol. 3, pages 217–271

LUCIUS APULEIUS, fl. 2nd century A.D.

"Cupid and Psyche"
from *The Golden Ass*
Vol. 3, pages 197–212

SUGGESTED READINGS IN THE *Syntopicon*

BEAUTY, Vol. 2, pages 112–125, especially
Topic 3: Beauty in relation to desire and love, as object or cause
Topic 4: Beauty and ugliness in relation to pleasure and pain
GOD, Vol. 2, pages 543–604, especially
Topic 1a: The nature and existence of the gods
Topic 1c: The intervention of the gods in the affairs of men: their judgment of the deserts of men
LOVE, Vol. 2, pages 1051–1082, especially
Topic 1d: The objects of love: the good, the true, the beautiful; God, man, things
Topic 1e: The intensity and power of love: its increase or decrease; its constructive or destructive force

RELATED AUTHORS AND WORKS IN *Great Books of the Western World*

Plato, Vol. 7, *Cratylus*, page 103; *Symposium*, pages 149–173
Virgil, Vol. 13, *Aeneid*, Bk. IV, pages 175–186
Dante, Vol. 21, *Divine Comedy*, Hell, Canto V, pages 7–8
Chaucer, Vol. 22, *Troilus and Cressida*, pages 1–155
Shakespeare, Vol. 26, *Romeo and Juliet*, pages 285–319
Freud, Vol. 54, *On Narcissism*, pages 404–406; *The Ego and the Id*, pages 708–712

RELATED AUTHORS AND WORKS IN *Gateway to the Great Books*

Anderson, *I'm a Fool*, Vol. 2, pages 511–520
Anonymous, *Aucassin and Nicolette*, Vol. 2, pages 523–551
Bacon, *Of Beauty*, Vol. 5, page 94; *Of Love*, Vol. 10, pages 351–352
Balzac, *Passion in the Desert*, Vol. 3, pages 436–447
Dostoevsky, *White Nights*, Vol. 3, pages 276–319
Galsworthy, *Apple-Tree*, Vol. 3, pages 323–367
Hawthorne, *Rappaccini's Daughter*, Vol. 3, pages 128–152
Pater, "Art of Life," Vol. 10, pages 258–261
Turgenev, *First Love*, Vol. 3, pages 217–271

MATTHEW ARNOLD, 1822–1888

The Study of Poetry
Vol. 5, pages 19–41

SUGGESTED READINGS IN THE *Syntopicon*

POETRY, Vol. 3, pages 400–419, especially
  Topic 2: The origin and development of poetry: the materials
    of myth and legend
  Topic 5b: Poetry contrasted with history and philosophy:
    the dispraise and defense of the poet
  Topic 8a(2): Poetic truth: verisimilitude or plausibility;
    the possible, the probable, and the necessary

TRUTH, Vol. 3, pages 915–938, especially
  Topic 4b: Truth in science and poetry: the truth of fact
    and the truth of fiction

RELATED AUTHORS AND WORKS IN *Great Books of the Western World*

Aristotle, Vol. 9, *On Poetics*, pages 681–699
Montaigne, Vol. 25, *Of Books*, pages 199–200
Cervantes, Vol. 29, *Don Quixote*, First Part, Chap. 32, pages
  117–120; Chaps. 47–50, pages 184–194
Bacon, Vol. 30, *Advancement of Learning*, Second Book, pages
  38–39
Descartes, Vol. 31, *Discourse on Method*, Part I, pages 42–43
Fielding, Vol. 37, *Tom Jones*, Bk. II, Chap. 1, pages 19–20; Bk.
  VII, Chap. 1, pages 121–123; Bk. VIII, Chap. 1, pages
  152–155; Bk. IX, Chap. 1, pages 189–191; Bk. XIV,
  Chap. 1, pages 296–298; Bk. XVI, Chap. 5, pages
  345–348
Kant, Vol. 42, *Critique of Judgement*, First Part, Sect. I, Bk. II,
  pages 532–537, especially 532, 535
James, W., Vol. 53, *Principles of Psychology*, Chap. XXI, pages
  641–643

RELATED AUTHORS AND WORKS IN *Gateway to the Great Books*

Bacon, *Of Beauty*, Vol. 5, page 94; *Of Truth*, Vol. 10, pages
  346–347
De Quincey, *Literature of Knowledge and Literature of Power*,
  Vol. 5, pages 358–361
Eliot, T. S., *Dante*, Vol. 5, pages 317–403; *Tradition
  and the Individual Talent*, pages 404–411

Hazlitt, *My First Acquaintance With Poets,* Vol. 5, pages
264–279; *Of Persons One Would Wish to Have Seen,*
pages 284–295
Johnson, *Preface to Shakespeare,* Vol. 5, pages 316–353
Lamb, *Sanity of True Genius,* Vol. 5, pages 308–310
Mill, J. S., "Childhood and Youth," Vol. 6, pages 5–47
Pater, "Art of Life," Vol. 10, pages 258–261
Sainte-Beuve, *What Is a Classic?,* Vol. 5, pages 65–75
Santayana, *Lucretius,* Vol. 10, pages 365–390; *Goethe's Faust,*
pages 391–419
Schiller, *On Simple and Sentimental Poetry,* Vol. 5, pages
155–211
Schopenhauer, *On Style,* Vol. 5, pages 124–136
Shelley, *Defence of Poetry,* Vol. 5, pages 216–242
Whitman, *Preface to Leaves of Grass,* Vol. 5, pages 247–259
Woolf, *How Should One Read a Book?,* Vol. 5, pages 5–14

Sweetness and Light
Vol. 5, pages 42–61

SUGGESTED READINGS IN THE *Syntopicon*

BEAUTY, Vol. 2, pages 112–125, especially

Topic 1*a*: The beautiful and the good: beauty as a kind
of fitness or order

PROGRESS, Vol. 3, pages 437–453, especially

Topic 1*b*: Optimism or meliorism: the doctrine of human
perfectibility
Topic 6: Intellectual or cultural progress: its sources
and impediments

VIRTUE AND VICE, Vol. 3, pages 975–1009, especially

Topic 4*d*(4): The influence on moral character of poetry,
music, and other arts: the guidance of history
and example

RELATED AUTHORS AND WORKS IN *Great Books of the Western World*

Plato, Vol. 7, *Symposium,* pages 162–164
Cervantes, Vol. 29, *Don Quixote,* First Part, Chaps. 47–50, pages
184–194
Bacon, Vol. 30, *Advancement of Learning,* pages 1–101, *passim*
Fielding, Vol. 37, *Tom Jones,* Bk. VII, Chap. 1, pages 121–123
Rousseau, Vol. 38, *Discourse on the Origin of Inequality,* First
Part, pages 338–348
Kant, Vol. 42, *Critique of Judgement,* First Part, Sect. I, Bk. II,
pages 520–523

ARNOLD, *Sweetness and Light*
continued

RELATED AUTHORS AND WORKS IN *Gateway to the Great Books*

Bacon, *Of Beauty*, Vol. 5, page 94
Chekhov, *Darling*, Vol. 3, pages 452–462
Eliot, T. S., *Tradition and the Individual Talent*, Vol. 5,
    pages 404–411
Epictetus, *Enchiridion*, Vol. 10, pages 236–254
Erskine, *Moral Obligation to Be Intelligent*, Vol. 10, pages 5–13
Guizot, "Civilization," Vol. 6, pages 302–317
Hume, *Of the Standard of Taste*, Vol. 5, pages 103–119
Pater, "Art of Life," Vol. 10, pages 258–261
Ruskin, *Idealist's Arraignment of the Age*, Vol. 7, pages 126–136
Sainte-Beuve, *What Is a Classic?*, Vol. 5, pages 65–75
Shelley, *Defence of Poetry*, Vol. 5, pages 216–242
Tolstoy, *What Men Live By*, Vol. 3, pages 707–727
Voltaire, "English Men and Ideas," Vol. 7, pages 332–378
Whitman, *Preface to Leaves of Grass*, Vol. 5, pages 247–259

SIR FRANCIS BACON, 1561–1626

Of Beauty
Vol. 5, page 94

SUGGESTED READINGS IN THE *Syntopicon*

BEAUTY, Vol. 2, pages 112–125, especially
    Topic 1a: The beautiful and the good: beauty as a kind
        of fitness or order
    Topic 1c: The elements of beauty: unity, proportion, clarity
TRUTH, Vol. 3, pages 915–938, especially
    Topic 1c: The relation of truth, goodness, and beauty

RELATED AUTHORS AND WORKS IN *Great Books of the Western World*

Plato, Vol. 7, *Phaedrus*, pages 124–129
Plotinus, Vol. 17, *First Ennead*, Sixth Tractate, pages 21–26
Aquinas, Vol. 19, *Summa Theologica*, First Part, Q 5, Art. 4,
    pages 25–26; Part I–II, Q 27, Art. 1, page 737
Pascal, Vol. 33, *Pensées*, Sect. I, page 176
Kant, Vol. 42, *Critique of Judgement*, First Part, Sect. I, Bk. I,
    pages 476–495

RELATED AUTHORS AND WORKS IN *Gateway to the Great Books*

Apuleius, "Cupid and Psyche," Vol. 3, pages 197–212
Arnold, *Study of Poetry*, Vol. 5, pages 19–41; *Sweetness and Light*, pages 42–61
De Quincey, *On the Knocking at the Gate in Macbeth*, Vol. 5, pages 362–366
Fabre, *Laboratory of the Open Fields*, Vol. 8, pages 97–104
Hume, *Of the Standard of Taste*, Vol. 5, pages 103–119
Pater, "Art of Life," Vol. 10, pages 258–261
Schopenhauer, *On the Comparative Place of Interest and Beauty in Works of Art*, Vol. 5, pages 143–150

Of Discourse
Vol. 5, pages 95–96

SUGGESTED READINGS IN THE *Syntopicon*

DIALECTIC, Vol. 2, pages 345–357, especially
Topic 2b(2): The technique of question and answer
OPINION, Vol. 3, pages 303–322, especially
Topic 2c: Reasoning and argument concerning matters of opinion: comparison of demonstration and persuasion, principles and assumptions, axioms and postulates
RHETORIC, Vol. 3, pages 645–664, especially
Topic 2a: The devices of rhetoric: figures of speech; the extension and contraction of discourse

RELATED AUTHORS AND WORKS IN *Great Books of the Western World*

Plato, Vol. 7, *Republic*, Bks. VI–VII, pages 383–398
Aristotle, Vol. 8, *Topics*, Bk. VIII, pages 211–223; Vol. 9, *Rhetoric*, Bk. I, Chaps. 1–2, pages 593–598; Bk. II, Chaps. 18–26, pages 639–653
Montaigne, Vol. 25, *Of the Art of Conference*, pages 446–457
Bacon, Vol. 30, *Advancement of Learning*, Second Book, pages 62–69
Mill, J. S., Vol. 43, *On Liberty*, Chap. 2, pages 274–293

RELATED AUTHORS AND WORKS IN *Gateway to the Great Books*

Dewey, "Process of Thought," Vol. 10, pages 92–213
Dickens, "Full and Faithful Report of the Memorable Trial of Bardell Against Pickwick," Vol. 2, pages 391–448
Kipling, *Mowgli's Brothers*, Vol. 2, pages 126–141
Mill, J. S., "Childhood and Youth," Vol. 6, pages 5–47
Tolstoy, *Three Hermits*, Vol. 3, pages 700–706
Voltaire, "Philosophy of Common Sense," Vol. 10, pages 453–474

SIR FRANCIS BACON
continued

Of Studies
Vol. 5, pages 97–98

SUGGESTED READINGS IN THE *Syntopicon*

EDUCATION, Vol. 2, pages 376–399, especially
Topic 5c: The nature of learning: its several modes
MIND, Vol. 3, pages 171–203, especially
Topic 1a(3): The functioning of intellect: the acts
of understanding, judgment, and reasoning

RELATED AUTHORS AND WORKS IN *Great Books of the Western World*

Plato, Vol. 7, *Republic*, Bks. VI–VII, pages 385–401
Aquinas, Vol. 19, *Summa Theologica*, First Part, Q 85, Art. 1–Q
87, Art. 3, pages 451–468
Montaigne, Vol. 25, *Of Books*, pages 194–200
Bacon, Vol. 30, *Advancement of Learning*, First Book, pages 2–28
Descartes, Vol. 31, *Rules for the Direction of the Mind*, Rules
VIII–XII, pages 12–25; *Discourse on Method*, Part I,
pages 42–44

RELATED AUTHORS AND WORKS IN *Gateway to the Great Books*

De Quincey, *Literature of Knowledge and Literature of Power*,
Vol. 5, pages 358–361
Erskine, *Moral Obligation to Be Intelligent*, Vol. 10, pages 5–13
Franklin, *Proposals Relating to the Education of Youth
in Pennsylvania*, Vol. 6, pages 536–542
Mill, J. S., "Childhood and Youth," Vol. 6, pages 5–47
Sainte-Beuve, *What Is a Classic?*, Vol. 5, pages 65–75
Schopenhauer, *On Some Forms of Literature*, Vol. 5, pages
137–142; *On Education*, Vol. 7, pages 197–203
Tolstoy, *Three Hermits*, Vol. 3, pages 700–706
Woolf, *How Should One Read a Book?*, Vol. 5, pages 5–14

Of Youth and Age
Vol. 7, pages 3–4

SUGGESTED READINGS IN THE *Syntopicon*

FAMILY, Vol. 2, pages 486–514, especially
Topic 6c: The condition of immaturity
Topic 6e: The initiation of children into adult life

MAN, Vol. 3, pages 1–41, especially
Topic 6c: The ages of man: infancy, youth, maturity,
senescence

RELATED AUTHORS AND WORKS IN *Great Books of the Western World*

Plato, Vol. 7, *Republic*, Bk. I, page 296; Bk. VI, page 381;
Bk. VII, page 401
Aristotle, Vol. 8, *On the Soul*, Bk. I, Chap. 4, page 638; Vol. 9,
Nicomachean Ethics, Bk. I, Chap. 4, page 340; Bk. VI,
Chap. 8, page 391; *Politics*, Bk. VII, Chap. 13, page 537;
Bk. VIII, Chap. 7, page 548; *Rhetoric*, Bk. II, Chaps. 12–16,
pages 636–638
Montaigne, Vol. 25, *Of Age*, pages 156–158; *All Things Have Their
Season*, page 339; *Upon Some Verses of Virgil*, pages
406–408, 432–434
Shakespeare, Vol. 26, *As You Like It*, Act II, Scene VII, pages
607–609; Vol. 27, *King Lear*, pages 244–283, especially Act I,
Scene I, pages 244–247
Swift, Vol. 36, *Gulliver's Travels*, Part III, Chap. X, pages 127–129
Hamilton, Madison, Jay, Vol. 43, *Federalist*, No. 79, page 234
Boswell, Vol. 44, *Life of Samuel Johnson*, pages 126, 360, 381,
407–408
Tolstoy, Vol. 51, *War and Peace*, Bk. 8, Chaps. II–IV, pages
305–310; Bk. 13, Chap. XVII, pages 584–585
James, W., Vol. 53, *Principles of Psychology*, Chap. XI, page 270;
Chap. XV, page 409; Chap. XXIV, pages 711–712

RELATED AUTHORS AND WORKS IN *Gateway to the Great Books*

Cicero, *On Old Age*, Vol. 10, pages 317–343
Conrad, *Youth*, Vol. 2, pages 210–236
Galsworthy, *Apple-Tree*, Vol. 3, pages 323–367
Hazlitt, *On the Feeling of Immortality in Youth*, Vol. 10, pages
565–570
Lamb, *Dream Children*, Vol. 5, pages 304–307
Mill, J. S., "Childhood and Youth," Vol. 6, pages 5–47
Plutarch, *Of Bashfulness*, Vol. 7, pages 97–109; *Contentment*,
Vol. 10, pages 264–281
Singer, *Spinoza of Market Street*, Vol. 3, pages 466–480
Swift, *Resolutions When I Come to be Old*, Vol. 7, page 32
Turgenev, *First Love*, Vol. 3, pages 217–271

SIR FRANCIS BACON
continued

Of Parents and Children
Of Marriage and Single Life
Vol. 7, pages 5–8

SUGGESTED READINGS IN THE *Syntopicon*

FAMILY, Vol. 2, pages 486–514, especially
Topic 4: The institution of marriage: its nature and purpose
Topic 4c: Matrimony and celibacy
Topic 6: Parents and children: fatherhood, motherhood
Topic 6a: The desire for offspring
Topic 7c: Patterns of friendship in the family: man and wife;
parents and children; brothers and sisters
Topic 8: Historical observations on the institution of marriage
and the family
LOVE, Vol. 2, pages 1051–1082, especially
Topic 2b(4): Patterns of love and friendship in the family
Topic 2d: Conjugal love: its sexual, fraternal, and romantic
components
VIRTUE AND VICE, Vol. 3, pages 975–1009, especially
Topic 4d(1): The influence of parental authority
on the formation of character

RELATED AUTHORS AND WORKS IN *Great Books of the Western World*

Plato, Vol. 7, *Republic,* Bk. V, pages 361–365
Aristotle, Vol. 9, *Nicomachean Ethics,* Bk. VIII, Chaps. 7–14,
pages 410–416; *Politics,* Bk. VII, Chaps. 16–17, pages 539–542
Chaucer, Vol. 22, *Canterbury Tales,* Wife of Bath's Prologue,
pages 256–269; Merchant's Prologue, page 318; Epilogue
to the Merchant's Tale, page 338
Rabelais, Vol. 24, *Gargantua and Pantagruel,* Bk. I, Chaps.
1–11, pages 3–15; Bk. II, Chap. 8, pages 81–83; Bk. III,
Chaps. 9–49, pages 144–223; Bk. IV, Chap. 9, pages 248–250
Montaigne, Vol. 25, *Of the Affection of Fathers to Their Children,*
pages 183–192; *Upon Some Verses of Virgil,* pages 406–434
Shakespeare, Vol. 26, *King Henry IV,* First Part, Act III, Scene II,
pages 452–454; Vol. 27, *King Lear,* pages 244–283
Locke, Vol. 35, *Concerning Civil Government,* Chap. VI,
pages 36–42
Tolstoy, Vol. 51, *War and Peace,* Bk. 3, Chaps. I–VI, pages
111–131; First Epilogue, Chaps. V–XVI, pages 650–674

Dostoevsky, Vol. 52, *Brothers Karamazov*, Part I, Bk. I, pages
1–11; Bk. II, Chap. 6, pages 32–37; Bk. III, Chap. 9, pages
70–73; Part II, Bk. IV, Chap. 2, pages 88–90; Part III, Bk.
VIII, Chap. 4, pages 206–209; Part IV, Bk. XI, Chaps. 7–8,
pages 324–336; Bk. XII, pages 348–401
Freud, Vol. 54, *New Introductory Lectures on Psycho-Analysis*,
Lecture 33, pages 856–863

RELATED AUTHORS AND WORKS IN *Gateway to the Great Books*

Chekhov, *Darling*, Vol. 3, pages 452–462
Dickens, "Full and Faithful Report of the Memorable Trial
of Bardell Against Pickwick," Vol. 2, pages 391–448
Dinesen, *Sorrow-Acre*, Vol. 3, pages 615–641
Eliot, G., *Lifted Veil*, Vol. 3, pages 157–193
Galsworthy, *Apple-Tree*, Vol. 3, pages 323–367
Hawthorne, *Rappaccini's Daughter*, Vol. 3, pages 128–152
Lawrence, *Rocking-Horse Winner*, Vol. 3, pages 512–525
Mill, J. S., "Childhood and Youth," Vol. 6, pages 5–47
Molière, *Doctor in Spite of Himself*, Vol. 4, pages 52–81
Synge, *Riders to the Sea*, Vol. 4, pages 342–352
Turgenev, *First Love*, Vol. 3, pages 217–271

Of Great Place
Vol. 7, pages 9–11

SUGGESTED READINGS IN THE *Syntopicon*

HONOR, Vol. 2, pages 728–748, especially
Topic 2: Honor and fame in the life of the individual
Topic 2b: Honor as an object of desire and as a factor in virtue
and happiness
Topic 3: The social realization of honor and fame
Topic 3b: The conditions of honor or fame and the causes
of dishonor or infamy
Topic 5a: Honor as a motivation of heroism
STATE, Vol. 3, pages 826–865, especially
Topic 8: The offices of state: the statesman, king, or prince
Topic 8b: The qualities or virtues necessary for the good
statesman or king
Topic 8e: The advantages and disadvantages of participation
in political life
VIRTUE AND VICE, Vol. 3, pages 975–1009, especially
Topic 7d: The virtues which constitute the good or successful
ruler: the vices associated with the possession
of power

BACON, *Of Great Place*
continued

Of Seditions and Troubles
Vol. 7, pages 12–17

OLIGARCHY, Vol. 3, pages 270–281, especially
Topic 3: The instability of oligarchical government
REVOLUTION, Vol. 3, pages 626–644, especially
Topic 1b: The definition of treason or sedition: the revolutionist
as a treasonable conspirator
Topic 3b: Ways of retaining power and combatting revolution

RELATED AUTHORS AND WORKS IN *Great Books of the Western World*

Thucydides, Vol. 6, *History of the Peloponnesian War*, Bk. III,
Chap. IX, pages 425–428
Plato, Vol. 7, *Republic*, Bks. VIII–IX, pages 401–421
Aristotle, Vol. 9, *Politics*, Bk. V, pages 502–519
Machiavelli, Vol. 23, *Prince*, Chap. VIII, pages 12–14; Chap.
XXVI, pages 36–37
Hobbes, Vol. 23, *Leviathan*, Part II, Chaps. 29–30, pages 148–159
Shakespeare, Vol. 26, *King Richard II*, pages 320–351; *Julius
Caesar*, pages 568–596; Vol. 27, *Coriolanus*, pages 351–392
Locke, Vol. 35, *Concerning Civil Government*, Chaps. XVI–XIX,
pages 65–81
Hamilton, Madison, Jay, Vol. 43, *Federalist*, Nos. 9–10, pages 47–53
Marx and Engels, Vol. 50, *Manifesto of the Communist Party*,
pages 419–434
Tolstoy, Vol. 51, *War and Peace*, First Epilogue, Chap. XIV,
pages 668–669

RELATED AUTHORS AND WORKS IN *Gateway to the Great Books*

Burke, *Letter to the Sheriffs of Bristol*, Vol. 7, pages 237–271
Hugo, "Battle with the Cannon," Vol. 2, pages 146–154
Lincoln, *Address at Cooper Institute*, Vol. 6, pages 737–746;
First Inaugural Address, pages 747–755; *Letter to Horace
Greeley*, pages 756–757; *Gettysburg Address*, page 759
Macaulay, *Machiavelli*, Vol. 7, pages 295–329
O'Neill, *Emperor Jones*, Vol. 4, pages 357–382
Paine, "Call to Patriots—December 23, 1776," Vol. 6, pages
461–468
Tacitus, *Life of Gnaeus Julius Agricola*, Vol. 6, pages 274–298
Thoreau, *Plea for Captain John Brown*, Vol. 6, pages 714–732
Washington, *Circular Letter to the Governors of All the States
on Disbanding the Army*, Vol. 6, pages 474–483;
Farewell Address, pages 484–497
Whitman, *Death of Abraham Lincoln*, Vol. 6, pages 174–183

SIR FRANCIS BACON
continued

Of Custom and Education
Vol. 7, pages 18–19

SUGGESTED READINGS IN THE *Syntopicon*

CUSTOM AND CONVENTION, Vol. 2, pages 268–285, especially
Topic 2: The origin, development, and transmission of customs
Topic 5*b*: The effect of custom on the training and character
of men
Topic 7*d*: The influence of custom on the liberty
of the individual
Topic 8: Custom in relation to order and progress: the factors
of tradition and invention
EDUCATION, Vol. 2, pages 376–399, especially
Topic 4*c*: The role of the state in moral education: law, custom,
public opinion
GOOD AND EVIL, Vol. 2, pages 605–636, especially
Topic 6*d*: The possibility of moral knowledge: the subjectivity
or conventionality of judgments of good and evil
HABIT, Vol. 2, pages 665–683, especially
Topic 6: The force of habit in human life
Topic 7: The social significance of habit: habit in relation to law
LAW, Vol. 2, pages 962–990, especially
Topic 5*f*: The relation of positive law to custom
VIRTUE AND VICE, Vol. 3, pages 975–1009, especially
Topic 4*d*(3): The guidance of laws and customs: the limits
of positive law with respect to commanding
virtue and prohibiting vice

RELATED AUTHORS AND WORKS IN *Great Books of the Western World*

Plato, Vol. 7, *Republic*, Bks. II–III, pages 320–339
Aristotle, Vol. 9, *Nicomachean Ethics*, Bk. II, Chaps. 1–4, pages
348–351; Bk. X, Chap. 9, pages 434–436; *Politics*, Bk. VII,
Chap. 13–Bk. VIII, Chap. 7, pages 536–548
Augustine, Vol. 18, *Confessions*, Bk. I, pages 4–8
Aquinas, Vol. 20, *Summa Theologica*, Part I–II, Q 97, Art. 3,
pages 237–238
Montaigne, Vol. 25, *Of Custom*, pages 42–51; *Of Cannibals*, pages
91–98; *Use Makes Perfect*, pages 176–181; *Of Cruelty*, pages
200–208; *Of Virtue*, pages 340–343

Descartes, Vol. 31, *Discourse on Method*, Part I, page 44; Part II, pages 46, 48; Part III, pages 48–51
Spinoza, Vol. 31, *Ethics*, Part I, Appendix, pages 369–372
Mill, J. S., Vol. 43, *On Liberty*, Chap. 3, pages 293–302
James, W., Vol. 53, *Principles of Psychology*, Chap. IV, pages 68–83
Freud, Vol. 54, *Civilization and Its Discontents*, Chap. VIII, pages 799–801

RELATED AUTHORS AND WORKS IN *Gateway to the Great Books*

Butler, "Customs and Opinions of the Erewhonians," Vol. 2, pages 483–506
Faraday, *Observations on Mental Education*, Vol. 7, pages 208–232
Kipling, *Mowgli's Brothers*, Vol. 2, pages 126–141
Mill, J. S., "Childhood and Youth," Vol. 6, pages 5–47
Pater, "Art of Life," Vol. 10, pages 258–261
Schopenhauer, *On Education*, Vol. 7, pages 197–203
Swift, *Essay on Modern Education*, Vol. 7, pages 33–39
Twain, "Learning the River," Vol. 6, pages 50–98

Of Followers and Friends
Vol. 7, pages 20–21

SUGGESTED READINGS IN THE *Syntopicon*

HONOR, Vol. 2, pages 728–748, especially
Topic 4c: Honor as a political technique: the uses of praise, prestige, public opinion
JUSTICE, Vol. 2, pages 850–879, especially
Topic 9e: The just distribution of honors, ranks, offices, suffrage
LOVE, Vol. 2, pages 1051–1082, especially
Topic 2b(3): The types of friendship: friendships based on utility, pleasure, or virtue

RELATED AUTHORS AND WORKS IN *Great Books of the Western World*

Plato, Vol. 7, *Lysis*, pages 14–25
Aristotle, Vol. 9, *Nicomachean Ethics*, Bk. VIII, Chaps. 2–8, pages 407–411; Bk. VIII, Chap. 13, pages 414–415
Machiavelli, Vol. 23, *Prince*, Chap. XVII, page 24; Chaps. XXI–XXII, pages 31–33
Montaigne, Vol. 25, *Of Recompenses of Honor*, pages 181–183
Shakespeare, Vol. 27, *King Lear*, Act III, pages 262–269
Gibbon, Vol. 41, *Decline and Fall of the Roman Empire*, Chap. LIII, pages 317–319

BACON, *Of Followers and Friends*
continued

RELATED AUTHORS AND WORKS IN *Gateway to the Great Books*

Cicero, *On Friendship*, Vol. 10, pages 286–316
La Bruyère, *Characters*, Vol. 6, pages 102–105
Maupassant, *Two Friends*, Vol. 2, pages 159–164
Molière, *Misanthrope*, Vol. 4, pages 6–51
Sheridan, *School for Scandal*, Vol. 4, pages 85–159

Of Usury
Vol. 7, pages 22–24

SUGGESTED READINGS IN THE *Syntopicon*

JUSTICE, Vol. 2, pages 850–879, especially
Topic 8*d*: Justice and the use of money: usury and interest rates
WEALTH, Vol. 3, pages 1038–1070, especially
Topic 5*e*: The rate of interest on money: the condemnation of usury
Topic 6*d*(1): The distinction of profit from rent, interest, and wages

RELATED AUTHORS AND WORKS IN *Great Books of the Western World*

Aristotle, Vol. 9, *Politics*, Bk. I, Chaps. 9–10, pages 450–452
Shakespeare, Vol. 26, *Merchant of Venice*, Act I, Scene III, pages 409–411
Pascal, Vol. 33, *Provincial Letters*, Letter VIII, pages 53–57
Smith, Vol. 39, *Wealth of Nations*, Bk. I, Chap. IX, pages 37–41
Marx, Vol. 50, *Capital*, Part VIII, Chap. XXXI, pages 371–373

RELATED AUTHORS AND WORKS IN *Gateway to the Great Books*

Hume, *Of Money*, Vol. 7, pages 62–71

Of Riches
Vol. 7, pages 25–27

SUGGESTED READINGS IN THE *Syntopicon*

HAPPINESS, Vol. 2, pages 684–710, especially
Topic 2*b*(1): The contribution of the goods of fortune to happiness: wealth, health, longevity
JUSTICE, Vol. 2, pages 850–879, especially
Topic 8*d*: Justice and the use of money: usury and interest rates

NATURE, Vol. 3, pages 225–250, especially
Topic 5b: Natural inclinations and natural needs with respect
to property and wealth
NECESSITY AND CONTINGENCY, Vol. 3, pages 251–269,
especially
Topic 5e: Economic necessities or luxuries
VIRTUE AND VICE, Vol. 3, pages 975–1009, especially
Topic 6c: The relation of virtue to wealth
WEALTH, Vol. 3, pages 1038–1070, especially
Topic 10: The moral aspects of wealth and poverty
Topic 10a: The nature of wealth as a good: its place
in the order of goods and its relation to happiness
Topic 10c: Temperance and intemperance with respect
to wealth: liberality, magnificence, miserliness,
avarice

RELATED AUTHORS AND WORKS IN *Great Books of the Western World*

Aristophanes, Vol. 5, *Plutus*, pages 629–642
Aristotle, Vol. 9, *Nicomachean Ethics*, Bk. IV, Chaps. 1–2, pages
366–370; *Politics*, Bk. I, Chaps. 9–12, pages 450–454
Montaigne, Vol. 25, *That the Relish of Good and Evil Depends
in a Great Measure Upon the Opinion We Have of Them*,
pages 122–125
Pascal, Vol. 33, *Provincial Letters*, Letter XII, pages 91–94
Marx and Engels, Vol. 50, *Manifesto of the Communist Party*,
Chap. II, pages 425–429
Tolstoy, Vol. 51, *War and Peace*, Book 14, Chap. XII, page 605
Dostoevsky, Vol. 52, *Brothers Karamazov*, Part II, Bk. V, Chap.
5, pages 130–132; Bk. VI, Chap. 3, pages 164–166

RELATED AUTHORS AND WORKS IN *Gateway to the Great Books*

Bunin, *Gentleman from San Francisco*, Vol. 3, pages 102–123
Fitzgerald, *Diamond as Big as the Ritz*, Vol. 3, pages 397–431
Hume, *Of Money*, Vol. 7, pages 62–71
La Bruyère, *Characters*, Vol. 6, pages 102–105
Lawrence, *Rocking-Horse Winner*, Vol. 3, pages 512–525
Pushkin, *Queen of Spades*, Vol. 3, pages 484–507
Twain, *Man That Corrupted Hadleyburg*, Vol. 2, pages 346–386

SIR FRANCIS BACON
continued

The Sphinx
Vol. 8, pages 2–4

SUGGESTED READINGS IN THE *Syntopicon*

KNOWLEDGE, Vol. 2, pages 880–920, especially
  Topic 2: Man's natural desire and power to know
  Topic 8: The use and value of knowledge
MAN, Vol. 3, pages 1–41, especially
  Topic 2b: The sciences of human nature: anthropology
    and psychology; rational and empirical psychology;
    experimental and clinical psychology
  Topic 10c: Man as an integral part of the universe: his station
    in the cosmos
REASONING, Vol. 3, pages 546–568, especially
  Topic 5b: Scientific reasoning: the theory of demonstration
SCIENCE, Vol. 3, pages 682–705, especially
  Topic 1b: Science as the discipline of experimental inquiry
    and the organization of experimental knowledge:
    the scientific spirit
  Topic 3: The relation of science to action and production
  Topic 4: The nature of scientific knowledge
  Topic 7: The evaluation of science

RELATED AUTHORS AND WORKS IN *Great Books of the Western World*

Sophocles, Vol. 5, *Oedipus the King,* pages 99–102
Descartes, Vol. 31, *Discourse on Method,* Part VI, pages 60–67
Kant, Vol. 42, *Critique of Pure Reason,* pages 248–250
Goethe, Vol. 47, *Faust,* First Part, pages 11–18

RELATED AUTHORS AND WORKS IN *Gateway to the Great Books*

Campbell, *Measurement,* Vol. 9, pages 204–221
Emerson, *Nature,* Vol. 10, pages 512–524
Guizot, "Civilization," Vol. 6, pages 302–317
Mill, J. S., *Nature,* Vol. 10, pages 477–508
Tyndall, "Michael Faraday," Vol. 8, pages 8–28

Of Truth
Vol. 10, pages 346–347

Of Death
Vol. 10, pages 348–349

BACON, *Of Death*
continued

LIFE AND DEATH, Vol. 2, pages 1013–1034, especially
   Topic 7: The causes and occurrence of death: the transition
     from life to death
   Topic 8c: The contemplation and fear of death: the attitude
     of the hero, the philosopher, the martyr

RELATED AUTHORS AND WORKS IN *Great Books of the Western World*

Sophocles, Vol. 5, *Oedipus at Colonus*, pages 114–130; *Antigone*,
   pages 131–142
Plato, Vol. 7, *Apology*, pages 205–212; *Crito*, pages 213–219;
   Phaedo, pages 220–251
Aristotle, Vol. 9, *Nicomachean Ethics*, Bk. III, Chaps. 6–9, pages
   361–364
Lucretius, Vol. 12, *On the Nature of Things*, Bk. III, pages 35–44
Augustine, Vol. 18, *Confessions*, Bk. IX, pages 61–71
Montaigne, Vol. 25, *That to Study Philosophy Is to Learn to Die*,
   pages 28–36; *That the Relish of Good and Evil Depends*
   in a Great Measure Upon the Opinion We Have of Them,
   pages 115–118; *A Custom of the Isle of Cea*, pages 167–173;
   Apology for Raimond de Sebonde, pages 266–268
Shakespeare, Vol. 27, *Hamlet*, pages 29–72; *Measure for Measure*,
   pages 174–204
Spinoza, Vol. 31, *Ethics*, Part V, Props. 38–40, pages 461–462
Goethe, Vol. 47, *Faust*, First Part, pages 110–114; Second Part,
   Act V, pages 280–294
Tolstoy, Vol. 51, *War and Peace*, Bk. 12, Chap. XVI, pages
   560–562
Freud, Vol. 54, *Thoughts for the Times on War and Death*,
   pages 755–766

RELATED AUTHORS AND WORKS IN *Gateway to the Great Books*

Browne, "Immortality," Vol. 10, pages 575–580
Butler, "Customs and Opinions of the Erewhonians," Vol. 2, pages
   483–506
Cicero, *On Old Age*, Vol. 10, pages 317–343
Crane, *Open Boat*, Vol. 3, pages 5–26
Epictetus, *Enchiridion*, Vol. 10, pages 236–254
Epicurus, *Letter to Menoeceus*, Vol. 10, pages 230–233
Hazlitt, *On the Feeling of Immortality in Youth*, Vol. 10, pages
   565–570
Hemingway, *Killers*, Vol. 2, pages 169–177
Maupassant, *Two Friends*, Vol. 2, pages 159–164
O'Neill, *Emperor Jones*, Vol. 4, pages 357–382

Pliny, "Eruption of Vesuvius," Vol. 6, pages 264–270
Poe, *Masque of the Red Death*, Vol. 2, pages 278–283
Santayana, *Lucretius*, Vol. 10, pages 365–390
Synge, *Riders to the Sea*, Vol. 4, pages 342–352
Tolstoy, *Death of Ivan Ilyitch*, Vol. 3, pages 646–699
Whitman, *Preface to Leaves of Grass*, Vol. 5, pages 247–259;
    Death of Abraham Lincoln, Vol. 6, pages 174–183

Of Adversity
Vol. 10, page 350

SUGGESTED READINGS IN THE *Syntopicon*

OPPOSITION, Vol. 3, pages 323–341, especially
    Topic 5*d*: Opposition or strife as a productive principle
        or source of progress
PLEASURE AND PAIN, Vol. 3, pages 377–399, especially
    Topic 8*a*: Pleasure and pain in relation to virtue: the restraints
        of temperance and the endurance of courage

RELATED AUTHORS AND WORKS IN *Great Books of the Western World*

Augustine, Vol. 18, *City of God*, Bk. V, Chaps. 11–26, pages
    216–230
Spinoza, Vol. 31, *Ethics*, Part IV, Props. 46–73, pages 438–447
Milton, Vol. 32, *Areopagitica*, pages 390–391
Hegel, Vol. 46, *Philosophy of History*, Second Part, pages
    274–275, 278–281
Goethe, Vol. 47, *Faust*, Second Part, Act V, pages 277–282
Tolstoy, Vol. 51, *War and Peace*, Bk. 13, Chap. XII, pages
    577–578; Bk. 14, Chap. XII, pages 604–605; Bk. 15, Chaps.
    XII–XIII, pages 630–634

RELATED AUTHORS AND WORKS IN *Gateway to the Great Books*

Crane, *Open Boat*, Vol. 3, pages 5–26
Dinesen, *Sorrow-Acre*, Vol. 3, pages 615–641
Emerson, *Self-Reliance*, Vol. 10, pages 525–545
Flaubert, *Legend of St. Julian the Hospitaller*, Vol. 3, pages
    371–392
Gogol, *Overcoat*, Vol. 2, pages 452–478
Hugo, "Battle with the Cannon," Vol. 2, pages 146–154
Ibsen, *Enemy of the People*, Vol. 4, pages 164–246
James, W., *Energies of Men*, Vol. 7, pages 157–170
Long, *Power Within Us*, Vol. 6, pages 246–261
Maupassant, *Two Friends*, Vol. 2, pages 159–164
O'Neill, *Emperor Jones*, Vol. 4, pages 357–382

BACON, *Of Adversity*
continued

Synge, *Riders to the Sea,* Vol. 4, pages 342–352
Tacitus, *Life of Gnaeus Julius Agricola,* Vol. 6, pages 274–298
Xenophon, "March to the Sea," Vol. 6, pages 196–222

Of Love
Vol. 10, pages 351–352

SUGGESTED READINGS IN THE *Syntopicon*

LOVE, Vol. 2, pages 1051–1082, especially
Topic 1e: The intensity and power of love: its increase
or decrease; its constructive or destructive force
Topic 2a: Lustful, sexual, or selfish love: concupiscent love
Topic 2b: Friendly, tender, or altruistic love: fraternal love

RELATED AUTHORS AND WORKS IN *Great Books of the Western World*

Plato, Vol. 7, *Phaedrus,* pages 115–141; *Symposium,* pages 149–173
Aristotle, Vol. 9, *Nicomachean Ethics,* Bks. VIII–IX, pages
406–426
Augustine, Vol. 18, *Confessions,* Bk. VIII, pages 55–61
Dante, Vol. 21, *Divine Comedy,* Purgatory, Cantos XVI–XVII,
pages 76–79
Shakespeare, Vol. 26, *Much Ado About Nothing,* pages 503–531;
As You Like It, pages 597–626; Vol. 27, *Othello,* pages
205–243
Spinoza, Vol. 31, *Ethics,* Part III, Props. 15–50, pages 401–411;
Prop. 59, page 417
Goethe, Vol. 47, *Faust,* First Part, pages 63–93, 108–114
Tolstoy, Vol. 51, *War and Peace,* Bk. 6, Chap. II, pages
236–237; Chaps. XVI–XVII, pages 257–260; Chap. XIX, pages
262–263; Chaps. XXI–XXIV, pages 264–271; Bk. 8,
Chaps. X–XXII, pages 320–341; Bk. 10, Chaps. XXXVI–XXXVII,
pages 461–465; Bk. 11, Chaps. XXXI–XXXII, pages
522–527; Bk. 12, Chaps. XIV–XVI, pages 555–562
Dostoevsky, Vol. 52, *Brothers Karamazov,* Part II, Bk. VI, pages
146–170; Part III, Bk. VII, Chap. 4, pages 189–191
Freud, Vol. 54, *Civilization and Its Discontents,* pages 767–802

RELATED AUTHORS AND WORKS IN *Gateway to the Great Books*

Anderson, *I'm a Fool,* Vol. 2, pages 511–520
Anonymous, *Aucassin and Nicolette,* Vol. 2, pages 523–551
Apuleius, "Cupid and Psyche," Vol. 3, pages 197–212
Balzac, *Passion in the Desert,* Vol. 3, pages 436–447

Chekhov, *Darling*, Vol. 3, pages 452–462
Cicero, *On Friendship*, Vol. 10, pages 286–316
Dinesen, *Sorrow-Acre*, Vol. 3, pages 615–641
Dostoevsky, *White Nights*, Vol. 3, pages 276–319
Eliot, G., *Lifted Veil*, Vol. 3, pages 157–193
Galsworthy, *Apple-Tree*, Vol. 3, pages 323–367
Hawthorne, *Rappaccini's Daughter*, Vol. 3, pages 128–152
Molière, *Misanthrope*, Vol. 4, pages 6–51
Sheridan, *School for Scandal*, Vol. 4, pages 85–159
Singer, *Spinoza of Market Street*, Vol. 3, pages 446–480
Tolstoy, *What Men Live By*, Vol. 3, pages 707–727
Turgenev, *First Love*, Vol. 3, pages 217–271
Wilde, *Happy Prince*, Vol. 2, pages 261–268

Of Friendship

Vol. 10, pages 353–358

SUGGESTED READINGS IN THE *Syntopicon*

HONOR, Vol. 2, pages 728–748, especially
Topic 2e: Honor as the pledge of friendship: the codes
of honor among social equals
LOVE, Vol. 2, pages 1051–1082, especially
Topic 2b: Friendly, tender, or altruistic love: fraternal love
Topic 3a: Friendship and love in relation to virtue
and happiness
Topic 3d: The heroism of friendship and the sacrifices of love
TRUTH, Vol. 3, pages 915–938, especially
Topic 8c: Truth in relation to love and friendship: the pleasant
and the unpleasant truth

RELATED AUTHORS AND WORKS IN *Great Books of the Western World*

Homer, Vol. 4, *Iliad*, Bks. XVI–XVIII, pages 112–136; Bk. XXIII,
pages 161–170
Plato, Vol. 7, *Lysis*, pages 14–25
Aristotle, Vol. 9, *Nicomachean Ethics*, Bks. VIII–IX,
pages 406–426
Augustine, Vol. 18, *Confessions*, Bk. VII, pages 43–52
Montaigne, Vol. 25, *Of Friendship*, pages 82–88
Spinoza, Vol. 31, *Ethics*, Part IV, Props. 70–73, pages 445–447;
Appendix I–XVII, pages 447–448
Melville, Vol. 48, *Moby Dick*, Chaps. 3–4, pages 8–22; Chap. 10,
pages 36–39
Tolstoy, Vol. 51, *War and Peace*, Bk. 12, Chap. XIII,
pages 554–555

BACON, *Of Friendship*
continued

RELATED AUTHORS AND WORKS IN *Gateway to the Great Books*

Anderson, *I'm a Fool*, Vol. 2, pages 511–520
Cicero, *On Friendship*, Vol. 10, pages 286–316
Kipling, *Mowgli's Brothers*, Vol. 2, pages 126–141
La Bruyère, *Characters*, Vol. 6, pages 102–105
Maupassant, *Two Friends*, Vol. 2, pages 159–164
Molière, *Misanthrope*, Vol. 4, pages 6–51
Scott, *Two Drovers*, Vol. 2, pages 182–205
Wilde, *Happy Prince*, Vol. 2, pages 261–268

Of Anger
Vol. 10, pages 359–360

SUGGESTED READINGS IN THE *Syntopicon*

EMOTION, Vol. 2, pages 413–436, especially
Topic 2*a*: Definitions of particular passions
Topic 2*b*: The order and connection of the passions
SIN, Vol. 3, pages 753–773, especially
Topic 2*c*(1): The classification and order of mortal sins

RELATED AUTHORS AND WORKS IN *Great Books of the Western World*

Homer, Vol. 4, *Iliad*, Bk. I, pages 3–9; Bks. XVIII–XXIV,
pages 130–179
Sophocles, Vol. 5, *Ajax*, pages 143–155
Plato, Vol. 7, *Euthyphro*, pages 193–194
Aristotle, Vol. 9, *Nicomachean Ethics*, Bk. II, Chaps. 5–9,
pages 351–355; *Rhetoric*, Bk. II, Chaps. 2–4, pages 623–626
Plotinus, Vol. 17, *Fourth Ennead*, Fourth Tractate, pages 172–173
Dante, Vol. 21, *Divine Comedy*, Hell, Canto VII, pages 9–10;
Purgatory, Canto XVI, pages 76–78
Hobbes, Vol. 23, *Leviathan*, Part I, Chap. 6, pages 61–65
Montaigne, Vol. 25, *Of Anger*, pages 344–347
Shakespeare, Vol. 27, *King Lear*, pages 244–283; *Timon of Athens*,
pages 393–420
Spinoza, Vol. 31, *Ethics*, Part IV, Props. 34–37, pages 432–436;
Props. 45–46, page 438
Milton, Vol. 32, *Paradise Lost*, Bk. I, pages 93–110
Locke, Vol. 35, *Essay Concerning Human Understanding*,
Bk. II, Chap. XX, page 177
James, W., Vol. 53, *Principles of Psychology*, Chap. XXIV,
pages 717–718

RELATED AUTHORS AND WORKS IN *Gateway to the Great Books*

Flaubert, *Legend of St. Julian the Hospitaller*, Vol. 3,
pages 371–392
Plutarch, *Contentment*, Vol. 10, pages 264–281
Poe, *Tell-Tale Heart*, Vol. 2, pages 273–277
Scott, *Two Drovers*, Vol. 2, pages 182–205
For other works by Bacon in *Great Books of the Western World*,
see Vol. 30

HONORÉ DE BALZAC, 1799–1850

A Passion in the Desert
Vol. 3, pages 436–447

SUGGESTED READINGS IN THE *Syntopicon*

ANIMAL, Vol. 2, pages 19–49, especially
Topic 1a(1): Animal sensitivity: its degrees and differentiations
Topic 1c(2): Comparison of animal with human intelligence
Topic 12a: The taming of animals
Topic 13: The attribution of human qualities or virtues
to animals: personification in allegory and satire
EMOTION, Vol. 2, pages 413–436, especially
Topic 1c: Instinctive emotional reactions in animals and men
Topic 5b: The acquisition and retention of power: love or fear
SIGN AND SYMBOL, Vol. 3, pages 730–752, especially
Topic 1c: The things of nature functioning symbolically:
the book of nature
Topic 3a: Verbal ambiguity: indefiniteness or multiplicity
of meaning

RELATED AUTHORS AND WORKS IN *Great Books of the Western World*

Homer, Vol. 4, *Odyssey*, Bk. XVII, lines 290–327, page 280
Aristotle, Vol. 9, *History of Animals*, Bk. IX, Chap. 1,
pages 133–136; Chap. 44, pages 154–155; *Nicomachean
Ethics*, Bk. VI, Chap. 7, page 390
Montaigne, Vol. 25, *Of Cruelty*, pages 206–208; *Apology
for Raimond de Sebonde*, pages 208–294
Swift, Vol. 36, *Gulliver's Travels*, Part IV, pages 135–184
Melville, Vol. 48, *Moby Dick*, Chaps. 132–135, pages 394–419
Darwin, Vol. 49, *Descent of Man*, Part I, Chaps. III–IV,
pages 292–309 and *passim*

BALZAC, *A Passion in the Desert*
continued

RELATED AUTHORS AND WORKS IN *Gateway to the Great Books*

Anderson, *I'm a Fool*, Vol. 2, pages 511–520
Apuleius, "Cupid and Psyche," Vol. 3, pages 197–212
Bacon, *Sphinx*, Vol. 8, pages 2–4; *Of Love*, Vol. 10, pages 351–352
Emerson, *Thoreau*, Vol. 6, pages 150–165
Flaubert, *Legend of St. Julian the Hospitaller*, Vol. 3, pages 371–392
Galsworthy, *Apple-Tree*, Vol. 3, pages 323–367
Hawthorne, *Rappaccini's Daughter*, Vol. 3, pages 128–152
Huxley, *On the Relations of Man to the Lower Animals*, Vol. 8, pages 160–204
Kipling, *Mowgli's Brothers*, Vol. 2, pages 126–141
Lawrence, *Rocking-Horse Winner*, Vol. 3, pages 512–525

CLAUDE BERNARD, 1813–1878

Experimental Considerations Common to Living Things and Inorganic Bodies
Vol. 8, pages 266–290

SUGGESTED READINGS IN THE *Syntopicon*

ANIMAL, Vol. 2, pages 19–49, especially
Topic 1e: The conception of the animal as a machine or automaton
CAUSE, Vol. 2, pages 155–178, especially
Topic 2: Comparison of causes in animate and inanimate nature
Topic 5b: Cause in philosophical and scientific method: the role of causes in definition, demonstration, experiment, hypothesis
EXPERIENCE, Vol. 2, pages 468–485, especially
Topic 5: The theory of experimentation in scientific method
HYPOTHESIS, Vol. 2, pages 749–760, especially
Topic 4: The role of hypotheses in science

LIFE AND DEATH, Vol. 2, pages 1013–1034, especially
  Topic 2: Continuity or discontinuity between living
    and non-living things: comparison of vital powers
    and activities with the potentialities and motions
    of inert bodies
MECHANICS, Vol. 3, pages 80–112, especially
  Topic 4c: The mechanistic account of the phenomena of life
MEDICINE, Vol. 3, pages 113–132, especially
  Topic 2a: The scientific foundations of the art of medicine:
    the contrast between the empiric and the artist
    in medicine

RELATED AUTHORS AND WORKS IN *Great Books of the Western World*

Hippocrates, Vol. 10, *Oath*, page xiii; *On Ancient Medicine*,
  pages 1–5
Galen, Vol. 10, *On the Natural Faculties*, Bk. I, pages 173–183
Descartes, Vol. 31, *Discourse on Method*, Part V, pages 56–60
Newton, Vol. 34, *Mathematical Principles of Natural Philosophy*,
  Preface, pages 1–2; Bk. III, pages 270–271
James, W., Vol. 53, *Principles of Psychology*, Chap. V, pages 84–95
Freud, Vol. 54, *New Introductory Lectures on Psycho-Analysis*,
  Lecture 35, page 884

RELATED AUTHORS AND WORKS IN *Gateway to the Great Books*

Fabre, *Laboratory of the Open Fields*, Vol. 8, pages 97–104;
  Sacred Beetle, pages 105–119
Huxley, *On the Relations of Man to the Lower Animals*, Vol. 8
  pages 160–204
Pavlov, *Scientific Study of the So-Called Psychical Processes
  in the Higher Animals*, Vol. 8, pages 294–309
Wöhler, *On the Artificial Production of Urea*, Vol. 8,
  pages 312–314

KEES BOEKE, 1884–

Cosmic View
Vol. 8, pages 600–644

SUGGESTED READINGS IN THE *Syntopicon*

ELEMENT, Vol. 2, pages 400–412, especially
  Topic 3a: Element and atom: qualitative and quantitative
    indivisibility

BOEKE, *Cosmic View*
continued

INFINITY, Vol. 2, pages 816–834, especially
Topic 3: The infinite in quantity
Topic 4*b*: The infinite divisibility of matter: the issue
concerning atoms
MATHEMATICS, Vol. 3, pages 42–62, especially
Topic 5*a*: The art of measurement
QUANTITY, Vol. 3, pages 527–545
WORLD, Vol. 3, pages 1118–1140, especially
Topic 2: The universe and man: macrocosm and microcosm
Topic 5: The number of worlds: the uniqueness of this world;
the possibility or actuality of other worlds
Topic 7: The space of the world: astronomical theories
concerning the size or extent of the universe

RELATED AUTHORS AND WORKS IN *Great Books of the Western World*

Plato, Vol. 7, *Protagoras*, pages 38–64; *Timaeus*, pages 442–477
Pascal, Vol. 33, *Pensées*, Sect. II, pages 181–184; *On Geometrical
Demonstration*, pages 434–439
Newton, Vol. 34, *Mathematical Principles of Natural Philosophy*,
pages 8–11
Fourier, Vol. 45, *Analytical Theory of Heat*, Chap. II, Sect. IX,
pages 249–251
Faraday, Vol. 45, *Experimental Researches in Electricity*,
pages 850–855

RELATED AUTHORS AND WORKS IN *Gateway to the Great Books*

Campbell, *Measurement*, Vol. 9, pages 204–221
Epicurus, *Letter to Herodotus*, Vol. 10, pages 216–229
Galileo, *Starry Messenger*, Vol. 8, pages 330–355
Haldane, *On Being the Right Size*, Vol. 8, pages 149–154
Kasner and Newman, *New Names for Old*, Vol. 9, pages 121–136;
Beyond the Googol, pages 137–162
Santayana, *Lucretius*, Vol. 10, pages 365–390
Voltaire, *Micromégas*, Vol. 2, pages 241–256; "English Men
and Ideas," Vol. 7, pages 332–378

SIR THOMAS BROWNE, 1605-1682

"Immortality"
from *Urn-Burial*
Vol. 10, pages 575-580

SUGGESTED READINGS IN THE *Syntopicon*

IMMORTALITY, Vol. 2, pages 784-804, especially
Topic 1: The desire for immortality: the fear of death
Topic 6b: Enduring fame: survival in the memory
LIFE AND DEATH, Vol. 2, pages 1013-1034, especially
Topic 8d: The ceremonials of death: the rites of burial in war and peace

RELATED AUTHORS AND WORKS IN *Great Books of the Western World*

Homer, Vol. 4, *Iliad*, Bk. XXIV, pages 171-179
Aeschylus, Vol. 5, *Choephoroe*, pages 70-80
Sophocles, Vol. 5, *Antigone*, pages 131-142
Euripides, Vol. 5, *Alcestis*, pages 237-247
Herodotus, Vol. 6, *History*, Ninth Book, pages 305-306
Plato, Vol. 7, *Symposium*, pages 165-167; *Phaedo*, pages 230-235
Montaigne, Vol. 25, *That to Study Philosophy Is to Learn to Die*, pages 33-36; *Apology for Raimond de Sebonde*, pages 264-268
Shakespeare, Vol. 27, *Hamlet*, pages 29-72; *Winter's Tale*, pages 489-523
Bacon, Vol. 30, *Advancement of Learning*, First Book, pages 27-28

RELATED AUTHORS AND WORKS IN *Gateway to the Great Books*

Bacon, *Of Death*, Vol. 10, pages 348-349
Butler, "Customs and Opinions of the Erewhonians," Vol. 2, pages 483-506
Cicero, *On Old Age*, Vol. 10, pages 317-343
Emerson, *Thoreau*, Vol. 6, pages 150-165
Hazlitt, *On the Feeling of Immortality in Youth*, Vol. 10, pages 565-570
Maupassant, *Two Friends*, Vol. 2, pages 159-164
Poe, *Masque of the Red Death*, Vol. 2, pages 278-283
Synge, *Riders to the Sea*, Vol. 4, pages 342-352
Tolstoy, *Death of Ivan Ilyitch*, Vol. 3, pages 646-699
Whitman, *Death of Abraham Lincoln*, Vol. 6, pages 174-183

IVAN BUNIN, 1870–1953

The Gentleman from San Francisco
Vol. 3, pages 102–123

SUGGESTED READINGS IN THE *Syntopicon*

HAPPINESS, Vol. 2, pages 684–710, especially
Topic 2b(1): The contribution of the goods of fortune
to happiness: wealth, health, longevity
Topic 4b: The attainability of happiness: the fear of death
and the tragic view of human life
Topic 5a: The happiness of the individual in relation
to the happiness or good of other men

OPPOSITION, Vol. 3, pages 323–341, especially
Topic 4e: Conflict in human life: opposed types of men
and modes of life
Topic 5b: The class war: the opposition of the rich
and the poor, the propertied and the propertyless,
capital and labor, producers and consumers

WEALTH, Vol. 3, pages 1038–1070, especially
Topic 10a: The nature of wealth as a good: its place
in the order of goods and its relation to happiness
Topic 10c: Temperance and intemperance with respect
to wealth: liberality, magnificence, miserliness,
avarice

RELATED AUTHORS AND WORKS IN *Great Books of the Western World*

Plato, Vol. 7, *Republic*, Bk. I, pages 295–310
Tacitus, Vol. 15, *Annals*, Bk. II, page 31; Bk. III, pages 57–58
Goethe, Vol. 47, *Faust*, First Part, pages 37–38; Second Part,
Act I, pages 146–151
Marx, Vol. 50, *Capital*, Part II, Chap. IV, pages 71–73; Part VII,
Chap. XXIV, pages 292–295; Marx and Engels, *Manifesto
of the Communist Party*, Chap. II, pages 425–427

RELATED AUTHORS AND WORKS IN *Gateway to the Great Books*

Anderson, *I'm a Fool*, Vol. 2, pages 511–520
Anonymous, *Aucassin and Nicolette*, Vol. 2, pages 523–551
Bacon, *Of Riches*, Vol. 7, pages 25–27
Cicero, *On Old Age*, Vol. 10, pages 317–343
Fitzgerald, *Diamond as Big as the Ritz*, Vol. 3, pages 397–431
Galsworthy, *Apple-Tree*, Vol. 3, pages 323–367
Hume, *Of Money*, Vol. 7, pages 62–71
Lawrence, *Rocking-Horse Winner*, Vol. 3, pages 512–525

O'Neill, *Emperor Jones*, Vol. 4, pages 357–382
Plutarch, *Contentment*, Vol. 10, pages 264–281
Pushkin, *Queen of Spades*, Vol. 3, pages 484–507
Synge, *Riders to the Sea*, Vol. 4, pages 342–352
Tolstoy, *What Men Live By*, Vol. 3, pages 707–727
Twain, *Man That Corrupted Hadleyburg*, Vol. 2, pages 346–386

EDMUND BURKE, 1729–1797

Letter to the Sheriffs of Bristol
Vol. 7, pages 237–271

SUGGESTED READINGS IN THE *Syntopicon*

GOVERNMENT, Vol. 2, pages 637–664, especially
Topic 5*b*: The government of dependencies: colonial
government; the government of conquered peoples
JUSTICE, Vol. 2, pages 850–879, especially
Topic 6*c*: The inalienability of natural rights: their violation
by tyranny and despotism
Topic 9*b*: Justice as the moral principle of political
organization: the bond of men in states
LAW, Vol. 2, pages 962–990, especially
Topic 7*d*: Tyranny and treason or sedition as illegal acts:
the use of force without authority
LIBERTY, Vol. 2, pages 991–1012, especially
Topic 6*c*: The struggle for sovereign independence against
the yoke of imperialism or colonial subjugation
REVOLUTION, Vol. 3, pages 626–644, especially
Topic 6: The justice of revolution
Topic 7: Empire and revolution: the justification of colonial
rebellion and the defense of imperialism
WAR AND PEACE, Vol. 3, pages 1010–1037, especially
Topic 4*b*: The factors responsible for civil strife
Topic 11*b*: Justice and fraternity as principles of peace
among men

RELATED AUTHORS AND WORKS IN *Great Books of the Western World*

Thucydides, Vol. 6, *History of the Peloponnesian War*,
Third Book, Chap. IX, pages 424–429
Machiavelli, Vol. 23, *Prince*, Chaps. IV–IX, pages 7–16

BURKE, *Letter to the Sheriffs of Bristol*
continued

Smith, Vol. 39, *Wealth of Nations*, Bk. IV, Chap. VII,
pages 260–279
Kant, Vol. 42, *Science of Right*, Second Part, pages 439–441
Constitution of the United States of America, Vol. 43, Art. I,
Sect. 9, page 13; Art. III, Sect. 3, pages 15–16;
Amendments I–X, pages 17–18
Hamilton, Madison, Jay, Vol. 43, *Federalist*, No. 84, pages 251–256
Mill, J. S., Vol. 43, *Representative Government*, Chaps. 17–18,
pages 428–442

RELATED AUTHORS AND WORKS IN *Gateway to the Great Books*

Bacon, *Of Seditions and Troubles*, Vol. 7, pages 12–17
Calhoun, "Concurrent Majority," Vol. 7, pages 276–290
Carlyle, *Hero as King*, Vol. 6, pages 110–145
Great Documents, *Virginia Declaration of Rights*, Vol. 6, pages
415–417; *Declaration of Independence*, pages 418–421;
Declaration of the Rights of Man and of the Citizen,
pages 412–414
Jefferson, "Virginia Constitution," Vol. 6, pages 502–517;
First Inaugural Address, pages 518–521
Lincoln, *First Inaugural Address*, Vol. 6, pages 747–755
Paine, "A Call to Patriots—December 23, 1776," Vol. 6,
pages 461–468
Washington, *Farewell Address*, Vol. 6, pages 484–497

JOHN BAGNELL BURY, 1861–1927

Herodotus
Vol. 6, pages 364–383

SUGGESTED READINGS IN THE *Syntopicon*

CUSTOM AND CONVENTION, Vol. 2, pages 268–285, especially
Topic 3: The conflict of customs: their variation from place
to place
HISTORY, Vol. 2, pages 711–727, especially
Topic 1: History as knowledge and as literature: its kinds
and divisions; its distinction from poetry, myth,
philosophy, and science
Topic 3: The writing of history: research and narration

Topic 4a(2): Material forces in history: economic, physical,
and geographic factors
Topic 5a: The relation of the gods or God to human history:
the dispensations of providence

TIME, Vol. 3, pages 896–914, especially
Topic 8: Historical time

RELATED AUTHORS AND WORKS IN *Great Books of the Western World*

Homer, Vol. 4, *Iliad*, Bks. I–II, pages 3–18
Aeschylus, Vol. 5, *Prometheus Bound*, pages 40–51; *Agamemnon*,
pages 52–69; *Eumenides*, pages 81–91
Thucydides, Vol. 6, *History of the Peloponnesian War*, First Book,
Chap. I, pages 349–355
Aristotle, Vol. 9, *On Poetics*, Chap. 9, page 686
Plutarch, Vol. 14, *Pericles*, pages 121–141
Bacon, Vol. 30, *Advancement of Learning*, Second Book,
pages 32–39
Fielding, Vol. 37, *Tom Jones*, Bk. II, Chap. 1, pages 19–20;
Bk. VIII, Chap. 1, pages 152–155; Bk. IX, Chap. 1,
pages 189–191
Gibbon, Vol. 40, *Decline and Fall of the Roman Empire*, Chaps.
IX–X, pages 88–98; Chap. XXVI, pages 409–415; Vol. 41,
Chap. XLVIII, pages 161–163
Melville, Vol. 48, *Moby Dick*, Extracts, pages xi–xx; Chap. 45,
pages 150–156; Chaps. 55–57, pages 195–203; Chaps. 82–83,
pages 267–271

RELATED AUTHORS AND WORKS IN *Gateway to the Great Books*

De Quincey, *Literature of Knowledge and Literature of Power;*
Vol. 5, pages 358–366
Hume, *Of the Study of History*, Vol. 7, pages 89–92
Lucian, *Way to Write History*, Vol. 6, pages 387–406
Sainte-Beuve, *What Is a Classic?*, Vol. 5, pages 65–89

For Herodotus' *History* in *Great Books of the Western World*,
see Vol. 6, pages 1–314

SAMUEL BUTLER, 1835–1902

"Customs and Opinions of the Erewhonians"
from *Erewhon*
Vol. 2, pages 483–506

SUGGESTED READINGS IN THE *Syntopicon*

CUSTOM AND CONVENTION, Vol. 2, pages 268–285, especially
Topic 3: The conflict of customs: their variation from place
to place
Topic 6b: The force of custom with respect to law
Topic 7d: The influence of custom on the liberty
of the individual

JUSTICE, Vol. 2, pages 850–879, especially
Topic 1f: Justice as a custom or moral sentiment based
on considerations of utility
Topic 9c: The criteria of justice in various forms of government
and diverse constitutions

LAW, Vol. 2, pages 962–990, especially
Topic 5f: The relation of positive law to custom
Topic 6e(1): The nature and causes of crime
Topic 6e(3): The punishment of crime

RELATED AUTHORS AND WORKS IN *Great Books of the Western World*

Aristophanes, Vol. 5, *Wasps*, pages 507–525
Aristotle, Vol. 9, *Nicomachean Ethics*, Bk. V, Chaps. ι–2,
pages 376–378; Chaps. 6–8, pages 381–384
Rabelais, Vol. 24, *Gargantua and Pantagruel*, Bk. I. Chaps. 52–57,
pages 60–66
Bacon, Vol. 30, *New Atlantis*, pages 200–203, 207–208
Swift, Vol. 36, *Gulliver's Travels*, Part IV, pages 135–184

RELATED AUTHORS AND WORKS IN *Gateway to the Great Books*

Bacon, *Of Custom and Education*, Vol. 7, pages 18–19; *Of Death*,
Vol. 10, pages 348–349
Dickens, "Full and Faithful Report of the Memorable Trial
of Bardell Against Pickwick," Vol. 2, pages 391–448
Great Documents, *Declaration of Independence*, Vol. 6, pages
418–421; *Universal Declaration of Human Rights*,
pages 452–456
Ibsen, *Enemy of the People*, Vol. 4, pages 164–246
Molière, *Misanthrope*, Vol. 4, pages 6–51; *Doctor in Spite
of Himself*, pages 52–81

Ruskin, *Idealist's Arraignment of the Age*, Vol. 7, pages 126–136
Sheridan, *School for Scandal*, Vol. 4, pages 85–159
Thoreau, *Civil Disobedience*, Vol. 6, pages 695–713
Twain, *Man That Corrupted Hadleyburg*, Vol. 2, pages 346–386
For Butler's translations of *The Iliad* and *The Odyssey* in *Great Books of the Western World*, see Vol. 4

JOHN C. CALHOUN, 1782–1850

"The Concurrent Majority"
from *A Disquisition on Government*
Vol. 7, pages 276–290

SUGGESTED READINGS IN THE *Syntopicon*

CONSTITUTION, Vol. 2, pages 233–251, especially
Topic 9*b*: Types of representation: diverse methods of selecting representatives
DEMOCRACY, Vol. 2, pages 303–322, especially
Topic 2*a*: Lawless mob-rule: the tyranny of the majority
Topic 5*b*(1): Majority rule and minority or proportional representation
Topic 5*c*: The distribution of functions and powers: checks and balances in representative democracy
GOVERNMENT, Vol. 2, pages 637–664, especially
Topic 1*a*: The origin and necessity of government: the issue concerning anarchy
Topic 1*h*: Self-government: expressions of the popular will; elections; voting

RELATED AUTHORS AND WORKS IN *Great Books of the Western World*

Plato, Vol. 7, *Laws*, Bk. VI, pages 697–705
Aristotle, Vol. 9, *Politics*, Bk. I, Chap. 2, pages 445–446; Bk. III, Chaps. 1–5, pages 471–475
Hobbes, Vol. 23, *Leviathan*, Part I, Chaps. 13–14, pages 84–87
Rousseau, Vol. 38, *Social Contract*, Bk. IV, Chaps. 4–7, pages 428–435
Smith, Vol. 39, *Wealth of Nations*, Bk. IV, Chap. VII, pages 269–271
Constitution of the United States of America, Vol. 43, pages 11–20
Hamilton, Madison, Jay, Vol. 43, *Federalist*, Nos. 41–51, pages 132–165; No. 85, pages 256–259

CALHOUN, "The Concurrent Majority"
continued

Mill, J. S., Vol. 43, *Representative Government,* Chaps. 6–7,
    pages 366–380
Tolstoy, Vol. 51, *War and Peace,* Second Epilogue, Chaps. IV–V,
    pages 680–684

RELATED AUTHORS AND WORKS IN *Gateway to the Great Books*

Adams, "United States in 1800," Vol. 6, pages 322–359
Burke, *Letter to the Sheriffs of Bristol,* Vol. 7, pages 237–271
Ibsen, *Enemy of the People,* Vol. 4, pages 164–246
Jefferson, "Virginia Constitution," Vol. 6, pages 502–517
Lincoln, *First Inaugural Address,* Vol. 6, pages 747–765
Thoreau, *Civil Disobedience,* Vol. 6, pages 695–713
Tocqueville, "Observations on American Life and Government,"
    Vol. 6, pages 564–690
Washington, *Farewell Address,* Vol. 6, pages 484–497

TOMMASO CAMPANELLA, 1568–1639

"Arguments for and against Galileo"
from *The Defenses of Galileo*
Vol. 8, pages 359–364

SUGGESTED READINGS IN THE *Syntopicon*

ASTRONOMY, Vol. 2, pages 87–111, especially
    Topic 5: Astronomy and cosmology: the theory of the world
        or universe as reflecting astronomical conceptions
    Topic 6: Astronomy and theology: astronomy as affecting
        views of God, creation, the divine plan, and the moral
        hierarchy
    Topic 13: The history of astronomy
SCIENCE, Vol. 3, pages 682–705, especially
    Topic 1b: Science as the discipline of experimental inquiry
        and the organization of experimental knowledge:
        the scientific spirit
    Topic 2a: The relation between science and religion:
        the conception of sacred theology as a science
    Topic 6b: The place of science in society: the social conditions
        favorable to the advancement of science

RELATED AUTHORS AND WORKS IN *Great Books of the Western World*

Aristotle, Vol. 8, *On the Heavens*, pages 359–405
Ptolemy, Vol. 16, *Almagest*, Bk. I, pages 7–12
Copernicus, Vol. 16, *On the Revolutions of the Heavenly Spheres*, Introduction–Bk. I, pages 505–545
Kepler, Vol. 16, *Epitome of Copernican Astronomy*, Bk. IV, pages 853–854, 888–893, 915–916, 929–933
Galileo, Vol. 28, *Dialogues Concerning the Two New Sciences*, pages 127–260
Descartes, Vol. 31, *Discourse on Method*, Parts V–VI, pages 54–67

RELATED AUTHORS AND WORKS IN *Gateway to the Great Books*

Bacon, *Of Truth*, Vol. 10, pages 346–347
Galileo, *Starry Messenger*, Vol. 8, pages 330–355
Voltaire, "English Men and Ideas," Vol. 7, pages 332–378

For Galileo's *Dialogues Concerning the Two New Sciences* in *Great Books of the Western World*, see Vol. 28

NORMAN ROBERT CAMPBELL, 1880–1949

Measurement
Vol. 9, pages 204–221

SUGGESTED READINGS IN THE *Syntopicon*

MATHEMATICS, Vol. 3, pages 42–62, especially
Topic 2*b*: The being of mathematical objects: their real, ideal, or mental existence
Topic 5*a*: The art of measurement
MECHANICS, Vol. 3, pages 80–112, especially
Topic 3*a*: Number and the continuum: the theory of measurement
QUANTITY, Vol. 3, pages 527–545, especially
Topic 6*b*: Mathematical procedures in measurement: superposition, congruence; ratio and proportion; parameters and coordinates
Topic 6*c*: Physical procedures in measurement: experiment and observation; clocks, rules, balances

CAMPBELL, *Measurement*
continued

RELATED AUTHORS AND WORKS IN *Great Books of the Western World*

Plato, Vol. 7, *Republic*, Bk. VII, pages 391–398
Euclid, Vol. 11, *Elements*, Bk. V, pages 81–98
Nicomachus, Vol. 11, *Introduction to Arithmetic*, Bk. I,
    pages 811–817
Berkeley, Vol. 35, *Principles of Human Knowledge*, pages 436–439

RELATED AUTHORS AND WORKS IN *Gateway to the Great Books*

Bacon, *Sphinx*, Vol. 8, pages 2–4
Boeke, *Cosmic View*, Vol. 8, pages 442–446
Dantzig, *Fingerprints*, Vol. 9, pages 165–177; *Empty Column*,
    pages 178–189
Einstein and Infeld, "Rise and Decline of Classical Physics,"
    Vol. 8, pages 490–560
Kasner and Newman, *New Names for Old*, Vol. 9, pages 121–136;
    Beyond the Googol, pages 137–162
Russell, *Definition of Number*, Vol. 9, pages 111–117
Voltaire, *Micromégas*, Vol. 2, pages 241–256

Numerical Laws and the Use of Mathematics in Science
Vol. 9, pages 222–238

SUGGESTED READINGS IN THE *Syntopicon*

MATHEMATICS, Vol. 3, pages 42–62, especially
    Topic 5: The applications of mathematics to physical
        phenomena: the utility of mathematics
MECHANICS, Vol. 3, pages 80–112, especially
    Topic 3: The use of mathematics in mechanics: the dependence
        of progress in mechanics on mathematical discovery
PHYSICS, Vol. 3, pages 363–376, especially
    Topic 3: The role of mathematics in the natural sciences:
        observation and measurement in relation
        to mathematical formulations
SCIENCE, Vol. 3, pages 682–705, especially
    Topic 5c: The use of mathematics in science: calculation
        and measurement

RELATED AUTHORS AND WORKS IN *Great Books of the Western World*

Plato, Vol. 7, *Timaeus*, pages 442–477
Galileo, Vol. 28, *Dialogues Concerning the Two New Sciences*,
    Third Day, pages 197–237

Bacon, Vol. 30, *Novum Organum,* First Book, pages 107–136
Newton, Vol. 34, *Mathematical Principles of Natural Philosophy,*
Bk. II, Sects. I–III, pages 159–189
Kant, Vol. 42, *Critique of Pure Reason,* pages 69–72

RELATED AUTHORS AND WORKS IN *Gateway to the Great Books*

Einstein and Infeld, "Rise and Decline of Classical Physics,"
Vol. 8, pages 490–560
Euler, *Seven Bridges of Königsberg,* Vol. 9, pages 193–201
Forsyth, *Mathematics in Life and Thought,* Vol. 9, pages 26–46
Haldane, *On Being the Right Size,* Vol. 8, pages 149–154
Helmholtz, *On the Conservation of Force,* Vol. 8, pages 451–484
Mendeleev, "Genesis of a Law of Nature," Vol. 8, pages 442–446
Poincaré, *Mathematical Creation,* Vol. 9, pages 294–304
Russell, *Study of Mathematics,* Vol. 9, pages 84–94
Whitehead, "On Mathematical Method," Vol. 9, pages 51–67;
On the Nature of a Calculus, pages 68–78

THOMAS CARLYLE, 1795–1881

The Hero as King
Vol. 6, pages 110–145

SUGGESTED READINGS IN THE *Syntopicon*

ARISTOCRACY, Vol. 2, pages 50–63, especially
Topic 1*a*: Aristocracy as a good form of government
Topic 4: Aristocracy and the issue of rule by men as opposed
to rule by law

HISTORY, Vol. 2, pages 711–727, especially
Topic 4*a*(4): The role of the individual in history: the great
man, hero, or leader

HONOR, Vol. 2, pages 728–748, especially
Topic 3*a*: The reaction of the community to its good or great
men
Topic 5*b*: Hero-worship: the exaltation of leaders
Topic 5*d*: The estimation of the role of the hero in history

LAW, Vol. 2, pages 962–990, especially
Topic 6*b*: The exemption of the sovereign person
from the coercive force of law

CARLYLE, *The Hero as King*
continued

LIBERTY, Vol. 2, pages 991–1012, especially
  Topic 6b: The struggle for civil liberty and economic freedom:
    the overthrow of tyrants, despots, and oppressors
MONARCHY, Vol. 3, pages 204–224, especially
  Topic 2: The theory of royalty
  Topic 3: The use and abuse of monarchical power

RELATED AUTHORS AND WORKS IN *Great Books of the Western World*

Homer, Vol. 4, *Iliad*, pages 3–179
Sophocles, Vol. 5, *Oedipus the King*, pages 99–113
Plato, Vol. 7, *Republic*, Bks. V–VI, pages 369–383; *Statesman*,
  pages 598–604
Aristotle, Vol. 9, *Politics*, Bk. III, Chaps. 14–18, pages 483–487
Virgil, Vol. 13, *Aeneid*, pages 103–379
Machiavelli, Vol. 23, *Prince*, pages 1–37, especially Chaps. 15–21,
  pages 22–33
Hobbes, Vol. 23, *Leviathan*, Part II, Chap. 29, pages 149–153
Rabelais, Vol. 24, *Gargantua and Pantagruel*, Bks. I–II,
  pages 1–126
Shakespeare, Vol. 26, *King Henry VI*, First Part, pages 1–32;
  King Henry VI, Second Part, pages 33–68; *King Henry VI*,
  Third Part, pages 69–104; *King Richard III*, pages 105–148;
  King Richard II, pages 320–351; *King Henry IV*, First Part,
  pages 434–466; *King Henry IV*, Second Part, pages 467–502;
  King Henry V, pages 532–567; *Julius Caesar*, pages 568–596;
  Vol. 27, *Antony and Cleopatra*, pages 311–350; *Coriolanus*,
  pages 351–392
Locke, Vol. 35, *Concerning Civil Government*, Chap. VII, pages
  44–46; Chap. VIII, pages 48–51; Chap. XIV, pages 62–64;
  Chaps. XVII–XIX, pages 70–81
Hegel, Vol. 46, *Philosophy of History*, Introduction III, pages
  162–170; Second Part, pages 280–283; Fourth Part, pages
  360–362
Tolstoy, Vol. 51, *War and Peace*, Second Epilogue, pages 675–696

RELATED AUTHORS AND WORKS IN *Gateway to the Great Books*

Bacon, *Of Great Place*, Vol. 7, pages 9–11
Burke, *Letter to the Sheriffs of Bristol*, Vol. 7, pages 237–271
Emerson, *Self-Reliance*, Vol. 10, pages 525–545
Galton, "Classification of Human Ability," Vol. 8, pages 227–261
Hawthorne, *Sketch of Abraham Lincoln*, Vol. 6, pages 168–171
Hume, *Of the Study of History*, Vol. 7, pages 89–92

Ibsen, *Enemy of the People*, Vol. 4, pages 164–246
James, W., *Great Men and Their Environment*, Vol. 7, pages
171–194
Jefferson, "Biographical Sketches," Vol. 6, pages 522–528
Macaulay, *Machiavelli*, Vol. 7, pages 295–329
O'Neill, *Emperor Jones*, Vol. 4, pages 353–382
Shaw, *Man of Destiny*, Vol. 4, pages 300–338
Tacitus, *Life of Gnaeus Julius Agricola*, Vol. 6, pages 274–298
Washington, *Circular Letter to the Governors of All the States
on Disbanding the Army*, Vol. 6, pages 474–483; *Farewell
Address*, pages 484–497
Whitman, *Death of Abraham Lincoln*, Vol. 6, pages 174–183

RACHEL L. CARSON, 1907–1964

The Sunless Sea
Vol. 8, pages 132–146

SUGGESTED READINGS IN THE *Syntopicon*

ANIMAL, Vol. 2, pages 19–49, especially
Topic 11: The habitat of animals
EVOLUTION, Vol. 2, pages 451–467, especially
Topic 5a: The struggle for existence: its causes
and consequences
Topic 6b: The geographical distribution of the forms of life
in relation to the genealogy of existing species
SCIENCE, Vol. 3, pages 682–705, especially
Topic 1b: Science as the discipline of experimental inquiry
and the organization of experimental knowledge:
the scientific spirit
Topic 2b: The comparison of science with poetry and history

RELATED AUTHORS AND WORKS IN *Great Books of the Western World*

Plato, Vol. 7, *Phaedrus*, pages 138–140
Aristotle, Vol. 9, *History of Animals*, Bks. V–VI, pages 73–89;
Bk. VIII, pages 115–132; Bk. IX, pages 140–144
Darwin, Vol. 49, *Origin of Species*, Chaps. III–IV, pages 32–64;
Chaps. XII–XIII, pages 181–206

RELATED AUTHORS AND WORKS IN *Gateway to the Great Books*

Conrad, *Youth*, Vol. 2, pages 210–236
Crane, *Open Boat*, Vol. 3, pages 5–26
Darwin, *Autobiography*, Vol. 8, pages 47–93

CARSON, *The Sunless Sea*
continued

Fabre, *Laboratory of the Open Fields,* Vol. 8, pages 97–104;
  Sacred Beetle, pages 105–119
Haldane, *On Being the Right Size,* Vol. 8, pages 149–154
Huxley, *On the Relations of Man to the Lower Animals,*
  Vol. 8, pages 160–204; *On a Piece of Chalk,* Vol. 8, pages 205–222
Lyell, "Geological Evolution," Vol. 8, pages 319–324
Malthus, "Principle of Population," Vol. 7, pages 502–530

ANTON CHEKHOV, 1860–1904

The Darling
Vol. 3, pages 452–462

SUGGESTED READINGS IN THE *Syntopicon*

CHANCE, Vol. 2, pages 179–192, especially
  Topic 6a: Chance and fortune in the life of the individual
DESIRE, Vol. 2, pages 323–344, especially
  Topic 2d: The satisfaction of desire: possession and enjoyment
  Topic 4b: The attachment of desires: fixations, projections,
    identifications, transferences
HAPPINESS, Vol. 2, pages 684–710, especially
  Topic 2b(5): The importance of friendship and love
    for happiness
LOVE, Vol. 2, pages 1051–1082, especially
  Topic 1e: The intensity and power of love: its increase
    or decrease; its constructive or destructive force

RELATED AUTHORS AND WORKS IN *Great Books of the Western World*

Plato, Vol. 7, *Symposium,* pages 157–159; 164–165
Montaigne, Vol. 25, *Upon Some Verses of Virgil,* pages 432–433
Shakespeare, Vol. 26, *Romeo and Juliet,* Act II, pages 293–300

RELATED AUTHORS AND WORKS IN *Gateway to the Great Books*

Anonymous, *Aucassin and Nicolette,* Vol. 2, pages 523–551
Arnold, *Sweetness and Light,* Vol. 5, pages 42–61

Bacon, *Of Marriage and Single Life*, Vol. 7, pages 7–8; *Of Love*,
  Vol. 10, pages 351–352
Galsworthy, *Apple-Tree*, Vol. 3, pages 323–367
Plutarch, *Contentment*, Vol. 10, pages 264–281
Turgenev, *First Love*, Vol. 3, pages 217–271
Wilde, *Happy Prince*, Vol. 2, pages 261–268

The Cherry Orchard
Vol. 4, pages 249–294

SUGGESTED READINGS IN THE *Syntopicon*

ARISTOCRACY, Vol. 2, pages 50–63, especially
  Topic 7: Historic and poetic exemplifications of aristocracy
CHANGE, Vol. 2, pages 193–217, especially
  Topic 12*b*: The love and hatred of change
HISTORY, Vol. 2, pages 711–727, especially
  Topic 4*b*: The laws and patterns of historical change: cycles,
    progress, evolution
PROGRESS, Vol. 3, pages 437–453, especially
  Topic 5: Forces operating against social progress: emotional
    opposition to change or novelty; political conservatism

RELATED AUTHORS AND WORKS IN *Great Books of the Western World*

Aeschylus, Vol. 5, *Eumenides*, pages 81–91
Sophocles, Vol. 5, *Antigone*, pages 131–142
Montaigne, Vol. 25, *Of Vanity*, pages 462–465
Rousseau, Vol. 38, *Discourse on the Origin of Inequality*,
  pages 333–366
Gibbon, Vol. 40, *Decline and Fall of the Roman Empire*,
  General Observations, pages 632–634
Boswell, Vol. 44, *Life of Samuel Johnson*, pages 189–190
Tolstoy, Vol. 51, *War and Peace*, Second Epilogue, pages 675–696

RELATED AUTHORS AND WORKS IN *Gateway to the Great Books*

Anonymous, *Aucassin and Nicolette*, Vol. 2, pages 523–551
Ibsen, *Enemy of the People*, Vol. 4, pages 164–246
La Bruyère, *Characters*, Vol. 6, pages 102–105
Pater, "Art of Life," Vol. 10, pages 258–261
Ruskin, *Idealist's Arraignment of the Age*, Vol. 7, pages 126–136
Tacitus, *Life of Gnaeus Julius Agricola*, Vol. 6, pages 274–298

CICERO, 106–43 B.C.

On Friendship
Vol. 10, pages 286–316

SUGGESTED READINGS IN THE *Syntopicon*

HONOR, Vol. 2, pages 728–748, especially
Topic 2e: Honor as the pledge of friendship: the codes of honor among social equals

LOVE, Vol. 2, pages 1051–1082, especially
Topic 2b(3): The types of friendship: friendships based on utility, pleasure, or virtue
Topic 3a: Friendship and love in relation to virtue and happiness

STATE, Vol. 3, pages 826–865, especially
Topic 3e: Love and justice as the bond of men in states: friendship and patriotism

RELATED AUTHORS AND WORKS IN *Great Books of the Western World*

Homer, Vol. 4, *Iliad*, Bks. XVI–XVIII, pages 112–136; Bk. XXIII, pages 161–170
Plato, Vol. 7, *Lysis*, pages 14–25
Aristotle, Vol. 9, *Nicomachean Ethics*, Bks. VIII–X, Chap. 4, pages 406–428
Montaigne, Vol. 25, *Of Friendship*, pages 82–88
Cervantes, Vol. 29, *Don Quixote*, Chaps. 33–34, pages 120–134
Spinoza, Vol. 31, *Ethics*, Part II, Prop. 22, page 383; Prop. 35, pages 385–386; Props. 41–44, pages 388–390; Part IV, Props. 35–36, pages 433–434
Melville, Vol. 48, *Moby Dick*, Chaps. 3–4, pages 8–22; Chap. 10, pages 36–39
Tolstoy, Vol. 51, *War and Peace*, Bk. 12, Chap. XIII, pages 554–555
James, W., Vol. 53, *Principles of Psychology*, Chap. X, pages 189–191

RELATED AUTHORS AND WORKS IN *Gateway to the Great Books*

Bacon, *Of Followers and Friends*, Vol. 7, pages 20–21; *Of Love*, Vol. 10, pages 351–352; *Of Friendship*, pages 353–358
Kipling, *Mowgli's Brothers*, Vol. 2, pages 126–141
La Bruyère, *Characters*, Vol. 6, pages 102–105
Maupassant, *Two Friends*, Vol. 2, pages 159–164
Scott, *Two Drovers*, Vol. 2, pages 182–205

On Old Age
Vol. 10, pages 317–343

CICERO, *On Old Age*
continued

Dinesen, *Sorrow-Acre*, Vol. 3, pages 615–641
Epictetus, *Enchiridion*, Vol. 10, pages 236–254
Epicurus, *Letter to Menoeceus*, Vol. 10, pages 230–233
Flaubert, *Legend of St. Julian the Hospitaller*, Vol. 3, pages 371–392
Hazlitt, *On the Feeling of Immortality in Youth*, Vol. 10, pages 565–570
Pater, "Art of Life," Vol. 10, pages 258–261
Plutarch, *Contentment*, Vol. 10, pages 264–281
Singer, *Spinoza of Market Street*, Vol. 3, pages 466–480
Swift, *Resolutions when I Come to be Old*, Vol. 7, page 32
Tolstoy, *Death of Ivan Ilyitch*, Vol. 3, pages 646–699; *Three Hermits*, pages 700–706
Whitman, *Death of Abraham Lincoln*, Vol. 6, pages 174–183

KARL VON CLAUSEWITZ, 1780–1831

What Is War?
Vol. 7, pages 479–497

SUGGESTED READINGS IN THE *Syntopicon*

WAR AND PEACE, Vol. 3, pages 1010–1037, especially
Topic 1: War as the reign of force: the state of war and the state of nature
Topic 3*a*: The distinction between just and unjust warfare: wars of defense and wars of conquest
Topic 7: The inevitability of war: the political necessity of military preparations

RELATED AUTHORS AND WORKS IN *Great Books of the Western World*

Homer, Vol. 4, *Iliad*, pages 3–179
Plato, Vol. 7, *Republic*, Bk. II, pages 318–319
Machiavelli, Vol. 23, *Prince*, Chaps. XII–XIV, pages 17–22
Rabelais, Vol. 24, *Gargantua and Pantagruel*, Chaps. 25–33, pages 30–41
Locke, Vol. 35, *Concerning Civil Government*, Chaps. II–III, pages 25–29; Chap. XVI, pages 65–70
Kant, Vol. 42, *Science of Right*, Second Part, pages 452–455
Hamilton, Madison, Jay, Vol. 43, *Federalist*, Nos. 3–9, pages 33–49

Hegel, Vol. 46, *Philosophy of Right,* Third Part, Sub-sect. III, pages 107–110

Tolstoy, Vol. 51, *War and Peace,* Bk. 9, Chap. I, pages 342–344; Chaps. IX–XI, pages 358–365; Bk. 10, Chap. I, pages 389–391; Chap. XIX, pages 430–432; Chap. XXV, page 440; Bk. 11, Chaps. I–V, pages 469–476; Bk. 13, Chaps. I–X, pages 563–575; Chaps. XVII–XIX, pages 585–587; Bk. 14, Chaps. I–II, pages 588–590; Bk. 15, Chaps. IV–V, pages 618–621; First Epilogue, Chaps. I–IV, pages 645–650

Freud, Vol. 54, *Civilization and Its Discontents,* Chap. V, pages 785–789

RELATED AUTHORS AND WORKS IN *Gateway to the Great Books*

Dante, "On World Government," Vol. 7, pages 383–399

Great Documents, *Charter of the United Nations,* Vol. 6, pages 422–451

Hugo, "Battle with the Cannon," Vol. 2, pages 146–154

Kant, *Perpetual Peace,* Vol. 7, pages 441–475

Lincoln, *Meditation on the Divine Will,* Vol. 6, page 758

Maupassant, *Two Friends,* Vol. 2, pages 159–164

Prescott, "Land of Montezuma," Vol. 6, pages 231–243

Rousseau, *Lasting Peace Through the Federation of Europe,* Vol. 7, pages 405–436

Shaw, *Man of Destiny,* Vol. 4, pages 300–338

Washington, *Circular Letter to the Governors of All the States on Disbanding the Army,* Vol. 6, pages 474–483

WILLIAM KINGDON CLIFFORD, 1845–1879

The Postulates of the Science of Space
Vol. 9, pages 243–259

SUGGESTED READINGS IN THE *Syntopicon*

HYPOTHESIS, Vol. 2, pages 749–760, especially

Topic 3: The foundations of mathematics: postulates, assumptions

MATHEMATICS, Vol. 3, pages 42–62, especially

Topic 1c: The certainty and exactitude of mathematical knowledge: the *a priori* foundations of arithmetic and geometry

Topic 4b: The operations of geometry

CLIFFORD, *The Postulates of the Science of Space*
continued

QUANTITY, Vol. 3, pages 527–545, especially
　　Topic 3: The magnitudes of geometry: the relations
　　　　of dimensionality
　　Topic 3a: Straight lines: their length and their relations; angles,
　　　　perpendiculars, parallels
　　Topic 3d: Surfaces
　　Topic 5a: Space: the matrix of figures and distances
SPACE, Vol. 3, pages 811–825, especially
　　Topic 3c: Geometrical space, its kinds and properties: spatial
　　　　relationships and configurations
　　Topic 5: The mode of existence of geometrical objects: their
　　　　character as abstractions; their relation to intelligible
　　　　matter

RELATED AUTHORS AND WORKS IN *Great Books of the Western World*

Aristotle, Vol. 8, *Physics*, Bks. III–IV, Chaps. 4–8; 1–9, pages
　　280–297
Euclid, Vol. 11, *Elements*, Bk. I, pages 1–29
Ptolemy, Vol. 16, *Almagest*, Bk. I, pages 5–33
Copernicus, Vol. 16, *On the Revolutions of the Heavenly Spheres*,
　　Bk. I, pages 511–545
Descartes, Vol. 31, *Rules for the Direction of the Mind*, Rule XIV,
　　pages 28–33
Kant, Vol. 42, *Critique of Pure Reason*, pages 211–218
James, W., Vol. 53, *Principles of Psychology*, Chap. XX, pages
　　540–635; Chap. XXVIII, pages 874–882

RELATED AUTHORS AND WORKS IN *Gateway to the Great Books*

Einstein and Infeld, "Rise and Decline of Classical Physics," Vol. 8,
　　pages 490–560
Poincaré, *Space*, Vol. 9, pages 265–293
Russell, *Study of Mathematics*, Vol. 9, pages 84–94; *Mathematics
　　and the Metaphysicians*, pages 95–110
Voltaire, *Micromégas*, Vol. 2, pages 241–256; "English Men
　　and Ideas," Vol. 7, pages 332–378

The Ethics of Belief
Vol. 10, pages 16–36

SUGGESTED READINGS IN THE *Syntopicon*

KNOWLEDGE, Vol. 2, pages 880–920, especially
Topic 4b: Knowledge, belief, and opinion: their relation
or distinction
OPINION, Vol. 3, pages 303–322, especially
Topic 2d: Reason, experience, and authority as sources
of opinion
REASONING, Vol. 3, pages 546–568, especially
Topic 4a: Immediate inference: its relation to mediated
inference or reasoning
Topic 5a: The fact and the reasoned fact: mere belief
distinguished from belief on rational grounds

RELATED AUTHORS AND WORKS IN *Great Books of the Western World*

Plato, Vol. 7, *Republic,* Bk. V, pages 370–373
Bacon, Vol. 30, *Advancement of Learning,* Second Book, pages
47–48, 60–61; *Novum Organum,* First Book, pages 109–116
Descartes, Vol. 31, *Discourse on Method,* Parts I–IV, pages 44–54
Pascal, Vol. 33, *Pensées,* Sects. III–IV, pages 205–225; *Preface
to the Treatise on the Vacuum,* pages 355–358
Locke, Vol. 35, *Essay Concerning Human Understanding,* Bk. IV,
Chaps. XVIII–XXI, pages 380–395
Hume, Vol. 35, *Enquiry Concerning Human Understanding,* Sects.
X–XI, pages 488–503
Kant, Vol. 42, *Critique of Pure Reason,* pages 109–111
Freud, Vol. 54, *New Introductory Lectures on Psycho-Analysis,*
Lecture 35, pages 873–884

RELATED AUTHORS AND WORKS IN *Gateway to the Great Books*

Adams, *Saint Thomas Aquinas,* Vol. 10, pages 422–450
Bacon, *Of Truth,* Vol. 10, pages 346–347
Dewey, "Process of Thought," Vol. 10, pages 92–213
Dickens, "Full and Faithful Report of the Memorable Trial
of Bardell Against Pickwick," Vol. 2, pages 391–448
Emerson, *Montaigne; or, the Skeptic,* Vol. 10, pages 546–562
Erskine, *Moral Obligation to Be Intelligent,* Vol. 10, pages 5–13
Faraday, *Observations on Mental Education,* Vol. 7, pages 208–232
James, W., *Will to Believe,* Vol. 10, pages 39–57; *Sentiment
of Rationality,* pages 58–87
Laplace, "Probability," Vol. 9, pages 325–338
Peirce, *Red and the Black,* Vol. 9, pages 342–348
Voltaire, "Philosophy of Common Sense," Vol. 10, pages 453–474

JOSEPH CONRAD, 1857–1924

Youth
Vol. 2, pages 210–236

SUGGESTED READINGS IN THE *Syntopicon*

COURAGE, Vol. 2, pages 252–267, especially
   Topic 6: The formation or training of the courageous man
EDUCATION, Vol. 2, pages 376–399, especially
   Topic 5*f*: Learning apart from teachers and books: the role
      of experience
EXPERIENCE, Vol. 2, pages 468–485, especially
   Topic 8: Variety of experience as an ideal of human life
HONOR, Vol. 2, pages 728–748, especially
   Topic 2*c*: Honor as due self-esteem: magnanimity
      or proper pride
MAN, Vol. 3, pages 1–41, especially
   Topic 6*c*: The ages of man: infancy, youth, maturity,
      senescence
MEMORY AND IMAGINATION, Vol. 3, pages 133–157, especially
   Topic 4*a*: Memory in the life of the individual: personal
      identity and continuity

RELATED AUTHORS AND WORKS IN *Great Books of the Western World*

Plutarch, Vol. 14, *Demosthenes,* pages 691–695
Rabelais, Vol. 24, *Gargantua and Pantagruel,* Bk. I, Chap. 23,
   pages 28–29
Montaigne, Vol. 25, *Of the Education of Children,* pages 75–76
Melville, Vol. 48, *Moby Dick,* Chap. 24, page 82; Chap. 26,
   pages 83–85

RELATED AUTHORS AND WORKS IN *Gateway to the Great Books*

Anderson, *I'm a Fool,* Vol. 2, pages 511–520
Bacon, *Of Youth and Age,* Vol. 7, pages 3–4
Crane, *Open Boat,* Vol. 3, pages 5–26
Defoe, *Robinson Crusoe,* Vol. 2, pages 5–141
De Quincey, *Literature of Knowledge and Literature of Power,*
   Vol. 5, pages 358–366
Dinesen, *Sorrow-Acre,* Vol. 3, pages 615–641
Hazlitt, *On the Feeling of Immortality in Youth,* Vol. 10,
   pages 565–570
Melville, *Billy Budd,* Vol. 3, pages 31–98
Turgenev, *First Love,* Vol. 3, pages 217–271
Twain, "Learning the River," Vol. 6, pages 50–98

STEPHEN CRANE, 1871-1900

The Open Boat
Vol. 3, pages 5-26

SUGGESTED READINGS IN THE *Syntopicon*

CAUSE, Vol. 2, pages 155-178, especially
   Topic 3: Causality and freedom
CHANCE, Vol. 2, pages 179-192, especially
   Topic 2b: The relation of chance to fate, providence,
     and predestination
COURAGE, Vol. 2, pages 252-267, especially
   Topic 3: The passions in the sphere of courage: fear, daring,
     anger, hope, despair
FATE, Vol. 2, pages 515-525, especially
   Topic 1: The decrees of fate and the decisions of the gods
LIFE AND DEATH, Vol. 2, pages 1013-1034, especially
   Topic 8a: The love of life: the instinct of self-preservation;
     the life instinct
MAN, Vol. 3, pages 1-41, especially
   Topic 10d: The finiteness and insufficiency of man: his sense
     of being dependent and ordered to something
     beyond himself
WORLD, Vol. 3, pages 1118-1140, especially
   Topic 6c: The rationality or intelligibility of the universe
   Topic 6d: The goodness and beauty of the universe: its evil
     and imperfections

RELATED AUTHORS AND WORKS IN *Great Books of the Western World*

Homer, Vol. 4, *Odyssey*, Bk. V, pages 208-213
Euripides, Vol. 5, *Alcestis*, pages 237-247
Plato, Vol. 7, *Laws*, Bk. X, pages 767-768
Virgil, Vol. 13, *Aeneid*, Bk. I, pages 103-123
Dante, Vol. 21, *Divine Comedy*, Hell, Canto XXVI, pages 38-39
Montaigne, Vol. 25, *That the Relish of Good and Evil Depends
   in a Great Measure Upon the Opinion We Have of Them*,
   pages 115-119
Shakespeare, Vol. 27, *Pericles*, Act III, Scene I, pages 433-434;
   Tempest, Act I, Scene I, pages 524-525
Melville, Vol. 48, *Moby Dick*, Chap. 42, pages 144-145
Tolstoy, Vol. 51, *War and Peace*, Second Epilogue, pages 675-696

CRANE, *The Open Boat*
continued

RELATED AUTHORS AND WORKS IN *Gateway to the Great Books*

Bacon, *Of Death*, Vol. 10, pages 348–349; *Of Adversity*, page 350
Bunin, *Gentleman from San Francisco*, Vol. 3, pages 102–123
Conrad, *Youth*, Vol. 2, pages 210–236
Defoe, *Robinson Crusoe*, Vol. 2, pages 5–121
De Quincey, *Literature of Knowledge and Literature of Power*,
Vol. 5, pages 358–366
Dinesen, *Sorrow-Acre*, Vol. 3, pages 615–641
Emerson, *Self-Reliance*, Vol. 10, pages 525–545
James, W., *Energies of Men*, Vol. 7, pages 157–170
Synge, *Riders to the Sea*, Vol. 4, pages 342–352

JEAN DE CRÈVECOEUR, 1735–1813

"The Making of Americans"
from *Letters from an American Farmer*

Vol. 6, pages 546–559

SUGGESTED READINGS IN THE *Syntopicon*

DEMOCRACY, Vol. 2, pages 303–322, especially
Topic 4a: Liberty and equality for all under law
LABOR, Vol. 2, pages 921–940, especially
Topic 7f: The relation of economic to political freedom:
economic democracy
LIBERTY, Vol. 2, pages 991–1012, especially
Topic 1f: The freedom of equals under government:
the equality of citizenship
PROGRESS, Vol. 3, pages 437–453, especially
Topic 4c: The growth of political freedom: the achievement
of citizenship and civil rights
RELIGION, Vol. 3, pages 588–625, especially
Topic 6e: Religious liberty: freedom of conscience; religious
toleration

RELATED AUTHORS AND WORKS IN *Great Books of the Western World*

Plato, Vol. 7, *Laws*, Bk. III, pages 674–676; Bk. IV, pages 681–682
Aristotle, Vol. 9, *Athenian Constitution*, Chaps. 5–42, pages 554–572
Locke, Vol. 35, *Letter Concerning Toleration*, pages 1–22

Smith, Vol. 39, *Wealth of Nations*, Bk. I, Chap. X, pages 51–56
Hamilton, Madison, Jay, Vol. 43, *Federalist*, No. 10, pages 50–51;
No. 35, pages 113–114
Mill, J. S., Vol. 43, *On Liberty*, Chap. 1, pages 267–274

RELATED AUTHORS AND WORKS IN *Gateway to the Great Books*

Adams, "United States in 1800," Vol. 6, pages 322–359
Great Documents, *Virginia Declaration of Rights*, Vol. 6, pages
415–417
Hawthorne, *Sketch of Abraham Lincoln*, Vol. 6, pages 168–171
Hume, *Of Refinement in the Arts*, Vol. 7, pages 52–61
Jefferson, *First Inaugural Address*, Vol. 6, pages 518–521
Lincoln, *Address at Cooper Institute*, Vol. 6, pages 737–746
Tocqueville, "Observations on American Life and Government,"
Vol. 6, pages 564–690
Whitman, *Preface to Leaves of Grass*, Vol. 5, pages 247–259

EVE CURIE, 1904–

The Discovery of Radium
Vol. 8, pages 32–42

SUGGESTED READINGS IN THE *Syntopicon*

ELEMENT, Vol. 2, pages 400–412, especially
Topic 1: The concept of element
Topic 3: The theory of the elements in natural philosophy,
physics, and chemistry
PHYSICS, Vol. 3, pages 363–376, especially
Topic 4: The experimental method in the study of nature
SCIENCE, Vol. 3, pages 682–705, especially
Topic 1*b*: Science as the discipline of experimental inquiry
and the organization of experimental knowledge:
the scientific spirit
Topic 5: Scientific method
Topic 6: The development of the sciences
SPACE, Vol. 3, pages 811–825, especially
Topic 2*c*: Space as a medium of physical action: the ether
and action-at-a-distance; the phenomena
of gravitation, radiation, and electricity

RELATED AUTHORS AND WORKS IN *Great Books of the Western World*

Descartes, Vol. 31, *Discourse on Method*, Part VI, pages 60–67
Lavoisier, Vol. 45, *Elements of Chemistry*, pages 1–133

CURIE, *The Discovery of Radium*
continued

RELATED AUTHORS AND WORKS IN *Gateway to the Great Books*

Darwin, *Autobiography*, Vol. 8, pages 47–93
Einstein and Infeld, "Rise and Decline of Classical Physics,"
    Vol. 8, pages 490–560
Faraday, *Chemical History of a Candle*, Vol. 8, pages 368–439
Galton, "Classification of Human Ability," Vol. 8, pages 227–261
James, W., *Energies of Men*, Vol. 7, pages 157–170
Mendeleev, "Genesis of a Law of Nature," Vol. 8, pages 442–446
Poincaré, *Mathematical Creation*, Vol. 9, pages 294–304
Tyndall, "Michael Faraday," Vol. 8, pages 8–28
Wöhler, *On the Artificial Production of Urea*, Vol. 8, pages 312–314
Woolf, *Art of Biography*, Vol. 6, pages 186–192

DANTE ALIGHIERI, 1265–1321

"On World Government"
from *De Monarchia*
Vol. 7, pages 383–399

SUGGESTED READINGS IN THE *Syntopicon*

CITIZEN, Vol. 2, pages 218–232, especially
    Topic 7: Political citizenship and membership in the city of God
    Topic 8: The idea of world citizenship: the political
        brotherhood of man
JUSTICE, Vol. 2, pages 850–879, especially
    Topic 1e: Justice as an act of will or duty fulfilling obligations
        to the common good: the harmonious action
        of individual wills under a universal law
        of freedom
WAR AND PEACE, Vol. 3, pages 1010–1037, especially
    Topic 11d: World government and world peace

RELATED AUTHORS AND WORKS IN *Great Books of the Western World*

Aurelius, Vol. 12, *Meditations*, Bks. III–IV, pages 262–264
Kant, Vol. 42, *Science of Right*, Second Part, pages 455–458
Hegel, Vol. 46, *Philosophy of Right*, Third Part, Sub-sect. III,
    pages 108–109
Tolstoy, Vol. 51, *War and Peace*, Bk. 6, Chap. VII, pages 244–245

Dostoevsky, Vol. 52, *Brothers Karamazov*, Part II, Bk. V, Chap. 5, page 133
Freud, Vol. 54, *Thoughts for the Times on War and Death*, Chap. I, pages 755–761

RELATED AUTHORS AND WORKS IN *Gateway to the Great Books*

Clausewitz, *What Is War?*, Vol. 7, pages 479–497
Great Documents, *Charter of the United Nations*, Vol. 6, pages 422–451; *Universal Declaration of Human Rights*, pages 452–456
Guizot, "Civilization," Vol. 6, pages 302–317
Kant, *Perpetual Peace*, Vol. 7, pages 441–475
Rousseau, *Lasting Peace through the Federation of Europe*, Vol. 7, pages 405–436

For Dante's *Divine Comedy* in *Great Books of the Western World*, see Vol. 21

TOBIAS DANTZIG, 1884–1956

Fingerprints
The Empty Column
Vol. 9, pages 165–189

SUGGESTED READINGS IN THE *Syntopicon*

MATHEMATICS, Vol. 3, pages 42–62, especially
Topic 2: The objects of mathematics: number, figure, extension, relation, order
Topic 2a: The apprehension of mathematical objects: by intuition, abstraction, imagination, construction; the forms of time and space
Topic 2b: The being of mathematical objects: their real, ideal, or mental existence
QUANTITY, Vol. 3, pages 527–545, especially
Topic 4: Discrete quantities: number and numbering

RELATED AUTHORS AND WORKS IN *Great Books of the Western World*

Plato, Vol. 7, *Republic*, Bk. VII, pages 391–398
Aristotle, Vol. 8, *Metaphysics*, Bk. X, Chaps. 1–7, pages 578–585; Bk. XI, Chaps. 1–9, pages 587–594; Bk. XIII, Chap. 6–Bk. XIV, Chap. 6, pages 611–626
Kant, Vol. 42, *Critique of Pure Reason*, Introduction, pages 15–20; pages 29–33; pages 211–217

DANTZIG, *Fingerprints, The Empty Column*
continued

James, W., Vol. 53, *Principles of Psychology,* Chap. XXVIII, pages 869–881

RELATED AUTHORS AND WORKS IN *Gateway to the Great Books*

Campbell, *Measurement,* Vol. 9, pages 204–221
Forsyth, *Mathematics, in Life and Thought,* Vol. 9, pages 26–46
Hogben, *Mathematics, the Mirror of Civilization,* Vol. 9, pages 3–23
Kasner and Newman, *New Names for Old,* Vol. 9, pages 121–136; *Beyond the Googol,* pages 137–162
Poincaré, *Mathematical Creation,* Vol. 9, pages 294–304
Russell, *Definition of Number,* Vol. 9, pages 111–117
Whitehead, *On the Nature of a Calculus,* Vol. 9, pages 68–78

CHARLES ROBERT DARWIN, 1809–1882

Autobiography
Vol. 8, pages 47–93

SUGGESTED READINGS IN THE *Syntopicon*

EDUCATION, Vol. 2, pages 376–399, especially
Topic 4*b*: The influence of the family in moral training
Topic 5*e*: The emotional aspect of learning: pleasure, desire, interest
Topic 5*f*: Learning apart from teachers and books: the role of experience

EVOLUTION, Vol. 2, pages 451–467, especially
Topic 5: The theory of evolution: the origin of new species from a common ancestry

SCIENCE, Vol. 3, pages 682–705, especially
Topic 2*b*: The comparison of science with poetry and history
Topic 5*a*: The role of experience: observation and experiment

RELATED AUTHORS AND WORKS IN *Great Books of the Western World*

Montaigne, Vol. 25, *Use Makes Perfect,* pages 176–181; *Of Experience,* pages 520–522
Descartes, Vol. 31, *Discourse on Method,* Parts I–III, pages 41–51; *Meditation II,* pages 77–81
James, Vol. 53, *Principles of Psychology,* Chap. VII, pages 121–126; Chap. X, pages 191–197

Freud, Vol. 54, *New Introductory Lectures on Psycho-Analysis*, Lecture 35, page 884

RELATED AUTHORS AND WORKS IN *Gateway to the Great Books*

Balzac, *Passion in the Desert*, Vol. 3, pages 436–447
Carson, *Sunless Sea*, Vol. 8, pages 132–146
Curie, *Discovery of Radium*, Vol. 8, pages 32–42
De Quincey, *Literature of Knowledge and Literature of Power*, Vol. 5, pages 358–361
Dewey, "Process of Thought," Vol. 10, pages 92–213
Eiseley, "On Time," Vol. 8, pages 123–129
Fabre, *Laboratory of the Open Fields*, Vol. 8, pages 97–104; *Sacred Beetle*, pages 105–119
Galton, "Classification of Human Ability," Vol. 8, pages 227–261
Huxley, *On a Piece of Chalk*, Vol. 8, pages 205–222; *On the Relations of Man to the Lower Animals*, pages 106–204
Lamb, *Sanity of True Genius*, Vol. 5, pages 308–310
Lyell, "Geological Evolution," Vol. 8, pages 319–324
Malthus, "Principle of Population," Vol. 7, pages 502–530
Mill, J. S., "Childhood and Youth," Vol. 6, pages 5–47
Poincaré, *Mathematical Creation*, Vol. 9, pages 294–304
Tyndall, "Michael Faraday," Vol. 8, pages 8–28
Woolf, *Art of Biography*, Vol. 6, pages 186–192

For other works by Darwin in *Great Books of the Western World*, see Vol. 49

DANIEL DEFOE, 1660–1731

Robinson Crusoe
Vol. 2, pages 5–121

SUGGESTED READINGS IN THE *Syntopicon*

EDUCATION, Vol. 2, pages 376–399, especially
Topic 5*f*: Learning apart from teachers and books: the role of experience

EXPERIENCE, Vol. 2, pages 468–485, especially
Topic 4*b*: Verification by experience: experience as the ultimate test of truth
Topic 6*a*: Experience as indispensable to sound judgment and prudence

D E F O E , *Robinson Crusoe*
continued

LABOR, Vol. 2, pages 921–940, especially
    Topic 1*d*: The social necessity of labor and the moral obligation
        to work
    Topic 1*e*: The honor of work and the virtue of productivity:
        progress through the invention of arts
        for the conquest of nature

RELATED AUTHORS AND WORKS IN *Great Books of the Western World*

Sophocles, Vol. 5, *Philoctetes,* pages 182–195
Aristotle, Vol. 9, *Politics,* Bk. I, pages 445–455
Epictetus, Vol. 12, *Discourses,* Bk. III, Chap. 13, pages 188–189
Montaigne, Vol. 25, *Of Solitude,* pages 107–112
Shakespeare, Vol. 27, *Tempest,* Act I, pages 524–531
Mill, J. S., Vol. 43, *Utilitarianism,* Chap. 2, pages 447–457
James, W., Vol. 53, *Principles of Psychology,* Chap. IV, page 81;
    Chap. XI, pages 275–291; Chap. XIX, pages 502–507

RELATED AUTHORS AND WORKS IN *Gateway to the Great Books*

Conrad, *Youth,* Vol. 2, pages 210–236
Crane, *Open Boat,* Vol. 3, pages 5–26
Emerson, *Thoreau,* Vol. 6, pages 150–165; *Self-Reliance,* Vol. 10,
    pages 525–545
Fabre, *Sacred Beetle,* Vol. 8, pages 105–119
Long, *Power within Us,* Vol. 6, pages 246–261
O'Neill, *Emperor Jones,* Vol. 4, pages 357–382
Sainte-Beuve, *What Is a Classic?,* Vol. 5, pages 65–75
Tolstoy, *Three Hermits,* Vol. 3, pages 700–706
Twain, "Learning the River," Vol. 6, pages 50–98
Voltaire, "Philosophy of Common Sense," Vol. 10, pages 453–474

THOMAS DE QUINCEY, 1785–1859

Literature of Knowledge and Literature of Power
Vol. 5, pages 358–361

SUGGESTED READINGS IN THE *Syntopicon*

ART, Vol. 2, pages 64–86, especially
    Topic 2*b*: The role of matter and form in artistic and natural
        production

Topic 10a: The influence of the arts on character
and citizenship: the role of the arts in the training
of youth
POETRY, Vol. 3, pages 400–419, especially
Topic 5: Poetry in relation to knowledge
Topic 5a: The aim of poetry to instruct as well as to delight:
the pretensions or deceptions of the poet as teacher

RELATED AUTHORS AND WORKS IN *Great Books of the Western World*

Plato, Vol. 7, *Republic*, Bks. II–III, pages 320–339; Bk. X,
pages 427–434
Augustine, Vol. 18, *City of God*, Bk. II, Chaps. 8–15, pages 153–157
Rabelais, Vol. 24, *Gargantua and Pantagruel*, Bk. I, Author's
Prologue, pages 1–3
Montaigne, Vol. 25, *Of the Education of Children*, page 62;
Apology for Raimond de Sebonde, page 245
Cervantes, Vol. 29, *Don Quixote*, First Part, Chap. 32, pages
117–120; Chaps. 47–50, pages 184–194
Kant, Vol. 42, *Critique of Judgement*, First Part, Sect. I, Bk. II,
pages 520–528
Goethe, Vol. 47, *Faust*, Prelude on the Stage, pages 2–6

RELATED AUTHORS AND WORKS IN *Gateway to the Great Books*

Arnold, *Sweetness and Light*, Vol. 5, pages 42–61
Bacon, *Of Studies*, Vol. 5, pages 97–98
Bury, *Herodotus*, Vol. 6, pages 364–383
Conrad, *Youth*, Vol. 2, pages 210–236
Crane, *Open Boat*, Vol. 3, pages 5–26
Darwin, *Autobiography*, Vol. 8, pages 47–93
Dinesen, *Sorrow-Acre*, Vol. 3, pages 615–641
Eliot, T. S., *Dante*, Vol. 5, pages 371–403
Hawthorne, *Rappaccini's Daughter*, Vol. 3, pages 128–152
Hugo, "Battle with the Cannon," Vol. 2, pages 146–154
Ibsen, *Enemy of the People*, Vol. 4, pages 164–246
Johnson, *Preface to Shakespeare*, Vol. 5, pages 316–353
Melville, *Billy Budd*, Vol. 3, pages 31–98
Mill, J. S., "Childhood and Youth," Vol. 6, pages 5–47
Molière, *Misanthrope*, Vol. 4, pages 6–51
Sainte-Beuve, *Montaigne*, Vol. 5, pages 76–89
Santayana, *Lucretius*, Vol. 10, pages 365–390; *Goethe's Faust*,
pages 391–419
Schiller, *On Simple and Sentimental Poetry*, Vol. 5, pages 155–211
Schopenhauer, *On Some Forms of Literature*, Vol. 5, pages
137–142; *On the Comparative Place of Interest and Beauty
in Works of Art*, pages 143–150

DE QUINCEY, *Literature of Knowledge and Power*
continued

Shelley, *Defence of Poetry*, Vol. 5, pages 216–242
Tolstoy, *Death of Ivan Ilyitch*, Vol. 3, pages 646–699

On the Knocking at the Gate in Macbeth
Vol. 5, pages 362–366

SUGGESTED READINGS IN THE *Syntopicon*

BEAUTY, Vol. 2, pages 112–125, especially
    Topic 2: Beauty in nature and in art
KNOWLEDGE, Vol. 2, pages 880–920, especially
    Topic 6b(4): Knowledge in relation to the faculties
        of understanding, judgment, and reason;
        and to the work of intuition, imagination,
        and understanding
MEMORY AND IMAGINATION, Vol. 3, pages 133–157, especially
    Topic 6c(2): The schema of the imagination as mediating
        between concepts of the understanding
        and the sensory manifold of intuition:
        the transcendental unity of apperception

RELATED AUTHORS AND WORKS IN *Great Books of the Western World*

Shakespeare, Vol. 27, *Macbeth*, pages 284–310, especially pages
    291–292
Kant, Vol. 42, *Critique of Pure Reason*, Part I, pages 23–110;
    Critique of Judgement, Introduction, pages 463–476
Hegel, Vol. 46, *Philosophy of History*, Second Part, pages 264–268
James, W., Vol. 53, *Principles of Psychology*, Chap. X, pages
    232–235

RELATED AUTHORS AND WORKS IN *Gateway to the Great Books*

Bacon, *Of Beauty*, Vol. 5, page 94
Flaubert, *Legend of St. Julian the Hospitaller*, Vol. 3, pages
    371–392
Hemingway, *Killers*, Vol. 2, pages 169–177
Johnson, *Preface to Shakespeare*, Vol. 5, pages 316–353
Lamb, *My First Play*, Vol. 5, pages 300–303
Schopenhauer, *On the Comparative Place of Interest and Beauty
    in Works of Art*, Vol. 5, pages 143–150

JOHN DEWEY, 1859–1952

"The Process of Thought"
from *How We Think*
Vol. 10, pages 92–213

SUGGESTED READINGS IN THE *Syntopicon*

DEFINITION, Vol. 2, pages 286–302, especially
Topic 1*b*: The purpose of definition: the clarification of ideas
HYPOTHESIS, Vol. 2, pages 749–760, especially
Topic 1: The use of hypotheses in the process of dialectic
IDEA, Vol. 2, pages 761–783, especially
Topic 1*b*: Ideas or conceptions as that by which the mind
thinks or knows
Topic 5*d*: The order of concepts in the stages of learning:
the more and the less general
Topic 5*e*: The association, comparison, and discrimination
of ideas: the stream of thought or consciousness
JUDGMENT, Vol. 2, pages 835–849, especially
Topic 1: Judgment as an act or faculty of the mind: its contrast
with the act of conception or with the faculties
of understanding and reason
Topic 7*c*: Reasoning as a sequence of judgments: the chain
of reasoning
Topic 8*b*: Analytic and synthetic judgments: trifling
and instructive propositions
KNOWLEDGE, Vol. 2, pages 880–920, especially
Topic 6*b*(4): Knowledge in relation to the faculties
of understanding, judgment, and reason;
and to the work of intuition, imagination,
and understanding
LANGUAGE, Vol. 2, pages 941–961, especially
Topic 1*a*: The role of language in thought
Topic 5*a*: The abuse of words: ambiguity, imprecision,
obscurity
Topic 8: Grammar and rhetoric: the effective use of language
in teaching and persuasion
MIND, Vol. 3, pages 171–203, especially
Topic 1*a*(2): The cooperation of intellect and sense:
the dependence of thought upon imagination
and the direction of imagination by reason

DEWEY, "The Process of Thought"
continued

REASONING, Vol. 3, pages 546–568, especially
Topic 1: Definitions or descriptions of reasoning: the process
of thought
Topic 1c: The role of sense, memory, and imagination
in reasoning: perceptual inference, rational
reminiscence, the collation of images
Topic 5a: The fact and the reasoned fact: mere belief
distinguished from belief on rational grounds
Topic 5b(2): Definitions used as means in reasoning;
definitions as the end of reasoning
Topic 5b(3): A priori and a posteriori reasoning: from causes
or from effects: from principles
or from experience; analysis and synthesis
SENSE, Vol. 3, pages 706–729, especially
Topic 3d(1): The functions of the common sense:
discrimination, comparison, association, collation
or perception

RELATED AUTHORS AND WORKS IN *Great Books of the Western World*

Plato, Vol. 7, *Republic*, Bks. VI–VII, pages 383–398
Aristotle, Vol. 8, *Posterior Analytics*, Bk. I, Chaps. 1–3, pages
97–100
Aquinas, Vol. 19, *Summa Theologica*, First Part, Q 14, Arts. 1–12,
pages 75–86
Hobbes, Vol. 23, *Leviathan*, Part I, Chaps. 4–5, pages 56–59
Bacon, Vol. 30, *Advancement of Learning*, Second Book, pages
56–69; *Novum Organum*, First Book, pages 109–116
Descartes, Vol. 31, *Rules for the Direction of the Mind*, Rules
V–XIV, pages 7–32
Locke, Vol. 35, *Essay Concerning Human Understanding*, Bk. IV,
pages 307–395
Kant, Vol. 42, *Critique of Pure Reason*, pages 23–110
James, W., Vol. 53, *Principles of Psychology*, Chap. XIII, pages
315–341

RELATED AUTHORS AND WORKS IN *Gateway to the Great Books*

Bacon, *Of Discourse*, Vol. 5, pages 95–96
Clifford, *Ethics of Belief*, Vol. 10, pages 16–36
Darwin, *Autobiography*, Vol. 8, pages 47–93
Einstein and Infeld, "Rise and Decline of Classical Physics,"
Vol. 8, pages 490–560
Erskine, *Moral Obligation to Be Intelligent*, Vol. 10, pages 5–13
Faraday, *Observations on Mental Education*, Vol. 7, pages 208–232

Forsyth, *Mathematics, in Life and Thought,* Vol. 9, pages 26–46
James, W., *Will to Believe,* Vol. 10, pages 39–57; *Sentiment
of Rationality,* pages 58–87
Poincaré, *Mathematical Creation,* Vol. 9, pages 294–304
Schopenhauer, *On Education,* Vol. 7, pages 197–203

CHARLES DICKENS, 1812–1870

"A Full and Faithful Report of the Memorable Trial of Bardell against Pickwick"

from *The Pickwick Papers*
Vol. 2, pages 391–448

SUGGESTED READINGS IN THE *Syntopicon*

CUSTOM AND CONVENTION, Vol. 2, pages 268–285, especially
Topic 5*a*: The conventional determination of moral judgments:
the moral evaluation of conventions
Topic 6*a*: Constitutions, social contracts, positive laws,
and manners as conventions
Topic 6*b*: The force of custom with respect to law
LAW, Vol. 2, pages 962–990, especially
Topic 5*g*: The application of positive law to cases: the casuistry
of the judicial process; the conduct of a trial;
the administration of justice
Topic 9: The legal profession and the study of law: praise
and dispraise of lawyers and judges
VIRTUE AND VICE, Vol. 3, pages 975–1009, especially
Topic 4*e*(3): Circumstances as affecting the morality
of human acts

RELATED AUTHORS AND WORKS IN *Great Books of the Western World*

Rabelais, Vol. 24, *Gargantua and Pantagruel,* Bk. II, Chaps. 10–13,
pages 85–92; Bk. III, Chaps. 39–44, pages 204–215
Montaigne, Vol. 25, *Of Experience,* pages 516–520
Shakespeare, Vol. 26, *Merchant of Venice,* Act IV, Scene I,
pages 425–430
Cervantes, Vol. 29, *Don Quixote,* Second Part, Chap. 49, pages
352–356
Swift, Vol. 36, *Gulliver's Travels,* Part I, Chap. IV, pages 22–23
Boswell, Vol. 44, *Life of Samuel Johnson,* pages 251–252

DICKENS, "Bardell against Pickwick"
continued

RELATED AUTHORS AND WORKS IN *Gateway to the Great Books*

Butler, "Customs and Opinions of the Erewhonians," Vol. 2,
pages 483–506
Clifford, *Ethics of Belief*, Vol. 10, pages 16–36
Melville, *Billy Budd*, Vol. 3, pages 31–98
Scott, *Two Drovers*, Vol. 2, pages 182–205

ISAK DINESEN, 1885–1962

Sorrow-Acre
Vol. 3, pages 615–641

SUGGESTED READINGS IN THE *Syntopicon*

ARISTOCRACY, Vol. 2, pages 50–63, especially
Topic 4: Aristocracy and the issue of rule by men as opposed
to rule by law
Topic 7: Historic and poetic exemplifications of aristocracy
LOVE, Vol. 2, pages 1051–1082, especially
Topic 2*b*(4): Patterns of love and friendship in the family
Topic 3*d*: The heroism of friendship and the sacrifices of love
OPINION, Vol. 3, pages 303–322, especially
Topic 6*b*: The inexactitude of moral principles as applied
to particular cases
TYRANNY, Vol. 3, pages 939–956, especially
Topic 2*b*: The degeneration of oligarchy: the tyranny
of the wealthy

RELATED AUTHORS AND WORKS IN *Great Books of the Western World*

Sophocles, Vol. 5, *Antigone*, pages 131–142
Euripides, Vol. 5, *Trojan Women*, pages 276–280
Plato, Vol. 7, *Statesman*, pages 596–604
Montaigne, Vol. 25, *Of Three Good Women*, pages 358–362
Shakespeare, Vol. 26, *King Henry VI*, First Part, Act IV,
Scenes V–VII, pages 23–26
Montesquieu, Vol. 38, *Spirit of Laws*, Bk. V, Chap. 8, pages 23–25

RELATED AUTHORS AND WORKS IN *Gateway to the Great Books*

Bacon, *Of Parents and Children*, Vol. 7, pages 5–6; *Of Adversity*,
Vol. 10, page 350; *Of Love*, pages 351–352

Cicero, *On Old Age*, Vol. 10, pages 317–343
Conrad, *Youth*, Vol. 2, pages 210–236
Crane, *Open Boat*, Vol. 3, pages 5–26
Fitzgerald, *Diamond as Big as the Ritz*, Vol. 3, pages 397–431
Hazlitt, *On the Feeling of Immortality in Youth*, Vol. 10,
    pages 565–570
Hemingway, *Killers*, Vol. 2, pages 169–177
Hugo, "Battle with the Cannon," Vol. 2, pages 146–154
Long, *Power within Us*, Vol. 6, pages 246–261
Maupassant, *Two Friends*, Vol. 2, pages 159–164
Melville, *Billy Budd*, Vol. 3, pages 31–98
Synge, *Riders to the Sea*, Vol. 4, pages 342–352
Tolstoy, *Death of Ivan Ilyitch*, Vol. 3, pages 646–699; *What Men
    Live By*, pages 707–727

FYODOR DOSTOEVSKY, 1821–1881

White Nights
Vol. 3, pages 276–319

SUGGESTED READINGS IN THE *Syntopicon*

DESIRE, Vol. 2, pages 323–344, especially
    Topic 5*a*: Desire ruling imagination: daydreaming and fantasy
HAPPINESS, Vol. 2, pages 684–710, especially
    Topic 2*b*(5): The importance of friendship and love
        for happiness
    Topic 4*a*: Man's capacity for happiness: differences in human
        nature with respect to happiness
LOVE, Vol. 2, pages 1051–1082, especially
    Topic 2*b*(1):The relation between love and friendship
    Topic 2*b*(2): Self-love in relation to the love of others
    Topic 3*d*: The heroism of friendship and the sacrifices of love

RELATED AUTHORS AND WORKS IN *Great Books of the Western World*

Plato, Vol. 7, *Phaedrus*, pages 126–129; *Symposium*, pages 155–157,
    164–167
Dante, Vol. 21, *Divine Comedy*, Hell, Canto V, pages 7–8
Shakespeare, Vol. 26, *Love's Labour's Lost*, Act IV, Scene III,
    pages 268–272
Fielding, Vol. 37, *Tom Jones*, Bk. VI, Chaps. 7–8, pages 108–111
James, W., Vol. 53, *Principles of Psychology*, Chap. X, pages
    204–211

DOSTOEVSKY, *White Nights*
continued

RELATED AUTHORS AND WORKS IN *Gateway to the Great Books*

Anderson, *I'm a Fool*, Vol. 2, pages 511–520
Anonymous, *Aucassin and Nicolette*, Vol. 2, pages 523–551
Apuleius, "Cupid and Psyche," Vol. 3, pages 197–212
Bacon, *Of Love*, Vol. 10, pages 351–352
Galsworthy, *Apple-Tree*, Vol. 3, pages 323–367
Lamb, *Dream Children*, Vol. 5, pages 304–307
Pater, "Art of Life," Vol. 10, pages 258–261
Turgenev, *First Love*, Vol. 3, pages 217–271

For Dostoevsky's *The Brothers Karamazov* in *Great Books of the Western World*, see Vol. 52

SIR ARTHUR EDDINGTON, 1882–1944

The Running-Down of the Universe
Vol. 8, pages 565–580

SUGGESTED READINGS IN THE *Syntopicon*

CHANCE, Vol. 2, pages 179–192, especially
　　Topic 4: Cause and chance in relation to knowledge
　　　　　　and opinion: the theory of probability
CHANGE, Vol. 2, pages 193–217, especially
　　Topic 5: The measure of motion
　　Topic 13: The problem of the eternity of motion or change
MECHANICS, Vol. 3, pages 80–112, especially
　　Topic 6e: Work and energy: their conservation; perpetual
　　　　　　motion
SPACE, Vol. 3, pages 811–825, especially
　　Topic 2: Space, void, and motion
TIME, Vol. 3, pages 896–914, especially
　　Topic 2c: The creation of time: the priority of eternity to time;
　　　　　　the immutability of the world after the end of time
　　Topic 3: The mode of existence of time
WORLD, Vol. 3, pages 1118–1140, especially
　　Topic 1b: The universe as a machine: the system of its moving
　　　　　　parts

RELATED AUTHORS AND WORKS IN *Great Books of the Western World*

Aristotle, Vol. 8, *Physics*, Bk. VIII, pages 334–352
Lucretius, Vol. 12, *On the Nature of Things*, Bks. I–II, pages 12–19
Newton, Vol. 34, *Mathematical Principles of Natural Philosophy*,
  Bk. III, pages 284–285
Faraday, Vol. 45, *Experimental Researches in Electricity*, pages
  850–855

RELATED AUTHORS AND WORKS IN *Gateway to the Great Books*

Emerson, *Montaigne; or, the Skeptic*, Vol. 10, pages 546–562
Epicurus, *Letter to Herodotus*, Vol. 10, pages 216–229
Helmholtz, *On the Conservation of Force*, Vol. 8, pages 451–484
Jeans, *Beginnings and Endings*, Vol. 8, pages 585–596
Poincaré, *Chance*, Vol. 9, pages 305–320
Santayana, *Lucretius*, Vol. 10, pages 365–390
Voltaire, *Micromégas*, Vol. 2, pages 241–256; "English Men
  and Ideas," Vol. 7, pages 332–378

ALBERT EINSTEIN, 1879–1955
and LEOPOLD INFELD, 1898–

"The Rise and Decline of Classical Physics"
from *The Evolution of Physics*
Vol. 8, pages 490–560

SUGGESTED READINGS IN THE *Syntopicon*

ASTRONOMY, Vol. 2, pages 87–111, especially
  Topic 2: The method of astronomy
  Topic 8c(2): The form of celestial motion: circles, the equant,
    ellipses
  Topic 8c(3): The laws of celestial motion: celestial
    mechanics
CHANGE, Vol. 2, pages 193–217
ELEMENT, Vol. 2, pages 400–412, especially
  Topic 5: The theory of atomism: critiques of atomism
INFINITY, Vol. 2, pages 816–834, especially
  Topic 3: The infinite in quantity
  Topic 4: The infinity of matter
MATHEMATICS, Vol. 3, pages 42–62, especially
  Topic 5b: Mathematical physics: the mathematical structure
    of nature

EINSTEIN and INFELD, "Classical Physics"
continued

MECHANICS, Vol. 3, pages 80–112

PHYSICS, Vol. 3, pages 363–376, especially

Topic 1*b*: The relation of the philosophy of nature
to mathematics: mathematical method
and mathematical principles in natural philosophy

Topic 3: The role of mathematics in the natural sciences:
observation and measurement in relation
to mathematical formulations

Topic 4*b*: Experimental discovery: inductive generalization
from experiment; the role of theory or hypothesis
in experimentation

Topic 4*d*: Experimental measurement: the application
of mathematical formulae

Topic 5: The utility of physics: the invention of machines;
the techniques of engineering; the mastery of nature

QUANTITY, Vol. 3, pages 527–545

SCIENCE, Vol. 3, pages 682–705, especially

Topic 1*b*: Science as the discipline of experimental inquiry
and the organization of experimental knowledge:
the scientific spirit

Topic 4: The nature of scientific knowledge

Topic 5: Scientific method

SPACE, Vol. 3, pages 811–825, especially

Topic 2: Space, void, and motion

RELATED AUTHORS AND WORKS IN *Great Books of the Western World*

Lucretius, Vol. 12, *On the Nature of Things*, pages 1–97
Copernicus, Vol. 16, *On the Revolutions of the Heavenly
Spheres*, Translator's Introduction, pages 481–495; Bk. I,
pages 511–532; Bk. V, pages 732–810
Kepler, Vol. 16, *Epitome of Copernican Astronomy*, Bks. IV–V,
pages 845–989
Gilbert, Vol. 28, *On the Loadstone*, pages 1–121
Galileo, Vol. 28, *Dialogues Concerning the Two New Sciences*,
Third and Fourth Days, pages 197–260
Newton, Vol. 34, *Mathematical Principles of Natural Philosophy*,
pages 1–372; *Optics*, pages 377–544
Huygens, Vol. 34, *Treatise on Light*, pages 551–619
Fourier, Vol. 45, *Analytical Theory of Heat*, pages 169–251
Faraday, Vol. 45, *Experimental Researches in Electricity*,
pages 265–319, 595–629, 631–845

RELATED AUTHORS AND WORKS IN *Gateway to the Great Books*
Campbell, *Measurement*, Vol. 9, pages 204–221; *Numerical Laws and the Use of Mathematics in Science*, pages 222–238
Clifford, *Postulates of the Science of Space*, Vol. 9, pages 243–259
Curie, *Discovery of Radium*, Vol. 8, pages 32–42
Dewey, "Process of Thought," Vol. 10, pages 92–213
Epicurus, *Letter to Herodotus*, Vol. 10, pages 216–229
Faraday, *Chemical History of a Candle*, Vol. 8, pages 368–439
Forsyth, *Mathematics, in Life and Thought*, Vol. 9, pages 26–46
Galileo, *Starry Messenger*, Vol. 8, pages 330–355
Helmholtz, *On the Conservation of Force*, Vol. 8, pages 451–484
Mendeleev, "Genesis of a Law of Nature," Vol. 8, pages 442–446
Poincaré, *Space*, Vol. 9, pages 265–293
Russell, *Mathematics and the Metaphysicians*, Vol. 9, pages 95–110
Tyndall, "Michael Faraday," Vol. 8, pages 8–28
Voltaire, "English Men and Ideas," Vol. 7, pages 332–378
Whitehead, "On Mathematical Method," Vol. 9, pages 51–67

LOREN EISELEY, 1907–

"On Time"
from *The Immense Journey*
Vol. 8, pages 123–129

SUGGESTED READINGS IN THE *Syntopicon*
ANIMAL, Vol. 2, pages 19–49, especially
Topic 2*b*: Analogies of structure and function among different classes of animals
Topic 2*c*: Continuity and discontinuity in the scale of animal life: gradation from lower to higher forms
Topic 11*b*: The relation between animals and their environments
EVOLUTION, Vol. 2, pages 451–467, especially
Topic 4: The problem of evolution: the origin of plant and animal species
Topic 5: The theory of evolution: the origin of new species from a common ancestry
Topic 6: The facts of evolution: evidences bearing on the history of life on earth
HABIT, Vol. 2, pages 665–683, especially
Topic 3: The instincts or innate habits of animals and men

EISELEY, "On Time"
continued

SCIENCE, Vol. 3, pages 682–705, especially
  Topic 2b: The comparison of science with poetry and history
TIME, Vol. 3, pages 896–914, especially
  Topic 3: The mode of existence of time
  Topic 6: The knowledge of time and the experience of duration
  Topic 8a: Prehistoric and historic time: the antiquity of man

RELATED AUTHORS AND WORKS IN *Great Books of the Western World*

Augustine, Vol. 18, *Confessions*, Bk. XII, pages 99–110
Darwin, Vol. 49, *Origin of Species*, pages 1–243; *Descent of Man*,
  Chaps. I–II, pages 255–284; Chaps. IV–VII, pages 308–351;
  Chaps. XV–XVI, pages 500–525

RELATED AUTHORS AND WORKS IN *Gateway to the Great Books*

Boeke, *Cosmic View*, Vol. 8, pages 600–644
Carson, *Sunless Sea*, Vol. 8, pages 132–146
Darwin, *Autobiography*, Vol. 8, pages 47–93
Huxley, *On the Relations of Man to the Lower Animals*, pages
  160–204; *On a Piece of Chalk*, Vol. 8, pages 205–222
Jeans, *Beginnings and Endings*, Vol. 8, pages 585–596
Lyell, "Geological Evolution," Vol. 8, pages 319–324
Voltaire, *Micromégas*, Vol. 2, pages 241–256

GEORGE ELIOT, 1819–1880

The Lifted Veil
Vol. 3, pages 157–193

SUGGESTED READINGS IN THE *Syntopicon*

EMOTION, Vol. 2, pages 413–436, especially
  Topic 1a: Emotion in relation to feelings of pleasure and pain
  Topic 2c: The opposition of particular emotions to one another
  Topic 4c: The moral significance of temperamental type
    or emotional disposition
MAN, Vol. 3, pages 1–41, especially
  Topic 2b: The sciences of human nature: anthropology
    and psychology; rational and empirical psychology;
    experimental and clinical psychology

Topic 6a: The cause and range of human inequalities: differences in ability, inclination, temperament, habit
Topic 6b: The differences between men and women: their equality or inequality
PROPHECY, Vol. 3, pages 454–471, especially
Topic 1a: Prophecy as the reading of fate, the foretelling of fortune, the beholding of the future

RELATED AUTHORS AND WORKS IN *Great Books of the Western World*

Homer, Vol. 4, *Odyssey*, Bk. XI, pages 243–249
Sophocles, Vol. 5, *Oedipus the King*, pages 102–103; *Oedipus at Colonus*, pages 126–128; *Antigone*, pages 139–140
Virgil, Vol. 13, *Aeneid*, Bk. VI, pages 211–235
Goethe, Vol. 47, *Faust*, First Part, pages 37–49; Second Part, Act II, pages 197–198
Melville, Vol. 48, *Moby Dick*, Chap. 19, pages 68–70; Chap. 117, pages 364–365; Chap. 135, pages 415–418

RELATED AUTHORS AND WORKS IN *Gateway to the Great Books*

Anderson, *I'm a Fool*, Vol. 2, pages 511–520
Bacon, *Of Marriage and Single Life*, Vol. 7, pages 7–8; *Of Love*, Vol. 10, pages 351–352
Hawthorne, *Rappaccini's Daughter*, Vol. 3, pages 128–152
Lawrence, *Rocking-Horse Winner*, Vol. 3, pages 512–525
Long, *Power within Us*, Vol. 6, pages 246–261
Mann, *Mario and the Magician*, Vol. 3, pages 573–610
Plutarch, *Of Bashfulness*, Vol. 7, pages 97–109
Pushkin, *Queen of Spades*, Vol. 3, pages 484–507
Stevenson, *Strange Case of Dr. Jekyll and Mr. Hyde*, Vol. 2, pages 288–341

THOMAS STEARNS ELIOT, 1888–1965

Dante
Vol. 5, pages 371–403

SUGGESTED READINGS IN THE *Syntopicon*

IDEA, Vol. 2, pages 761–783, especially
Topic 4b(4): Univocal and analogical terms
LANGUAGE, Vol. 2, pages 941–961, especially
Topic 9: The language of poetry

T. S. ELIOT, Dante
continued

PHILOSOPHY, Vol. 3, pages 342–362, especially
Topic 1*d*: The relation of philosophy to myth, poetry,
and history
POETRY, Vol. 3, pages 400–419, especially
Topic 8*b*: Critical standards and artistic rules with respect
to the language of poetry: the distinction
between prose and verse; the measure of excellence
in style
Topic 8*c*: The interpretation of poetry

RELATED AUTHORS AND WORKS IN *Great Books of the Western World*

Plato, Vol. 7, *Protagoras*, pages 52–57
Aristotle, Vol. 9, *On Poetics*, pages 681–699
Cervantes, Vol. 29, *Don Quixote*, Second Part, Chap. 16,
pages 251–252
Kant, Vol. 42, *Critique of Judgement*, Introduction–First Part,
Sect. I, Bk. I, pages 474–483
Goethe, Vol. 47, *Faust*, Second Part, Act III, page 227

RELATED AUTHORS AND WORKS IN *Gateway to the Great Books*

Adams, *Saint Thomas Aquinas*, Vol. 10, pages 422–450
Arnold, *Study of Poetry*, Vol. 5, pages 19–41
De Quincey, *Literature of Knowledge and Literature of Power*,
Vol. 5, pages 359–362
Dante, "On World Government," Vol. 7, pages 383–399
Hazlitt, *On Swift*, Vol. 5, pages 280–283
Johnson, *Preface to Shakespeare*, Vol. 5, pages 316–353
Sainte-Beuve, *What Is a Classic?*, Vol. 5, pages 65–75
Schopenhauer, *On Style*, Vol. 5, pages 124–136
Shelley, *Defence of Poetry*, Vol. 5, pages 216–242
Woolf, *How Should One Read a Book?*, Vol. 5, pages 5–14

For Dante's *Divine Comedy* in *Great Books of the Western World*,
see Vol. 21

Tradition and the Individual Talent
Vol. 5, pages 404–411

SUGGESTED READINGS IN THE *Syntopicon*

MEMORY AND IMAGINATION, Vol. 3, pages 133–157, especially
Topic 4*b*: Memory in the life of the group or race: instinct,
legend, and tradition

POETRY, Vol. 3, pages 400–419, especially
Topic 3: The inspiration or genius of the poet: the influence
of the poetic tradition
Topic 6a: The expression of emotion in poetry

RELATED AUTHORS AND WORKS IN *Great Books of the Western World*

Plato, Vol. 7, *Ion*, pages 142–148
Fielding, Vol. 37, *Tom Jones*, Bk. XII, Chap. 1, pages 246–247;
Bk. XIII, Chap. 1, pages 273–274
Kant, Vol. 42, *Critique of Judgement*, First Part, Sect. I, Bk. II,
pages 513–514, 518–520, 525–537
Goethe, Vol. 47, *Faust*, Prelude on the Stage, pages 2–6

RELATED AUTHORS AND WORKS IN *Gateway to the Great Books*

Arnold, *Study of Poetry*, Vol. 5, pages 19–41; *Sweetness and Light*,
pages 42–61
Emerson, *Thoreau*, Vol. 6, pages 150–165
Guizot, "Civilization," Vol. 6, pages 302–317
Hazlitt, *My First Acquaintance with Poets*, Vol. 5, pages 264–279;
Of Persons One Would Wish to Have Seen, pages 284–295
Hume, *Of the Study of History*, Vol. 7, pages 89–92
James, W., *Great Men and Their Environment*, Vol. 7,
pages 171–194
Lamb, *Sanity of True Genius*, Vol. 5, pages 308–310
Lawrence, *Rocking-Horse Winner*, Vol. 3, pages 512–525
Sainte-Beuve, *What Is a Classic?*, Vol. 5, pages 65–75
Schopenhauer, *On Education*, Vol. 7, pages 197–203
Shelley, *Defence of Poetry*, Vol. 5, pages 216–242
Stevenson, *Lantern-Bearers*, Vol. 7, pages 112–121
Whitman, *Preface to Leaves of Grass*, Vol. 5, pages 247–259
Woolf, *How Should One Read a Book?*, Vol. 5, pages 5–14

RALPH WALDO EMERSON, 1803–1882

Thoreau
Vol. 6, pages 150–165

SUGGESTED READINGS IN THE *Syntopicon*

ANIMAL, Vol. 2, pages 19–49, especially
Topic 12c: Friendship or love between animals and men
EDUCATION, Vol. 2, pages 376–399, especially
Topic 5f: Learning apart from teachers and books: the role
of experience

EMERSON, *Thoreau*
continued

LAW, Vol. 2, pages 962–990, especially
    Topic 6c: The force of tyrannical, unjust, or bad laws:
        the right of rebellion or disobedience
LIBERTY, Vol. 2, pages 991–1012, especially
    Topic 3d: Freedom from conflict and freedom for individuality
        as conditions of happiness
NATURE, Vol. 3, pages 225–250, especially
    Topic 3a: The rationality of nature: the maxims and laws
        of nature

RELATED AUTHORS AND WORKS IN *Great Books of the Western World*

Lucretius, Vol. 12, *On the Nature of Things*, Bk. V, pages 71–80
Epictetus, Vol. 12, *Discourses*, Bk. IV, Chap. 1, pages 213–223
Rabelais, Vol. 24, *Gargantua and Pantagruel*, Bk. I, Chaps. 23–24,
    pages 26–30
Montaigne, Vol. 25, *Of Cruelty*, pages 206–208; *Of Experience*,
    pages 516–543
Milton, Vol. 32, *Areopagitica*, pages 381–412
Sterne, Vol. 36, *Tristram Shandy*, Bk. VII, Chap. 32, pages 483–485

RELATED AUTHORS AND WORKS IN *Gateway to the Great Books*

Balzac, *Passion in the Desert*, Vol. 3, pages 436–447
Defoe, *Robinson Crusoe*, Vol. 2, pages 5–121
Eliot, T. S., *Tradition and the Individual Talent*, Vol. 5,
    pages 404–411
Emerson, *Nature*, Vol. 10, pages 512–524; *Self-Reliance*,
    pages 525–545
Great Documents, *Declaration of Independence*, Vol. 6,
    pages 418–421
Kipling, *Mowgli's Brothers*, Vol. 2, pages 126–141
Lamb, *Sanity of True Genius*, Vol. 5, pages 308–310
Long, *Power within Us*, Vol. 6, pages 246–261
Plutarch, *Contentment*, Vol. 10, pages 264–281
Ruskin, *Idealist's Arraignment of the Age*, Vol. 7, pages 126–136
Stevenson, *Lantern-Bearers*, Vol. 7, pages 112–121
Thoreau, *Civil Disobedience*, Vol. 6, pages 695–713; *Plea
    for Captain John Brown*, pages 714–732
Tocqueville, "Observations on American Life and Government,"
    Vol. 6, pages 564–690
Woolf, *Art of Biography*, Vol. 6, pages 186–192

Nature

Vol. 10, pages 512–524

SUGGESTED READINGS IN THE *Syntopicon*

BEAUTY, Vol. 2, pages 112–125, especially
Topic 2: Beauty in nature and in art
CHANGE, Vol. 2, pages 193–217, especially
Topic 4: Motion and rest: contrary motions
NATURE, Vol. 3, pages 225–250, especially
Topic 1*b*: Nature as the universe or the totality of things:
the identification of God and nature; the distinction
between *natura naturans* and *natura naturata*
Topic 2*b*: Nature and convention: the state of nature
and the state of society
Topic 3*a*: The rationality of nature: the maxims and laws
of nature

RELATED AUTHORS AND WORKS IN *Great Books of the Western World*

Plato, Vol. 7, *Timaeus*, pages 447–450
Plotinus, Vol. 17, *Third Ennead*, Eighth Tractate, pages 129–131;
Sixth Ennead, Third Tractate, pages 295–297
Montaigne, Vol. 25, Author to the Reader, page ix; *Of Repentance*,
pages 388–395; *Of Experience*, pages 516–543
Spinoza, Vol. 31, *Ethics*, Part I, Props. 1–32, pages 355–367
Newton, Vol. 34, *Mathematical Principles of Natural Philosophy*,
Def. III, page 5; Laws I–III, page 14
Kant, Vol. 42, *Critique of Judgement*, First Part, Sect. I, Bk. II,
pages 521–528

RELATED AUTHORS AND WORKS IN *Gateway to the Great Books*

Adams, *Saint Thomas Aquinas*, Vol. 10, pages 422–450
Bacon, *Sphinx*, Vol. 8, pages 2–4
Emerson, *Thoreau*, Vol. 6, pages 150–165
Epicurus, *Letter to Herodotus*, Vol. 10, pages 216–229
Fabre, *Laboratory of the Open Fields*, Vol. 8, pages 97–104;
Sacred Beetle, pages 105–119
Huxley, *On the Relations of Man to the Lower Animals*, Vol. 8,
pages 160–204
James, W., *Will to Believe*, Vol. 10, pages 39–57
Long, *Power within Us*, Vol. 6, pages 246–261
Mill, J. S., *Nature*, Vol. 10, pages 477–508
Santayana, *Lucretius*, Vol. 10, pages 365–390
Voltaire, "Philosophy of Common Sense," Vol. 10, pages 453–474

RALPH WALDO EMERSON
continued

Self-Reliance
Vol. 10, pages 525–545

SUGGESTED READINGS IN THE *Syntopicon*

CUSTOM AND CONVENTION, Vol. 2, pages 268–285, especially
  Topic 9a: Custom as a source of opinion and belief:
    its influence on judgments of beauty
HONOR, Vol. 2, pages 728–748, especially
  Topic 2c: Honor as due self-esteem: magnanimity
    or proper pride
OPINION, Vol. 3, pages 303–322, especially
  Topic 3a: The truth of knowledge and of right opinion:
    their difference with respect to manner of acquisition,
    stability, and teachability
  Topic 5a: Rights and duties with respect to the expression
    of opinion
WISDOM, Vol. 3, pages 1102–1117, especially
  Topic 1a: Diverse conceptions of natural wisdom: the supreme
    form of human knowledge

RELATED AUTHORS AND WORKS IN *Great Books of the Western World*

Aeschylus, Vol. 5, *Agamemnon*, pages 61–62
Plato, Vol. 7, *Apology*, pages 208–209
Aristotle, Vol. 9, *Nicomachean Ethics*, Bk. IV, Chaps. 2–4,
  pages 368–372
Montaigne, Vol. 25, *Of Presumption*, pages 307–320
Spinoza, Vol. 31, *Ethics*, Part IV, Prop. 18, pages 428–429
Pascal, Vol. 33, *Pensées*, Sect. II, pages 191–192
Kant, Vol. 42, *Critique of Pure Reason*, pages 240–243
Boswell, Vol. 44, *Life of Samuel Johnson*, pages 221–224

RELATED AUTHORS AND WORKS IN *Gateway to the Great Books*

Adams, "United States in 1800," Vol. 6, pages 322–359
Bacon, *Of Adversity*, Vol. 10, page 350
Carlyle, *Hero as King*, Vol. 6, pages 110–145
Crane, *Open Boat*, Vol. 3, pages 5–26
Defoe, *Robinson Crusoe*, Vol. 2, pages 5–121
Emerson, *Thoreau*, Vol. 6, pages 150–165
Ibsen, *Enemy of the People*, Vol. 4, pages 164–246
Lamb, *Sanity of True Genius*, Vol. 5, pages 308–310
Long, *Power within Us*, Vol. 6, pages 246–261

Sainte-Beuve, *Montaigne*, Vol. 5, pages 76–89
Shaw, *Man of Destiny*, Vol. 4, pages 300–338
Tocqueville, "Observations on American Life and Government,"
Vol. 6, pages 564–690
Twain, "Learning the River," Vol. 6, pages 50–98
Washington, *Farewell Address*, Vol. 6, pages 484–497

Montaigne; or, the Skeptic
Vol. 10, pages 546–562

SUGGESTED READINGS IN THE *Syntopicon*

KNOWLEDGE, Vol. 2, pages 880–920, especially

Topic 5c: Dogmatism, skepticism, and the critical attitude
with respect to the extent, certainty, and finality
of human knowledge

MIND, Vol. 3, pages 171–203, especially

Topic 5b: The natural limits of the mind: the unknowable;
objects which transcend its powers; reason's critical
determination of its own limits or boundaries

RELATION, Vol. 3, pages 569–587, especially

Topic 6b: Absolute and relative with respect to truth

TRUTH, Vol. 3, pages 915–938, especially

Topic 7a: The impossibility of knowing the truth: the restriction
of all human judgments to degrees of probability;
the denial of axioms and of the possibility
of demonstration

RELATED AUTHORS AND WORKS IN *Great Books of the Western World*

Plato, Vol. 7, *Euthydemus*, pages 65–84
Montaigne, Vol. 25, *Apology for Raimond de Sebonde*, pages
208–294
Bacon, Vol. 30, *Advancement of Learning*, First Book, pages 15–17
Pascal, Vol. 33, *Pensées*, Sect. III, pages 205–217
Hume, Vol. 35, *Enquiry Concerning Human Understanding*,
Sect. IV, Part II–Sect. V, Part I, pages 460–466

RELATED AUTHORS AND WORKS IN *Gateway to the Great Books*

Bacon, *Of Truth*, Vol. 10, pages 346–347
Clifford, *Ethics of Belief*, Vol. 10, pages 16–36
Eddington, *Running-Down of the Universe*, Vol. 8, pages 565–580
Eliot, G., *Lifted Veil*, Vol. 3, pages 157–193
James, W., *Will to Believe*, Vol. 10, pages 39–57
Sainte-Beuve, *Montaigne*, Vol. 5, pages 76–89
Xenophon, "Character of Socrates," Vol. 6, pages 223–226

EMERSON, *Montaigne; or, the Skeptic*
continued

For Montaigne's *Essays* in *Great Books of the Western World*, see Vol. 25

EPICTETUS, *c.* 60–*c.* 138

The Enchiridion
Vol. 10, pages 236–254

SUGGESTED READINGS IN THE *Syntopicon*

DESIRE, Vol. 2, pages 323–344, especially
  Topic 6*a*: The regulation of desire by reason: the discipline of moral virtue or duty
DUTY, Vol. 2, pages 358–375, especially
  Topic 2: Comparison of the ethics of duty with the ethics of happiness, pleasure, or utility
GOOD AND EVIL, Vol. 2, pages 605–636, especially
  Topic 3*b*: Goodness in the order of freedom and will
  Topic 4*c*: Goods of the body and goods of the soul
  Topic 4*d*: Intrinsic and external goods: intrinsic worth and extrinsic value
LIFE AND DEATH, Vol. 2, pages 1013–1034, especially
  Topic 8*c*: The contemplation and fear of death: the attitude of the hero, the philosopher, the martyr

RELATED AUTHORS AND WORKS IN *Great Books of the Western World*

Plato, Vol. 7, *Republic*, Bk. IV, pages 346–356; Bk. IX, pages 421–425
Aurelius, Vol. 12, *Meditations*, Bks. III–VII, pages 259–283
Augustine, Vol. 18, *City of God*, Bk. XII, Chaps. 4–10, pages 344–349
Montaigne, Vol. 25, *That the Relish of Good and Evil Depends in a Great Measure Upon the Opinion We Have of Them*, pages 115–125
Bacon, Vol. 30, *Advancement of Learning*, Second Book, pages 69–81
Spinoza, Vol. 31, *Ethics*, Part IV, Appendix, pages 447–450
Kant, Vol. 42, *Fundamental Principles of the Metaphysic of Morals*, First–Second Sections, pages 256–267; Third Section, pages 280–283; *Critique of Practical Reason*, Part I, Bk. II, Chaps. I–II, pages 340–342

Mill, J. S., Vol. 43, *Utilitarianism*, Chap. 2, pages 447–457
Hegel, Vol. 46, *Philosophy of Right*, First Part, pages 23–31, *passim*

RELATED AUTHORS AND WORKS IN *Gateway to the Great Books*

Arnold, *Sweetness and Light*, Vol. 5, pages 42–61
Bacon, *Of Death*, Vol. 10, pages 348–349
Cicero, *On Old Age*, Vol. 10, pages 317–343
Epicurus, *Letter to Menoeceus*, Vol. 10, pages 230–233
Pater, "Art of Life," Vol. 10, pages 258–261
Plutarch, *Contentment*, Vol. 10, pages 264–281
Xenophon, "Character of Socrates," Vol. 6, pages 223–226

For Epictetus' *Discourses* in *Great Books of the Western World*, see Vol. 12, pages 100–250

EPICURUS, *c.* 341–*c.* 270 B.C.

Letter to Herodotus
Vol. 10, pages 216–229

SUGGESTED READINGS IN THE *Syntopicon*

ELEMENT, Vol. 2, pages 400–412, especially
Topic 5c: Atoms and the void as the ultimate constituents of reality
INFINITY, Vol. 2, pages 816–834, especially
Topic 4b: The infinite divisibility of matter: the issue concerning atoms
MATTER, Vol. 3, pages 63–79, especially
Topic 2b: The motions of matter or bodies
SOUL, Vol. 3, pages 791–810, especially
Topic 3d: The denial of soul as an immaterial principle, form, or substance: the atomic theory of the soul

RELATED AUTHORS AND WORKS IN *Great Books of the Western World*

Aristotle, Vol. 8, *Physics*, Bk. IV, Chaps. 6–9, pages 292–297
Lucretius, Vol. 12, *On the Nature of Things*, Bks. I–II, pages 1–30
Plotinus, Vol. 17, *Fourth Ennead*, Seventh Tractate, pages 191–200
Bacon, Vol. 30, *Novum Organum*, Second Book, pages 162–168
Newton, Vol. 34, *Optics*, Bk. III, Part I, pages 536–544
Kant, Vol. 42, *Critique of Pure Reason*, pages 137–140, 161–163; *Critique of Judgement*, Second Part, First-Second Division, pages 556–567

E P I C U R U S , *Letter to Herodotus*
continued

RELATED AUTHORS AND WORKS IN *Gateway to the Great Books*

Boeke, *Cosmic View,* Vol. 8, pages 600–644
Eddington, *Running-Down of the Universe,* Vol. 8, pages 565–580
Einstein and Infeld, "Rise and Decline of Classical Physics," Vol. 8,
    pages 490–560
Emerson, *Nature,* Vol. 10, pages 512–524
Faraday, *Chemical History of a Candle,* Vol. 8, pages 368–439
Pater, "Art of Life," Vol. 10, pages 258–261
Santayana, *Lucretius,* Vol. 10, pages 365–390
Swift, *Modest Proposal,* Vol. 7, pages 42–49
Voltaire, *Micromégas,* Vol. 2, pages 241–256

Letter to Menoeceus
Vol. 10, pages 230–233

SUGGESTED READINGS IN THE *Syntopicon*

DESIRE, Vol. 2, pages 323–344, especially
    Topic 6a: The regulation of desire by reason: the discipline
        of moral virtue or duty
PLEASURE AND PAIN, Vol. 3, pages 377–399, especially
    Topic 6a: Pleasure as the only good or as the measure
        of goodness in all other things
PRUDENCE, Vol. 3, pages 472–487, especially
    Topic 3b: Prudence as a factor in the formation and
        maintenance of moral virtue: the determination
        of the relative or subjective mean

RELATED AUTHORS AND WORKS IN *Great Books of the Western World*

Plato, Vol. 7, *Philebus,* pages 609–639
Aristotle, Vol. 9, *Nicomachean Ethics,* Bk. II, Chaps. 2–9, pages
    349–355; Bk. VI, pages 387–394
Lucretius, Vol. 12, *On the Nature of Things,* Bk. I, pages 10–14
Epictetus, Vol. 12, *Discourses,* Bk. I, pages 105–138
Aurelius, Vol. 12, *Meditations,* Bks. III–VII, pages 259–285
Montaigne, Vol. 25, *That to Study Philosophy Is to Learn to Die,*
    pages 28–36
Spinoza, Vol. 31, *Ethics,* Part III, Props. 55–58, pages 413–415
Kant, Vol. 42, *Fundamental Principles of the Metaphysic
    of Morals,* First Section, pages 256–259; *Critique of Practical
    Reason,* Part I, Bk. II, Chaps. I–II, pages 340–342
Mill, J. S., Vol. 43, *Utilitarianism,* Chap. 2, pages 447–457

RELATED AUTHORS AND WORKS IN *Gateway to the Great Books*

Bacon, *Of Death*, Vol. 10, pages 348–349
Cicero, *On Old Age*, Vol. 10, pages 317–343
Epictetus, *Enchiridion*, Vol. 10, pages 236–254
Pater, "Art of Life," Vol. 10, pages 258–261
Plutarch, *Contentment*, Vol. 10, pages 264–281
Poe, *Masque of the Red Death*, Vol. 2, pages 278–283
Sainte-Beuve, *Montaigne*, Vol. 5, pages 76–89
Santayana, *Lucretius*, Vol. 10, pages 365–390
Xenophon, "Character of Socrates," Vol. 6, pages 223–226

JOHN ERSKINE, 1879–1951

The Moral Obligation to Be Intelligent
Vol. 10, pages 5–13

SUGGESTED READINGS IN THE *Syntopicon*

GOOD AND EVIL, Vol. 2, pages 605–636, especially
  Topic 6c: The goodness of knowledge or wisdom: the use
    of knowledge
VIRTUE AND VICE, Vol. 3, pages 975–1009, especially
  Topic 1a: The relation between knowledge and virtue
WILL, Vol. 3, pages 1071–1101, especially
  Topic 1: The existence and nature of will: its relation to reason
    or mind and to desire or emotion

RELATED AUTHORS AND WORKS IN *Great Books of the Western World*

Plato, Vol. 7, *Protagoras*, pages 45–64; *Meno*, pages 183–190;
  Republic, Bk. I, pages 306–308
Aristotle, Vol. 9, *Nicomachean Ethics*, Bk. I, Chaps. 7–9, pages
  342–345; Bk. VI, Chap. 12–Bk. VII, Chap. 5, pages 393–399
Montaigne, Vol. 25, *Apology for Raimond de Sebonde*, pages
  233–242
Spinoza, Vol. 31, *Ethics*, Part II, Props. 48–49, pages 391–394
Milton, Vol. 32, *Paradise Lost*, Bk. IV, pages 163–164; Bk. IX,
  pages 262–265, 269–271; *Areopagitica*, pages 390–391
Hume, Vol. 35, *Enquiry Concerning Human Understanding*, Sect. I,
  pages 451–455
Mill, J. S., Vol. 43, *Utilitarianism*, Chap. 2, pages 448–452

RELATED AUTHORS AND WORKS IN *Gateway to the Great Books*

Arnold, *Sweetness and Light*, Vol. 5, pages 42–61
Bacon, *Of Studies*, Vol. 5, pages 97–98

ERSKINE, *The Moral Obligation to Be Intelligent*
continued

Clifford, *Ethics of Belief*, Vol. 10, pages 16–36
Dewey, "Process of Thought," Vol. 10, pages 92–213
Faraday, *Observations on Mental Education*, Vol. 7, pages 208–232
James, W., *Will to Believe*, Vol. 10, pages 39–57
Mill, J. S., "Childhood and Youth," Vol. 6, pages 5–47
Sainte-Beuve, *Montaigne*, Vol. 5, pages 76–89
Schopenhauer, *On Education*, Vol. 7, pages 197–203
Voltaire, "Philosophy of Common Sense," Vol. 10, pages 453–474
Xenophon, "Character of Socrates," Vol. 6, pages 223–226

LEONHARD EULER, 1707–1783

The Seven Bridges of Königsberg
Vol. 9, pages 193–201

SUGGESTED READINGS IN THE *Syntopicon*

MATHEMATICS, Vol. 3, pages 42–62, especially
Topic 3: Method in mathematics: the model of mathematical thought
Topic 3d: Symbols and formulae: the attainment of generality
SPACE, Vol. 3, pages 811–825, especially
Topic 3c: Geometrical space, its kinds and properties: spatial relationships and configurations

RELATED AUTHORS AND WORKS IN *Great Books of the Western World*

Archimedes, Vol. 11, *Method Treating of Mechanical Problems*, pages 569–592
Descartes, Vol. 31, *Geometry*, pages 295–353
Newton, Vol. 34, *Mathematical Principles of Natural Philosophy*, Definitions–Bk. I, Sect. II, pages 5–42; Bk. II, Sects. I–V, pages 159–203

RELATED AUTHORS AND WORKS IN *Gateway to the Great Books*

Campbell, *Numerical Laws and the Use of Mathematics in Science*, Vol. 9, pages 222–238
Whitehead, "On Mathematical Method," Vol. 9, pages 51–67

JEAN HENRI FABRE, 1823–1915

A Laboratory of the Open Fields
The Sacred Beetle
Vol. 8, pages 97–119

SUGGESTED READINGS IN THE *Syntopicon*

ANIMAL, Vol. 2, pages 19–49, especially
Topic 1d: The habits or instincts of animals: types of animal habit or instinct; the habits or instincts of different classes of animals
Topic 11: The habitat of animals

LABOR, Vol. 2, pages 921–940, especially
Topic 1f: The degradation of labor: the alienation of the laborer's work in chattel slavery, serfdom, and industrial wage slavery

SCIENCE, Vol. 3, pages 682–705, especially
Topic 1b: Science as the discipline of experimental inquiry and the organization of experimental knowledge: the scientific spirit
Topic 5a: The role of experience: observation and experiment

RELATED AUTHORS AND WORKS IN *Great Books of the Western World*

Aristotle, Vol. 9, *History of Animals*, Bk. V, Chap. 15–Bk. VI, Chap. 6, pages 73–89; Bk. VIII, pages 114–133; Bk. IX, Chaps. 9–13, pages 140–144
Harvey, Vol. 28, *Anatomical Exercises on the Generation of Animals*, Introduction, pages 331–337
Bacon, Vol. 30, *Novum Organum*, First Book, pages 107–118
Kant, Vol. 42, *Critique of Pure Reason*, pages 146–149
Darwin, Vol. 49, *Origin of Species*, Chap. VIII, pages 119–135; *Descent of Man*, Chap. IV, pages 304–312

RELATED AUTHORS AND WORKS IN *Gateway to the Great Books*

Bacon, *Of Beauty*, Vol. 5, page 94
Balzac, *Passion in the Desert*, Vol. 3, pages 436–447
Bernard, *Experimental Considerations Common to Living Things and Inorganic Bodies*, Vol. 8, pages 266–290
Carson, *Sunless Sea*, Vol. 8, pages 132–146
Darwin, *Autobiography*, Vol. 8, pages 47–93
Defoe, *Robinson Crusoe*, Vol. 2, pages 5–121
Emerson, *Nature*, Vol. 10, pages 512–524
Haldane, *On Being the Right Size*, Vol. 8, pages 149–154

FABRE, *A Laboratory*
of the Open Fields, The Sacred Beetle
continued

Huxley, *On the Relations of Man to the Lower Animals,* Vol. 8,
pages 160–204
Kipling, *Mowgli's Brothers,* Vol. 2, pages 126–141

MICHAEL FARADAY, 1791–1867

Observations on Mental Education
Vol. 7, pages 208–232

SUGGESTED READINGS IN THE *Syntopicon*

JUDGMENT, Vol. 2, pages 835–849, especially

Topic 1: Judgment as an act or faculty of the mind: its contrast
with the act of conception or with the faculties
of understanding and reason

Topic 8a: Self-evident and demonstrable propositions:
immediate and mediated, intuitive and reasoned
judgments

Topic 10: The truth and falsity of judgments

KNOWLEDGE, Vol. 2, pages 880–920, especially

Topic 6b(4): Knowledge in relation to the faculties
of understanding, judgment, and reason;
and to the work of intuition, imagination,
and understanding

Topic 10: The growth of human knowledge: the history
of man's progress and failures in the pursuit
of knowledge

REASONING, Vol. 3, pages 546–568, especially

Topic 5a: The fact and the reasoned fact: mere belief
distinguished from belief on rational grounds

RELATED AUTHORS AND WORKS IN *Great Books of the Western World*

Plato, Vol. 7, *Sophist,* pages 570–577
Aristotle, Vol. 8, *On the Soul,* Bk. III, Chaps. 3–8, pages 659–664;
Vol. 9, *Nicomachean Ethics,* Bk. VI, Chaps. 3–11, pages 388–393
Montaigne, Vol. 25, *Apology for Raimond de Sebonde,*
pages 276–278
Bacon, Vol. 30, *Advancement of Learning,* Second Book, pages 42–48,
55–60
Descartes, Vol. 31, *Discourse on Method,* Parts I–IV, pages 41–54

Hume, Vol. 35, *Enquiry Concerning Human Understanding,*
Sect. IV, Part II–Sect. V, Part II, pages 460–469
Kant, Vol. 42, *Critique of Judgement,* Introduction, pages 467–475
James, W., Vol. 53, *Principles of Psychology,* Chap. X, pages
232–235

RELATED AUTHORS AND WORKS IN *Gateway to the Great Books*

Bacon, *Of Custom and Education,* Vol. 7, pages 18–19
Clifford, *Ethics of Belief,* Vol. 10, pages 16–36
Dewey, "Process of Thought," Vol. 10, pages 92–213
Erskine, *Moral Obligation to Be Intelligent,* Vol. 10, pages 5–13
Franklin, *Proposals Relating to the Education of Youth
in Pennsylvania,* Vol. 6, pages 536–542
James, W., *Will to Believe,* Vol. 10, pages 39–57; *Sentiment
of Rationality,* pages 58–87
Schopenhauer, *On Education,* Vol. 7, pages 197–203
Swift, *Essay on Modern Education,* Vol. 7, pages 33–39

The Chemical History of a Candle
Vol. 8, pages 368–439

SUGGESTED READINGS IN THE *Syntopicon*

ANIMAL, Vol. 2, pages 19–49, especially
Topic 5d: The respiratory system: breathing, lungs, gills
CHANGE, Vol. 2, pages 193–217, especially
Topic 6c: Comparison of change in living and non-living things
Topic 9a: Physical and chemical change: compounds
and mixtures
MECHANICS, Vol. 3, pages 80–112, especially
Topic 7a: Light: the corpuscular and the wave theory
Topic 7c: The theory of heat

RELATED AUTHORS AND WORKS IN *Great Books of the Western World*

Gilbert, Vol. 28, *On the Loadstone,* pages 1–121
Lavoisier, Vol. 45, *Elements of Chemistry,* First Part,
Chap. V–Second Part, pages 22–86
Fourier, Vol. 45, *Analytical Theory of Heat,* pages 169–251

RELATED AUTHORS AND WORKS IN *Gateway to the Great Books*

Curie, *Discovery of Radium,* Vol. 8, pages 32–42
Einstein and Infeld, "Rise and Decline of Classical Physics," Vol. 8,
pages 490–560
Epicurus, *Letter to Herodotus,* Vol. 10, pages 216–229
Helmholtz, *On the Conservation of Force,* Vol. 8, pages 451–484
Huxley, *On a Piece of Chalk,* Vol. 8, pages 205–222

FARADAY, *The Chemical History of a Candle*
continued

Mendeleev, "Genesis of a Law of Nature," Vol. 8, pages 442–446
Santayana, *Lucretius,* Vol. 10, pages 365–390
Tyndall, "Michael Faraday," Vol. 8, pages 8–28
Wöhler, *On the Artificial Production of Urea,* Vol. 8, pages 312–314

For Faraday's *Experimental Researches in Electricity* in *Great Books of the Western World,* see Vol. 45, pages 261–866

FRANCIS SCOTT FITZGERALD, 1896–1940

The Diamond as Big as the Ritz
Vol. 3, pages 397–431

SUGGESTED READINGS IN THE *Syntopicon*

MEMORY AND IMAGINATION, Vol. 3, pages 133–157, especially
  Topic 7b: The fantastic and the realistic in poetry: the probable
      and the possible in poetry and history

OPINION, Vol. 3, pages 303–322, especially
  Topic 6a: Good and evil as matters of opinion: moral standards
      as customs or conventions reflecting prevalent
      opinion

TYRANNY, Vol. 3, pages 939–956, especially
  Topic 2b: The degeneration of oligarchy: the tyranny
      of the wealthy

VIRTUE AND VICE, Vol. 3, pages 975–1009, especially
  Topic 6c: The relation of virtue to wealth

WEALTH, Vol. 3, pages 1038–1070, especially
  Topic 10a: The nature of wealth as a good: its place
      in the order of goods and its relation to happiness
  Topic 10b: Natural limits to the acquisition of wealth
      by individuals: the distinction between necessities
      and luxuries

RELATED AUTHORS AND WORKS IN *Great Books of the Western World*

Plato, Vol. 7, *Republic,* Bks. III–IV, pages 341–343
Dante, Vol. 21, *Divine Comedy,* Hell, Canto VII, pages 9–10
Machiavelli, Vol. 23, *Prince,* Chaps. 16–19, pages 22–26
Montaigne, Vol. 25, *Of the Inequality Amongst Us,* pages 126–131
Boswell, Vol. 44, *Life of Samuel Johnson,* pages 491–494

RELATED AUTHORS AND WORKS IN *Gateway to the Great Books*

Bacon, *Of Riches,* Vol. 7, pages 25–27
Bunin, *Gentleman from San Francisco,* Vol. 3, pages 102–123
Dinesen, *Sorrow-Acre,* Vol. 3, pages 615–641
Hemingway, *Killers,* Vol. 2, pages 169–177
James, H., *Pupil,* Vol. 3, pages 530–568
Lawrence, *Rocking-Horse Winner,* Vol. 3, pages 512–525
Macaulay, *Machiavelli,* Vol. 7, pages 295–329
Mann, *Mario and the Magician,* Vol. 3, pages 573–610
O'Neill, *Emperor Jones,* Vol. 4, pages 357–382
Pater, "Art of Life," Vol. 10, pages 258–261
Pushkin, *Queen of Spades,* Vol. 3, pages 484–507
Shaw, *Man of Destiny,* Vol. 4, pages 300–338
Twain, *Man That Corrupted Hadleyburg,* Vol. 2, pages 346–386

GUSTAVE FLAUBERT, 1821–1880

The Legend of St. Julian the Hospitaller
Vol. 3, pages 371–392

SUGGESTED READINGS IN THE *Syntopicon*

FATE, Vol. 2, pages 515–525, especially
Topic 1: The decrees of fate and the decisions of the gods
Topic 2: The fated or inevitable in human life
LOVE, Vol. 2, pages 1051–1082, especially
Topic 5a(2): Beatitude as the fruition of love
Topic 5b(1): The precepts of charity: the law of love
Topic 5b(2): The theological virtue of charity: its relation
to the other virtues
SIN, Vol. 3, pages 753–773, especially
Topic 4e: The prevention and purging of sin: purification
by sacrifice; the sacrament of penance; contrition,
confession, and absolution
Topic 7: Grace and good works in relation to salvation from sin

RELATED AUTHORS AND WORKS IN *Great Books of the Western World*

Sophocles, Vol. 5, *Oedipus the King,* pages 99–113
Euripides, Vol. 5, *Orestes,* pages 394–410
Plutarch, Vol. 14, *Alexander,* pages 540–544
Augustine, Vol. 18, *Confessions,* Bk. IX, pages 61–71
Dante, Vol. 21, *Divine Comedy,* Paradise, Cantos XXVI–XXXIII,
pages 145–157

FLAUBERT, *The Legend of St. Julian*
continued

RELATED AUTHORS AND WORKS IN *Gateway to the Great Books*

Anonymous, *Aucassin and Nicolette*, Vol. 2, pages 523–551
Bacon, *Of Adversity*, Vol. 10, page 350; *Of Anger*, pages 359–360
Balzac, *Passion in the Desert*, Vol. 3, pages 436–447
De Quincey, *On the Knocking at the Gate in Macbeth*, Vol. 5, pages 362–366
Hemingway, *Killers*, Vol. 2, pages 169–177
Huxley, *On the Relations of Man to the Lower Animals*, Vol. 8, pages 160–204
Kipling, *Mowgli's Brothers*, Vol. 2, pages 126–141
Lincoln, *Meditation on the Divine Will*, Vol. 6, page 758
Long, *Power within Us*, Vol. 6, pages 246–261
O'Neill, *Emperor Jones*, Vol. 4, pages 357–382
Poe, *Tell-Tale Heart*, Vol. 2, pages 273–277; *Masque of the Red Death*, pages 278–283
Scott, *Two Drovers*, Vol. 2, pages 182–205
Shaw, *Man of Destiny*, Vol. 4, pages 300–338
Stevenson, *Strange Case of Dr. Jekyll and Mr. Hyde*, Vol. 2, pages 288–341
Tolstoy, *What Men Live By*, Vol. 3, pages 707–727

ANDREW RUSSELL FORSYTH, 1858–1942

Mathematics, in Life and Thought
Vol. 9, pages 26–46

SUGGESTED READINGS IN THE *Syntopicon*

ELEMENT, Vol. 2, pages 400–412, especially
Topic 5c: Atoms and the void as the ultimate constituents of reality
Topic 5g: The explanation of natural phenomena by reference to the properties and motions of atoms
HYPOTHESIS, Vol. 2, pages 749–760, especially
Topic 3: The foundations of mathematics: postulates, assumptions
Topic 4: The role of hypotheses in science
MATHEMATICS, Vol. 3, pages 42–62, especially
Topic 5: The applications of mathematics to physical phenomena: the utility of mathematics

MECHANICS, Vol. 3, pages 80–112, especially
  Topic 1a: Matter, mass, and atoms: the primary qualities
    of bodies
  Topic 3: The use of mathematics in mechanics: the dependence
    of progress in mechanics on mathematical discovery
PHYSICS, Vol. 3, pages 363–376, especially
  Topic 1b: The relation of the philosophy of nature
    to mathematics: mathematical method
    and mathematical principles in natural philosophy
  Topic 3: The role of mathematics in the natural sciences:
    observation and measurement in relation
    to mathematical formulations
  Topic 4: The experimental method in the study of nature
SCIENCE, Vol. 3, pages 682–705, especially
  Topic 5: Scientific method

RELATED AUTHORS AND WORKS IN *Great Books of the Western World*

Euclid, Vol. 11, *Elements*, Bk. I, pages 1–29
Nicomachus, Vol. 11, *Introduction to Arithmetic*, Bk. I, pages
  811–814
Lucretius, Vol. 12, *On the Nature of Things*, Bk. I, pages 4–8; Bk.
  VI, pages 80–97
Copernicus, Vol. 16, *On the Revolutions of the Heavenly Spheres*,
  pages 505–556
Kepler, Vol. 16, *Epitome of Copernican Astronomy*, Bk. IV,
  pages 845–864, 895–905, 918–940
Ptolemy, Vol. 16, *Almagest*, Bk. I, pages 5–20
Galileo, Vol. 28, *Dialogues Concerning the Two New Sciences*,
  Third Day, pages 197–237
Newton, Vol. 34, *Mathematical Principles of Natural Philosophy*,
  Bk. I, Sects. I–II, pages 25–35; Sects. XI–XIII, pages 130–152;
  Bk. II, Sect. IX, pages 259–267; Bk. III, pages 269–372
Faraday, Vol. 45, *Experimental Researches in Electricity*,
  pages 298–301, 850–855

RELATED AUTHORS AND WORKS IN *Gateway to the Great Books*

Bernard, *Experimental Considerations Common to Living Things
  and Inorganic Bodies*, Vol. 8, pages 266–290
Campbell, *Numerical Laws and the Use of Mathematics in Science*,
  Vol. 9, pages 222–238
Dantzig, *Fingerprints*, Vol. 9, pages 165–177
Dewey, "Process of Thought," Vol. 10, pages 92–213
Einstein and Infeld, "Rise and Decline of Classical Physics," Vol. 8,
  pages 490–560
Hogben, *Mathematics, the Mirror of Civilization*, Vol. 9, pages 3–23

FORSYTH, *Mathematics, in Life and Thought*
continued

Peirce, *Red and the Black*, Vol. 9, pages 342–348
Russell, *Study of Mathematics*, Vol. 9, pages 84–94; *Mathematics and the Metaphysicians*, pages 95–110
Whitehead, "On Mathematical Method," Vol. 9, pages 51–67

BENJAMIN FRANKLIN, 1706–1790

A Proposal for Promoting Useful Knowledge among the British Plantations in America
Vol. 6, pages 533–535

SUGGESTED READINGS IN THE *Syntopicon*

ART, Vol. 2, pages 64–86, especially
Topic 6c: Art as the application of science: the productive powers of knowledge

KNOWLEDGE, Vol. 2, pages 880–920, especially
Topic 8a: The technical use of knowledge in the sphere of production: the applications of science in art

PHYSICS, Vol. 3, pages 363–376, especially
Topic 5: The utility of physics: the invention of machines; the techniques of engineering; the mastery of nature

PROGRESS, Vol. 3, pages 437–453, especially
Topic 3c: Man's progressive conquest of the forces of nature through science and invention

SCIENCE, Vol. 3, pages 682–705, especially
Topic 1b(1): The utility of science: the applications of experimental knowledge in the mastery of nature; machinery and inventions
Topic 1b(2): The effects of science on human life: the economic and social implications of technology

STATE, Vol. 3, pages 826–865, especially
Topic 7b: The importance of the arts and sciences in political life

RELATED AUTHORS AND WORKS IN *Great Books of the Western World*

Plato, Vol. 7, *Republic*, Bk. VII, pages 391–397
Rabelais, Vol. 24, *Gargantua and Pantagruel*, Bk. I, pages 1–67

Bacon, Vol. 30, *Advancement of Learning*, Second Book, pages 29–32; *New Atlantis*, pages 210–214
Descartes, Vol. 31, *Discourse on Method*, Part VI, pages 60–67
Swift, Vol. 36, *Gulliver's Travels*, Part III, pages 91–131
Hegel, Vol. 46, *Philosophy of History*, Fourth Part, Sect. II, Chap. 3, pages 346–348

RELATED AUTHORS AND WORKS IN *Gateway to the Great Books*

Jefferson, "Biographical Sketches," Vol. 6, pages 522–528
Schopenhauer, *On Education*, Vol. 7, pages 197–203
Tocqueville, "Observations on American Life and Government," Vol. 6, pages 564–690

Proposals Relating to the Education of Youth in Pennsylvania
Vol. 6, pages 536–542

SUGGESTED READINGS IN THE *Syntopicon*

EDUCATION, Vol. 2, pages 376–399, especially

Topic 1: The ends of education
Topic 1a: The ideal of the educated man
Topic 2: The kinds of education: physical, moral, liberal, professional, religious
Topic 4d: The effect upon character of poetry, music, and other arts: the role of history and examples

FAMILY, Vol. 2, pages 486–514, especially

Topic 6e: The initiation of children into adult life

HISTORY, Vol. 2, pages 711–727, especially

Topic 2: The light and lesson of history: its role in the education of the mind and in the guidance of human conduct

RELATED AUTHORS AND WORKS IN *Great Books of the Western World*

Plato, Vol. 7, *Republic*, Bks. II–III, pages 320–339
Aristotle, Vol. 9, *Politics*, Bks. VII–VIII, pages 527–548
Rabelais, Vol. 24, *Gargantua and Pantagruel*, Bk. I, Chaps. 14–16, pages 18–20; Chaps. 23–24, pages 26–30; Bk. II, Chap. 8, pages 81–83
Montaigne, Vol. 25, *Of the Education of Children*, pages 62–80
Bacon, Vol. 30, *Advancement of Learning*, First Book, pages 17–28
Descartes, Vol. 31, *Discourse on Method*, Part I, pages 41–44

RELATED AUTHORS AND WORKS IN *Gateway to the Great Books*

Adams, "United States in 1800," Vol. 6, pages 322–359
Bacon, *Of Studies*, Vol. 5, pages 97–98

FRANKLIN, *Proposals*
continued

Faraday, *Observations on Mental Education*, Vol. 7, pages 208–232
Jefferson, "Biographical Sketches," Vol. 6, pages 522–528
Mill, J. S., "Childhood and Youth," Vol. 6, pages 5–47
Schopenhauer, *On Education*, Vol. 7, pages 197–203
Swift, *Essay on Modern Education*, Vol. 7, pages 33–39
Tocqueville, "Observations on American Life and Government,"
Vol. 6, pages 564–690

GALILEO GALILEI, 1564–1642

The Starry Messenger
Vol. 8, pages 330–355

SUGGESTED READINGS IN THE *Syntopicon*

ASTRONOMY, Vol. 2, pages 87–111, especially

Topic 2: The method of astronomy
Topic 5: Astronomy and cosmology: the theory of the world
or universe as reflecting astronomical conceptions
Topic 6: Astronomy and theology: astronomy as affecting
views of God, creation, the divine plan, and the moral
hierarchy
Topic 8c: Celestial motion: periodicity and the great year
Topic 9: The particular heavenly bodies
Topic 13: The history of astronomy

MECHANICS, Vol. 3, pages 80–112, especially

Topic 4a: Terrestrial and celestial mechanics: the mechanics
of finite bodies and of particles or atoms
Topic 7a(1): The laws of reflection and refraction
Topic 7a(4): The medium of light: the ether

SCIENCE, Vol. 3, pages 682–705, especially

Topic 1b: Science as the discipline of experimental inquiry
and the organization of experimental knowledge:
the scientific spirit

WORLD, Vol. 3, pages 1118–1140, especially

Topic 1b: The universe as a machine: the system of its moving
parts

RELATED AUTHORS AND WORKS IN *Great Books of the Western World*

Aristotle, Vol. 8, *On the Heavens*, pages 359–405
Ptolemy, Vol. 16, *Almagest*, Bk. I, pages 7–12; Bk. III, pages 86–93

Copernicus, Vol. 16, *On the Revolutions of the Heavenly Spheres,*
Introduction-Bk. I, pages 505–545
Kepler, Vol. 16, *Epitome of Copernican Astronomy,* Bk. IV, Part II,
pages 888–893; Part III, pages 929–933; Bk. V, Part I,
pages 968–979

RELATED AUTHORS AND WORKS IN *Gateway to the Great Books*

Boeke, *Cosmic View,* Vol. 8, pages 600–644
Campanella, "Arguments for and against Galileo," Vol. 8,
pages 359–364
Einstein and Infeld, "Rise and Decline of Classical Physics," Vol. 8,
pages 490–560
Voltaire, *Micromégas,* Vol. 2, pages 241–256

For Galileo's *Dialogues Concerning the Two New Sciences* in *Great
Books of the Western World,* see Vol. 28, pages 129–260

JOHN GALSWORTHY, 1867–1933

The Apple-Tree
Vol. 3, pages 323–367

SUGGESTED READINGS IN THE *Syntopicon*

DESIRE, Vol. 2, pages 323–344, especially
Topic 3c: Desire and love: their distinction and connection
Topic 4a: The conflict of desires with one another
EMOTION, Vol. 2, pages 413–436, especially
Topic 4a: The conflict between reason and emotion
LOVE, Vol. 2, pages 1051–1082, especially
Topic 1c: The distinction between love and desire:
the generous and acquisitive aims
Topic 1e: The intensity and power of love: its increase
or decrease; its constructive or destructive force
Topic 3b: The demands of love and the restraints of virtue:
moderation in love; the order of loves
MEMORY AND IMAGINATION, Vol. 3, pages 133–157, especially
Topic 2c: The association of ideas: controlled and free
association; reminiscence and reverie

RELATED AUTHORS AND WORKS IN *Great Books of the Western World*

Plato, Vol. 7, *Phaedrus,* pages 120–129
Dante, Vol. 21, *Divine Comedy,* Hell, Canto V, pages 7–8
Rabelais, Vol. 24, *Gargantua and Pantagruel,* Bk. III, Chap. 31,
pages 188–191

GALSWORTHY, *The Apple-Tree*
continued

Montaigne, Vol. 25, *Of Three Commerces*, pages 398–399
Shakespeare, Vol. 26, *As You Like It*, pages 597–626; Vol. 27,
   Troilus and Cressida, Act II, Scene II, pages 113–115
James, W., Vol. 53, *Principles of Psychology*, Chap. X, pages
   204–209

RELATED AUTHORS AND WORKS IN *Gateway to the Great Books*

Anderson, *I'm a Fool*, Vol. 2, pages 511–520
Anonymous, *Aucassin and Nicolette*, Vol. 2, pages 523–551
Apuleius, "Cupid and Psyche," Vol. 3, pages 197–212
Bacon, *Of Youth and Age*, Vol. 7, pages 3–4; *Of Marriage
   and Single Life*, pages 7–8; *Of Love*, Vol. 10, pages 351–352
Balzac, *Passion in the Desert*, Vol. 3, pages 436–447
Bunin, *Gentleman from San Francisco*, Vol. 3, pages 102–123
Chekhov, *Darling*, Vol. 3, pages 452–462
Dostoevsky, *White Nights*, Vol. 3, pages 276–319
Hawthorne, *Rappaccini's Daughter*, Vol. 3, pages 128–152
Hazlitt, *On the Feeling of Immortality in Youth*, Vol. 10,
   pages 565–570

FRANCIS GALTON, 1822–1911

"The Classification of Human Ability"
from *Hereditary Genius*
Vol. 8, pages 227–261

SUGGESTED READINGS IN THE *Syntopicon*

ANIMAL, Vol. 2, pages 19–49, especially
   Topic 10: Heredity and environment: the genetic determination
      of individual differences and similarities
EVOLUTION, Vol. 2, pages 451–467, especially
   Topic 2: Genetic variation in the course of generations
FAMILY, Vol. 2, pages 486–514, especially
   Topic 6b: Eugenics: control of breeding; birth control
MAN, Vol. 3, pages 1–41, especially
   Topic 2b: The sciences of human nature: anthropology
      and psychology; rational and empirical psychology;
      experimental and clinical psychology
   Topic 6: Individual differences among men

RELATED AUTHORS AND WORKS IN *Great Books of the Western World*

Plato, Vol. 7, *Republic*, Bk. V, pages 361–363

Hume, Vol. 35, *Enquiry Concerning Human Understanding,*
Sect. I, pages 451–455

Darwin, Vol. 49, *Descent of Man,* Chap. II, pages 275–277; Chap.
V, pages 323–328; Chap. VIII, pages 391–394

James, W., Vol. 53, *Principles of Psychology,* Chap. VII, pages
120–129; Chap. XXVIII, pages 853–858, 890–897

RELATED AUTHORS AND WORKS IN *Gateway to the Great Books*

Curie, *Discovery of Radium,* Vol. 8, pages 32–42

Darwin, *Autobiography,* Vol. 8, pages 47–93

Huxley, *On the Relations of Man to the Lower Animals,* Vol. 8,
pages 160–204

James, W., *Energies of Men,* Vol. 7, pages 157–170; *Great Men
and Their Environment,* pages 171–194

Laplace, "Probability," Vol. 9, pages 325–338

Mill, J. S., "Childhood and Youth," Vol. 6, pages 5–47

Poincaré, *Mathematical Creation,* Vol. 9, pages 294–304

Tyndall, "Michael Faraday," Vol. 8, pages 8–28

NIKOLAI GOGOL, 1809–1852

The Overcoat
Vol. 2, pages 452–478

SUGGESTED READINGS IN THE *Syntopicon*

HAPPINESS, Vol. 2, pages 684–710, especially

Topic 2*b*(1): The contribution of the goods of fortune
to happiness: wealth, health, longevity

Topic 4*a*: Man's capacity for happiness: differences in human
nature with respect to happiness

STATE, Vol. 3, pages 826–865, especially

Topic 5*c*: The classes or sub-groups arising from the division
of labor or distinctions of birth: the social hierarchy

WEALTH, Vol. 3, pages 1038–1070, especially

Topic 8*c*: The causes of poverty: competition, incompetence,
indigence, expropriation, unemployment; the poverty
of the proletariat as dispossessed of the instruments
of production

WISDOM, Vol. 3, pages 1102–1117, especially

Topic 4: The praise of folly: the wisdom of fools and innocents

GOGOL, *The Overcoat*
continued

RELATED AUTHORS AND WORKS IN *Great Books of the Western World*

Cervantes, Vol. 29, *Don Quixote*, Second Part, Chap. 43, pages 334–336

Rousseau, Vol. 38, *Discourse on Political Economy*, pages 381–382

Boswell, Vol. 44, *Life of Samuel Johnson*, pages 144–145

Tolstoy, Vol. 51, *War and Peace*, Second Epilogue, pages 685–686

RELATED AUTHORS AND WORKS IN *Gateway to the Great Books*

Bacon, *Of Adversity*, Vol. 10, page 350

Plutarch, *Contentment*, Vol. 10, pages 264–281

Singer, *Spinoza of Market Street*, Vol. 3, pages 466–480

Swift, *Modest Proposal*, Vol. 7, pages 42–49

Synge, *Riders to the Sea*, Vol. 4, pages 342–352

Tolstoy, *Death of Ivan Ilyitch*, Vol. 3, pages 646–699

Wilde, *Happy Prince*, Vol. 2, pages 261–268

GREAT DOCUMENTS

The English Bill of Rights
Declaration of the Rights of Man and of the Citizen
The Virginia Declaration of Rights
The Declaration of Independence
Charter of the United Nations
Universal Declaration of Human Rights
Vol. 6, pages 409–456

SUGGESTED READINGS IN THE *Syntopicon*

CITIZEN, Vol. 2, pages 218–232, especially

Topic 4: The rights, duties, privileges, and immunities of citizenship

CONSTITUTION, Vol. 2, pages 233–251, especially

Topic 7b: The safeguards of constitutional government: bills of rights; separation of powers; impeachment

JUSTICE, Vol. 2, pages 850–879, especially

Topic 6: Justice and liberty: the theory of human rights

Topic 6b: The relation between natural and positive rights, innate and acquired rights, private and public rights: their correlative duties

Topic 6c: The inalienability of natural rights: their violation by tyranny and despotism

Topic 6e: Justice and natural rights as the source of civil liberty

LAW, Vol. 2, pages 962–990, especially

Topic 4e: The relation of natural law to natural rights and natural justice

Topic 7c: The priority of natural to civil law: the inviolability or inalienability of natural rights

LIBERTY, Vol. 2, pages 991–1012, especially

Topic 1g: The juridical protection of liberties: bills of rights; the separation of powers

RELATED AUTHORS AND WORKS IN *Great Books of the Western World*

Sophocles, Vol. 5, *Antigone*, pages 134–135

Aquinas, Vol. 20, *Summa Theologica*, Part I–II, Q 95, Art. 2, pages 227–228; Q 100, Art. 1, pages 251–252

Hobbes, Vol. 23, *Leviathan*, Part II, Chap. XXI, pages 112–117

Milton, Vol. 32, *Areopagitica*, pages 381–412

Locke, Vol. 35, *Concerning Civil Government*, Chap. II, pages 25–28

Montesquieu, Vol. 38, *Spirit of Laws*, Bk. I, Chaps. 1–3, pages 1–3

Rousseau, Vol. 38, *Social Contract*, Bk. II, Chaps. 4–5, pages 396–399

Kant, Vol. 42, *Science of Right*, First Part, page 434; Second Part, pages 435–436, 456–457

Articles of Confederation, Vol. 43, pages 5–9

Constitution of the United States of America, Vol. 43, pages 11–20

Hamilton, Madison, Jay, Vol. 43, *Federalist*, No. 84, pages 251–253

Mill, J. S., Vol. 43, *On Liberty*, pages 267–323; *Utilitarianism*, Chap. 5, pages 472–476

RELATED AUTHORS AND WORKS IN *Gateway to the Great Books*

Adams, "United States in 1800," Vol. 6, pages 322–359

Burke, *Letter to the Sheriffs of Bristol*, Vol. 7, pages 237–271

Butler, "Customs and Opinions of the Erewhonians," Vol. 2, pages 483–506

Clausewitz, *What Is War?*, Vol. 7, pages 479–497

Crèvecoeur, "Making of Americans," Vol. 6, pages 546–559

Dante, "On World Government," Vol. 7, pages 383–399

Emerson, *Thoreau*, Vol. 6, pages 150–165

Jefferson, "Virginia Constitution," Vol. 6, pages 502–517; *First Inaugural Address*, pages 518–521

Lincoln, *Address at Cooper Institute*, Vol. 6, pages 737–746; *First Inaugural Address*, pages 747–755; *Letter to Horace Greeley*, pages 756–757; *Gettysburg Address*, page 759

Paine, "Call to Patriots—December 23, 1776," Vol. 6, pages 461–468

GREAT DOCUMENTS
continued

Thoreau, *Civil Disobedience*, Vol. 6, pages 695–713
Tocqueville, "Observations on American Life and Government,"
Vol. 6, pages 564–690
Tolstoy, *What Men Live By*, Vol. 3, pages 707–727
Voltaire, "English Men and Ideas," Vol. 7, pages 332–378
Whitman, *Death of Abraham Lincoln*, Vol. 6, pages 174–183

FRANÇOIS GUIZOT, 1787–1874

"Civilization"
from *History of Civilization in Europe*
Vol. 6, pages 302–317

SUGGESTED READINGS IN THE *Syntopicon*

ART, Vol. 2, pages 64–86, especially
    Topic 12: The history of the arts: progress in art as measuring
    stages of civilization
HISTORY, Vol. 2, pages 711–727, especially
    Topic 4c: The spirit of the time as conditioning the politics
    and culture of a period
LIBERTY, Vol. 2, pages 991–1012, especially
    Topic 6a: The historical significance of freedom: stages
    in the realization of freedom; the beginning and end
    of the historical process
PROGRESS, Vol. 3, pages 437–453, especially
    Topic 6: Intellectual or cultural progress: its sources
    and impediments

RELATED AUTHORS AND WORKS IN *Great Books of the Western World*

Hobbes, Vol. 23, *Leviathan*, Introduction, page 47; Part II,
    pages 99–164
Bacon, Vol. 30, *Advancement of Learning*, First Book, pages 1–28
Rousseau, Vol. 38, *Discourse on the Origin of Inequality*, First Part,
    pages 334–348
Gibbon, Vol. 40, *Decline and Fall of the Roman Empire*, Chap. XL,
    pages 668–671; Vol. 41, Chap. LXXI, pages 590–598
Mill, J. S., Vol. 43, *On Liberty*, Chaps. 2–3, pages 274–302

Hegel, Vol. 46, *Philosophy of History*, Introduction III,
pages 156–190
Darwin, Vol. 49, *Descent of Man*, Chap. V, pages 320–330
Freud, Vol. 54, *Civilization and Its Discontents*, Chap. III,
pages 776–781

RELATED AUTHORS AND WORKS IN *Gateway to the Great Books*

Adams, "United States in 1800," Vol. 6, pages 322–359
Arnold, *Sweetness and Light*, Vol. 5, pages 42–61
Bacon, *Sphinx*, Vol. 8, pages 2–4
Eliot, T. S., *Tradition and the Individual Talent*, Vol. 5,
pages 404–411
Hume, *Of the Standard of Taste*, Vol. 5, pages 103–119;
Of Refinement in the Arts, Vol. 7, pages 52–61; *Of the Study
of History*, pages 89–92
Jefferson, *First Inaugural Address*, Vol. 6, pages 518–521
Lucian, *Way to Write History*, Vol. 6, pages 387–406
Macaulay, *Machiavelli*, Vol. 7, pages 295–329

J. B. S. HALDANE, 1892–1964

On Being the Right Size
Vol. 8, pages 149–154

SUGGESTED READINGS IN THE *Syntopicon*

ANIMAL, Vol. 2, pages 19–49, especially
Topic 2b: Analogies of structure and function among different
classes of animals
Topic 3: The anatomy of animals
CHANGE, Vol. 2, pages 193–217, especially
Topic 8: Change of size
DEMOCRACY, Vol. 2, pages 303–322, especially
Topic 5a: The distinction between direct democracy
and representative, or republican, government:
the territorial limits of democracy
QUANTITY, Vol. 3, pages 527–545, especially
Topic 5d: Mass: its relation to weight

RELATED AUTHORS AND WORKS IN *Great Books of the Western World*

Aristotle, Vol. 9, *History of Animals*, Bk. I, Chaps. 1–15,
pages 7–16; *On the Parts of Animals*, Bks. II–IV, pages 170–229

HALDANE, *On Being the Right Size*
continued

Galileo, Vol. 28, *Dialogues Concerning the Two New Sciences,*
Third Day, pages 197–237
Swift, Vol. 36, *Gulliver's Travels,* Parts I–II, pages 3–87
Darwin, Vol. 49, *Origin of Species,* Chap. VI, pages 85–91

RELATED AUTHORS AND WORKS IN *Gateway to the Great Books*

Boeke, *Cosmic View,* Vol. 8, pages 600–644
Campbell, *Numerical Laws and the Use of Mathematics in Science,*
Vol. 9, pages 222–238
Carson, *Sunless Sea,* Vol. 8, pages 132–146
Fabre, *Laboratory of the Open Fields,* Vol. 8, pages 97–104;
Sacred Beetle, pages 105–119

NATHANIEL HAWTHORNE, 1804–1864

Rappaccini's Daughter
Vol. 3, pages 128–152

SUGGESTED READINGS IN THE *Syntopicon*

BEAUTY, Vol. 2, pages 112–125, especially
Topic 3: Beauty in relation to desire and love, as object or cause
EMOTION, Vol. 2, pages 413–436, especially
Topic 3*a*: Madness or frenzy due to emotional excess:
excessively emotional or emotionally over-determined
behavior
FAMILY, Vol. 2, pages 486–514, especially
Topic 6*d*: The care and government of children: the rights
and duties of the child; parental despotism
and tyranny
GOOD AND EVIL, Vol. 2, pages 605–636, especially
Topic 3*f*: The sources of evil in human life
LIFE AND DEATH, Vol. 2, pages 1013–1034, especially
Topic 7: The causes and occurrence of death: the transition
from life to death
MAN, Vol. 3, pages 1–41, especially
Topic 5*b*: Abnormalities due to defect or conflict of powers:
feeble-mindedness, neuroses, insanity, madness

RELATED AUTHORS AND WORKS IN *Great Books of the Western World*

Euripides, Vol. 5, *Electra*, pages 327–339
Shakespeare, Vol. 27, *King Lear*, Act I, pages 244–254
Goethe, Vol. 47, *Faust*, Second Part, Act I, pages 156–160

RELATED AUTHORS AND WORKS IN *Gateway to the Great Books*

Anonymous, *Aucassin and Nicolette*, Vol. 2, pages 523–551
Apuleius, "Cupid and Psyche," Vol. 3, pages 197–212
Bacon, *Of Parents and Children*, Vol. 7, pages 5–6; *Of Love*, Vol. 10, pages 351–352
Balzac, *Passion in the Desert*, Vol. 3, pages 436–447
Eliot, G., *Lifted Veil*, Vol. 3, pages 157–193
Galsworthy, Apple-Tree, Vol. 3, pages 323–367
Lawrence, *Rocking-Horse Winner*, Vol. 3, pages 515–525
Mann, *Mario and the Magician*, Vol. 3, pages 573–610
Poe, *Tell-Tale Heart*, Vol. 2, pages 273–277; *Masque of the Red Death*, pages 278–283
Stevenson, *Strange Case of Dr. Jekyll and Mr. Hyde*, Vol. 2, pages 288–341
Turgenev, *First Love*, Vol. 3, pages 217–271

Sketch of Abraham Lincoln
Vol. 6, pages 168–171

SUGGESTED READINGS IN THE *Syntopicon*

ARISTOCRACY, Vol. 2, pages 50–63, especially
Topic 6: The selection of the best men for public office:
the aristocratic theory of representation in modern
constitutional government

HISTORY, Vol. 2, pages 711–727, especially
Topic 4a(4): The role of the individual in history: the great
man, hero, or leader

HONOR, Vol. 2, pages 728–748, especially
Topic 3a: The reaction of the community to its good
or great men

STATE, Vol. 3, pages 826–865, especially
Topic 8d: Statecraft: the art or science of governing; political
prudence
Topic 8d(2): The occasions and uses of rhetoric

RELATED AUTHORS AND WORKS IN *Great Books of the Western World*

Aristotle, Vol. 9, *Politics*, Bk. III, Chaps. 10–13, pages 478–483
Plutarch, Vol. 14, *Pericles*, pages 121–141

HAWTHORNE, *Sketch of Abraham Lincoln*
continued

Shakespeare, Vol. 26, *King Henry IV*, First Part, pages 434–466;
King Henry IV, Second Part, pages 467–502
Locke, Vol. 35, *Concerning Civil Government*, Chap. VIII,
pages 48–51
Hamilton, Madison, Jay, Vol. 43, *Federalist*, No. 68, page 206
Hegel, Vol. 46, *Philosophy of History*, Introduction III,
pages 162–170
Tolstoy, Vol. 51, *War and Peace*, First Epilogue, Chaps. I–IV,
pages 645–650; Second Epilogue, pages 675–696

RELATED AUTHORS AND WORKS IN *Gateway to the Great Books*

Adams, "United States in 1800," Vol. 6, pages 322–359, especially
Chap. VI, pages 343–359
Bacon, *Of Great Place*, Vol. 7, pages 9–11
Carlyle, *Hero as King*, Vol. 6, pages 110–145
Crèvecoeur, "Making of Americans," Vol. 6, pages 546–559
James, W., *Great Men and Their Environment*, Vol. 7, pages 171–194
Jefferson, "Biographical Sketches," Vol. 6, pages 522–528
Lincoln, *Address at Cooper Institute*, Vol. 6, pages 737–746; *First
Inaugural Address*, pages 747–755; *Letter to Horace Greeley*,
pages 756–757; *Meditation on the Divine Will*, page 758;
Gettysburg Address, page 759; *Second Inaugural Address*,
pages 760–761; *Last Public Address*, pages 762–765
Thoreau, *Plea for Captain John Brown*, Vol. 6, pages 714–732
Tocqueville, "Observations on American Life and Government,"
Vol. 6, pages 564–690
Whitman, *Death of Abraham Lincoln*, Vol. 6, pages 174–183
Woolf, *Art of Biography*, Vol. 6, pages 186–192
Xenophon, "Character of Socrates," Vol. 6, pages 223–226

WILLIAM HAZLITT, 1778–1830

My First Acquaintance with Poets
Vol. 5, pages 264–279

SUGGESTED READINGS IN THE *Syntopicon*

MEMORY AND IMAGINATION, Vol. 3, pages 133–157, especially
Topic 3*d*: Memory as the muse of poetry and history:
the dependence of history on the memory of men

POETRY, Vol. 3, pages 400–419, especially
Topic 5b: Poetry contrasted with history and philosophy: the dispraise and defense of the poet
Topic 8b: Critical standards and artistic rules with respect to the language of poetry: the distinction between prose and verse; the measure of excellence in style

RELATED AUTHORS AND WORKS IN *Great Books of the Western World*

Plato, Vol. 7, *Republic*, Bks. II–III, pages 320–333
Bacon, Vol. 30, *Advancement of Learning*, Second Book, pages 32–34
Pascal, Vol. 33, *Pensées*, Sect. I, pages 173–174, 177–178
James, W., Vol. 53, *Principles of Psychology*, Chap. XXII, pages 686–689

RELATED AUTHORS AND WORKS IN *Gateway to the Great Books*

Arnold, *Study of Poetry*, Vol. 5, pages 19–41
Eliot, T. S., *Tradition and the Individual Talent*, Vol. 5, pages 404–411
Lamb, *Sanity of True Genius*, Vol. 5, pages 308–310
Schiller, *On Simple and Sentimental Poetry*, Vol. 5, pages 155–211
Schopenhauer, *On Some Forms of Literature*, Vol. 5, pages 137–142
Woolf, *How Should One Read a Book?*, Vol. 5, pages 5–14

On Swift
Vol. 5, pages 280–283

SUGGESTED READINGS IN THE *Syntopicon*

POETRY, Vol. 3, pages 400–419, especially
Topic 8b: Critical standards and artistic rules with respect to the language of poetry: the distinction between prose and verse; the measure of excellence in style
TRUTH, Vol. 3, pages 915–938, especially
Topic 4b: Truth in science and poetry: the truth of fact and the truth of fiction

RELATED AUTHORS AND WORKS IN *Great Books of the Western World*

Plato, Vol. 7, *Republic*, Bks. II–III, pages 320–324, 328–333
Montaigne, Vol. 25, *Of Books*, pages 199–200
Cervantes, Vol. 29, *Don Quixote*, First Part, Chaps. 47–50, pages 183–193

RELATED AUTHORS AND WORKS IN *Gateway to the Great Books*

Schopenhauer, *On Style*, Vol. 5, pages 124–136

HAZLITT, *On Swift*
continued

Swift, *Resolutions when I Come to Be Old*, Vol. 7, page 32; *Essay on Modern Education*, pages 33–39; *Meditation upon a Broomstick*, pages 40–41; *Modest Proposal*, pages 42–49

For Swift's *Gulliver's Travels* in *Great Books of the Western World*, see Vol. 36, pages ix–184

Of Persons One Would Wish to Have Seen
Vol. 5, pages 284–295

SUGGESTED READINGS IN THE *Syntopicon*

ART, Vol. 2, pages 64–86, especially
Topic 7a: Art as a source of pleasure or delight

BEAUTY, Vol. 2, pages 112–125, especially
Topic 5: Judgments of beauty: the objective and the subjective in aesthetic judgments or judgments of taste

POETRY, Vol. 3, pages 400–419, especially
Topic 3: The inspiration or genius of the poet: the influence of the poetic tradition

RELATED AUTHORS AND WORKS IN *Great Books of the Western World*

Homer, Vol. 4, *Odyssey*, Bk. XI, pages 243–249
Plato, Vol. 7, *Ion*, pages 142–148; *Republic*, Bk. X, pages 427–441
Virgil, Vol. 13, *Aeneid*, Bk. VI, pages 211–235
Montaigne, Vol. 25, *Of Books*, pages 195–197
Kant, Vol. 42, *Critique of Judgement*, First Part, Sect. I, Bk. I, pages 476–483
James, W., Vol. 53, *Principles of Psychology*, Chap. XXV, pages 755–758

RELATED AUTHORS AND WORKS IN *Gateway to the Great Books*

Arnold, *Study of Poetry*, Vol. 5, pages 19–41
Eliot, T. S., *Tradition and the Individual Talent*, Vol. 5, pages 404–411
Hume, *Of the Standard of Taste*, Vol. 5, pages 103–119
Lamb, *Dream Children*, Vol. 5, pages 304–307
Sainte-Beuve, *What Is a Classic?*, Vol. 5, pages 65–75; *Montaigne*, pages 76–89
Schiller, *On Simple and Sentimental Poetry*, Vol. 5, pages 155–211
Xenophon, "Character of Socrates," Vol. 6, pages 223–226

On the Feeling of Immortality in Youth
Vol. 10, pages 565–570

SUGGESTED READINGS IN THE *Syntopicon*

IMMORTALITY, Vol. 2, pages 784–804, especially
Topic 1: The desire for immortality: the fear of death
LIFE AND DEATH, Vol. 2, pages 1013–1034, especially
Topic 8a: The love of life: the instinct of self-preservation;
the life instinct

RELATED AUTHORS AND WORKS IN *Great Books of the Western World*

Plato, Vol. 7, *Symposium*, pages 165–167; *Phaedo*, pages 230–235
Lucretius, Vol. 12, *On the Nature of Things*, Bk. III, pages 30–44,
passim
Aquinas, Vol. 19, *Summa Theologica*, First Part, Q 75, Art. 6,
pages 383–384
Montaigne, Vol. 25, *That to Study Philosophy Is to Learn to Die*,
pages 33–36
James, W., Vol. 53, *Principles of Psychology*, Chap. XI, page 270;
Chap. XV, pages 409–411

RELATED AUTHORS AND WORKS IN *Gateway to the Great Books*

Anonymous, *Aucassin and Nicolette*, Vol. 2, pages 523–551
Bacon, *Of Youth and Age*, Vol. 7, pages 3–4; *Of Death*, Vol. 10,
pages 348–349
Browne, "Immortality," Vol. 10, pages 575–580
Cicero, *On Old Age*, Vol. 10, pages 317–343
Conrad, *Youth*, Vol. 2, pages 210–236
Dinesen, *Sorrow-Acre*, Vol. 3, pages 615–641
Galsworthy, *Apple-Tree*, Vol. 3, pages 323–367
Long, *Power within Us*, Vol. 6, pages 246–261
Pater, "Art of Life," Vol. 10, pages 258–261

H. L. F. VON HELMHOLTZ, 1821–1894

On the Conservation of Force
Vol. 8, pages 451–484

SUGGESTED READINGS IN THE *Syntopicon*

MECHANICS, Vol. 3, pages 80–112

HELMHOLTZ, *On the Conservation of Force*
continued

PHYSICS, Vol. 3, pages 363–376

QUANTITY, Vol. 3, pages 527–545, especially
Topic 5: Physical quantities

REASONING, Vol. 3, pages 546–568, especially
Topic 5*b*: Scientific reasoning: the theory of demonstration
Topic 6*c*: Inductive and deductive inference in the philosophy
of nature and the natural sciences

SCIENCE, Vol. 3, pages 682–705, especially
Topic 1*b*(2): The effects of science on human life:
the economic and social implications
of technology
Topic 3: The relation of science to action and production

RELATED AUTHORS AND WORKS IN *Great Books of the Western World*

Lucretius, Vol. 12, *On the Nature of Things,* Bk. II, pages 15–22
Galileo, Vol. 28, *Dialogues Concerning the Two New Sciences,*
pages 129–260
Newton, Vol. 34, *Mathematical Principles of Natural Philosophy,*
pages 1–372
Fourier, Vol. 45, *Analytical Theory of Heat,* pages 169–251
Faraday, Vol. 45, *Experimental Researches in Electricity,*
pages 273–302, 603–607, 670–673, 758–778, 795–848
James, W., Vol. 53, *Principles of Psychology,* Chap. XXVIII,
pages 878–884

RELATED AUTHORS AND WORKS IN *Gateway to the Great Books*

Campbell, *Numerical Laws and the Use of Mathematics in Science,*
Vol. 9, pages 222–238
Eddington, *Running-Down of the Universe,* Vol. 8, pages 565–580
Einstein and Infeld, "Rise and Decline of Classical Physics," Vol. 8,
pages 490–560
Faraday, *Chemical History of a Candle,* Vol. 8, pages 368–439
Santayana, *Lucretius,* Vol. 10, pages 365–390
Tyndall, "Michael Faraday," Vol. 8, pages 8–28

ERNEST HEMINGWAY, 1899–1961

The Killers
Vol. 2, pages 169–177

SUGGESTED READINGS IN THE *Syntopicon*

JUSTICE, Vol. 2, pages 850–879, especially
Topic 10c: The justice of punishment for unjust acts:
the distinction between retribution and vengeance
LAW, Vol. 2, pages 962–990, especially
Topic 6e(1): The nature and causes of crime
Topic 6e(3): The punishment of crime
LIFE AND DEATH, Vol. 2, pages 1013–1034, especially
Topic 8c: The contemplation and fear of death: the attitude
of the hero, the philosopher, the martyr
PUNISHMENT, Vol. 3, pages 488–512, especially
Topic 1b: The retributive purpose of punishment:
the *lex talionis;* retaliation and revenge; the righting
of a wrong

RELATED AUTHORS AND WORKS IN *Great Books of the Western World*

Aeschylus, Vol. 5, *Eumenides,* pages 81–91
Sophocles, Vol. 5, *Electra,* pages 156–169
Euripides, Vol. 5, *Orestes,* pages 398–400
Plato, Vol. 7, *Apology,* pages 200–212
Shakespeare, Vol. 26, *King Richard III,* pages 105–148; Vol. 27,
Measure for Measure, pages 174–204; *Macbeth,* pages 284–310
Milton, Vol. 32, *Paradise Lost,* Bk. III, pages 135–151
Hegel, Vol. 46, *Philosophy of Right,* First Part, pages 37–39
Melville, Vol. 48, *Moby Dick,* Chap. 36, pages 118–122

RELATED AUTHORS AND WORKS IN *Gateway to the Great Books*

Bacon, *Of Death,* Vol. 10, pages 348–349
De Quincey, *On the Knocking at the Gate in Macbeth,* Vol. 5,
pages 362–366
Dinesen, *Sorrow-Acre,* Vol. 3, pages 615–641
Fitzgerald, *Diamond as Big as the Ritz,* Vol. 3, pages 397–431
Flaubert, *Legend of St. Julian the Hospitaller,* Vol. 3,
pages 371–392
Hugo, "Battle with the Cannon," Vol. 2, pages 146–154
O'Neill, *Emperor Jones,* Vol. 4, pages 357–382
Poe, *Tell-Tale Heart,* Vol. 2, pages 273–277; *Masque of the Red
Death,* pages 278–283

HEMINGWAY, *The Killers*
continued

Scott, *Two Drovers*, Vol. 2, pages 182–205
Tolstoy, *Death of Ivan Ilyitch*, Vol. 3, pages 646–699
Twain, *Man That Corrupted Hadleyburg*, Vol. 2, pages 346–386

LANCELOT HOGBEN, 1895–

Mathematics, the Mirror of Civilization
Vol. 9, pages 3–23

SUGGESTED READINGS IN THE *Syntopicon*

INFINITY, Vol. 2, pages 816–834, especially
Topic 3*a*: Number: the infinite of division and addition
Topic 3*b*: The infinite divisibility of continuous quantities: the infinitesimal; the method of exhaustion and the theory of limits
Topic 4*b*: The infinite divisibility of matter: the issue concerning atoms

MATHEMATICS, Vol. 3, pages 42–62, especially
Topic 5: The applications of mathematics to physical phenomena: the utility of mathematics

QUANTITY, Vol. 3, pages 527–545, especially
Topic 6: The measurements of quantities: the relation of magnitudes and multitudes; the units of measurement
Topic 7: Infinite quantity: the actual infinite and the potentially infinite quantity; the mathematical and physical infinite of the great and the small

RELATED AUTHORS AND WORKS IN *Great Books of the Western World*

Plato, Vol. 7, *Parmenides*, pages 486–511; *Timaeus*, pages 442–477
Descartes, Vol. 31, *Geometry*, Bk. II, pages 322–331
Newton, Vol. 34, *Mathematical Principles of Natural Philosophy*, Bk. III, pages 270–372
Kant, Vol. 42, *Critique of Pure Reason*, Introduction, pages 15–20; pages 29–33; pages 211–218
James, W., Vol. 53, *Principles of Psychology*, Chap. XXVIII, pages 874–882

RELATED AUTHORS AND WORKS IN *Gateway to the Great Books*
Dantzig, *Fingerprints,* Vol. 9, pages 165–177; *Empty Column,*
pages 178–189
Forsyth, *Mathematics, in Life and Thought,* Vol. 9, pages 26–46
Kasner and Newman, *New Names for Old,* Vol. 9, pages 121–136;
Beyond the Googol, pages 137–162
Poincaré, *Mathematical Creation,* Vol. 9, pages 294–304
Russell, *Study of Mathematics,* Vol. 9, pages 84–94; *Mathematics
and the Metaphysicians,* pages 95–110
Whitehead, "On Mathematical Method," Vol. 9, pages 51–67

VICTOR HUGO, 1802–1885

"The Battle with the Cannon"
from *Ninety-Three*
Vol. 2, pages 146–154

SUGGESTED READINGS IN THE *Syntopicon*

CITIZEN, Vol. 2, pages 218–232, especially
Topic 1: The individual in relation to the state
Topic 2b: The distinction between citizen and subject:
the distinction between the subjects
of a constitutional monarchy and of a despotism
JUSTICE, Vol. 2, pages 850–879, especially
Topic 1c: Justice as a moral virtue directing activity in relation
to others and to the community: the distinction
between the just man and the just act
Topic 10d: The correction of legal justice: equity
in the application of human law
PUNISHMENT, Vol. 3, pages 488–512, especially
Topic 2: Personal responsibility as a condition of just
punishment: the problem of collective responsibility
Topic 4b: The forms of punishment available to the state
Topic 4b(1): The death penalty: its justification
REVOLUTION, Vol. 3, pages 626–644, especially
Topic 1c: Revolution and counter-revolution: civil strife
distinguished from war between states
Topic 2a: Change in the form of government or constitution
Topic 3b: Ways of retaining power and combatting revolution
Topic 3c: The causes and effects of revolution under different
forms of government
Topic 3c(3): Rebellion against tyranny and despotism

HUGO, "The Battle with the Cannon"
continued

RELATED AUTHORS AND WORKS IN *Great Books of the Western World*

Sophocles, Vol. 5, *Ajax*, pages 143–155
Plato, Vol. 7, *Gorgias*, pages 270–276; *Republic*, Bks. I–II,
pages 300–315
Aquinas, Vol. 19, *Summa Theologica*, First Part, Q 21,
pages 124–127; Vol. 20, Part I–II, Q 60, Art. 3, pages 51–52;
Q 100, Art. 12, pages 264–265
Milton, Vol. 32, *Paradise Lost*, Bks. I–II, pages 93–134
Freud, Vol. 54, *Thoughts for the Times on War and Death*,
pages 755–766

RELATED AUTHORS AND WORKS IN *Gateway to the Great Books*

Bacon, *Of Seditions and Troubles*, Vol. 7, pages 12–17;
Of Adversity, Vol. 10, page 350
Conrad, *Youth*, Vol. 2, pages 210–236
De Quincey, *Literature of Knowledge and Literature of Power*,
Vol. 5, pages 358–361
Dinesen, *Sorrow-Acre*, Vol. 3, pages 615–641
Hemingway, *Killers*, Vol. 2, pages 169–177
Maupassant, *Two Friends*, Vol. 2, pages 159–164
Melville, *Billy Budd*, Vol. 3, pages 31–98
Paine, "Call to Patriots—December 23, 1776," Vol. 6, pages 461–468
Scott, *Two Drovers*, Vol. 2, pages 182–205

DAVID HUME, 1711–1776

Of the Standard of Taste
Vol. 5, pages 103–119

SUGGESTED READINGS IN THE *Syntopicon*

ART, Vol. 2, pages 64–86, especially
Topic 7*b*: The judgment of excellence in art
BEAUTY, Vol. 2, pages 112–125, especially
Topic 5: Judgments of beauty: the objective and the subjective
in aesthetic judgments or judgments of taste
GOOD AND EVIL, Vol. 2, pages 605–636, especially
Topic 3*a*: Human nature and the determination of the good
for man: the real and the apparent good; particular
goods and the good in general

OPINION, Vol. 3, pages 303–322, especially

Topic 6a: Good and evil as matters of opinion: moral standards as customs or conventions reflecting prevalent opinion

RELATED AUTHORS AND WORKS IN *Great Books of the Western World*

Aquinas, Vol. 19, *Summa Theologica*, First Part, Q 5, Arts. 3–4, pages 25–26; Part I–II, Q 27, Art. 1, page 737

Montaigne, Vol. 25, *That the Relish of Good and Evil Depends in a Great Measure Upon the Opinion We Have of Them*, pages 115–119

Descartes, Vol. 31, *Discourse on Method*, Part II, pages 44, 46; Part III, pages 48–49

Spinoza, Vol. 31, *Ethics*, Part I, Appendix, pages 369–372

Pascal, Vol. 33, *Pensées*, Sect. I, page 176; Sect. VI, page 238

Kant, Vol. 42, *Critique of Judgement*, pages 463–613

RELATED AUTHORS AND WORKS IN *Gateway to the Great Books*

Arnold, *Sweetness and Light*, Vol. 5, pages 42–61

Bacon, *Of Beauty*, Vol. 5, page 94

Guizot, "Civilization," Vol. 6, pages 302–317

Hazlitt, *Of Persons One Would Wish to Have Seen*, Vol. 5, pages 284–295

Lamb, *My First Play*, Vol. 5, pages 300–303

Sainte-Beuve, *What Is a Classic?*, Vol. 5, pages 65–75

Schopenhauer, *On the Comparative Place of Interest and Beauty in Works of Art*, Vol. 5, pages 143–150

Woolf, *How Should One Read a Book?*, Vol. 5, pages 5–14

Of Refinement in the Arts
Vol. 7, pages 52–61

SUGGESTED READINGS IN THE *Syntopicon*

ART, Vol. 2, pages 64–86, especially

Topic 9b: The production of wealth: the industrial arts

LABOR, Vol. 2, pages 921–940, especially

Topic 1b: Labor, leisure, and happiness: the servile, political, and contemplative life

Topic 1e: The honor of work and the virtue of productivity: progress through the invention of arts for the conquest of nature

Topic 6: The wages of labor: kinds of wage payments

HUME, *Of Refinement in the Arts*
continued

NECESSITY AND CONTINGENCY, Vol. 3, pages 251–269,
especially
Topic 5e: Economic necessities or luxuries
PROGRESS, Vol. 3, pages 437–453, especially
Topic 3: Economic progress
TEMPERANCE, Vol. 3, pages 866–881, especially
Topic 5b: The temperance of a people: luxurious indulgences;
the intemperance of the mob

RELATED AUTHORS AND WORKS IN *Great Books of the Western World*

Plato, Vol. 7, *Republic*, Bk. II, pages 316–319
Aristotle, Vol. 8, *Metaphysics*, Bk. I, Chap. 1, pages 499–500; Vol. 9,
Politics, Bk. VII, Chaps. 1–9, pages 527–533
Lucretius, Vol. 12, *On the Nature of Things*, Bk. V, pages 73–80
Smith, Vol. 39, *Wealth of Nations*, Bk. I, Chap. I, pages 3–6; Chap.
X, pages 42–62; Bk. III, pages 163–181; Bk. IV, Chap. IX,
pages 288–300
Marx, Vol. 50, *Capital*, Part III, Chaps. VIII–IX, pages 100–111;
Part IV, Chaps. XIV–XV, pages 173–188

RELATED AUTHORS AND WORKS IN *Gateway to the Great Books*

Adams, "United States in 1800," Vol. 6, pages 322–359
Crèvecoeur, "Making of Americans," Vol. 6, pages 546–559
Guizot, "Civilization," Vol. 6, pages 302–317
Hogben, *Mathematics, the Mirror of Civilization*, Vol. 9, pages 3–23
Ruskin, *Idealist's Arraignment of the Age*, Vol. 7, pages 126–136

Of Money
Vol. 7, pages 62–71

Of the Balance of Trade
Vol. 7, pages 72–84

Of Taxes
Vol. 7, pages 85–88

SUGGESTED READINGS IN THE *Syntopicon*

LABOR, Vol. 2, pages 921–940, especially
Topic 5: The organization of production: the position of labor
in different economies
Topic 6: The wages of labor: kinds of wage payments

PROGRESS, Vol. 3, pages 437–453, especially

Topic 3: Economic progress

STATE, Vol. 3, pages 826–865, especially

Topic 2d: The economic aspect of the state: differentiation
of states according to their economic systems

Topic 7a: Wealth and political welfare

Topic 9a: Commerce and trade between states: commercial
rivalries and trade agreements; free trade and tariffs

WEALTH, Vol. 3, pages 1038–1070, especially

Topic 3: The production of wealth in the political community

Topic 4: The exchange of wealth or the circulation
of commodities: the processes of commerce or trade

Topic 5: Money

Topic 9: Political economy: the nature of the science
of economics

RELATED AUTHORS AND WORKS IN *Great Books of the Western World*

Plato, Vol. 7, *Republic*, Bk. II, pages 316–319
Aristotle, Vol. 9, *Politics*, Bk. I, Chaps. 9–10, pages 450–452
Rousseau, Vol. 38, *Discourse on Political Economy*, pages 367–385
Smith, Vol. 39, *Wealth of Nations*, Bk. I, Chaps. I–V, pages 3–20;
Chap. VIII, pages 27–37; Bk. II, Chap. II, pages 121–142; Bk.
IV, Chap. IX, pages 288–300
Marx, Vol. 50, *Capital*, Part I, Chaps. I–III, pages 33–68; Part IV,
Chap. XIV, pages 171–176

RELATED AUTHORS AND WORKS IN *Gateway to the Great Books*

Adams, "United States in 1800," Vol. 6, pages 322–359
Bacon, *Of Usury*, Vol. 7, pages 22–24; *Of Riches*, pages 25–27
Bunin, *Gentleman from San Francisco*, Vol. 3, pages 102–123
Burke, *Letter to the Sheriffs of Bristol*, Vol. 7, pages 237–271
Voltaire, "English Men and Ideas: On Trade," Vol. 7, pages
338–339

Of the Study of History
Vol. 7, pages 89–92

SUGGESTED READINGS IN THE *Syntopicon*

EDUCATION, Vol. 2, pages 376–399, especially

Topic 4d: The effect upon character of poetry, music, and other
arts: the role of history and examples

HISTORY, Vol. 2, pages 711–727, especially

Topic 2: The light and lesson of history: its role
in the education of the mind and in the guidance
of human conduct

HUME, *Of the Study of History*
continued

RELATED AUTHORS AND WORKS IN *Great Books of the Western World*

Plato, Vol. 7, *Laws*, Bk. III, pages 663–676
Aristotle, Vol. 9, *On Poetics*, Chap. 9, page 686; Chap. 23, page 695
Plutarch, Vol. 14, *Pericles*, pages 121–122
Machiavelli, Vol. 23, *Prince*, Chaps. XV–XXI, pages 22–33
Montaigne, Vol. 25, *Of Books*, pages 197–199
Bacon, Vol. 30, *Advancement of Learning*, Second Book,
    pages 32–38
Fielding, Vol. 37, *Tom Jones*, Bk. VIII, Chap. 1, pages 152–155
Smith, Vol. 39, *Wealth of Nations*, Bk. V, Chap. I, Art. II,
    pages 331–343
Hamilton, Madison, Jay, Vol. 43, *Federalist*, Nos. 18–20, pages 71–78
Tolstoy, Vol. 51, *War and Peace*, Second Epilogue, pages 675–696
Dostoevsky, Vol. 52, *Brothers Karamazov*, Part IV, Bk. X, Chap. 5,
    pages 291–292

RELATED AUTHORS AND WORKS IN *Gateway to the Great Books*

Bury, *Herodotus*, Vol. 6, pages 364–383
Carlyle, *Hero as King*, Vol. 6, pages 110–145
Eliot, T. S., *Tradition and the Individual Talent*, Vol. 5,
    pages 404–411
Guizot, "Civilization," Vol. 6, pages 302–317
Lucian, *Way to Write History*, Vol. 6, pages 387–406
Macaulay, *Machiavelli*, Vol. 7, pages 295–329
Schopenhauer, *On Education*, Vol. 7, pages 197–203
Woolf, *How Should One Read a Book?*, Vol. 5, pages 5–14

For Hume's *Enquiry Concerning Human Understanding*
in *Great Books of the Western World*, see Vol. 35, pages 451–509

THOMAS HENRY HUXLEY, 1825–1895

On the Relations of Man to the Lower Animals
Vol. 8, pages 160–204

SUGGESTED READINGS IN THE *Syntopicon*

ANIMAL, Vol. 2, pages 19–49, especially
    Topic 1c: The distinction between animal and human nature
    Topic 2: The classification of animals
EVOLUTION, Vol. 2, pages 451–467

MAN, Vol. 3, pages 1–41, especially

Topic 1c: The conception of man as an animal, differing only in degree of intelligence and of other qualities possessed by other animals

Topic 4a: Man's vegetative powers: comparison with similar functions in plants and animals

Topic 4b: Man's sensitive and appetitive powers: comparison with similar functions in other animals

Topic 8: The origin or genealogy of man

Topic 10e: Man's comparison of himself with other creatures and with the universe as a whole

NATURE, Vol. 3, pages 225–250, especially

Topic 1c: Nature as the complex of the objects of sense: the realm of things existing under the determination of universal laws

RELATED AUTHORS AND WORKS IN *Great Books of the Western World*

Aristotle, Vol. 9, *History of Animals*, pages 7–158

Montaigne, Vol. 25, *Apology for Raimond de Sebonde*, pages 208–294

Darwin, Vol. 49, *Origin of Species*, pages 1–243; *Descent of Man*, pages 253–600

James, W., Vol. 53, *Principles of Psychology*, Chap. XXII, pages 679–686; Chap. XXIV, pages 704–706

Freud, Vol. 54, *Beyond the Pleasure Principle*, pages 651–654

RELATED AUTHORS AND WORKS IN *Gateway to the Great Books*

Balzac, *Passion in the Desert*, Vol. 3, pages 436–447

Bernard, *Experimental Considerations Common to Living Things and Inorganic Bodies*, Vol. 8, pages 266–290

Carson, *Sunless Sea*, Vol. 8, pages 132–146

Darwin, *Autobiography*, Vol. 8, pages 47–93

Eiseley, "On Time," Vol. 8, pages 123–129

Emerson, *Nature*, Vol. 10, pages 512–524

Fabre, *Laboratory of the Open Fields*, Vol. 8, pages 97–104; *Sacred Beetle*, pages 105–119

Flaubert, *Legend of St. Julian the Hospitaller*, Vol. 3, pages 371–392

Galton, "Classification of Human Ability," Vol. 8, pages 227–261

Kipling, *Mowgli's Brothers*, Vol. 2, pages 126–141

Mill, J. S., *Nature*, Vol. 10, pages 477–508

Pavlov, *Scientific Study of the So-Called Psychical Processes in the Higher Animals*, Vol. 8, pages 294–309

THOMAS HENRY HUXLEY
continued

On a Piece of Chalk
Vol. 8, pages 205–222

SUGGESTED READINGS IN THE *Syntopicon*

CHANGE, Vol. 2, pages 193–217, especially
    Topic 6c: Comparison of change in living and non-living things
    Topic 9a: Physical and chemical change: compounds
        and mixtures
EVOLUTION, Vol. 2, pages 451–467, especially
    Topic 6: The facts of evolution: evidences bearing
        on the history of life on earth
SCIENCE, Vol. 3, pages 682–705, especially
    Topic 1b: Science as the discipline of experimental inquiry
        and the organization of experimental knowledge:
        the scientific spirit

RELATED AUTHORS AND WORKS IN *Great Books of the Western World*

Darwin, Vol. 49, *Origin of Species*, Chaps. III–IV, pages 32–64;
    Chaps. X–XIII, pages 152–206; Chap. XV, pages 230–243

RELATED AUTHORS AND WORKS IN *Gateway to the Great Books*

Carson, *Sunless Sea*, Vol. 8, pages 132–146
Darwin, *Autobiography*, Vol. 8, pages 47–93
Eiseley, "On Time," Vol. 8, pages 123–129
Faraday, *Chemical History of a Candle*, Vol. 8, pages 368–439
Lyell, "Geological Evolution," Vol. 8, pages 319–324

HENRIK IBSEN, 1828–1906

An Enemy of the People
Vol. 4, pages 164–246

SUGGESTED READINGS IN THE *Syntopicon*

COURAGE, Vol. 2, pages 252–267, especially
    Topic 7a: The courage required of citizens and statesmen:
        the political recognition of courage
DEMOCRACY, Vol. 2, pages 303–322, especially
    Topic 2a: Lawless mob-rule: the tyranny of the majority

HONOR, Vol. 2, pages 728–748, especially
    Topic 3a: The reaction of the community to its good
        or great men
TRUTH, Vol. 3, pages 915–938, especially
    Topic 8b: The expediency of the political lie

RELATED AUTHORS AND WORKS IN *Great Books of the Western World*

Sophocles, Vol. 5, *Oedipus the King*, pages 99–113; *Philoctetes*,
    pages 182–184
Plato, Vol. 7, *Republic*, Bk. IV, pages 342–356
Montaigne, Vol. 25, *Of Presumption*, pages 314–316
Hamilton, Madison, Jay, Vol. 43, *Federalist*, No. 10, pages 49–53;
    No. 51, pages 164–165
Mill, J. S., Vol. 43, *Representative Government*, Chaps. 6–7, pages
    366–380
Boswell, Vol. 44, *Life of Samuel Johnson*, pages 212; 498–499

RELATED AUTHORS AND WORKS IN *Gateway to the Great Books*

Bacon, *Of Adversity*, Vol. 10, page 350
Butler, "Customs and Opinions of the Erewhonians," Vol. 2,
    pages 483–506
Calhoun, "Concurrent Majority," Vol. 7, pages 276–290
Carlyle, *Hero as King*, Vol. 6, pages 110–145
Chekhov, *Cherry Orchard*, Vol. 4, pages 249–294
Emerson, *Self-Reliance*, Vol. 10, pages 525–545
Ruskin, *Idealist's Arraignment of the Age*, Vol. 7, pages 126–136
Thoreau, *Civil Disobedience*, Vol. 6, pages 695–713
Tocqueville, "Observations on American Life and Government,"
    Vol. 6, pages 564–690
Voltaire, "English Men and Ideas: On Inoculation," Vol. 7,
    pages 339–343
Xenophon, "Character of Socrates," Vol. 6, pages 223–226

HENRY JAMES, 1843–1916

The Pupil
Vol. 3, pages 530–568

SUGGESTED READINGS IN THE *Syntopicon*

CUSTOM AND CONVENTION, Vol. 2, pages 268–285, especially
    Topic 5a: The conventional determination of moral judgments:
        the moral evaluation of conventions
DESIRE, Vol. 2, pages 323–344, especially
    Topic 7a(3): The accumulation of wealth

HENRY JAMES, *The Pupil*
continued

EDUCATION, Vol. 2, pages 376–399, especially
Topic 4*b*: The influence of the family in moral training
FAMILY, Vol. 2, pages 486–514, especially
Topic 6*e*: The initiation of children into adult life
TRUTH, Vol. 3, pages 915–938, especially
Topic 8*c*: Truth in relation to love and friendship: the pleasant
and the unpleasant truth
WEALTH, Vol. 3, pages 1038–1070, especially
Topic 10*c*: Temperance and intemperance with respect
to wealth: liberality, magnificence, miserliness,
avarice
Topic 10*e*(3): The choice between God and Mammon:
the love of money as the root of all evil

RELATED AUTHORS AND WORKS IN *Great Books of the Western World*

Plato, Vol. 7, *Laws*, Bk. VII, pages 713–716
Montaigne, Vol. 25, *Of the Education of Children*, pages 62–80
Fielding, Vol. 37, *Tom Jones*, Bk. XIV, Chap. 8, pages 310–313

RELATED AUTHORS AND WORKS IN *Gateway to the Great Books*

Bacon, *Of Riches*, Vol. 7, pages 25–27
Fitzgerald, *Diamond as Big as the Ritz*, Vol. 3, pages 397–431
Franklin, *Proposals Relating to the Education of Youth
in Pennsylvania*, Vol. 6, pages 536–542
Lawrence, *Rocking-Horse Winner*, Vol. 3, pages 512–525
Pater, "Art of Life," Vol. 10, pages 258–261
Twain, *Man That Corrupted Hadleyburg*, Vol. 2, pages 346–386

WILLIAM JAMES, 1842–1910

On a Certain Blindness in Human Beings
Vol. 7, pages 141–156

SUGGESTED READINGS IN THE *Syntopicon*

MAN, Vol. 3, pages 1–41, especially
Topic 2*a*: Immediate self-consciousness: man's intimate
or introspective knowledge of himself
Topic 10*e*: Man's comparison of himself with other creatures
and with the universe as a whole

MIND, Vol. 3, pages 171–203, especially
    Topic 1d(1): The origin of the mind's simple ideas: sensation
        and reflection
PLEASURE AND PAIN, Vol. 3, pages 377–399, especially
    Topic 4b: Sensuous pleasure: the affective quality of sensations
    Topic 4c: Intellectual pleasure: the pleasures of reflection
        and contemplation
SENSE, Vol. 3, pages 706–729, especially
    Topic 3d(2): Memory and imagination as interior powers
        of sense
    Topic 6: The role of sense in the perception of beauty:
        the beautiful and the pleasing to sense; sensible
        and intelligible beauty

RELATED AUTHORS AND WORKS IN *Great Books of the Western World*

Plato, Vol. 7, *Philebus*, pages 609–639
Aristotle, Vol. 9, *Rhetoric*, Bk. I, Chap. 11, pages 613–615
Aquinas, Vol. 19, *Summa Theologica*, Part I–II, Q 11,
    pages 666–669
Montaigne, Vol. 25, *Of Experience*, pages 537–543
Pascal, Vol. 33, *Pensées*, Sect. II, pages 181–184
Tolstoy, Vol. 51, *War and Peace*, Bk. 12, Chaps. XII–XIII,
    pages 551–555; Bk. 13, Chaps. XI–XII, pages 575–578;
    Chap. XIV, pages 580–582; Bk. 14, Chaps. XII–XV,
    pages 604–609; Bk. 15, Chaps. XII–XIII, pages 630–634
Dostoevsky, Vol. 52, *Brothers Karamazov*, Part II, Bk. VI,
    pages 146–170
James, W., Vol. 53, *Principles of Psychology*, Chap. XI, pages
    260–298

RELATED AUTHORS AND WORKS IN *Gateway to the Great Books*

Pater, "Art of Life," Vol. 10, pages 258–261
Plutarch, *Contentment*, Vol. 10, pages 264–281
Schopenhauer, *On the Comparative Place of Interest and Beauty
    in Works of Art*, Vol. 5, pages 143–150

The Energies of Men
Vol. 7, pages 157–170

SUGGESTED READINGS IN THE *Syntopicon*

DESIRE, Vol. 2, pages 323–344, especially
    Topic 2c: Desire as a cause of action: motivation or purpose;
        voluntariness
MIND, Vol. 3, pages 171–203, especially
    Topic 2c(2): The influence of mental activity on bodily states

WILLIAM JAMES, *The Energies of Men*
continued

WILL, Vol. 3, pages 1071–1101, especially

Topic 3: The functioning of will in human conduct and thought

Topic 3*a*: The role of the will in behavior

Topic 9*a*: The distinction between men of strong and weak will: cultivation of will power

RELATED AUTHORS AND WORKS IN *Great Books of the Western World*

Aquinas, Vol. 19, *Summa Theologica*, Part I–II, Q 17, pages 686–693

James, W., Vol. 53, *Principles of Psychology*, Chap. XXVII, pages 838–850

Freud, Vol. 54, *Selected Papers on Hysteria*, Chaps. 1–3, pages 25–59

RELATED AUTHORS AND WORKS IN *Gateway to the Great Books*

Bacon, *Of Adversity*, Vol. 10, page 350

Crane, *Open Boat*, Vol. 3, pages 5–26

Curie, *Discovery of Radium*, Vol. 8, pages 32–42

Galton, "Classification of Human Ability," Vol. 8, pages 227–261

Hugo, "Battle with the Cannon," Vol. 2, pages 146–154

Long, *Power within Us*, Vol. 6, pages 246–261

O'Neill, *Emperor Jones*, Vol. 4, pages 357–382

Great Men and Their Environment
Vol. 7, pages 171–194

SUGGESTED READINGS IN THE *Syntopicon*

ANIMAL, Vol. 2, pages 19–49, especially

Topic 10: Heredity and environment: the genetic determination of individual differences and similarities

Topic 11*b*: The relation between animals and their environments

EVOLUTION, Vol. 2, pages 451–467, especially

Topic 3: The process of heredity

Topic 3*a*: The inheritance of acquired characteristics: the use and disuse of parts

FATE, Vol. 2, pages 515–525, especially

Topic 2: The fated or inevitable in human life

HISTORY, Vol. 2, pages 711–727, especially

Topic 4*a*(4): The role of the individual in history: the great man, hero, or leader

STATE, Vol. 3, pages 826–865, especially
Topic 8c: The education or training of the statesman or prince
WILL, Vol. 3, pages 1071–1101, especially
Topic 7b: The factors of freedom and necessity
in the philosophy of history

RELATED AUTHORS AND WORKS IN *Great Books of the Western World*

Herodotus, Vol. 6, *History*, Bk. VII, pages 214–220
Plutarch, Vol. 14, *Theseus*, pages 1–15; *Pericles*, pages 121–141
Machiavelli, Vol. 23, *Prince*, Chap. VI, pages 8–10; Chap. XXV,
pages 35–36
Hegel, Vol. 46, *Philosophy of History*, Introduction, Part III,
pages 156–190
Darwin, Vol. 49, *Descent of Man*, Part I, Chap. II, pages 266–286
Tolstoy, Vol. 51, *War and Peace*, Bk. 9, Chap. I, pages 342–344;
Bk. 13, pages 563–587; First Epilogue, Chaps. I–IV, pages
645–650; Second Epilogue, pages 675–696

RELATED AUTHORS AND WORKS IN *Gateway to the Great Books*

Bacon, *Of Great Place*, Vol. 7, pages 9–11
Carlyle, *Hero as King*, Vol. 6, pages 110–145
Eliot, T. S., *Tradition and the Individual Talent*, Vol. 5,
pages 404–411
Galton, "Classification of Human Ability," Vol. 8, pages 227–261
Hawthorne, *Sketch of Abraham Lincoln*, Vol. 6, pages 168–171
Hazlitt, *Of Persons One Would Wish to Have Seen*, Vol. 5,
pages 284–295
Lamb, *Sanity of True Genius*, Vol. 5, pages 308–310
Mill, J. S., "Childhood and Youth," Vol. 6, pages 5–47
Shaw, *Man of Destiny*, Vol. 4, pages 300–338
Tacitus, *Life of Gnaeus Julius Agricola*, Vol. 6, pages 274–298
Xenophon, "Character of Socrates," Vol. 6, pages 223–226

The Will to Believe
Vol. 10, pages 39–57

SUGGESTED READINGS IN THE *Syntopicon*

HYPOTHESIS, Vol. 2, pages 749–760, especially
Topic 2: Hypothetical reasoning and hypothetical constructions
in philosophy
KNOWLEDGE, Vol. 2, pages 880–920, especially
Topic 6c(4): The distinction between *a priori* and *a posteriori*
knowledge; the transcendental, or speculative,
and the empirical

WILLIAM JAMES, *The Will to Believe*
continued

OPINION, Vol. 3, pages 303–322, especially
   Topic 2*b*: The will as cause of assent in acts of opinion
WILL, Vol. 3, pages 1071–1101, especially
   Topic 3*b*(1): The distinction between knowledge and opinion
      in relation to the willful in thought: the will
      to believe and wishful thinking
   Topic 5*a*(1): The freedom of the will as consisting in a freely
      determined choice or a free judgment
      of the reason

RELATED AUTHORS AND WORKS IN *Great Books of the Western World*

Descartes, Vol. 31, *Discourse on Method*, Parts II–IV, pages 44–54,
   especially pages 48–54
Spinoza, Vol. 31, *Ethics*, Part I, Prop. 34–Appendix, pages
   369–372; Part II, Props. 48–49, pages 391–394
Pascal, Vol. 33, *Provincial Letters*, Letter XVIII, pages 153–159;
   Pensées, Sects. III–IV, pages 205–225, especially pages 214–216
Locke, Vol. 35, *Concerning Human Understanding*, Bk. II,
   Chap. XXI, pages 190–199; Bk. IV, Chap. XIX, pages
   384–388
Hume, Vol. 35, *Enquiry Concerning Human Understanding*,
   Sect. IV–Sect. V, Part I, pages 458–466; Sects. X–XI,
   pages 488–503
Kant, Vol. 42, *Critique of Pure Reason*, Introduction, pages 14–22;
   pages 23–66; pages 240–243
Dostoevsky, Vol. 52, *Brothers Karamazov*, Part II, Bk. V,
   Chaps. 3–5, pages 117–137; Part III, Bk. VII, Chaps. 1–2, pages
   171–180; Chap. 4, pages 189–191; Part IV, Bk. XI, Chap. 4,
   pages 310–317; Chap. 9, pages 337–346
Freud, Vol. 54, *Civilization and Its Discontents*, Parts I–II,
   pages 767–776; *New Introductory Lectures on Psycho-Analysis*,
   Lecture 35, pages 873–884

RELATED AUTHORS AND WORKS IN *Gateway to the Great Books*

Bacon, *Of Truth*, Vol. 10, pages 346–347
Clifford, *Ethics of Belief*, Vol. 10, pages 16–36
Dewey, "Process of Thought," Vol. 10, pages 92–213
Emerson, *Montaigne; or, the Skeptic*, Vol. 10, pages 546–562
Erskine, *Moral Obligation to Be Intelligent*, Vol. 10, pages 5–13
Faraday, *Observations on Mental Education*, Vol. 7, pages 208–232

The Sentiment of Rationality
Vol. 10, pages 58–87

SUGGESTED READINGS IN THE *Syntopicon*

KNOWLEDGE, Vol. 2, pages 880–920, especially
Topic 4*b*: Knowledge, belief, and opinion: their relation
or distinction

OPINION, Vol. 3, pages 303–322, especially
Topic 3*b*: Certain and probable, adequate and inadequate
knowledge: degrees of certitude; modes of assent

PHILOSOPHY, Vol. 3, pages 342–362, especially
Topic 3*b*: The philosopher's appeal to first principles
and to definitions
Topic 4*b*: Philosophy as a moral discipline: the consolation
of philosophy
Topic 6*c*: The philosopher as a man of reason: the limits
of reason; its supplementation by experience or faith

PRINCIPLE, Vol. 3, pages 420–436, especially
Topic 5: The skeptical denial of first principles or axioms:
the denial that any propositions elicit the universal
assent of mankind

UNIVERSAL AND PARTICULAR, Vol. 3, pages 957–974,
especially
Topic 4*c*: The abstraction of universal concepts
from the particulars of sense

RELATED AUTHORS AND WORKS IN *Great Books of the Western World*

Plato, Vol. 7, *Republic*, Bks. VI–VII, pages 383–398
Aristotle, Vol. 8, *Metaphysics*, Bk. IV, pages 522–532; Vol. 9,
Nicomachean Ethics, Bk. I, Chaps. 1–4, pages 339–340;
Chaps. 7–8, pages 342–345; Bk. X, Chap. 8, pages 432–434
Descartes, Vol. 31, *Discourse on Method*, Parts I–IV, pages 41–54
Spinoza, Vol. 31, *Ethics*, Part IV, Appendix, pages 447–450
Pascal, Vol. 33, *Pensées*, Sect. IV, pages 221–225
Locke, Vol. 35, *Concerning Human Understanding*, Bk. IV,
Chaps. XVII–XX, pages 371–394
Berkeley, Vol. 35, *Principles of Human Knowledge*, Introduction,
pages 405–409
Hume, Vol. 35, *Enquiry Concerning Human Understanding*,
Sect. XII, Parts I–III, pages 503–509
Kant, Vol. 42, *Critique of Pure Reason*, pages 129–173; *Critique
of Judgement*, Part II, pages 603–606

WILLIAM JAMES, *The Sentiment of Rationality*
continued

Goethe, Vol. 47, *Faust*, First Part, pages 30, 44–48; Second Part,
Act II, pages 161–173
Darwin, Vol. 49, *Descent of Man*, Part I, Chaps. III–V,
pages 287–330
Dostoevsky, Vol. 52, *Brothers Karamazov*, Part II, Bk. V,
Chaps. 3–4, pages 117–127; Part III, Bk. VII, Chap. 2, pages
177–180; Chap. 4, pages 189–191

RELATED AUTHORS AND WORKS IN *Gateway to the Great Books*

Clifford, *Ethics of Belief*, Vol. 10, pages 16–36
Dewey, "Process of Thought," Vol. 10, pages 92–213
Faraday, *Observations on Mental Education*, Vol. 7, pages 208–232
Mill, J. S., *Nature*, Vol. 10, pages 477–508
Poincaré, *Mathematical Creation*, Vol. 9, pages 294–304

For James's *Principles of Psychology* in *Great Books of the Western
World*, see Vol. 53

SIR JAMES JEANS, 1877–1946

Beginnings and Endings
Vol. 8, pages 585–596

SUGGESTED READINGS IN THE *Syntopicon*

CHANGE, Vol. 2, pages 193–217, especially
Topic 5: The measure of motion
Topic 13: The problem of the eternity of motion or change
MECHANICS, Vol. 3, pages 80–112, especially
Topic 6e: Work and energy: their conservation; perpetual
motion
PROGRESS, Vol. 3, pages 437–453, especially
Topic 6b: Progress in philosophy and in the sciences
SPACE, Vol. 3, pages 811–825, especially
Topic 2: Space, void, and motion
TIME, Vol. 3, pages 896–914, especially
Topic 2c: The creation of time: the priority of eternity to time;
the immutability of the world after the end of time
WORLD, Vol. 3, pages 1118–1140, especially
Topic 1b: The universe as a machine: the system of its moving
parts

RELATED AUTHORS AND WORKS IN *Great Books of the Western World*

Aristotle, Vol. 8, *Physics*, Bk. VIII, pages 334–352
Lucretius, Vol. 12, *On the Nature of Things*, Bks. I–II, pages 12–19
Augustine, Vol. 18, *Confessions*, Bk. XII, pages 99–110
Aquinas, Vol. 20, *Summa Theologica*, Treatise on the Last Things,
pages 997–1085
Newton, Vol. 34, *Mathematical Principles of Natural Philosophy*,
Bk. III, pages 284–285
Faraday, Vol. 45, *Experimental Researches in Electricity*,
pages 850–855

RELATED AUTHORS AND WORKS IN *Gateway to the Great Books*

Eddington, *Running-Down of the Universe*, Vol. 8, pages 565–580
Eiseley, "On Time," Vol. 8, pages 123–129
Santayana, *Lucretius*, Vol. 10, pages 365–390

THOMAS JEFFERSON, 1743–1826

"The Virginia Constitution"
from *Notes on Virginia*
Vol. 6, pages 502–517

SUGGESTED READINGS IN THE *Syntopicon*

DEMOCRACY, Vol. 2, pages 303–322, especially
Topic 4*b*: The democratic realization of popular sovereignty:
the safeguarding of natural rights
Topic 4*c*: The infirmities of democracy in practice
and the reforms or remedies for these defects
Topic 5*b*(1): Majority rule and minority or proportional
representation
Topic 5*c*: The distribution of functions and powers: checks
and balances in representative democracy
LIBERTY, Vol. 2, pages 991–1012, especially
Topic 6*c*: The struggle for sovereign independence against
the yoke of imperialism or colonial subjugation

RELATED AUTHORS AND WORKS IN *Great Books of the Western World*

Plato, Vol. 7, *Laws*, Bk. VI, pages 697–705
Aristotle, Vol. 9, *Politics*, Bk. III, Chaps. 6–13, pages 475–483
Locke, Vol. 35, *Concerning Civil Government*, Chaps. XII–XIII,
pages 58–62
Hamilton, Madison, Jay, Vol. 43, *Federalist*, No. 45, pages 147–148

JEFFERSON, "The Virginia Constitution"
continued

Mill, J. S., Vol. 43, *Representative Government*, Chaps. 6–7,
pages 366–380; Chaps. 12–13, pages 401–409

RELATED AUTHORS AND WORKS IN *Gateway to the Great Books*

Burke, *Letter to the Sheriffs of Bristol*, Vol. 7, pages 237–271
Calhoun, "Concurrent Majority," Vol. 7, pages 276–290
Great Documents, *Virginia Declaration of Rights*, Vol. 6,
    pages 415–417; *Declaration of Independence*, pages 418–421
Lincoln, *First Inaugural Address*, Vol. 6, pages 747–755
Thoreau, *Civil Disobedience*, Vol. 6, pages 695–713
Washington, *Farewell Address*, Vol. 6, pages 484–497

First Inaugural Address
Vol. 6, pages 518–521

SUGGESTED READINGS IN THE *Syntopicon*

DEMOCRACY, Vol. 2, pages 303–322, especially
    Topic 4*b*: The democratic realization of popular sovereignty:
        the safeguarding of natural rights
    Topic 5*b*(1): Majority rule and minority or proportional
        representation

GOVERNMENT, Vol. 2, pages 637–664, especially
    Topic 5*d*: Confederation and federal union: the division
        of jurisdiction between state and federal
        governments

LIBERTY, Vol. 2, pages 991–1012, especially
    Topic 1*a*: The birthright of freedom
    Topic 2*b*: Liberty of conscience and religious freedom

RELATED AUTHORS AND WORKS IN *Great Books of the Western World*

Plato, Vol. 7, *Laws*, Bk. III, pages 667–670
Locke, Vol. 35, *Letter Concerning Toleration*, pages 1–22
Kant, Vol. 42, *Science of Right*, Second Part, pages 435–458
Articles of Confederation, Vol. 43, pages 5–9

RELATED AUTHORS AND WORKS IN *Gateway to the Great Books*

Adams, "United States in 1800," Vol. 6, pages 322–359
Burke, *Letter to the Sheriffs of Bristol*, Vol. 7, pages 237–271
Crèvecoeur, "Making of Americans," Vol. 6, pages 546–559
Great Documents, Vol. 6, pages 409–456
Guizot, "Civilization," Vol. 6, pages 302–317
Lincoln, *First Inaugural Address*, Vol. 6, pages 747–755

Paine, "Call to Patriots—December 23, 1776," Vol. 6, pages 461–468
Tocqueville, "Observations on American Life and Government,"
Vol. 6, pages 564–690
Washington, *Farewell Address*, Vol. 6, pages 484–497

Biographical Sketches
Vol. 6, pages 522–528

SUGGESTED READINGS IN THE *Syntopicon*

HONOR, Vol. 2, pages 728–748, especially
Topic 1: The relation of honor and fame: praise and reputation
JUSTICE, Vol. 2, pages 850–879, especially
Topic 9b: Justice as the moral principle of political
organization: the bond of men in states
PRUDENCE, Vol. 3, pages 472–487, especially
Topic 1: The nature of prudence: as practical wisdom,
as a virtue or quality of the deliberative mind

RELATED AUTHORS AND WORKS IN *Great Books of the Western World*

Plutarch, Vol. 14, *Solon*, pages 64–77; *Pericles*, pages 121–141;
Marcus Cato, pages 276–290; *Alexander*, pages 540–576;
Caesar, pages 577–604

RELATED AUTHORS AND WORKS IN *Gateway to the Great Books*

Carlyle, *Hero as King*, Vol. 6, pages 110–145
Hawthorne, *Sketch of Abraham Lincoln*, Vol. 6, pages 168–171
La Bruyère, *Characters*, Vol. 6, pages 102–105
Tacitus, *Life of Gnaeus Julius Agricola*, Vol. 6, pages 274–298
Washington, *Circular Letter to the Governors of All the States
on Disbanding the Army*, Vol. 6, pages 474–483; *Farewell
Address*, pages 484–497
Woolf, *Art of Biography*, Vol. 6, pages 186–192

SAMUEL JOHNSON, 1709–1784

Preface to Shakespeare
Vol. 5, pages 316–353

SUGGESTED READINGS IN THE *Syntopicon*

ART, Vol. 2, pages 64–86, especially
Topic 5: The sources of art in experience, imagination,
and inspiration

JOHNSON, *Preface to Shakespeare*
continued

MEMORY AND IMAGINATION, Vol. 3, pages 133–157,
especially
Topic 7a: The use of imagination in the production
and appreciation of works of art

POETRY, Vol. 3, pages 400–419, especially
Topic 3: The inspiration or genius of the poet: the influence
of the poetic tradition
Topic 4a: Epic and dramatic poetry
Topic 8a(1): The poetic unities: comparison of epic
and dramatic unity
Topic 8a(2): Poetic truth: verisimilitude or plausibility;
the possible, the probable, and the necessary

RELATED AUTHORS AND WORKS IN *Great Books of the Western World*

Plato, Vol. 7, *Republic*, Bk. III, pages 328–331
Aristotle, Vol. 9, *On Poetics*, pages 681–699
Cervantes, Vol. 29, *Don Quixote*, First Part, Chap. 48,
pages 185–187; Second Part, Chap. 16, pages 251–252
Bacon, Vol. 30, *Advancement of Learning*, Second Book,
pages 38–39
Fielding, Vol. 37, *Tom Jones*, Bk. V, Chap. 1, pages 73–75; Bk. VII,
Chap. 1, pages 121–123; Bk. VIII, Chap. 1, pages 152–155;
Bk. IX, Chap. 1, pages 189–191; Bk. XIII, Chap. 1,
pages 273–274; Bk. XIV, Chap. 1, pages 296–298; Bk. XVI,
Chap. 5, pages 347–348

RELATED AUTHORS AND WORKS IN *Gateway to the Great Books*

Arnold, *Study of Poetry*, Vol. 5, pages 19–41
De Quincey, *Literature of Knowledge and Literature of Power*,
Vol. 5, pages 358–361; *On the Knocking at the Gate
in Macbeth*, pages 362–366
Eliot, T. S., *Tradition and the Individual Talent*, Vol. 5,
pages 404–411
Lamb, *My First Play*, Vol. 5, pages 300–303
Sainte-Beuve, *What Is a Classic?*, Vol. 5, pages 65–75
Schiller, *On Simple and Sentimental Poetry*, Vol. 5, pages 155–211
Schopenhauer, *On Some Forms of Literature*, Vol. 5, pages 137–142
Woolf, *How Should One Read a Book?*, Vol. 5, pages 5–14

For the works of Shakespeare in *Great Books of the Western World*,
see Vols. 26–27

For Boswell's *Life of Samuel Johnson* in *Great Books of the Western
World*, see Vol. 44

IMMANUEL KANT, 1724–1804

Perpetual Peace
Vol. 7, pages 441–475

KANT, *Perpetual Peace*

continued

Mill, J. S., Vol. 43, *Representative Government*, Chaps. 17–18,
pages 428–442
Hegel, Vol. 46, *Philosophy of Right*, Third Part, Sub-sect. III,
pages 106–109
Tolstoy, Vol. 51, *War and Peace*, Bk. 6, Chap. VII, pages 244–245;
Bk. 9, Chaps. I–VII, pages 342–355; First Epilogue,
Chaps. I–IV, pages 645–650
Freud, Vol. 54, *Thoughts for the Times on War and Death*,
pages 755–766

RELATED AUTHORS AND WORKS IN *Gateway to the Great Books*

Clausewitz, *What Is War?*, Vol. 7, pages 479–497
Dante, "On World Government," Vol. 7, pages 383–399
Guizot, "Civilization," Vol. 6, pages 302–317
Rousseau, *Lasting Peace through the Federation of Europe*, Vol. 7,
pages 405–436

For other works by Kant in *Great Books of the Western World*,
see Vol. 42, especially *The Science of Right*, pages 395–458

EDWARD KASNER, 1878–1955
and JAMES R. NEWMAN, 1907–1966

New Names for Old
Beyond the Googol
Vol. 9, pages 121–162

SUGGESTED READINGS IN THE *Syntopicon*

CHANGE, Vol. 2, pages 193–217, especially
Topic 1: The nature and reality of change or motion
Topic 5: The measure of motion
Topic 7*d*: The properties of variable motion: the laws of motion
INFINITY, Vol. 2, pages 816–834, especially
Topic 3: The infinite in quantity
Topic 4: The infinity of matter
LOGIC, Vol. 2, pages 1035–1050, especially
Topic 4*a*: Mathematical analysis and reasoning: the search
for a universal method

MATHEMATICS, Vol. 3, pages 42–62, especially
  Topic 2: The objects of mathematics: number, figure, extension, relation, order
  Topic 2b: The being of mathematical objects: their real, ideal, or mental existence
  Topic 3d: Symbols and formulae: the attainment of generality
  Topic 4: Mathematical techniques
QUANTITY, Vol. 3, pages 527–545, especially
  Topic 4: Discrete quantities: number and numbering
SCIENCE, Vol. 3, pages 682–705, especially
  Topic 2b: The comparison of science with poetry and history

RELATED AUTHORS AND WORKS IN *Great Books of the Western World*

Plato, Vol. 7, *Parmenides*, pages 486–511, especially pages 495–505
Aristotle, Vol. 8, *Physics*, Bk. IV, Chaps. 10–14, pages 297–304; Bk. VI, Chaps. 1–10, pages 312–325
Euclid, Vol. 11, *Elements*, Bks. I–II, pages 5–31; Bk. X, pages 191–300; Bk. XII, pages 338–368
Archimedes, Vol. 11, *Sand-Reckoner*, pages 520–526
Descartes, Vol. 31, *Rules for the Direction of the Mind*, Rules XIV–XXI, pages 28–40
Pascal, Vol. 33, *On Geometrical Demonstration*, pages 434–439
Berkeley, Vol. 35, *Principles of Human Knowledge*, pages 432–439

RELATED AUTHORS AND WORKS IN *Gateway to the Great Books*

Boeke, *Cosmic View*, Vol. 8, pages 600–644
Campbell, *Measurement*, Vol. 9, pages 204–221
Dantzig, *Fingerprints*, Vol. 9, pages 165–177; *Empty Column*, pages 178–189
Hogben, *Mathematics, the Mirror of Civilization*, Vol. 9, pages 3–23
Russell, *Definition of Number*, Vol. 9, pages 111–117; *Mathematics and the Metaphysicians*, pages 95–110

RUDYARD KIPLING, 1865–1936

Mowgli's Brothers
Vol. 2, pages 126–141

SUGGESTED READINGS IN THE *Syntopicon*

ANIMAL, Vol. 2, pages 19–49, especially
  Topic 1: General theories about the animal nature
  Topic 12c: Friendship or love between animals and men

KIPLING, *Mowgli's Brothers*
continued

Topic 13: The attribution of human qualities or virtues
to animals: personification in allegory and satire
COURAGE, Vol. 2, pages 252–267, especially
Topic 6: The formation or training of the courageous man
CUSTOM AND CONVENTION, Vol. 2, pages 268–285, especially
Topic 7a: Custom as unifying a community
EDUCATION, Vol. 2, pages 376–399, especially
Topic 3: The training of the body and the cultivation of bodily
skills: gymnastics, manual work

RELATED AUTHORS AND WORKS IN *Great Books of the Western World*

Homer, Vol. 4, *Odyssey*, Bk. XVII, page 280
Aristotle, Vol. 9, *History of Animals*, Bk. IX, Chap. 1, pages 133–135
Plutarch, Vol. 14, *Romulus*, pages 15–20
Milton, Vol. 32, *Paradise Lost*, Bk. IV, pages 152–174; Bk. VIII,
pages 232–246
Swift, Vol. 36, *Gulliver's Travels*, Part IV, pages 135–184
Darwin, Vol. 49, *Origin of Species*, pages v–251; *Descent of Man*,
pages 253–659

RELATED AUTHORS AND WORKS IN *Gateway to the Great Books*

Bacon, *Of Custom and Education*, Vol. 7, pages 18–19;
Of Friendship, Vol. 10, pages 353–358
Balzac, *Passion in the Desert*, Vol. 3, pages 436–447
Cicero, *On Friendship*, Vol. 10, pages 286–316
Emerson, *Thoreau*, Vol. 6, pages 150–165
Fabre, *Laboratory of the Open Fields*, Vol. 8, pages 97–104
Flaubert, *Legend of St. Julian the Hospitaller*, Vol. 3, pages 371–392
Huxley, *On the Relations of Man to the Lower Animals*, Vol. 8,
pages 160–204
Lawrence, *Rocking-Horse Winner*, Vol. 3, pages 515–525
Schopenhauer, *On Education*, Vol. 7, pages 197–203

JEAN DE LA BRUYÈRE, 1645–1696

Characters
Vol. 6, pages 102–105

SUGGESTED READINGS IN THE *Syntopicon*

ARISTOCRACY, Vol. 2, pages 50–63, especially
  Topic 3: The causes of degeneration or instability
    in aristocracies: aristocracy and revolution
CUSTOM AND CONVENTION, Vol. 2, pages 268–285, especially
  Topic 5: Custom and convention in the moral order
  Topic 5a: The conventional determination of moral judgments:
    the moral evaluation of conventions
HISTORY, Vol. 2, pages 711–727, especially
  Topic 2: The light and lesson of history: its role
    in the education of the mind and in the guidance
    of human conduct
HONOR, Vol. 2, pages 728–748, especially
  Topic 1: The relation of honor and fame: praise and reputation
VIRTUE AND VICE, Vol. 3, pages 975–1009, especially
  Topic 9: The advance or decline of human morality

RELATED AUTHORS AND WORKS IN *Great Books of the Western World*

Aristotle, Vol. 9, *Nicomachean Ethics*, Bks. III–IV, pages 355–376
Augustine, Vol. 18, *City of God*, Bk. V, Chaps. 12–20, pages 216–226
Swift, Vol. 36, *Gulliver's Travels*, Part I, Chap. IV, pages 20–23;
  Part II, Chaps. VII, pages 76–80
Hegel, Vol. 46, *Philosophy of History*, Introduction III,
  pages 182–186
Tolstoy, Vol. 51, *War and Peace*, First Epilogue, Chaps. XIII–XIV,
  pages 665–669

RELATED AUTHORS AND WORKS IN *Gateway to the Great Books*

Bacon, *Of Great Place*, Vol. 7, pages 9–11; *Of Followers
  and Friends*, pages 20–21; *Of Riches*, pages 25–27;
  Of Friendship, Vol. 10, pages 353–358
Chekhov, *Cherry Orchard*, Vol. 4, pages 249–294
Cicero, *On Friendship*, Vol. 10, pages 286–316
Jefferson, *Biographical Sketches*, Vol. 6, pages 522–528
Molière, *Misanthrope*, Vol. 4, pages 6–51
Plutarch, *Contentment*, Vol. 10, pages 264–281
Pushkin, *Queen of Spades*, Vol. 3, pages 484–507
Sheridan, *School for Scandal*, Vol. 4, pages 85–159
Xenophon, "Character of Socrates," Vol. 6, pages 223–226

CHARLES LAMB, 1775–1834

My First Play
Vol. 5, pages 300–303

SUGGESTED READINGS IN THE *Syntopicon*

ART, Vol. 2, pages 64–86, especially
    Topic 7a: Art as a source of pleasure or delight
KNOWLEDGE, Vol. 2, pages 880–920, especially
    Topic 6b(4): Knowledge in relation to the faculties
        of understanding, judgment, and reason;
        and to the work of intuition, imagination,
        and understanding
MEMORY AND IMAGINATION, Vol. 3, pages 133–157, especially
    Topic 7a: The use of imagination in the production
        and appreciation of works of art
POETRY, Vol. 3, pages 400–419, especially
    Topic 7d: Spectacle and song in drama

RELATED AUTHORS AND WORKS IN *Great Books of the Western World*

Aristotle, Vol. 9, *On Poetics*, pages 682–689, *passim*
Shakespeare, Vol. 27, *Hamlet*, pages 29–72
Cervantes, Vol. 29, *Don Quixote*, First Part, Chap. 48,
    pages 185–187
Fielding, Vol. 37, *Tom Jones*, Bk. VII, Chap. 1, pages 121–123;
    Bk. XVI, Chap. 5, pages 347–348
Kant, Vol. 42, *Critique of Judgement*, Introduction, pages 471–473;
    First Part, Sect. I, Bk. I, pages 476–483
Goethe, Vol. 47, *Faust*, Prelude on the Stage, pages 2–6
Freud, Vol. 54, *Civilization and Its Discontents*, Chap. II,
    pages 773–775

RELATED AUTHORS AND WORKS IN *Gateway to the Great Books*

De Quincey, *On the Knocking at the Gate in Macbeth*, Vol. 5,
    pages 362–366
Hume, *Of the Standard of Taste*, Vol. 5, pages 103–119
Johnson, *Preface to Shakespeare*, Vol. 5, pages 316–353
Schopenhauer, *On Some Forms of Literature*, Vol. 5, pages 137–142

Dream Children, a Reverie
Vol. 5, pages 304–307

SUGGESTED READINGS IN THE *Syntopicon*

MEMORY AND IMAGINATION, Vol. 3, pages 133–157,
especially
Topic 4a: Memory in the life of the individual: personal
identity and continuity
Topic 8c: The expression of desire in daydreaming or fantasy
SENSE, Vol. 3, pages 706–729, especially
Topic 3d(2): Memory and imagination as interior powers
of sense

RELATED AUTHORS AND WORKS IN *Great Books of the Western World*

Aristotle, Vol. 8, *On Memory and Reminiscence*, pages 690–695
Virgil, Vol. 13, *Aeneid*, Bk. VI, pages 211–235
Plotinus, Vol. 17, *Fourth Ennead*, Third Tractate, pages 155–159
Pascal, Vol. 33, *Pensées*, Sect. II, pages 186–189
Locke, Vol. 35, *Concerning Human Understanding*, Bk. II,
Chap. XXVII, pages 222–227
Freud, Vol. 54, *Interpretation of Dreams*, pages 135–398

RELATED AUTHORS AND WORKS IN *Gateway to the Great Books*

Bacon, *Of Youth and Age*, Vol. 7, pages 3–4
Dostoevsky, *White Nights*, Vol. 3, pages 276–319
Flaubert, *Legend of St. Julian the Hospitaller*, Vol. 3, pages 371–392
Hazlitt, *Of Persons One Would Wish to Have Seen*, Vol. 5,
pages 284–295
Lawrence, *Rocking-Horse Winner*, Vol. 3, pages 512–525
Wilde, *Happy Prince*, Vol. 2, pages 261–268

Sanity of True Genius
Vol. 5, pages 308–310

SUGGESTED READINGS IN THE *Syntopicon*

ART, Vol. 2, pages 64–86, especially
Topic 5: The sources of art in experience, imagination,
and inspiration
POETRY, Vol. 3, pages 400–419, especially
Topic 3: The inspiration or genius of the poet: the influence
of the poetic tradition
Topic 5b: Poetry contrasted with history and philosophy:
the dispraise and defense of the poet

LAMB, *Sanity of True Genius*
continued

RELATED AUTHORS AND WORKS IN *Great Books of the Western World*

Plato, Vol. 7, *Ion*, pages 142–148
Fielding, Vol. 37, *Tom Jones*, Bk. XII, Chap. 1, pages 246–247;
Bk. XIII, Chap. 1, pages 273–274
Kant, Vol. 42, *Critique of Judgement*, First Part, Sect. I,
pages 525–534
James, W., Vol. 53, *Principles of Psychology*, Chap. XXII, pages
686–689

RELATED AUTHORS AND WORKS IN *Gateway to the Great Books*

Arnold, *Study of Poetry*, Vol. 5, pages 19–41
Eliot, T. S., *Tradition and the Individual Talent*, Vol. 5,
pages 404–411
Emerson, *Thoreau*, Vol. 6, pages 150–165; *Self-Reliance*, Vol. 10,
pages 525–545
Hawthorne, *Sketch of Abraham Lincoln*, Vol. 6, pages 168–171
Hazlitt, *My First Acquaintance with Poets*, Vol. 5, pages 264–279
Poe, *Tell-Tale Heart*, Vol. 2, pages 273–277
Shelley, *Defence of Poetry*, Vol. 5, pages 216–242
Whitman, *Preface to Leaves of Grass*, Vol. 5, pages 247–259

PIERRE SIMON DE LAPLACE, 1749–1827

"Probability"
from *A Philosophical Essay on Probabilities*
Vol. 9, pages 325–338

SUGGESTED READINGS IN THE *Syntopicon*

CAUSE, Vol. 2, pages 155–178, especially
Topic 5d: The limits of our knowledge of causes
CHANCE, Vol. 2, pages 179–192
KNOWLEDGE, Vol. 2, pages 880–920, especially
Topic 4b: Knowledge, belief, and opinion: their relation
or distinction
NECESSITY AND CONTINGENCY, Vol. 3, pages 251–269,
especially
Topic 3: Necessity and contingency in the realm of change:
chance and determinism

RELATED AUTHORS AND WORKS IN *Great Books of the Western World*

Aristotle, Vol. 8, *Physics*, Bk. II, Chaps. 4–6, pages 272–275

Pascal, Vol. 33, *Pensées*, Sect. III, pages 213–217; *Correspondence with Fermat on the Theory of Probabilities*, pages 474–487

Hume, Vol. 35, *Enquiry Concerning Human Understanding*, Sect. VI, pages 469–470

RELATED AUTHORS AND WORKS IN *Gateway to the Great Books*

Clifford, *Ethics of Belief*, Vol. 10, pages 16–36

Faraday, *Observations on Mental Education*, Vol. 7, pages 208–232

Galton, "Classification of Human Ability," Vol. 8, pages 227–261

Peirce, *Red and the Black*, Vol. 9, pages 342–348

Poincaré, *Chance*, Vol. 9, pages 305–320

Pushkin, *Queen of Spades*, Vol. 3, pages 484–507

DAVID HERBERT LAWRENCE, 1885–1930

The Rocking-Horse Winner
Vol. 3, pages 512–525

SUGGESTED READINGS IN THE *Syntopicon*

EMOTION, Vol. 2, pages 413–436, especially

Topic 3a: Madness or frenzy due to emotional excess: excessively emotional or emotionally over-determined behavior

FAMILY, Vol. 2, pages 486–514, especially

Topic 7d: The emotional impact of family life upon the child: the domestic triangle; the symbolic roles of father and mother

LOVE, Vol. 2, pages 1051–1082, especially

Topic 1e: The intensity and power of love: its increase or decrease; its constructive or destructive force

WEALTH, Vol. 3, pages 1038–1070, especially

Topic 10c: Temperance and intemperance with respect to wealth: liberality, magnificence, miserliness, avarice

RELATED AUTHORS AND WORKS IN *Great Books of the Western World*

Euripides, Vol. 5, *Hippolytus*, pages 225–236

Shakespeare, Vol. 27, *Hamlet*, pages 29–72

Dostoevsky, Vol. 52, *Brothers Karamazov*, Part II, Bk. IV, Chaps. 6–7, pages 100–109

LAWRENCE, *The Rocking-Horse Winner*
continued

Freud, Vol. 54, *General Introduction to Psycho-Analysis*, Part II, Lecture 13, pages 528–531; Part III, Lecture 21, pages 580–585

RELATED AUTHORS AND WORKS IN *Gateway to the Great Books*

Bacon, *Of Parents and Children*, Vol. 7, pages 5–6; *Of Riches*, pages 25–27

Balzac, *Passion in the Desert*, Vol. 3, pages 436–447

Bunin, *Gentleman from San Francisco*, Vol. 3, pages 102–123

Eliot, G., *Lifted Veil*, Vol. 3, pages 157–193

Eliot, T. S., *Tradition and the Individual Talent*, Vol. 5, pages 404–411

Fitzgerald, *Diamond as Big as the Ritz*, Vol. 3, pages 397–431

Hawthorne, *Rappaccini's Daughter*, Vol. 3, pages 128–152

James, H., *Pupil*, Vol. 3, pages 530–568

Kipling, *Mowgli's Brothers*, Vol. 2, pages 126–141

Lamb, *Dream Children*, Vol. 5, pages 304–307

Poe, *Tell-Tale Heart*, Vol. 2, pages 273–277

Pushkin, *Queen of Spades*, Vol. 3, pages 484–507

Stevenson, *Strange Case of Dr. Jekyll and Mr. Hyde*, Vol. 2, pages 288–341

Wilde, *Happy Prince*, Vol. 2, pages 261–268

ABRAHAM LINCOLN, 1809–1865

Address at Cooper Institute
First Inaugural Address
Letter to Horace Greeley
Second Inaugural Address
Last Public Address
Vol. 6, pages 737–757; 760–765

SUGGESTED READINGS IN THE *Syntopicon*

CONSTITUTION, Vol. 2, pages 233–251, especially

Topic 7*b*: The safeguards of constitutional government: bills of rights; separation of powers: impeachment

GOVERNMENT, Vol. 2, pages 637–664, especially

Topic 5*d*: Confederation and federal union: the division of jurisdiction between state and federal governments

LIBERTY, Vol. 2, pages 991-1012, especially

Topic 5a: Man's freedom in relation to fate or to the will of God

REVOLUTION, Vol. 3, pages 626-644, especially

Topic 2c: Change in the extent of the state or empire: dissolution, secession, liberation, federation

SLAVERY, Vol. 3, pages 774-790, especially

Topic 3b: Laws regulating slavery: the rights and duties of master and slave

Topic 3c: The emancipation or manumission of slaves: the rebellion of slaves

Topic 3d: Criticisms of the institution of slavery: the injustice of slavery; its transgression of inalienable human rights

STATE, Vol. 3, pages 826-865, especially

Topic 3g: The identity and continuity of a state: the dissolution of the body politic or civil society

WAR AND PEACE, Vol. 3, pages 1010-1037, especially

Topic 5a: The moral consequences of war: its effects on the happiness and virtue of men and on the welfare of women and children

Topic 5b: The political consequences of war: its effects on different forms of government

WEALTH, Vol. 3, pages 1038-1070, especially

Topic 7b(1): Chattel slaves as property

RELATED AUTHORS AND WORKS IN *Great Books of the Western World*

Plato, Vol. 7, *Laws*, Bk. III, pages 667-671; Bk. X, pages 766-769

Aristotle, Vol. 9, *Politics*, Bk. I, Chaps. 4-7, pages 447-449

Aquinas, Vol. 20, *Summa Theologica*, Part I-II, Q 105, Art. 4, pages 318-321

Milton, Vol. 32, *Samson Agonistes*, pages 335-378

Locke, Vol. 35, *Concerning Civil Government*, Chaps. II-IV, pages 25-30; Chap. XVI, pages 65-68

Montesquieu, Vol. 38, *Spirit of Laws*, Bk. XV, Chaps. 9-18, pages 111-115

Rousseau, Vol. 38, *Discourse on Political Economy*, pages 370-377; *Social Contract*, Bk. I, Chap. 4, pages 389-390

Kant, Vol. 42, *Science of Right*, Introduction, pages 400-402; First Part, pages 421-422

Articles of Confederation, Vol. 43, pages 5-9

Constitution of the United States of America, Vol. 43, Amendment 13, Sect. I, page 18

LINCOLN, *Public Papers*
  continued

Hamilton, Madison, Jay, Vol. 43, *Federalist*, Nos. 18–20,
  pages 71–78; No. 41, pages 132–136; No. 43, pages 139–144;
  No. 54, pages 170–172
Freud, Vol. 54, *Thoughts for the Times on War and Death*, Chap.
  I, pages 756–761

RELATED AUTHORS AND WORKS IN *Gateway to the Great Books*

Adams, "United States in 1800," Vol. 6, pages 322–359
Bacon, *Of Seditions and Troubles*, Vol. 7, pages 12–17
Burke, *Letter to the Sheriffs of Bristol*, Vol. 7, pages 237–271
Calhoun, "Concurrent Majority," Vol. 7, pages 276–290
Crèvecoeur, "Making of Americans," Vol. 6, pages 546–559
Great Documents, *English Bill of Rights*, Vol. 6, pages 409–411;
  Virginia Declaration of Rights, pages 415–417; *Declaration
  of Independence*, pages 418–421
Guizot, "Civilization," Vol. 6, pages 302–317
Hawthorne, *Sketch of Abraham Lincoln*, Vol. 6, pages 168–171
Jefferson, "Virginia Constitution," Vol. 6, pages 502–517; *First
  Inaugural Address*, pages 518–521
Paine, "Call to Patriots—December 23, 1776," Vol. 6, pages 461–468
Thoreau, *Civil Disobedience*, Vol. 6, pages 695–713; *Plea
  for Captain John Brown*, pages 714–732
Tocqueville, "Observations on American Life and Government,"
  Vol. 6, pages 564–690
Washington, *Circular Letter to the Governors of All the States
  on Disbanding the Army*, Vol. 6, pages 474–483; *Farewell
  Address*, pages 484–497
Whitman, *Death of Abraham Lincoln*, Vol. 6, pages 174–183

Meditation on the Divine Will
Vol. 6, page 758

SUGGESTED READINGS IN THE *Syntopicon*

  GOD, Vol. 2, pages 543–604, especially
    Topic 5g: God's will: divine choice
  WAR AND PEACE, Vol. 3, pages 1010–1037, especially
    Topic 2a: Civil war and war between states or international
      war

RELATED AUTHORS AND WORKS IN *Great Books of the Western World*

Aquinas, Vol. 19, *Summa Theologica*, First Part, Q 19,
  pages 108–119

Hegel, Vol. 46, *Philosophy of History*, Introduction, pages 158–160
Tolstoy, Vol. 51, *War and Peace*, Second Epilogue, pages 675–677

RELATED AUTHORS AND WORKS IN *Gateway to the Great Books*

Clausewitz, *What Is War?*, Vol. 7, pages 479–497
Flaubert, *Legend of St. Julian the Hospitaller*, Vol. 3, pages 371–392
Hawthorne, *Sketch of Abraham Lincoln*, Vol. 6, pages 168–171
Maupassant, *Two Friends*, Vol. 2, pages 159–164
Synge, *Riders to the Sea*, Vol. 4, pages 342–352
Whitman, *Death of Abraham Lincoln*, Vol. 6, pages 174–183

The Gettysburg Address
Vol. 6, page 759

SUGGESTED READINGS IN THE *Syntopicon*

COURAGE, Vol. 2, pages 252–267, especially
    Topic 7c: Courage in war
DEMOCRACY, Vol. 2, pages 303–322, especially
    Topic 4b: The democratic realization of popular sovereignty:
        the safeguarding of natural rights
LIBERTY, Vol. 2, pages 991–1012, especially
    Topic 1f: The freedom of equals under government:
        the equality of citizenship
WAR AND PEACE, Vol. 3, pages 1010–1037, especially
    Topic 2a: Civil war and war between states or international war

RELATED AUTHORS AND WORKS IN *Great Books of the Western World*

Thucydides, Vol. 6, *History of the Peloponnesian War*, Second Book,
    Chap. VI, pages 395–399
Plato, Vol. 7, *Laws*, Bk. IV, pages 681–682
Aristotle, Vol. 9, *Politics*, Bk. III, Chaps. 16–17, pages 485–487
Hobbes, Vol. 23, *Leviathan*, Part II, Chap. XVIII, pages 101–104
Locke, Vol. 35, *Concerning Civil Government*, Chaps. XI–XIII,
    pages 55–59
Hamilton, Madison, Jay, Vol. 43, *Federalist*, No. 84, pages 251–254

RELATED AUTHORS AND WORKS IN *Gateway to the Great Books*

Great Documents, *Declaration of Independence*, Vol. 6,
    pages 409–456
Hawthorne, *Sketch of Abraham Lincoln*, Vol. 6, pages 168–171
Whitman, *Death of Abraham Lincoln*, Vol. 6, pages 174–183

HANIEL LONG, 1888–1956

The Power within Us

Vol. 6, pages 246–261

SUGGESTED READINGS IN THE *Syntopicon*

COURAGE, Vol. 2, pages 252–267, especially
Topic 5: The motivations of courage: fame or honor, happiness,
love, duty, religious faith
EXPERIENCE, Vol. 2, pages 468–485, especially
Topic 7: Mystical or religious experience: experience
of the supernatural
HONOR, Vol. 2, pages 728–748, especially
Topic 5c: The occasions of heroism in war and peace
MAN, Vol. 3, pages 1–41, especially
Topic 13: The grandeur and misery of man
NATURE, Vol. 3, pages 225–250, especially
Topic 2b: Nature and convention: the state of nature
and the state of society
Topic 3c(4): Divine causality in relation to the course
of nature: the preservation of nature; providence;
miracles

RELATED AUTHORS AND WORKS IN *Great Books of the Western World*

Plato, Vol. 7, *Laches*, pages 26–37
Aristotle, Vol. 9, *Nicomachean Ethics*, Bk. III, Chaps. 6–9,
pages 361–364
Hobbes, Vol. 23, *Leviathan*, Part I, Chaps. 13–15, pages 84–96
Montaigne, Vol. 25, *Of Cannibals*, pages 91–98
Shakespeare, Vol. 27, *King Lear*, pages 244–283, especially Act III,
pages 262–269
Swift, Vol. 36, *Gulliver's Travels*, Part IV, pages 135–184
Rousseau, Vol. 38, *Discourse on the Origin of Inequality*,
First–Second Parts, pages 334–353; Appendix, pages 363–366
Freud, Vol. 54, *Civilization and Its Discontents*, Chap. III, pages
776–781; Chap. IV, pages 783–784; Chaps. V–VI, pages 787–789;
Chap. VII, pages 791–792; Chap. VIII, pages 799–802

RELATED AUTHORS AND WORKS IN *Gateway to the Great Books*

Bacon, *Of Great Place*, Vol. 7, pages 9–11; *Sphinx*, Vol. 8,
pages 2–4; *Of Adversity*, Vol. 10, page 350
Crane, *Open Boat*, Vol. 3, pages 5–26
Defoe, *Robinson Crusoe*, Vol. 2, pages 5–121

Dinesen, *Sorrow-Acre*, Vol. 3, pages 615–641
Eliot, G., *Lifted Veil*, Vol. 3, pages 157–193
Emerson, *Self-Reliance*, Vol. 10, pages 525–545
Flaubert, *Legend of St. Julian the Hospitaller*, Vol. 3, pages 371–392
Hazlitt, *On the Feeling of Immortality in Youth*, Vol. 10,
    pages 565–570
James, W., *Energies of Men*, Vol. 7, pages 157–170
O'Neill, *Emperor Jones*, Vol. 4, pages 357–382
Prescott, "Land of Montezuma," Vol. 6, pages 231–243
Synge, *Riders to the Sea*, Vol. 4, pages 342–352
Tolstoy, *Three Hermits*, Vol. 3, pages 700–706; *What Men Live By*,
    pages 707–727
Xenophon, "March to the Sea," Vol. 6, pages 196–222

LUCIAN, *c.* 125–*c.* 190

The Way to Write History
Vol. 6, pages 387–406

SUGGESTED READINGS IN THE *Syntopicon*

EDUCATION, Vol. 2, pages 376–399, especially
    Topic 4*d*: The effect upon character of poetry, music, and other
        arts: the role of history and examples
HISTORY, Vol. 2, pages 711–727, especially
    Topic 1: History as knowledge and as literature: its kinds
        and divisions; its distinction from poetry, myth,
        philosophy, and science
    Topic 3: The writing of history: research and narration

RELATED AUTHORS AND WORKS IN *Great Books of the Western World*

Herodotus, Vol. 6, *History*, First Book, pages 1–48; Second Book,
    pages 71–73
Thucydides, Vol. 6, *History of the Peloponnesian War*,
    First Book, Chap. I, pages 349–355
Plato, Vol. 7, *Republic*, Bks. II–III, pages 320–333; Bk. X,
    pages 427–434
Aristotle, Vol. 9, *On Poetics*, Chap. 9, page 686
Montaigne, Vol. 25, *Of Books*, pages 194–200
Bacon, Vol. 30, *Advancement of Learning*, Second Book, pages 37–39
Fielding, Vol. 37, *Tom Jones*, Bk. II, Chap. 1, pages 19–20; Bk. VIII,
    Chap. 1, pages 152–155; Bk. IX, Chap. 1, pages 189–191
Hegel, Vol. 46, *Philosophy of History*, Introduction II–III,
    pages 155–158

LUCIAN, *The Way to Write History*
continued

Melville, Vol. 48, *Moby Dick*, Chap. 45, pages 150–156;
Chaps. 82–83, pages 267–270
Tolstoy, Vol. 51, *War and Peace*, Second Epilogue, pages 675–696

RELATED AUTHORS AND WORKS IN *Gateway to the Great Books*

Bury, *Herodotus*, Vol. 6, pages 364–383
Guizot, "Civilization," Vol. 6, pages 302–317
Hume, *Of the Study of History*, Vol. 7, pages 89–92
Voltaire, *Micromégas*, Vol. 2, pages 241–256
Woolf, *How Should One Read a Book?*, Vol. 5, pages 5–14; *Art of Biography*, Vol. 6, pages 186–192

SIR CHARLES LYELL, 1797–1875

"Geological Evolution"
from *The Principles of Geology*
Vol. 8, pages 319–324

SUGGESTED READINGS IN THE *Syntopicon*

CHANGE, Vol. 2, pages 193–217, especially
Topic 11: The apprehension of change: by sense, by reason
Topic 13: The problem of the eternity of motion or change
EVOLUTION, Vol. 2, pages 451–467, especially
Topic 6a: The geological record: the significance of fossil remains
TIME, Vol. 3, pages 896–914, especially
Topic 6e: Knowledge of the past: the storehouse of memory; the evidences of the past in physical traces or remnants

RELATED AUTHORS AND WORKS IN *Great Books of the Western World*

Aristotle, Vol. 8, *Physics*, Bk. VIII, pages 336–340
Gilbert, Vol. 28, *On the Loadstone*, Bk. VI, pages 106–121
Darwin, Vol. 49, *Origin of Species*, Chaps. X–XI, pages 152–180; Chap. XV, pages 231–243

RELATED AUTHORS AND WORKS IN *Gateway to the Great Books*

Carson, *Sunless Sea*, Vol. 8, pages 132–146
Darwin, *Autobiography*, Vol. 8, pages 47–93

Eiseley, "On Time," Vol. 8, pages 123–129
Huxley, *On a Piece of Chalk*, Vol. 8, pages 205–222
Pliny, "Eruption of Vesuvius," Vol. 6, pages 264–270

THOMAS BABINGTON MACAULAY, 1800–1859

Machiavelli
Vol. 7, pages 295–329

SUGGESTED READINGS IN THE *Syntopicon*

ARISTOCRACY, Vol. 2, pages 50–63, especially
  Topic 3: The causes of degeneration or instability
    in aristocracies: aristocracy and revolution
EXPERIENCE, Vol. 2, pages 468–485, especially
  Topic 6b: The role of experience in politics: the lessons
    of history
HISTORY, Vol. 2, pages 711–727, especially
  Topic 2: The light and lesson of history: its role
    in the education of the mind and in the guidance
    of human conduct
LIBERTY, Vol. 2, pages 991–1012, especially
  Topic 6c: The struggle for sovereign independence against
    the yoke of imperialism or colonial subjugation
STATE, Vol. 3, pages 826–865, especially
  Topic 8c: The education or training of the statesman or prince
VIRTUE AND VICE, Vol. 3, pages 975–1009, especially
  Topic 7d: The virtues which constitute the good or successful
    ruler: the vices associated with the possession
    of power
WAR AND PEACE, Vol. 3, pages 1010–1037, especially
  Topic 10: The military arts and the military profession: their
    role in the state

RELATED AUTHORS AND WORKS IN *Great Books of the Western World*

Thucydides, Vol. 6, *History of the Peloponnesian War*, Third
  Book, pages 417–446
Plato, Vol. 7, *Seventh Letter*, pages 806–807
Aristotle, Vol. 9, *Politics*, Bk. VI, pages 520–526
Dante, Vol. 21, *Divine Comedy*, Paradise, Canto XVI,
  pages 130–132

MACAULAY, *Machiavelli*
continued

Montaigne, Vol. 25, *Observation on the Means to Carry on a War According to Julius Caesar*, pages 354–358
Gibbon, Vol. 40, *Decline and Fall of the Roman Empire*, pages 630–634
Hamilton, Madison, Jay, Vol. 43, *Federalist*, Nos. 1–10, pages 29–53; especially Nos. 3–5, pages 33–38

RELATED AUTHORS AND WORKS IN *Gateway to the Great Books*

Bacon, *Of Great Place*, Vol. 7, pages 9–11; *Of Seditions and Troubles*, pages 12–17
Carlyle, *Hero as King*, Vol. 6, pages 110–145
Clausewitz, *What Is War?*, Vol. 7, pages 479–497
Guizot, "Civilization," Vol. 6, pages 302–317
Hume, *Of the Study of History*, Vol. 7, pages 89–92
Pater, "Art of Life," Vol. 10, pages 258–261
Prescott, "Land of Montezuma," Vol. 6, pages 231–243

For Machiavelli's *The Prince* in *Great Books of the Western World*, see Vol. 23, pages 3–37

THOMAS ROBERT MALTHUS, 1766–1834

"The Principle of Population"
from *Population: the First Essay*
Vol. 7, pages 502–530

SUGGESTED READINGS IN THE *Syntopicon*

JUSTICE, Vol. 2, pages 850–879, especially
    Topic 8: Economic justice: justice in production, distribution, and exchange
STATE, Vol. 3, pages 826–865, especially
    Topic 4c: The size, diversity, and distribution of populations: the causes and effects of their increase or decrease
WEALTH, Vol. 3, pages 1038–1070, especially
    Topic 8c: The causes of poverty: competition, incompetence, indigence, expropriation, unemployment; the poverty of the proletariat as dispossessed of the instruments of production
    Topic 8d: Laws concerning poverty: the poor laws, the dole

RELATED AUTHORS AND WORKS IN *Great Books of the Western World*

Plato, Vol. 7, *Laws*, Bk. III, pages 663–667
Aristotle, Vol. 9, *Politics*, Bk. VII, Chaps. 4–5, pages 530–531
Montesquieu, Vol. 38, *Spirit of Laws*, Bk. XXIII,
    pages 187–200
Smith, Vol. 39, *Wealth of Nations*, Bk. I, Chap. VIII,
    pages 33–34
Darwin, Vol. 49, *Origin of Species*, Chap. III, pages 32–39

RELATED AUTHORS AND WORKS IN *Gateway to the Great Books*

Adams, "United States in 1800," Vol. 6, pages 322–359
Carson, *Sunless Sea*, Vol. 8, pages 132–146
Darwin, *Autobiography*, Vol. 8, pages 47–93
Guizot, "Civilization," Vol. 6, pages 302–317
Prescott, "Land of Montezuma," Vol. 6, pages 231–243
Swift, *Modest Proposal*, Vol. 7, pages 42–49

THOMAS MANN, 1875–1955

Mario and the Magician
Vol. 3, pages 573–610

SUGGESTED READINGS IN THE *Syntopicon*

GOOD AND EVIL, Vol. 2, pages 605–636, especially
    Topic 3e: Right and wrong: the social incidence of the good;
        doing or suffering good and evil
    Topic 3f: The sources of evil in human life
TYRANNY, Vol. 3, pages 939–956, especially
    Topic 1d: The character of the tyrannical man: the friends
        of the tyrant
    Topic 5c: The location of sovereignty in despotic
        and constitutional government: the sovereign person,
        the sovereign office, the sovereign people
    Topic 5d: The analogues of despotic and constitutional rule
        in the relation of the powers of the soul: the tyranny
        of the passions
WILL, Vol. 3, pages 1071–1101, especially
    Topic 3a(1): The distinction between the voluntary
        and the involuntary: the conditions of
        voluntariness; comparison of men and animals
        with respect to voluntary behavior

MANN, *Mario and the Magician*
continued

Topic 7a: Free will as a source of human dignity: its relation to slavery and civil liberty
Topic 9a: The distinction between men of strong and weak will: cultivation of will power

RELATED AUTHORS AND WORKS IN *Great Books of the Western World*

Plato, Vol. 7, *Gorgias*, pages 262–270; *Seventh Letter*, pages 800–814
Plutarch, Vol. 14, *Dion*, pages 781–802
James, W., Vol. 53, *Principles of Psychology*, Chap. XXVII, pages 836–850

RELATED AUTHORS AND WORKS IN *Gateway to the Great Books*

Eliot, G., *Lifted Veil*, Vol. 3, pages 157–193
Fitzgerald, *Diamond as Big as the Ritz*, Vol. 3, pages 397–431
Hawthorne, *Rappaccini's Daughter*, Vol. 3, pages 128–152
Macaulay, *Machiavelli*, Vol. 7, pages 295–329
Melville, *Billy Budd*, Vol. 3, pages 31–98
O'Neill, *Emperor Jones*, Vol. 4, pages 357–382
Poe, *Tell-Tale Heart*, Vol. 2, pages 273–277
Stevenson, *Strange Case of Dr. Jekyll and Mr. Hyde*, Vol. 2, pages 288–341
Twain, *Man That Corrupted Hadleyburg*, Vol. 2, pages 346–386

GUY DE MAUPASSANT, 1850–1893

Two Friends
Vol. 2, pages 159–164

SUGGESTED READINGS IN THE *Syntopicon*

COURAGE, Vol. 2, pages 252–267, especially
Topic 5: The motivations of courage: fame or honor, happiness, love, duty, religious faith
Topic 7a: The courage required of citizens and statesmen: the political recognition of courage
Topic 7c: Courage in war
HONOR, Vol. 2, pages 728–748, especially
Topic 3b: The conditions of honor or fame and the causes of dishonor or infamy
Topic 5a: Honor as a motivation of heroism
Topic 5c: The occasions of heroism in war and peace

NATURE, Vol. 3, pages 225–250, especially
Topic 2e: The natural and the unnatural or monstrous:
the normal and the abnormal
WAR AND PEACE, Vol. 3, pages 1010–1037, especially
Topic 1: War as the reign of force: the state of war
and the state of nature
Topic 5a: The moral consequences of war: its effects
on the happiness and virtue of men
and on the welfare of women and children
Topic 9: The folly and futility of war

RELATED AUTHORS AND WORKS IN *Great Books of the Western World*

Aristophanes, Vol. 5, *Lysistrata*, pages 583–599
Thucydides, Vol. 6, *History of the Peloponnesian War*, Second
Book, Chap. VI, page 397; Third Book, Chap. X, pages
429–438; Fifth Book, Chap. XVII, pages 504–508
Virgil, Vol. 13, *Eclogues*, Eclogue IX, pages 29–31
Swift, Vol. 36, *Gulliver's Travels*, Part I, pages 3–42
Tolstoy, Vol. 51, *War and Peace*, Bk. 12, Chaps. IX–XI,
pages 547–551

RELATED AUTHORS AND WORKS IN *Gateway to the Great Books*

Bacon, *Of Followers and Friends*, Vol. 7, pages 20–21; *Of Death*,
Vol. 10, pages 348–349; *Of Adversity*, page 350;
Of Friendship, pages 353–358
Browne, "Immortality," Vol. 10, pages 575–580
Cicero, *On Friendship*, Vol. 10, pages 286–316
Clausewitz, *What Is War?*, Vol. 7, pages 479–497
Dinesen, *Sorrow-Acre*, Vol. 3, pages 615–641
Hugo, "Battle with the Cannon," Vol. 2, pages 146–154
Lincoln, *Meditation on the Divine Will*, Vol. 6, page 758;
Gettysburg Address, page 759; *Second Inaugural Address*,
pages 760–761
Melville, *Billy Budd*, Vol. 3, pages 31–98
Paine, "Call to Patriots—December 23, 1776," Vol. 6, pages 461–468
Scott, *Two Drovers*, Vol. 2, pages 182–205
Synge, *Riders to the Sea*, Vol. 4, pages 342–352
Tacitus, *Life of Gnaeus Julius Agricola*, Vol. 6, pages 274–298
Whitman, *Death of Abraham Lincoln*, Vol. 6, pages 174–183

HERMAN MELVILLE, 1819–1891

Billy Budd
Vol. 3, pages 31–98

SUGGESTED READINGS IN THE *Syntopicon*

CAUSE, Vol. 2, pages 155–178, especially
   Topic 1*b*: The order of causes: the relation of cause and effect
DUTY, Vol. 2, pages 358–375, especially
   Topic 8: The tension between duty and instinct, desire, or love
GOOD AND EVIL, Vol. 2, pages 605–636, especially
   Topic 1*d*: The origin, nature, and existence of evil
   Topic 3*b*(2): The good will: its conditions and consequences
   Topic 3*e*: Right and wrong: the social incidence of the good;
      doing or suffering good and evil
LAW, Vol. 2, pages 962–990, especially
   Topic 5*h*: The defect of positive law: its need for correction
      or dispensation by equity
PUNISHMENT, Vol. 3, pages 488–512, especially
   Topic 2*a*: Free will in relation to responsibility
      and punishment: voluntariness in relation to guilt
      or fault; the accidental, the negligent,
      and the intentional

RELATED AUTHORS AND WORKS IN *Great Books of the Western World*

Euripides, Vol. 5, *Alcestis*, pages 237–247
Plato, Vol. 7, *Laws*, Bk. IX, pages 746–751
Aristotle, Vol. 9, *Nicomachean Ethics*, Bk. III, Chaps. 1–6,
   pages 355–361
Montaigne, Vol. 25, *That the Intention Is Judge of Our Actions*,
   pages 13–14
Tolstoy, Vol. 51, *War and Peace*, Second Epilogue, pages 688–694

RELATED AUTHORS AND WORKS IN *Gateway to the Great Books*

Bacon, *Of Truth*, Vol. 10, pages 346–347
Conrad, *Youth*, Vol. 2, pages 210–236
De Quincey, *Literature of Knowledge and Literature of Power*,
   Vol. 5, pages 358–361
Dinesen, *Sorrow-Acre*, Vol. 3, pages 615–641
Hemingway, *Killers*, Vol. 2, pages 169–177
Hugo, "Battle with the Cannon," Vol. 2, pages 146–154
Mann, *Mario and the Magician*, Vol. 3, pages 573–610
Maupassant, *Two Friends*, Vol. 2, pages 159–164

DMITRI MENDELEEV, 1834–1907

"The Genesis of a Law of Nature"
from *The Periodic Law of the Chemical Elements*
Vol. 8, pages 442–446

JOHN STUART MILL, 1806–1873

"Childhood and Youth"

from *Autobiography*
Vol. 6, pages 5–47

SUGGESTED READINGS IN THE *Syntopicon*

EDUCATION, Vol. 2, pages 376–399, especially
Topic 1a: The ideal of the educated man
Topic 5b: The means and methods of teaching
Topic 5d: The order of learning: the organization
of the curriculum
Topic 5f: Learning apart from teachers and books: the role
of experience
Topic 9: Historical and biographical observations concerning
the institutions and practices of education

FAMILY, Vol. 2, pages 486–514, especially
Topic 6e: The initiation of children into adult life

GOD, Vol. 2, pages 543–604, especially
Topic 10: The denial of God or the gods, or of a supernatural
order: the position of the atheist

HISTORY, Vol. 2, pages 711–727, especially
Topic 2: The light and lesson of history: its role
in the education of the mind and in the guidance
of human conduct

RELIGION, Vol. 3, pages 588–625, especially
Topic 7: Historical observations concerning religious beliefs,
institutions, and controversies

VIRTUE AND VICE, Vol. 3, pages 975–1009, especially
Topic 4d(1): The influence of parental authority
on the formation of character

RELATED AUTHORS AND WORKS IN *Great Books of the Western World*

Plato, Vol. 7, *Republic*, Bks. II–III, pages 320–339; Bk. VII,
pages 391–401
Aristotle, Vol. 9, *Politics*, Bk. VII, Chap. 14–Bk. VIII,
pages 537–548
Aurelius, Vol. 12, *Meditations*, Bk. I, pages 253–256
Augustine, Vol. 18, *Confessions*, Bk. I, pages 4–9
Rabelais, Vol. 24, *Gargantua and Pantagruel*, Bk. I, Chaps. 11–24,
pages 14–30; Bk. II, Chaps. 5–8, pages 75–83
Montaigne, Vol. 25, *Of the Education of Children*, pages 62–80

Descartes, Vol. 31, *Discourse on Method,* Part I, pages 41–44; Part VI, pages 60–67

Boswell, Vol. 44, *Life of Samuel Johnson,* pages 7–17

Goethe, Vol. 47, *Faust,* First Part, pages 44–48; Second Part, Act II, pages 164–166

RELATED AUTHORS AND WORKS IN *Gateway to the Great Books*

Arnold, *Sweetness and Light,* Vol. 5, pages 42–61

Bacon, *Of Discourse,* Vol. 5, pages 95–96; *Of Studies,* pages 97–98; *Of Youth and Age,* Vol. 7, pages 3–4; *Of Parents and Children,* pages 5–6; *Of Custom and Education,* pages 18–19

Darwin, *Autobiography,* Vol. 8, pages 47–93

De Quincey, *Literature of Knowledge and Literature of Power,* Vol. 5, pages 358–361

Eliot, G., *Lifted Veil,* Vol. 3, pages 157–193

Erskine, *Moral Obligation to Be Intelligent,* Vol. 10, pages 5–13

Franklin, *Proposals Relating to the Education of Youth in Pennsylvania,* Vol. 6, pages 536–542

Galton, "Classification of Human Ability," Vol. 8, pages 227–261

James, W., *Great Men and Their Environment,* Vol. 7, pages 171–194

Schopenhauer, *On Education,* Vol. 7, pages 197–203

Stevenson, *Lantern-Bearers,* Vol. 7, pages 112–121

Swift, *Essay on Modern Education,* Vol. 7, pages 33–39

Twain, "Learning the River," Vol. 6, pages 50–98

Woolf, *Art of Biography,* Vol. 6, pages 186–192

Nature

Vol. 10, pages 477–508

SUGGESTED READINGS IN THE *Syntopicon*

LAW, Vol. 2, pages 962–990, especially

Topic 4*d*: The natural law as underlying the precepts of virtue: its relation to the moral precepts of divine law

NATURE, Vol. 3, pages 225–250, especially

Topic 2*a*: Nature and art: the imitation of nature; co-operation with nature

Topic 2*b*: Nature and convention: the state of nature and the state of society

Topic 3*a*: The rationality of nature: the maxims and laws of nature

Topic 3*c*(4): Divine causality in relation to the course of nature: the preservation of nature; providence; miracles

JOHN STUART MILL, *Nature*
continued

RELATED AUTHORS AND WORKS IN *Great Books of the Western World*

Plato, Vol. 7, *Timaeus*, pages 447–455
Aristotle, Vol. 8, *Physics*, Bk. II, Chap. 1, pages 268–270;
    Metaphysics, Bk. V, Chap. 4, pages 534–535
Lucretius, Vol. 12, *On the Nature of Things*, Bks. I–II, pages 1–30
Epictetus, Vol. 12, *Discourses*, Bk. I, Chap. 11, pages 116–118;
    Chap. 26, pages 131–132
Aquinas, Vol. 19, *Summa Theologica*, First Part, Q 44–Q 46, Art. 2,
    pages 238–255; Q 103–105, pages 528–545
Hobbes, Vol. 23, *Leviathan*, Part I, Chap. 15, pages 91–96
Bacon, Vol. 30, *Novum Organum*, Second Book, pages 172–176
Spinoza, Vol. 31, *Ethics*, Part I, pages 355–372
Rousseau, Vol. 38, *Discourse on the Origin of Inequality*,
    pages 329–366
Kant, Vol. 42, *Critique of Judgement*, Second Part, pages 550–613

RELATED AUTHORS AND WORKS IN *Gateway to the Great Books*

Adams, *Saint Thomas Aquinas*, Vol. 10, pages 422–450
Bacon, *Sphinx*, Vol. 8, pages 2–4
Balzac, *Passion in the Desert*, Vol. 3, pages 436–447
Emerson, *Nature*, Vol. 10, pages 512–524
Huxley, *On the Relations of Man to the Lower Animals*, Vol. 8,
    pages 160–204
James, W., *Sentiment of Rationality*, Vol. 10, pages 58–87
Santayana, *Lucretius*, Vol. 10, pages 365–390
Voltaire, "Philosophy of Common Sense," Vol. 10, pages 453–474

For other works by Mill in *Great Books of the Western World*,
see Vol. 43, pages 263–476

MOLIÈRE, 1622–1673

The Misanthrope
Vol. 4, pages 6–51

SUGGESTED READINGS IN THE *Syntopicon*

EMOTION, Vol. 2, pages 413–436, especially
    Topic 4b(1): Moderation of the passions by reason: virtue,
        continence, avoidance of sin

LAW, Vol. 2, pages 962–990, especially
 Topic 3a(1): The natural moral law as the eternal law
  in human nature
MAN, Vol. 3, pages 1–41, especially
 Topic 12: Man as an object of laughter and ridicule: comedy
  and satire
OPINION, Vol. 3, pages 303–322, especially
 Topic 6a: Good and evil as matters of opinion: moral standards
  as customs or conventions reflecting prevalent
  opinion
PROGRESS, Vol. 3, pages 437–453, especially
 Topic 1c: Skeptical or pessimistic denials of progress:
  the golden age as past; the cyclical motion of history
VIRTUE AND VICE, Vol. 3, pages 975–1009, especially
 Topic 1d: Virtue as an intrinsic good: its relation to happiness
 Topic 2c: The appearances of virtue: imperfect or conditional
  virtues; the counterfeits of virtue; natural
  or temperamental dispositions which simulate virtue
 Topic 4e(3): Circumstances as affecting the morality of human
  acts
 Topic 6d: Virtue and honor
 Topic 6e: Virtue in relation to friendship and love

RELATED AUTHORS AND WORKS IN *Great Books of the Western World*

Aristophanes, Vol. 5, *Clouds*, pages 488–506
Dante, Vol. 21, *Divine Comedy*, Hell, Canto XXIII, pages 33–34
Montaigne, Vol. 25, *That the Intention Is Judge of Our Actions*,
 pages 13–14; *Apology for Raimond de Sebonde*, pages 215–219
Shakespeare, Vol. 27, *King Lear*, pages 244–283
Pascal, Vol. 33, *Pensées*, Sect. XIV, pages 349–350
Swift, Vol. 36, *Gulliver's Travels*, Part IV, pages 135–184

RELATED AUTHORS AND WORKS IN *Gateway to the Great Books*

Bacon, *Of Followers and Friends*, Vol. 7, pages 20–21; *Of Truth*,
 Vol. 10, pages 346–347; *Of Love*, pages 351–352;
 Of Friendship, pages 353–358
Butler, "Customs and Opinions of the Erewhonians," Vol. 2,
 pages 483–506
De Quincey, *Literature of Knowledge and Literature of Power*,
 Vol. 5, pages 358–361
Dickens, "Full and Faithful Report of the Memorable Trial
 of Bardell against Pickwick," Vol. 2, pages 391–448
La Bruyère, *Characters*, Vol. 6, pages 102–105

MOLIÈRE, *The Misanthrope*
continued

Ruskin, *Idealist's Arraignment of the Age*, Vol. 7, pages 126–136
Twain, *Man That Corrupted Hadleyburg*, Vol. 2, pages 346–386

The Doctor in Spite of Himself
Vol. 4, pages 52–81

SUGGESTED READINGS IN THE *Syntopicon*

MAN, Vol. 3, pages 1–41, especially
Topic 12: Man as an object of laughter and ridicule:
comedy and satire
POETRY, Vol. 3, pages 400–419, especially
Topic 4b: Tragedy and comedy
VIRTUE AND VICE, Vol. 3, pages 975–1009, especially
Topic 4e(3): Circumstances as affecting the morality of human
acts

RELATED AUTHORS AND WORKS IN *Great Books of the Western World*

Aristophanes, Vol. 5, *Birds*, pages 542–563
Rabelais, Vol. 24, *Gargantua and Pantagruel*, Bk. III, Chaps. 29–33,
pages 185–195
Shakespeare, Vol. 26, *Much Ado About Nothing*, pages 503–531
Swift, Vol. 36, *Gulliver's Travels*, Part IV, pages 135–184

RELATED AUTHORS AND WORKS IN *Gateway to the Great Books*

Butler, "Customs and Opinions of the Erewhonians," Vol. 2,
pages 483–506
Voltaire, "English Men and Ideas: On Inoculation," Vol. 7,
pages 339–343

EUGENE GLADSTONE O'NEILL,
1888–1953

The Emperor Jones
Vol. 4, pages 357–382

SUGGESTED READINGS IN THE *Syntopicon*

EMOTION, Vol. 2, pages 413–436, especially
Topic 3a: Madness or frenzy due to emotional excess:
excessively emotional or emotionally over-determined
behavior

GOOD AND EVIL, Vol. 2, pages 605–636, especially
Topic 3e: Right and wrong: the social incidence of the good; doing or suffering good and evil
MAN, Vol. 3, pages 1–41, especially
Topic 13: The grandeur and misery of man
SIN, Vol. 3, pages 753–773, especially
Topic 5: The remorse of conscience and feelings of guilt: the psychogenesis and pathological expression of the sense of sin

RELATED AUTHORS AND WORKS IN *Great Books of the Western World*

Sophocles, Vol. 5, *Ajax*, pages 143–155
Euripides, Vol. 5, *Orestes*, pages 394–400
Shakespeare, Vol. 27, *Macbeth*, Act II, Scene II, pages 291–292; Act III, Scenes II–IV, pages 296–299
Freud, Vol. 54, *Civilization and Its Discontents*, Chap. VII, pages 791–796

RELATED AUTHORS AND WORKS IN *Gateway to the Great Books*

Bacon, *Of Great Place*, Vol. 7, pages 9–11; *Of Seditions and Troubles*, pages 12–17; *Of Death*, Vol. 10, pages 348–349; *Of Adversity*, page 350
Bunin, *Gentleman from San Francisco*, Vol. 3, pages 102–123
Defoe, *Robinson Crusoe*, Vol. 2, pages 5–121
Fitzgerald, *Diamond as Big as the Ritz*, Vol. 3, pages 397–431
Flaubert, *Legend of St. Julian the Hospitaller*, Vol. 3, pages 371–392
Hemingway, *Killers*, Vol. 2, pages 169–177
James, W., *Energies of Men*, Vol. 7, pages 157–170
Long, *Power within Us*, Vol. 6, pages 246–261
Mann, *Mario and the Magician*, Vol. 3, pages 573–610
Poe, *Tell-Tale Heart*, Vol. 2, pages 273–277
Stevenson, *Strange Case of Dr. Jekyll and Mr. Hyde*, Vol. 2, pages 288–341

THOMAS PAINE, 1737–1809

"A Call to Patriots—December 23, 1776"
from *The Crisis*
Vol. 6, pages 461–468

SUGGESTED READINGS IN THE *Syntopicon*

COURAGE, Vol. 2, pages 252–267, especially
　Topic 7a: The courage required of citizens and statesmen:
　　the political recognition of courage
LIBERTY, Vol. 2, pages 991–1012, especially
　Topic 6c: The struggle for sovereign independence
　　against the yoke of imperialism
　　or colonial subjugation
REVOLUTION, Vol. 3, pages 626–644, especially
　Topic 3a: The aims of political revolution: the seizure of power;
　　the attainment of liberty, justice, equality
　Topic 6a: The right of rebellion: the circumstances justifying
　　civil disobedience or violent insurrection

RELATED AUTHORS AND WORKS IN *Great Books of the Western World*

Plato, Vol. 7, *Statesman,* pages 605–608
Locke, Vol. 35, *Concerning Civil Government,* Chaps. XVIII–XIX,
　pages 71–77
Hamilton, Madison, Jay, Vol. 43, *Federalist,* No. 45, pages 147–148
Tolstoy, Vol. 51, *War and Peace,* Bk. 12, Chap. IV, pages 537–539;
　Second Epilogue, Chaps. IV–V, pages 680–684

RELATED AUTHORS AND WORKS IN *Gateway to the Great Books*

Bacon, *Of Seditions and Troubles,* Vol. 7, pages 12–17
Burke, *Letter to the Sheriffs of Bristol,* Vol. 7, pages 237–271
Great Documents, *Declaration of Independence,* Vol. 6,
　pages 418–421
Jefferson, *First Inaugural Address,* Vol. 6, pages 518–521
Lincoln, *First Inaugural Address,* Vol. 6, pages 747–755
Maupassant, *Two Friends,* Vol. 2, pages 159–164
Washington, *Circular Letter to the Governors of All the States
　on Disbanding the Army,* Vol. 6, pages 474–483

WALTER PATER, 1839–1894

"The Art of Life"
from *The Renaissance*
Vol. 10, pages 258–261

SUGGESTED READINGS IN THE *Syntopicon*

ART, Vol. 2, pages 64–86, especially
Topic 7a: Art as a source of pleasure or delight
DESIRE, Vol. 2, pages 323–344, especially
Topic 7a(1): The pursuit of pleasure
EXPERIENCE, Vol. 2, pages 468–485, especially
Topic 8: Variety of experience as an ideal of human life

RELATED AUTHORS AND WORKS IN *Great Books of the Western World*

Plato, Vol. 7, *Republic*, Bk. VIII, pages 408–412
Aristotle, Vol. 9, *Rhetoric*, Bk. III, Chaps. 1–7, pages 653–660;
    On Poetics, Chaps. 4–15, pages 682–689
Montaigne, Vol. 25, *Of Solitude*, pages 107–112; *Of Vanity*,
    pages 458–462
Rousseau, Vol. 38, *Discourse on the Origin of Inequality*, Part I,
    pages 339–342
Goethe, Vol. 47, *Faust*, First Part, pages 37–44; Second Part,
    Act III, pages 235–243; Act V, pages 278, 281–282

RELATED AUTHORS AND WORKS IN *Gateway to the Great Books*

Arnold, *Study of Poetry*, Vol. 5, pages 19–41; *Sweetness and Light*,
    pages 42–61
Bacon, *Of Beauty*, Vol. 5, page 94; *Of Custom and Education*,
    Vol. 7, pages 18–19
Cicero, *On Old Age*, Vol. 10, pages 317–343
Dostoevsky, *White Nights*, Vol. 3, pages 276–319
Epictetus, *Enchiridion*, Vol. 10, pages 236–254
Epicurus, *Letter to Herodotus*, Vol. 10, pages 216–229; *Letter
    to Menoeceus*, pages 230–233
Hazlitt, *On the Feeling of Immortality in Youth*, Vol. 10,
    pages 565–570
James, W., *On a Certain Blindness in Human Beings*, Vol. 7,
    pages 141–156
Johnson, *Preface to Shakespeare*, Vol. 5, pages 316–353
Plutarch, *Contentment*, Vol. 10, pages 264–281
Santayana, *Goethe's Faust*, Vol. 10, pages 391–419
Shelley, *Defence of Poetry*, Vol. 5, pages 216–242

IVAN PETROVICH PAVLOV, 1849–1936

Scientific Study of the So-called Psychical Processes in the Higher Animals
Vol. 8, pages 294–309

SUGGESTED READINGS IN THE *Syntopicon*

ANIMAL, Vol. 2, pages 19–49, especially
Topic 1*e*: The conception of the animal as a machine or automaton

HABIT, Vol. 2, pages 665–683

MECHANICS, Vol. 3, pages 80–112, especially
Topic 4*c*: The mechanistic account of the phenomena of life

MEDICINE, Vol. 3, pages 113–132, especially
Topic 2*a*: The scientific foundations of the art of medicine: the contrast between the empiric and the artist in medicine

MEMORY AND IMAGINATION, Vol. 3, pages 133–157, especially
Topic 1: The faculties of memory and imagination in brutes and men

SENSE, Vol. 3, pages 706–729, especially
Topic 2*c*: Comparisons of human and animal sensitivity
Topic 3: The analysis of the power of sense: its organs and activities

RELATED AUTHORS AND WORKS IN *Great Books of the Western World*

Aristotle, Vol. 9, *History of Animals*, Bk. IV, pages 59–62
Descartes, Vol. 31, *Discourse on Method*, Part V, pages 56–60
Darwin, Vol. 49, *Descent of Man*, Chap. III, pages 293–298
James, W., Vol. 53, *Principles of Psychology*, Chap. IV, pages 68–83; Chap. XXIV, pages 705–712; Chap. XXVI, pages 827–835

RELATED AUTHORS AND WORKS IN *Gateway to the Great Books*

Bernard, *Experimental Considerations Common to Living Things and Inorganic Bodies*, Vol. 8, pages 266–290
Fabre, *Laboratory of the Open Fields*, Vol. 8, pages 97–104; *Sacred Beetle*, pages 105–119
Huxley, *On the Relations of Man to the Lower Animals*, Vol. 8, pages 160–204
Wöhler, *On the Artificial Production of Urea*, Vol. 8, pages 312–314

CHARLES SANDERS PEIRCE, 1839–1914

The Red and the Black
Vol. 9, pages 342–348

SUGGESTED READINGS IN THE *Syntopicon*

CHANCE, Vol. 2, pages 179–192, especially
Topic 4: Cause and chance in relation to knowledge
and opinion: the theory of probability
TRUTH, Vol. 3, pages 915–938, especially
Topic 2e: The distinction between truth and probability: its
relation to the distinction between knowledge
and opinion
Topic 4c: Truth in metaphysics, mathematics, and the empirical
sciences: the truth of principles, hypotheses,
and conclusions in the several speculative disciplines
Topic 4d: Truth and probability in rhetoric and dialectic
Topic 7a: The impossibility of knowing the truth:
the restriction of all human judgments to degrees
of probability; the denial of axioms
and of the possibility of demonstration

RELATED AUTHORS AND WORKS IN *Great Books of the Western World*

Pascal, Vol. 33, *Pensées*, Sect. III, pages 213–217; *Treatise
on the Arithmetical Triangle*, pages 460–468; *Correspondence
with Fermat on the Theory of Probabilities*, pages 474–487
Locke, Vol. 35, *Concerning Human Understanding*, Bk. IV,
Chap. III, pages 322–323; Chap. VI, pages 332–336;
Chaps. XV–XVII, pages 365–372

RELATED AUTHORS AND WORKS IN *Gateway to the Great Books*

Clifford, *Ethics of Belief*, Vol. 10, pages 16–36
Erskine, *Moral Obligation to Be Intelligent*, Vol. 10, pages 5–13
Faraday, *Observations on Mental Education*, Vol. 7, pages 208–232
Forsyth, *Mathematics, in Life and Thought*, Vol. 9, pages 26–46
James, W., *Will to Believe*, Vol. 10, pages 39–57
Laplace, "Probability," Vol. 9, pages 325–338
Lawrence, *Rocking-Horse Winner*, Vol. 3, pages 512–515
Poincaré, *Chance*, Vol. 9, pages 305–320
Pushkin, *Queen of Spades*, Vol. 3, pages 484–507

PLINY THE YOUNGER (GAIUS PLINIUS CAECILIUS SECUNDUS), *c.* 61–*c.* 113

"The Eruption of Vesuvius"
from *Letters*
Vol. 6, pages 264–270

SUGGESTED READINGS IN THE *Syntopicon*

COURAGE, Vol. 2, pages 252–267, especially
Topic 1: The nature of courage
Topic 6: The formation or training of the courageous man
HISTORY, Vol. 2, pages 711–727, especially
Topic 3: The writing of history: research and narration

RELATED AUTHORS AND WORKS IN *Great Books of the Western World*

Herodotus, Vol. 6, *History*, First Book, pages 1–48
Thucydides, Vol. 6, *History of the Peloponnesian War*, First Book, Chap. I, pages 349–355
Goethe, Vol. 47, *Faust*, Second Part, Act II, pages 183–195

RELATED AUTHORS AND WORKS IN *Gateway to the Great Books*

Bacon, *Of Death*, Vol. 10, pages 348–349
Lyell, "Geological Evolution," Vol. 8, pages 319–324
Prescott, "Land of Montezuma," Vol. 6, pages 231–243

PLUTARCH, *c.* 46–120

Of Bashfulness
Vol 7, pages 97–109

SUGGESTED READINGS IN THE *Syntopicon*

HONOR, Vol. 2, pages 728–748, especially
Topic 2a· The sense of honor and of shame: loyalty to the good
VIRTUE AND VICE, Vol. 3, pages 975–1009, especially
Topic 1c: The doctrine of virtue as a mean
between the extremes of vice
Topic 4· The natural causes or conditions of virtue
Topic 5: Psychological factors in the formation of moral virtue
Topic 6· Virtue in relation to other moral goods or principles

RELATED AUTHORS AND WORKS IN *Great Books of the Western World*

Aristotle, Vol. 9, *Nicomachean Ethics*, Bk. II, Chaps. 6–9, pages 351–355; Bk. III, Chap. 7–Bk. V, Chap. 11, pages 361–387; *Rhetoric*, Bk. II, Chap. 6, pages 629–631

Montaigne, Vol. 25, *Of Conscience*, pages 174–176; *Of Glory*, pages 300–307; *Of Repentance*, pages 388–395

RELATED AUTHORS AND WORKS IN *Gateway to the Great Books*

Anderson, *I'm a Fool*, Vol. 2, pages 511–520
Bacon, *Of Youth and Age*, Vol. 7, pages 3–4
Eliot, G., *Lifted Veil*, Vol. 3, pages 157–193
Melville, *Billy Budd*, Vol. 3, pages 31–98

Contentment
Vol. 10, pages 264–281

SUGGESTED READINGS IN THE *Syntopicon*

HAPPINESS, Vol. 2, pages 684–710, especially
Topic 2*a*: The marks of a happy man, the quality of a happy life
Topic 2*b*(1): The contribution of the goods of fortune to happiness: wealth, health, longevity
Topic 2*b*(7): The function of knowledge and wisdom in the happy life: the place of speculative activity and contemplation

LABOR, Vol. 2, pages 921–940, especially
Topic 1*b*: Labor, leisure, and happiness: the servile, political, and contemplative life

RELATED AUTHORS AND WORKS IN *Great Books of the Western World*

Plato, Vol. 7, *Phaedo*, pages 220–251; *Republic*, Bk. VII, pages 388–401
Aristotle, Vol. 9, *Nicomachean Ethics*, Bk. I, Chaps. 5–12, pages 340–347
Epictetus, Vol. 12, *Discourses*, Bk. III, Chap. XXIV, pages 203–210
Aquinas, Vol. 19, *Summa Theologica*, Part I–II, Q 1, Art. 7–Q 2, Art. 5, pages 614–619
Hobbes, Vol. 23, *Leviathan*, Part I, Chap. XI, pages 76–79
Montaigne, Vol. 25, *That to Study Philosophy Is to Learn to Die*, pages 28–36; *That the Relish of Good and Evil Depends in a Great Measure Upon the Opinion We Have of Them*, pages 115–125; *Of Glory*, pages 300–307
Spinoza, Vol. 31, *Ethics*, Part IV, Appendix, pages 447–450
Pascal, Vol. 33, *Pensées*, Sect. II, pages 179–204

PLUTARCH, *Contentment*
continued

Kant, Vol. 42, *Fundamental Principles of the Metaphysic
of Morals,* pages 256–287
Tolstoy, Vol. 51, *War and Peace,* Bk. 12, Chap. XIII, pages
554–555; Bk. 13, Chap. XII, pages 577–578; Chap. XIV, pages
580–582; Bk. 14, Chap. XII, pages 604–605; Chap. XV, pages
608–609; Bk. 15, Chaps. XII–XIII, pages 630–634; Chap. XIX,
pages 642–643

RELATED AUTHORS AND WORKS IN *Gateway to the Great Books*

Bacon, *Of Youth and Age,* Vol. 7, pages 3–4; *Of Great Place,*
pages 9–11; *Of Anger,* Vol. 10, pages 359–360
Bunin, *Gentleman from San Francisco,* Vol. 3, pages 102–123
Chekhov, *Darling,* Vol. 3, pages 452–462
Cicero, *On Old Age,* Vol. 10, pages 317–343
Emerson, *Thoreau,* Vol. 6, pages 150–165
Epictetus, *Enchiridion,* Vol. 10, pages 236–254
Epicurus, *Letter to Menoeceus,* Vol. 10, pages 230–233
Gogol, *Overcoat,* Vol. 2, pages 452–478
James, W., *On a Certain Blindness in Human Beings,* Vol. 7,
pages 141–156
La Bruyère, *Characters,* Vol. 6, pages 102–105
Pater, "Art of Life," Vol. 10, pages 258–261
Santayana, *Lucretius,* Vol. 10, pages 365–390
Tacitus, *Life of Gnaeus Julius Agricola,* Vol. 6, pages 274–298
Tolstoy, *Three Hermits,* Vol. 3, pages 700–706
Wilde, *Happy Prince,* Vol. 2, pages 261–268
Xenophon, "Character of Socrates," Vol. 6, pages 223–226

For Plutarch's *Lives of the Noble Grecians and Romans*
in *Great Books of the Western World,* see Vol. 14

EDGAR ALLAN POE, 1809–1849

The Tell-Tale Heart
Vol. 2, pages 273–277

SUGGESTED READINGS IN THE *Syntopicon*

EMOTION, Vol. 2, pages 413–436, especially
Topic 3*a*: Madness or frenzy due to emotional excess:
excessively emotional or emotionally over-determined
behavior

MEMORY AND IMAGINATION, Vol. 3, pages 133–157, especially

Topic 7b: The fantastic and the realistic in poetry: the probable and the possible in poetry and history

MIND, Vol. 3, pages 171–203, especially

Topic 8a: The distinction between sanity and madness: the criterion of lucidity or insight

PUNISHMENT, Vol. 3, pages 488–512, especially

Topic 2b: Sanity, maturity, and moral competence in relation to responsibility

RELATED AUTHORS AND WORKS IN *Great Books of the Western World*

Sophocles, Vol. 5, *Ajax*, pages 143–155

Euripides, Vol. 5, *Electra*, pages 327–339

Plato, Vol. 7, *Phaedrus*, pages 115–141

Shakespeare, Vol. 27, *Hamlet*, Act IV, Scene V, pages 59–62; *Othello*, Act IV, Scene I, pages 229–233

Melville, Vol. 48, *Moby Dick*, Chap. 41, pages 135–136; Chap. 44, pages 148–150

Dostoevsky, Vol. 52, *Brothers Karamazov*, Part III, Bk. VIII, Chap. 8, pages 228–235

RELATED AUTHORS AND WORKS IN *Gateway to the Great Books*

Bacon, *Of Anger*, Vol. 10, pages 359–360

Flaubert, *Legend of St. Julian the Hospitaller*, Vol. 3, pages 371–392

Hawthorne, *Rappaccini's Daughter*, Vol. 3, pages 128–152

Hemingway, *Killers*, Vol. 2, pages 169–177

Lamb, *Sanity of True Genius*, Vol. 5, pages 308–310

Lawrence, *Rocking-Horse Winner*, Vol. 3, pages 512–525

Mann, *Mario and the Magician*, Vol. 3, pages 573–610

Melville, *Billy Budd*, Vol. 3, pages 31–98

O'Neill, *Emperor Jones*, Vol. 4, pages 357–382

Pushkin, *Queen of Spades*, Vol. 3, pages 484–507

Scott, *Two Drovers*, Vol. 2, pages 182–205

Stevenson, *Strange Case of Dr. Jekyll and Mr. Hyde*, Vol. 2, pages 288–341

The Masque of the Red Death
Vol. 2, pages 278–283

SUGGESTED READINGS IN THE *Syntopicon*

LIFE AND DEATH, Vol. 2, pages 1013–1034, especially

Topic 8a: The love of life· the instinct of self-preservation; the life instinct

POE, *The Masque of the Red Death*
continued

Topic 8c: The contemplation and fear of death: the attitude
of the hero, the philosopher, the martyr
MEMORY AND IMAGINATION, Vol. 3, pages 133–157, especially
Topic 7b: The fantastic and the realistic in poetry: the probable
and the possible in poetry and history
POETRY, Vol. 3, pages 400–419, especially
Topic 6a: The expression of emotion in poetry

RELATED AUTHORS AND WORKS IN *Great Books of the Western World*

Euripides, Vol. 5, *Alcestis*, pages 242–243
Shakespeare, Vol. 26, *King Richard III*, Act I, Scene IV,
pages 114–117
Swift, Vol. 36, *Gulliver's Travels*, Part III, Chap. X, pages 124–129

RELATED AUTHORS AND WORKS IN *Gateway to the Great Books*

Bacon, *Of Death*, Vol. 10, pages 348–349
Browne, "Immortality," Vol. 10, pages 575–580
Epicurus, *Letter to Menoeceus*, Vol. 10, pages 230–233
Flaubert, *Legend of St. Julian the Hospitaller*, Vol. 3,
pages 371–392
Hawthorne, *Rappaccini's Daughter*, Vol. 3, pages 128–152
Hemingway, *Killers*, Vol. 2, pages 169–177
O'Neill, *Emperor Jones*, Vol. 4, pages 357–382
Synge, *Riders to the Sea*, Vol. 4, pages 342–352

HENRI POINCARÉ, 1854–1912

Space
Vol. 9, pages 265–293

SUGGESTED READINGS IN THE *Syntopicon*

MATHEMATICS, Vol. 3, pages 42–62, especially
Topic 1c: The certainty and exactitude of mathematical
knowledge: the *a priori* foundations of arithmetic
and geometry
Topic 4b: The operations of geometry
QUANTITY, Vol. 3, pages 527–545, especially
Topic 3: The magnitudes of geometry: the relations
of dimensionality

SPACE, Vol. 3, pages 811–825, especially
Topic 3c: Geometrical space, its kinds and properties: spatial relationships and configurations
Topic 5: The mode of existence of geometrical objects: their character as abstractions; their relation to intelligible matter

RELATED AUTHORS AND WORKS IN *Great Books of the Western World*

Aristotle, Vol. 8, *Physics*, Bk. III, Chap. 4–Bk. IV, Chap. 9, pages 280–297
Euclid, Vol. 11, *Elements*, Bk. I, pages 1–29
Descartes, Vol. 31, *Rules for the Direction of the Mind*, Rule XIV, pages 28–33
Newton, Vol. 34, *Mathematical Principles of Natural Philosophy*, pages 1–372
Kant, Vol. 42, *Critique of Pure Reason*, pages 211–218
James, W., Vol. 53, *Principles of Psychology*, Chap. XX, pages 540–635

RELATED AUTHORS AND WORKS IN *Gateway to the Great Books*

Clifford, *Postulates of the Science of Space*, Vol. 9, pages 243–259
Russell, *Mathematics and the Metaphysicians*, Vol. 9, pages 95–110
Voltaire, *Micromégas*, Vol. 2, pages 241–256; "English Men and Ideas," Vol. 7, pages 332–378

Mathematical Creation
Vol. 9, pages 294–304

SUGGESTED READINGS IN THE *Syntopicon*

INDUCTION, Vol. 2, pages 805–815, especially
Topic 2: The conditions or sources of induction: memory, experience, experiment
MATHEMATICS, Vol. 3, pages 42–62, especially
Topic 3: Method in mathematics: the model of mathematical thought
REASONING, Vol. 3, pages 546–568, especially
Topic 1b: Discursive reasoning contrasted with immediate intuition
Topic 1c: The role of sense, memory, and imagination in reasoning: perceptual inference, rational reminiscence, the collation of images

RELATED AUTHORS AND WORKS IN *Great Books of the Western World*

Aristotle, Vol. 8, *Metaphysics*, Bk. XIV, Chaps. 3–6, pages 622–626
Pascal, Vol. 33, *Pensées*, Sect. I, pages 171–173

POINCARÉ, *Mathematical Creation*
continued

James, W., Vol. 53, *Principles of Psychology*, Chap. XXVIII, pages 874–878

RELATED AUTHORS AND WORKS IN *Gateway to the Great Books*

Campbell, *Numerical Laws and the Use of Mathematics in Science*, Vol. 9, pages 222–238
Curie, *Discovery of Radium*, Vol. 8, pages 32–42
Dantzig, *Fingerprints*, Vol. 9, pages 165–177; *Empty Column*, pages 178–189
Darwin, *Autobiography*, Vol. 8, pages 47–93
Dewey, "Process of Thought," Vol. 10, pages 92–213
Galton, "Classification of Human Ability," Vol. 8, pages 227–261
Hogben, *Mathematics, the Mirror of Civilization*, Vol. 9, pages 3–23
Mendeleev, "Genesis of a Law of Nature," Vol. 8, pages 442–446
Russell, *Study of Mathematics*, Vol. 9, pages 84–94
Tyndall, "Michael Faraday," Vol. 8, pages 8–28
Whitehead, "On Mathematical Method," Vol. 9, pages 51–67

Chance
Vol. 9, pages 305–320

SUGGESTED READINGS IN THE *Syntopicon*

CAUSE, Vol. 2, pages 155–178, especially
Topic 5: Cause in relation to knowledge
CHANCE, Vol. 2, pages 179–192, especially
Topic 1: The conception of chance
Topic 2a: The relation of chance to causality: philosophical or scientific determinism
Topic 4: Cause and chance in relation to knowledge and opinion: the theory of probability
NECESSITY AND CONTINGENCY, Vol. 3, pages 251–269, especially
Topic 3: Necessity and contingency in the realm of change: chance and determinism
Topic 4: Necessity and contingency in the realm of thought

RELATED AUTHORS AND WORKS IN *Great Books of the Western World*

Aristotle, Vol. 8, *Physics*, Bk. II, Chaps. 4–6, pages 272–275
Pascal, Vol. 33, *Treatise on the Arithmetical Triangle*, pages 460–468; *Correspondence with Fermat on the Theory of Probabilities*, pages 474–487

Hume, Vol. 35, *Enquiry Concerning Human Understanding*, Sect. VI, pages 469–470

Locke, Vol. 35, *Concerning Human Understanding*, Bk. IV, Chaps. III–IV, pages 322–323; Chap. VI, pages 332–336; Chaps. XV–XVII, pages 365–372

RELATED AUTHORS AND WORKS IN *Gateway to the Great Books*

Eddington, *Running-Down of the Universe*, Vol. 8, pages 565–580
Laplace, "Probability," Vol. 9, pages 325–338
Lawrence, *Rocking-Horse Winner*, Vol. 3, pages 512–525
Peirce, *Red and the Black*, Vol. 9, pages 342–348
Pushkin, *Queen of Spades*, Vol. 3, pages 484–507

WILLIAM HICKLING PRESCOTT, 1796–1859

"The Land of Montezuma"
from *The Conquest of Mexico*
Vol. 6, pages 231–243

SUGGESTED READINGS IN THE *Syntopicon*

MONARCHY, Vol. 3, pages 204–224, especially
   Topic 5: The absolute government of colonies, dependencies, or conquered peoples

REVOLUTION, Vol. 3, pages 626–644, especially
   Topic 7: Empire and revolution: the justification of colonial rebellion and the defense of imperialism

SLAVERY, Vol. 3, pages 774–790, especially
   Topic 6d: The imperialistic subjection or enslavement of conquered peoples or colonial dependencies

STATE, Vol. 3, pages 826–865, especially
   Topic 9f: Colonization and imperialism: the economic and political factors in empire

TYRANNY, Vol. 3, pages 939–956, especially
   Topic 7: The ways of tyrants or despots to attain and maintain power

WAR AND PEACE, Vol. 3, pages 1010–1037, especially
   Topic 6a: Conquest, empire, political expansion as ends of war
   Topic 10c: The military virtues: the qualities of the professional soldier; education for war

PRESCOTT, "The Land of Montezuma"
continued

RELATED AUTHORS AND WORKS IN *Great Books of the Western World*

Herodotus, Vol. 6, *History*, First Book, pages 16–20, 23–31;
Fifth–Sixth Books, pages 160–213
Thucydides, Vol. 6, *History of the Peloponnesian War*, Third
Book, Chap. IX, pages 425–428; Fifth Book, Chap. XVII,
pages 504–508
Hobbes, Vol. 23, *Leviathan*, Part II, Chaps. 19–20, pages 107–111
Montaigne, Vol. 25, *Of Cannibals*, pages 91–98
Gibbon, Vol. 40, *Decline and Fall of the Roman Empire*, Chap. II,
pages 21–23; Chap. XXVI, pages 420–422; Chap. XXX, pages
477–491; Chap. XXXI, pages 521–523; Vol. 41, Chap. XLIII,
pages 51–54

RELATED AUTHORS AND WORKS IN *Gateway to the Great Books*

Clausewitz, *What Is War?*, Vol. 7, pages 479–497
Hume, *Of Refinement in the Arts*, Vol. 7, pages 52–61
Long, *Power within Us*, Vol. 6, pages 246–261
Macaulay, *Machiavelli*, Vol. 7, pages 295–329
Malthus, "Principle of Population," Vol. 7, pages 502–530
Pliny, "Eruption of Vesuvius," Vol. 6, pages 264–270
Tacitus, *Life of Gnaeus Julius Agricola*, Vol. 6, pages 274–298
Xenophon, "March to the Sea," Vol. 6, pages 196–222

ALEXANDER PUSHKIN, 1799–1837

The Queen of Spades
Vol. 3, pages 484–507

SUGGESTED READINGS IN THE *Syntopicon*

CHANCE, Vol. 2, pages 179–192, especially
Topic 5: The control of chance or contingency by art
Topic 6a: Chance and fortune in the life of the individual
DESIRE, Vol. 2, pages 323–344, especially
Topic 5c: Desire ruling action: the unchecked expression
of desires; incontinence
Topic 7a(2): The lust for power
Topic 7a(3): The accumulation of wealth

WILL, Vol. 3, pages 1071–1101, especially

Topic 2c(3): The several acts of the will with respect to means: their antecedents and consequences

Topic 9a: The distinction between men of strong and weak will: cultivation of will power

RELATED AUTHORS AND WORKS IN *Great Books of the Western World*

Plato, Vol. 7, *Laws*, Bk. IV, page 679

Pascal, Vol. 33, *Correspondence with Fermat on the Theory of Probabilities*, pages 474–487

Berkeley, Vol. 35, *Principles of Human Knowledge*, page 431

Hegel, Vol. 46, *Philosophy of Right*, Third Part, pages 64–67

Melville, Vol. 48, *Moby Dick*, Chap. 37, pages 122–123; Chap. 41, pages 136–138; Chap. 134, pages 409–411

Tolstoy, Vol. 51, *War and Peace*, Bk. 4, Chaps. XIII–XVI, pages 188–193

RELATED AUTHORS AND WORKS IN *Gateway to the Great Books*

Bacon, *Of Riches*, Vol. 7, pages 25–27

Bunin, *Gentleman from San Francisco*, Vol. 3, pages 102–123

Eliot, G., *Lifted Veil*, Vol. 3, pages 157–193

Fitzgerald, *Diamond as Big as the Ritz*, Vol. 3, pages 397–431

La Bruyère, *Characters*, Vol. 6, pages 102–105

Laplace, "Probability," Vol. 9, pages 325–338

Lawrence, *Rocking-Horse Winner*, Vol. 3, pages 512–525

Peirce, *Red and the Black*, Vol. 9, pages 342–348

Poe, *Tell-Tale Heart*, Vol. 2, pages 273–277

Poincaré, *Chance*, Vol. 9, pages 305–320

JEAN JACQUES ROUSSEAU, 1712–1778

A Lasting Peace through the Federation of Europe
Vol. 7, pages 405–436

SUGGESTED READINGS IN THE *Syntopicon*

GOVERNMENT, Vol. 2, pages 637–664, especially

Topic 5a: Foreign policy: the making of treaties; the conduct of war and peace

LAW, Vol. 2, pages 962–990, especially

Topic 1a: The end of law: peace, order, and the common good

ROUSSEAU, *A Lasting Peace*
continued

STATE, Vol. 3, pages 826–865, especially
    Topic 9e(1): The military problem of the state: preparation
        for conquest or defense
    Topic 9e(2): Treaties between states: alliances, leagues,
        confederacies, or hegemonies
WAR AND PEACE, Vol. 3, pages 1010–1037, especially
    Topic 5c: The economic consequences of war: the cost of war
        and the by-products of war
    Topic 6a: Conquest, empire, political expansion as ends of war
    Topic 11a: Law and government as indispensable conditions
        of civil peace: the political community as the unit
        of peace
    Topic 11c: International law and international peace: treaties,
        alliances, and leagues as instrumentalities
        of international peace

RELATED AUTHORS AND WORKS IN *Great Books of the Western World*

Plato, Vol. 7, *Laws*, Bk. III, pages 663–677
Hobbes, Vol. 23, *Leviathan*, Part I, Chaps. 13–14, pages 85–87;
    Chap. 15, pages 91–93
Locke, Vol. 35, *Concerning Civil Government*, Chap. XVI,
    pages 65–70
Montesquieu, Vol. 38, *Spirit of Laws*, Bk. X, pages 61–68
Smith, Vol. 39, *Wealth of Nations*, Bk. V, Part I, pages 301–309
Kant, Vol. 42, *Science of Right*, Second Part, pages 452–456
Hamilton, Madison, Jay, Vol. 43, *Federalist*, Nos. 3–9, pages 33–49
Mill, J. S., Vol. 43, *Representative Government*, Chaps. 15–17,
    pages 417–433
Freud, Vol. 54, *Thoughts for the Times on War and Death*,
    Chap. I, pages 755–761

RELATED AUTHORS AND WORKS IN *Gateway to the Great Books*

Clausewitz, *What Is War?*, Vol. 7, pages 479–497
Dante, "On World Government," Vol. 7, pages 383–399
Kant, *Perpetual Peace*, Vol. 7, pages 441–475
Washington, *Farewell Address*, Vol. 6, pages 484–497

For other works by Rousseau in *Great Books of the Western World*,
see Vol. 38, pages 319–439

JOHN RUSKIN, 1819–1900

An Idealist's Arraignment of the Age
Vol. 7, pages 126–136

SUGGESTED READINGS IN THE Syntopicon

ART, Vol. 2, pages 64–86, especially
  Topic 12: The history of the arts: progress in art as measuring
    stages of civilization
BEAUTY, Vol. 2, pages 112–125, especially
  Topic 4: Beauty and ugliness in relation to pleasure and pain
FAMILY, Vol. 2, pages 486–514, especially
  Topic 5: The position of women
LABOR, Vol. 2, pages 921–940, especially
  Topic 1a: The curse of labor: myths of a golden age
    and the decay of the world
  Topic 1e: The honor of work and the virtue of productivity:
    progress through the invention of arts
    for the conquest of nature
PROGRESS, Vol. 3, pages 437–453, especially
  Topic 1c: Skeptical or pessimistic denials of progress:
    the golden age as past; the cyclical motion of history
  Topic 6: Intellectual or cultural progress: its sources
    and impediments

RELATED AUTHORS AND WORKS IN Great Books of the Western World

Aristotle, Vol. 9, Politics, Bk. I, Chap. 4, page 447
Lucretius, Vol. 12, On the Nature of Things, Bk. V, pages 73–80
Hobbes, Vol. 23, Leviathan, Part IV, Chap. 46, pages 267–269
Bacon, Vol. 30, Advancement of Learning, Second Book,
  pages 29–39
Swift, Vol. 36, Gulliver's Travels, Part III, Chaps. IV–VI,
  pages 103–115
Rousseau, Vol. 38, Discourse on the Origin of Inequality, First
  Part, pages 336–340
Smith, Vol. 39, Wealth of Nations, Bk. I, Chap. III, pages 8–10
Freud, Vol. 54, Civilization and Its Discontents, Chap. III,
  pages 776–780

RELATED AUTHORS AND WORKS IN Gateway to the Great Books

Arnold, Sweetness and Light, Vol. 5, pages 42–61
Butler, "Customs and Opinions of the Erewhonians," Vol. 2,
  pages 483–506

RUSKIN, *An Idealist's Arraignment of the Age*
continued

Chekhov, *Cherry Orchard*, Vol. 4, pages 249–294
Emerson, *Thoreau*, Vol. 6, pages 150–165
Guizot, "Civilization," Vol. 6, pages 302–317
Hume, *Of Refinement in the Arts*, Vol. 7, pages 52–61
Ibsen, *Enemy of the People*, Vol. 4, pages 164–246
Pater, "Art of Life," Vol. 10, pages 258–261
Stevenson, *Lantern-Bearers*, Vol. 7, pages 112–121
Swift, *Essay on Modern Education*, Vol. 7, pages 33–39; *Modest Proposal*, pages 42–49
Tolstoy, *What Men Live By*, Vol. 3, pages 707–727

BERTRAND A. W. RUSSELL, 1872–

The Study of Mathematics
Vol. 9, pages 84–94

SUGGESTED READINGS IN THE *Syntopicon*

LOGIC, Vol. 2, pages 1035–1050, especially
 Topic 3: Logic as an art: its place in education
 Topic 4a: Mathematical analysis and reasoning: the search
  for a universal method
MATHEMATICS, Vol. 3, pages 42–62, especially
 Topic 1a: The distinction of mathematics from physics
  and metaphysics; its relation to logic
 Topic 1b: The service of mathematics to dialectic
  and philosophy: its place in liberal education
NECESSITY AND CONTINGENCY, Vol. 3, pages 251–269,
 especially
 Topic 4d: Mathematical necessity: necessity in the objects
  of mathematics and in mathematical reasoning

RELATED AUTHORS AND WORKS IN *Great Books of the Western World*

Plato, Vol. 7, *Republic*, Bk. VII, pages 391–398; *Philebus*, pages
 633–636; *Laws*, Bk. VII, pages 728–730
Aristotle, Vol. 8, *Metaphysics*, Bk. XIV, Chaps. 3–6, pages 622–626
Euclid, Vol. 11, *Elements*, Bks. I–II, pages 5–31
Pascal, Vol. 33, *Pensées*, Sect. I, pages 171–173; *On Geometrical Demonstration*, pages 430–439

Kant, Vol. 42, *Critique of Pure Reason,* pages 211–218
James, W., Vol. 53, *Principles of Psychology,* Chap. XXVIII,
    pages 874–878

RELATED AUTHORS AND WORKS IN *Gateway to the Great Books*

Campbell, *Numerical Laws and the Use of Mathematics
    in Science,* Vol. 9, pages 222–238
Clifford, *Postulates of the Science of Space,* Vol. 9, pages 243–259
Forsyth, *Mathematics, in Life and Thought,* Vol. 9, pages 26–46
Hogben, *Mathematics, the Mirror of Civilization,* Vol. 9,
    pages 3–23
Poincaré, *Mathematical Creation,* Vol. 9, pages 294–304
Whitehead, "On Mathematical Method," Vol. 9, pages 51–67

Mathematics and the Metaphysicians
Vol. 9, pages 95–110

SUGGESTED READINGS IN THE *Syntopicon*

CHANGE, Vol. 2, pages 193–217, especially
    Topic 5: The measure of motion
    Topic 7d: The properties of variable motion: the laws of motion
INFINITY, Vol. 2, pages 816–834, especially
    Topic 3: The infinite in quantity
LOGIC, Vol. 2, pages 1035–1050, especially
    Topic 4a: Mathematical analysis and reasoning: the search
        for a universal method
MATHEMATICS, Vol. 3, pages 42–62, especially
    Topic 3d: Symbols and formulae: the attainment of generality
    Topic 4: Mathematical techniques
    Topic 4d: The method of exhaustion: the theory of limits
        and the calculus

RELATED AUTHORS AND WORKS IN *Great Books of the Western World*

Plato, Vol. 7, *Parmenides,* pages 486–511
Aristotle, Vol. 8, *Organon,* pages 5–253; *Metaphysics,* Bk. IV,
    pages 523–532; Bk. XI, Chaps. 4–7, pages 589–593
Euclid, Vol. 11, *Elements,* Bks. I–II, pages 5–31; Bk. X, pages
    191–300; Bk. XII, pages 338–368
Archimedes, Vol. 11, *Quadrature of the Parabola,* pages 527–537;
    Method Treating of Mechanical Problems, pages 569–592
Newton, Vol. 34, *Mathematical Principles of Natural Philosophy,*
    Bk. I, Sect. I, pages 25–32
Sterne, Vol. 36, *Tristram Shandy,* Bk. I, Chap. 22, page 229; Bk. II,
    Chaps. 7–8, pages 244–246

RUSSELL, *Mathematics and the Metaphysicians*
continued

Kant, Vol. 42, *Critique of Pure Reason*, Introduction, pages 14–22;
pages 129–151
Hegel, Vol. 46, *Philosophy of History*, Introduction, pages 178–190

RELATED AUTHORS AND WORKS IN *Gateway to the Great Books*

Clifford, *Postulates of the Science of Space*, Vol. 9, pages 243–259
Einstein and Infeld, "Rise and Decline of Classical Physics," Vol. 8,
pages 490–560
Forsyth, *Mathematics, in Life and Thought*, Vol. 9, pages 26–46
Hogben, *Mathematics, the Mirror of Civilization*, Vol. 9,
pages 3–23
Kasner and Newman, *New Names for Old*, Vol. 9, pages 121–136;
Beyond the Googol, pages 137–162
Poincaré, *Space*, Vol. 9, pages 265–293
Whitehead, "On Mathematical Method," Vol. 9, pages 51–67;
On the Nature of a Calculus, pages 68–78

Definition of Number
Vol. 9, pages 111–117

SUGGESTED READINGS IN THE *Syntopicon*

DEFINITION, Vol. 2, pages 286–302, especially
Topic 1: The theory of definition
Topic 1a: The object of definition: definitions as arbitrary
and nominal or real and concerned with essence
Topic 4: The search for definitions and the methods
of defending them
INFINITY, Vol. 2, pages 816–834, especially
Topic 3a: Number: the infinite of division and addition
MATHEMATICS, Vol. 3, pages 42–62, especially
Topic 2: The objects of mathematics: number, figure, extension,
relation, order
QUANTITY, Vol. 3, pages 527–545, especially
Topic 4: Discrete quantities: number and numbering

RELATED AUTHORS AND WORKS IN *Great Books of the Western World*

Plato, Vol. 7, *Meno*, pages 174–190, especially pages 174–177,
180–182; *Republic*, Bk. VII, pages 391–398; *Theaetetus*,
pages 512–550, especially 544–549

Aristotle, Vol. 8, *Topics*, Bks. VI–VII, pages 192–211; *Metaphysics*, Bk. I, page 499; Bk. VII, Chap. 10–Bk. VIII, Chap. 6, pages 558–570
Euclid, Vol. 11, *Elements*, Bk. V, pages 81–98
Archimedes, Vol. 11, *Sand-Reckoner*, pages 520–526
Nicomachus, Vol. 11, *Introduction to Arithmetic*, Bk. I, pages 811–817; Bk. II, pages 831–841
Swift, Vol. 36, *Gulliver's Travels*, Part IV, pages 151–160

RELATED AUTHORS AND WORKS IN *Gateway to the Great Books*

Campbell, *Measurement*, Vol. 9, pages 204–221
Dantzig, *Fingerprints*, Vol. 9, pages 165–177; *Empty Column*, pages 178–189
Kasner and Newman, *New Names for Old*, Vol. 9, pages 121–136; *Beyond the Googol*, pages 137–162

CHARLES AUGUSTIN SAINTE-BEUVE, 1804–1869

What Is a Classic?
Vol. 5, pages 65–75

SUGGESTED READINGS IN THE *Syntopicon*

ART, Vol. 2, pages 64–86, especially
　Topic 7b: The judgment of excellence in art
BEAUTY, Vol. 2, pages 112–125, especially
　Topic 5: Judgments of beauty: the objective and the subjective in aesthetic judgments or judgments of taste
RHETORIC, Vol. 3, pages 645–664, especially
　Topic 2b: The canon of excellence in style
UNIVERSAL AND PARTICULAR, Vol. 3, pages 957–974, especially
　Topic 7c: The issue concerning the universality of aesthetic standards: the subjective universal

RELATED AUTHORS AND WORKS IN *Great Books of the Western World*

Aristotle, Vol. 9, *On Poetics*, pages 691–698
Montaigne, Vol. 25, *Of Books*, pages 194–200
Cervantes, Vol. 29, *Don Quixote*, Part I, Chaps. 47–48, pages 184–187
Pascal, Vol. 33, *Pensées*, Sect. I, pages 174–176

SAINTE-BEUVE, *What Is a Classic?*
continued

Fielding, Vol. 37, *Tom Jones*, Bk. VIII, Chap. 1, pages 152–155;
    Bk. XII, Chap. 1, pages 246–247
Boswell, Vol. 44, *Life of Samuel Johnson*, pages 167–168

RELATED AUTHORS AND WORKS IN *Gateway to the Great Books*

Arnold, *Study of Poetry*, Vol. 5, pages 19–41; *Sweetness and Light*,
    pages 42–61
Bacon, *Of Studies*, Vol. 5, pages 97–98
Bury, *Herodotus*, Vol. 6, pages 364–383
Eliot, T. S., *Dante*, Vol. 5, pages 371–403; *Tradition
    and the Individual Talent*, pages 404–411
Guizot, "Civilization," Vol. 6, pages 302–317
Hazlitt, *Of Persons One Would Wish to Have Seen*, Vol. 5,
    pages 284–295
Hume, *Of the Standard of Taste*, Vol. 5, pages 103–119
Johnson, *Preface to Shakespeare*, Vol. 5, pages 316–353
Schiller, *On Simple and Sentimental Poetry*, Vol. 5, pages 155–211
Schopenhauer, *On Style*, Vol. 5, pages 124–136
Shelley, *Defence of Poetry*, Vol. 5, pages 216–242

Montaigne
Vol. 5, pages 76–89

SUGGESTED READINGS IN THE *Syntopicon*

BEAUTY, Vol. 2, pages 112–125, especially
    Topic 5: Judgments of beauty: the objective and the subjective
        in aesthetic judgments or judgments of taste
MIND, Vol. 3, pages 171–203, especially
    Topic 9c: Reason as regulating human conduct: reason as
        the principle of virtue or duty
POETRY, Vol. 3, pages 400–419, especially
    Topic 8b: Critical standards and artistic rules with respect
        to the language of poetry: the distinction
        between prose and verse; the measure of excellence
        in style

RELATED AUTHORS AND WORKS IN *Great Books of the Western World*

Plato, Vol. 7, *Ion*, pages 142–148
Pascal, Vol. 33, *Pensées*, Sect. I, pages 174–175, 177–178
Kant, Vol. 42, *Critique of Judgement*, First Part, Sect. I, Bk. II,
    pages 513–525

RELATED AUTHORS AND WORKS IN *Gateway to the Great Books*

De Quincey, *Literature of Knowledge and Literature of Power*, Vol. 5, pages 358–361

Emerson, *Montaigne; Or, the Skeptic*, Vol. 10, pages 546–562

Epicurus, *Letter to Menoeceus*, Vol. 10, pages 230–233

Erskine, *Moral Obligation to Be Intelligent*, Vol. 10, pages 5–13

Voltaire, "Philosophy of Common Sense," Vol. 10, pages 453–474

For Montaigne's *Essays* in *Great Books of the Western World*, see Vol. 25

GEORGE SANTAYANA, 1863–1952

Lucretius
Vol. 10, pages 365–390

SUGGESTED READINGS IN THE *Syntopicon*

DESIRE, Vol. 2, pages 323–344, especially

Topic 6a: The regulation of desire by reason: the discipline of moral virtue or duty

ELEMENT, Vol. 2, pages 400–412, especially

Topic 5: The theory of atomism: critiques of atomism

LIFE AND DEATH, Vol. 2, pages 1013–1034, especially

Topic 8c: The contemplation and fear of death: the attitude of the hero, the philosopher, the martyr

MATTER, Vol. 3, pages 63–79, especially

Topic 3a: Matter as the sole existent: materialism, atomism

NATURE, Vol. 3, pages 225–250, especially

Topic 2d: Natural and violent motion

SOUL, Vol. 3, pages 791–810, especially

Topic 3d: The denial of soul as an immaterial principle, form, or substance: the atomic theory of the soul

RELATED AUTHORS AND WORKS IN *Great Books of the Western World*

Aurelius, Vol. 12, *Meditations*, Bk. IX, pages 295–296

Plotinus, Vol. 17, *Fourth Ennead*, Seventh Tractate, pages 191–200

Montaigne, Vol. 25, *That to Study Philosophy Is to Learn to Die*, pages 28–36; *Apology for Raimond de Sebonde*, pages 246–269

Spinoza, Vol. 31, *Ethics*, Part III, pages 395–422; Part IV, Props. 44–66, pages 437–444

SANTAYANA, *Lucretius*
continued

Pascal, Vol. 33, *Pensées*, Sect. II, pages 181–186; Sect. III, pages 213–217; Sect. IV, pages 217–218, 221–223; Sect. V, page 229–Sect. VI, page 241; Sect. VII, pages 266–267; Sect. IX, page 282

RELATED AUTHORS AND WORKS IN *Gateway to the Great Books*

Arnold, *Study of Poetry*, Vol. 5, pages 19–41
Bacon, *Of Death*, Vol. 10, pages 348–349
De Quincey, *Literature of Knowledge and Literature of Power*, Vol. 5, pages 358–361
Emerson, *Nature*, Vol. 10, pages 512–524
Epicurus, *Letter to Herodotus*, Vol. 10, pages 216–229; *Letter to Menoeceus*, pages 230–233
Mill, J. S., *Nature*, Vol. 10, pages 477–508
Plutarch, *Contentment*, Vol. 10, pages 264–281
Shelley, *Defence of Poetry*, Vol. 5, pages 216–242

For Lucretius' *On the Nature of Things* in *Great Books of the Western World*, see Vol. 12, pages 1–97

Goethe's Faust
Vol. 10, pages 391–419

SUGGESTED READINGS IN THE *Syntopicon*

DESIRE, Vol. 2, pages 323–344, especially
    Topic 7a(2): The lust for power
EXPERIENCE, Vol. 2, pages 468–485, especially
    Topic 8: Variety of experience as an ideal of human life
HAPPINESS, Vol. 2, pages 684–710, especially
    Topic 7b: The imperfection of temporal happiness: its failure to satisfy natural desire
PHILOSOPHY, Vol. 3, pages 342–362, especially
    Topic 1d: The relation of philosophy to myth, poetry, and history
WILL, Vol. 3, pages 1071–1101, especially
    Topic 2b(2): The sensitive determination of the will's acts by estimations of benefit and harm, or pleasure and pain: the impulsion of the passions

RELATED AUTHORS AND WORKS IN *Great Books of the Western World*

Lucretius, Vol. 12, *On the Nature of Things*, Bk. III, pages 30–31, 42–43

Spinoza, Vol. 31, *Ethics*, Part II, Prop. 44, pages 389–390; Parts IV–V, pages 422–463

Milton, Vol. 32, *Paradise Lost*, Bk. IX, pages 247–273; Bk. XII, pages 329–333; *Areopagitica*, pages 390–391

Mill, J. S., Vol. 43, *On Liberty*, Chap. 3, pages 293–302

Dostoevsky, Vol. 52, *Brothers Karamazov*, Part II, Bk. VI, Chaps. 2–3, pages 153–167

RELATED AUTHORS AND WORKS IN *Gateway to the Great Books*

Arnold, *Study of Poetry*, Vol. 5, pages 19–41

Bunin, *Gentleman from San Francisco*, Vol. 3, pages 102–123

De Quincey, *Literature of Knowledge and Literature of Power*, Vol. 5, pages 358–360

Guizot, "Civilization," Vol. 6, pages 302–317

Hawthorne, *Rappaccini's Daughter*, Vol. 3, pages 128–152

Mann, *Mario and the Magician*, Vol. 3, pages 573–610

O'Neill, *Emperor Jones*, Vol. 4, pages 357–382

Pater, "Art of Life," Vol. 10, pages 258–261

Pushkin, *Queen of Spades*, Vol. 3, pages 484–507

Ruskin, *Idealist's Arraignment of the Age*, Vol. 7, pages 126–136

Shaw, *Man of Destiny*, Vol. 4, pages 300–338

Shelley, *Defence of Poetry*, Vol. 5, pages 216–242

For Goethe's *Faust* in *Great Books of the Western World*, see Vol. 47

FRIEDRICH SCHILLER, 1759–1805

On Simple and Sentimental Poetry
Vol. 5, pages 155–211

SUGGESTED READINGS IN THE *Syntopicon*

ART, Vol. 2, pages 64–86, especially

Topic 2*a*: Causation in art and nature: artistic production compared with natural generation

Topic 7*b*: The judgment of excellence in art

NATURE, Vol. 3, pages 225–250, especially

Topic 2*a*: Nature and art: the imitation of nature; co-operation with nature

SCHILLER, *On Simple and Sentimental Poetry*
continued

POETRY, Vol. 3, pages 400–419, especially
Topic 3: The inspiration or genius of the poet: the influence
of the poetic tradition
Topic 4a: Epic and dramatic poetry
Topic 4b: Tragedy and comedy
Topic 8a(2): Poetic truth: verisimilitude or plausibility;
the possible, the probable, and the necessary

RELATED AUTHORS AND WORKS IN *Great Books of the Western World*

Plato, Vol. 7, *Ion*, pages 142–148; *Republic*, Bks. II–III, pages
320–334
Aristotle, Vol. 9, *On Poetics*, Chaps. 5–16, pages 683–690;
Chaps. 23–26, pages 695–699
Cervantes, Vol. 29, *Don Quixote*, Part I, Chaps. 47–48, pages
184–187
Bacon, Vol. 30, *Advancement of Learning*, Second Book, pages
33–34
Pascal, Vol. 33, *Pensées*, Sect. I, pages 175–176
Sterne, Vol. 36, *Tristram Shandy*, Bk. I, Chaps. 6–7, pages 195–196
Fielding, Vol. 37, *Tom Jones*, Bk. VIII, Chap. 1, pages 152–155;
Bk. X, Chap. 1, pages 204–205; Bk. XIII, Chap. 1, pages
273–274

RELATED AUTHORS AND WORKS IN *Gateway to the Great Books*

Anonymous, *Aucassin and Nicolette*, Vol. 2, pages 523–551
Arnold, *Study of Poetry*, Vol. 5, pages 19–41
Balzac, *Passion in the Desert*, Vol. 3, pages 436–447
De Quincey, *Literature of Knowledge and Literature of Power*,
Vol. 5, pages 358–361
Dinesen, *Sorrow-Acre*, Vol. 3, pages 615–641
Galsworthy, *Apple-Tree*, Vol. 3, pages 323–367
Guizot, "Civilization," Vol. 6, pages 302–317
Hazlitt, *My First Acquaintance with Poets*, Vol. 5, pages 264–279;
Of Persons One Would Wish to Have Seen, pages 284–295
Johnson, *Preface to Shakespeare*, Vol. 5, pages 316–353
Sainte-Beuve, *What Is a Classic?*, Vol. 5, pages 65–75
Schopenhauer, *On Some Forms of Literature*, Vol. 5, pages 137–142
Scott, *Two Drovers*, Vol. 2, pages 182–205
Shelley, *Defence of Poetry*, Vol. 5, pages 216–242
Tolstoy, *Three Hermits*, Vol. 3, pages 700–706
Whitman, *Preface to Leaves of Grass*, Vol. 5, pages 247–259

ARTHUR SCHOPENHAUER, 1788–1860

On Style
Vol. 5, pages 124–136

SUGGESTED READINGS IN THE *Syntopicon*

ART, Vol. 2, pages 64–86, especially
Topic 7*b*: The judgment of excellence in art
BEAUTY, Vol. 2, pages 112–125, especially
Topic 5: Judgments of beauty: the objective and the subjective
in aesthetic judgments or judgments of taste
POETRY, Vol. 3, pages 400–419, especially
Topic 8*b*: Critical standards and artistic rules with respect
to the language of poetry; the distinction
between prose and verse; the measure of excellence
in style
RHETORIC, Vol. 3, pages 645–664, especially
Topic 2*b*: The canon of excellence in style

RELATED AUTHORS AND WORKS IN *Great Books of the Western World*

Aristotle, Vol. 9, *Rhetoric*, Bk. III, Chaps. 1–13, pages 653–667
Montaigne, Vol. 25, *Of Books*, pages 194–200
Cervantes, Vol. 29, *Don Quixote*, Preface, pages xi–xiii; Second
Part, Chap. 16, pages 251–252
Bacon, Vol. 30, *Advancement of Learning*, Second Book,
pages 38–39, 62–68
Descartes, Vol. 31, *Discourse on Method*, Part I, page 43
Fielding, Vol. 37, *Tom Jones*, Bk. I, Chap. 1, pages 1–2; Bk. V,
Chap. 1, pages 73–75; Bk. VIII, Chap. 1, pages 152–155;
Bk. IX, Chap. 1, pages 189–191
Kant, Vol. 42, *Critique of Judgement*, First Part, Sect. I, Bk. I,
pages 476–482
Goethe, Vol. 47, *Faust*, First Part, page 15

RELATED AUTHORS AND WORKS IN *Gateway to the Great Books*

Arnold, *Study of Poetry*, Vol. 5, pages 19–41
Bacon, *Of Beauty*, Vol. 5, page 94
Eliot, T. S., *Dante*, Vol. 5, pages 371–403
Hazlitt, *On Swift*, Vol. 5, pages 280–283
Sainte-Beuve, *What Is a Classic?*, Vol. 5, pages 65–75

ARTHUR SCHOPENHAUER
continued

On Some Forms of Literature
Vol. 5, pages 137–142

SUGGESTED READINGS IN THE *Syntopicon*

ART, Vol. 2, pages 64–86, especially
> Topic 6a: The comparison and distinction of art and science

POETRY, Vol. 3, pages 400–419, especially
> Topic 5b: Poetry contrasted with history and philosophy:
> the dispraise and defense of the poet
> Topic 8a(2): Poetic truth: verisimilitude or plausibility;
> the possible, the probable, and the necessary

RELATED AUTHORS AND WORKS IN *Great Books of the Western World*

Plato, Vol. 7, *Republic*, Bk. X, pages 427–434
Aristotle, Vol. 9, *On Poetics*, pages 681–699
Cervantes, Vol. 29, *Don Quixote*, First Part, Chap. 6, pages 13–16;
    Chap. 32, pages 117–120; Chaps. 47–50, pages 184–194; Second
    Part, Chaps. 3–4, pages 212–217
Bacon, Vol. 30, *Advancement of Learning*, Second Book, pages
    32–39
Fielding, Vol. 37, *Tom Jones*, Bk. II, Chap. 1, pages 19–20; Bk. III,
    Chap. 1, page 35; Bk. IV, Chap. 1, pages 49–50; Bk. VIII,
    Chap. 1, pages 152–155; Bk. IX, Chap. 1, pages 189–191;
    Bk. X, Chap. 1, pages 204–205; Bk. XIII, Chap. 1, pages
    273–274; Bk. XVI, Chap. 5, pages 347–348
Boswell, Vol. 44, *Life of Samuel Johnson*, pages 446–450

RELATED AUTHORS AND WORKS IN *Gateway to the Great Books*

Bacon, *Of Studies*, Vol. 5, pages 97–98
De Quincey, *Literature of Knowledge and Literature of Power*,
    Vol. 5, pages 358–361
Hazlitt, *My First Acquaintance with Poets*, Vol. 5, pages 264–279
Johnson, *Preface to Shakespeare*, Vol. 5, pages 316–353
Lamb, *My First Play*, Vol. 5, pages 300–303
Schiller, *On Simple and Sentimental Poetry*, Vol. 5, pages 155–211
Shelley, *Defence of Poetry*, Vol. 5, pages 216–242

On the Comparative Place of Interest and Beauty in Works of Art
Vol. 5, pages 143–150

SUGGESTED READINGS IN THE *Syntopicon*

BEAUTY, Vol. 2, pages 112–125, especially
Topic 1*b*: Beauty and truth: the beautiful as an object
of contemplation
Topic 2: Beauty in nature and in art
POETRY, Vol. 3, pages 400–419, especially
Topic 8*a*(2): Poetic truth: verisimilitude or plausibility;
the possible, the probable, and the necessary

RELATED AUTHORS AND WORKS IN *Great Books of the Western World*

Aristotle, Vol. 9, *On Poetics*, pages 681–699
Plotinus, Vol. 17, *Fifth Ennead*, Eighth Tractate, pages 239–246
Fielding, Vol. 37, *Tom Jones*, Bk. XVI, Chap. 5, pages 347–348
Kant, Vol. 42, *Critique of Judgement*, First Part, Sects. I–II,
pages 476–549
Goethe, Vol. 47, *Faust*, Prelude on the Stage, pages 2–6
James, W., Vol. 53, *Principles of Psychology*, Chap. XXVIII, pages
886–888

RELATED AUTHORS AND WORKS IN *Gateway to the Great Books*

Bacon, *Of Beauty*, Vol. 5, page 94
De Quincey, *Literature of Knowledge and Literature of Power*,
Vol. 5, pages 358–361; *On the Knocking at the Gate
in Macbeth*, pages 362–366
Hume, *Of the Standard of Taste*, Vol. 5, pages 103–119
James, W., *On a Certain Blindness in Human Beings*, Vol. 7,
pages 141–156
Woolf, *How Should One Read a Book?*, Vol. 5, pages 5–14

On Education
Vol. 7, pages 197–203

SUGGESTED READINGS IN THE *Syntopicon*

EDUCATION, Vol. 2, pages 376–399, especially
Topic 1: The ends of education
Topic 5*b*: The means and methods of teaching
Topic 5*c*: The nature of learning: its several modes
Topic 5*f*: Learning apart from teachers and books: the role
of experience

SCHOPENHAUER, *On Education*
continued

EXPERIENCE, Vol. 2, pages 468–485, especially
Topic 2: Experience in relation to the acts of the mind
Topic 6*a*: Experience as indispensable to sound judgment
and prudence
KNOWLEDGE, Vol. 2, pages 880–920, especially
Topic 6*b*: The classification of knowledge according
to the faculties involved in knowing
MEMORY AND IMAGINATION, Vol. 3, pages 133–157,
especially
Topic 3: Remembering as an act of knowledge and as a source
of knowledge
Topic 6*c*(1): The abstraction of ideas from images: the image
as a condition of thought

RELATED AUTHORS AND WORKS IN *Great Books of the Western World*

Plato, Vol. 7, *Republic*, Bks. II–III, pages 320–339; Bks. VI–VII,
pages 383–398
Aristotle, Vol. 8, *On the Soul*, Bk. III, Chaps. 3–8, pages 659–664;
Vol. 9, *Nicomachean Ethics*, Bk. I, Chaps. 3–4, pages 339–340;
Bk. VI, pages 387–394, especially Chaps. 5–8, pages 389–391;
Politics, Bk. VII, Chap. 13–Bk. VIII, Chap. 7, pages 536–548
Montaigne, Vol. 25, *Of Pedantry*, pages 55–62; *Of the Education
of Children*, pages 62–80
Bacon, Vol. 30, *Advancement of Learning*, First Book, pages 1–28
Descartes, Vol. 31, *Rules for the Direction of the Mind*,
Rules XII–XIII, pages 18–27
James, W., Vol. 53, *Principles of Psychology*, Chap. XVI, pages
424–427; Chap. XXVI, pages 827–835; Chap. XXVIII,
pages 852–862
Freud, Vol. 54, *New Introductory Lectures on Psycho-Analysis*,
Lecture, 34, pages 868–871

RELATED AUTHORS AND WORKS IN *Gateway to the Great Books*

Bacon, *Of Studies*, Vol. 5, pages 97–98; *Of Custom and Education*,
Vol. 7, pages 18–19
Conrad, *Youth*, Vol. 2, pages 210–236
Dewey, "Process of Thought," Vol. 10, pages 92–213
Eliot, T. S., *Tradition and the Individual Talent*, Vol. 5, pages
404–411
Erskine, *Moral Obligation to Be Intelligent*, Vol. 10, pages 5–13
Faraday, *Observations on Mental Education*, Vol. 7, pages 208–232
Flaubert, *Legend of St. Julian the Hospitaller*, Vol. 3, pages 371–392

Franklin, *Proposal for Promoting Useful Knowledge among the British Plantations in America*, Vol. 6, pages 533–535; *Proposals Relating to the Education of Youth in Pennsylvania*, pages 536–542
Hume, *Of the Study of History*, Vol. 7, pages 89–92
James, H., *Pupil*, Vol. 3, pages 530–568
Kipling, *Mowgli's Brothers*, Vol. 2, pages 126–141
Mill, J. S., "Childhood and Youth," Vol. 6, pages 5–47
Swift, *Essay on Modern Education*, Vol. 7, pages 33–39
Twain, "Learning the River," Vol. 6, pages 50–98
Voltaire, *Micromégas*, Vol. 2, pages 241–256
Woolf, *How Should One Read a Book?*, Vol. 5, pages 5–14

SIR WALTER SCOTT, 1771–1832

The Two Drovers
Vol. 2, pages 182–205

SUGGESTED READINGS IN THE *Syntopicon*

CHANCE, Vol. 2, pages 179–192, especially
   Topic 1*a*: Chance as the coincidence of causes
   Topic 6*a*: Chance and fortune in the life of the individual
EMOTION, Vol. 2, pages 413–436, especially
   Topic 3*a*: Madness or frenzy due to emotional excess: excessively emotional or emotionally over-determined behavior
HONOR, Vol. 2, pages 728–748, especially
   Topic 2*c*: Honor as due self-esteem: magnanimity or proper pride
JUSTICE, Vol. 2, pages 850–879, especially
   Topic 6*a*: The relation of natural rights to natural law and natural justice
   Topic 10*c*: The justice of punishment for unjust acts: the distinction between retribution and vengeance

RELATED AUTHORS AND WORKS IN *Great Books of the Western World*

Homer, Vol. 4, *Iliad*, Bks. XXI–XXII, pages 148–160
Herodotus, Vol. 6, *History*, Third Book, pages 97–98
Shakespeare, Vol. 26, *Romeo and Juliet*, Act III, Scene III, pages 304–306; Vol. 27, *King Lear*, Act IV, Scene VI, page 275
Spinoza, Vol. 31, *Ethics*, Part III, page 408

SCOTT, *The Two Drovers*
continued

Locke, Vol. 35, *Concerning Civil Government,* Chaps. II–III, pages 25–29

RELATED AUTHORS AND WORKS IN *Gateway to the Great Books*

Bacon, *Of Friendship,* Vol. 10, pages 353–358; *Of Anger,* pages 359–360

Cicero, *On Friendship,* Vol. 10, pages 286–316

Flaubert, *Legend of St. Julian the Hospitaller,* Vol. 3, pages 371–392

Great Documents, *English Bill of Rights,* Vol. 6, pages 409–411

Hemingway, *Killers,* Vol. 2, pages 169–177

Hugo, "Battle with the Cannon," Vol. 2, pages 146–154

Maupassant, *Two Friends,* Vol. 2, pages 159–164

Melville, *Billy Budd,* Vol. 3, pages 31–98

Poe, *Tell-Tale Heart,* Vol. 2, pages 273–277

Schiller, *On Simple and Sentimental Poetry,* Vol. 5, pages 155–211

Synge, *Riders to the Sea,* Vol. 4, pages 342–352

GEORGE BERNARD SHAW, 1856–1950

The Man of Destiny
Vol. 4, pages 300–338

SUGGESTED READINGS IN THE *Syntopicon*

HISTORY, Vol. 2, pages 711–727, especially

Topic 4a(4): The role of the individual in history: the great man, hero, or leader

HONOR, Vol. 2, pages 728–748, especially

Topic 5b: Hero-worship: the exaltation of leaders

WAR AND PEACE, Vol. 3, pages 1010–1037, especially

Topic 10d: The principles of strategy and tactics: the military genius

RELATED AUTHORS AND WORKS IN *Great Books of the Western World*

Homer, Vol. 4, *Iliad,* pages 3–179

Plutarch, Vol. 14, *Caesar,* pages 577–604; *Marcus Brutus,* pages 802–824

Machiavelli, Vol. 23, *Prince,* Chap. 25–26, pages 35–37

Rabelais, Vol. 24, *Gargantua and Pantagruel,* Bk. I, pages 1–67

Shakespeare, Vol. 26, *King Henry V*, pages 532–567; *Julius Caesar*, pages 568–596

Hegel, Vol. 46, *Philosophy of History*, Introduction III, pages 162–170

Tolstoy, Vol. 51, *War and Peace*, Second Epilogue, pages 675–696

RELATED AUTHORS AND WORKS IN *Gateway to the Great Books*

Bacon, *Of Great Place*, Vol. 7, pages 9–11
Carlyle, *Hero as King*, Vol. 6, pages 110–145
Clausewitz, *What Is War?*, Vol. 7, pages 479–497
Emerson, *Self-Reliance*, Vol. 10, pages 525–545
James, W., *Great Men and Their Environment*, Vol. 7, pages 171–194
Mann, *Mario and the Magician*, Vol. 3, pages 573–610
O'Neill, *Emperor Jones*, Vol. 4, pages 357–382
Tacitus, *Life of Gnaeus Julius Agricola*, Vol. 6, pages 274–298

PERCY BYSSHE SHELLEY, 1792–1822

A Defence of Poetry
Vol. 5, pages 216–242

SUGGESTED READINGS IN THE *Syntopicon*

MEMORY AND IMAGINATION, Vol. 3, pages 133–157, especially
Topic 7a: The use of imagination in the production and appreciation of works of art

PHILOSOPHY, Vol. 3, pages 342–362, especially
Topic 1d: The relation of philosophy to myth, poetry, and history

POETRY, Vol. 3, pages 400–419, especially
Topic 3: The inspiration or genius of the poet: the influence of the poetic tradition
Topic 5a: The aim of poetry to instruct as well as to delight: the pretentions or deceptions of the poet as teacher
Topic 5b: Poetry contrasted with history and philosophy: the dispraise and defense of the poet
Topic 8c: The interpretation of poetry
Topic 9a: The influence of poetry on mind and character: its role in education

SCIENCE, Vol. 3, pages 682–705, especially
Topic 2b: The comparison of science with poetry and history

SHELLEY, A *Defence of Poetry*
continued

RELATED AUTHORS AND WORKS IN *Great Books of the Western World*

Plato, Vol. 7, *Ion*, pages 142–148; *Republic*, Bks. II–III, pages 320–333

Montaigne, Vol. 25, *Of Books*, pages 194–200

Cervantes, Vol. 29, *Don Quixote*, Second Part, Chap. 16, pages 251–252

Bacon, Vol. 30, *Advancement of Learning*, Second Book, pages 38–39

Fielding, Vol. 37, *Tom Jones*, Bk. XIII, Chap. 1, pages 273–274

Kant, Vol. 42, *Critique of Judgement*, First Part, Sect. I, Bk. II, pages 524–537

RELATED AUTHORS AND WORKS IN *Gateway to the Great Books*

Arnold, *Study of Poetry*, Vol. 5, pages 19–41; *Sweetness and Light*, pages 42–61

De Quincey, *Literature of Knowledge and Literature of Power*, Vol. 5, pages 358–361

Eliot, T. S., *Dante*, Vol. 5, pages 371–403; *Tradition and the Individual Talent*, pages 404–411

Lamb, *Sanity of True Genius*, Vol. 5, pages 308–310

Pater, "Art of Life," Vol. 10, pages 258–261

Poincaré, *Mathematical Creation*, Vol. 9, pages 294–304

Sainte-Beuve, *What Is a Classic?*, Vol. 5, pages 65–75

Santayana, *Lucretius*, Vol. 10, pages 365–390; *Goethe's Faust*, pages 391–419

Schiller, *On Simple and Sentimental Poetry*, Vol. 5, pages 155–211

Schopenhauer, *On Some Forms of Literature*, Vol. 5, pages 137–142

Whitman, *Preface to Leaves of Grass*, Vol. 5, pages 247–259

Woolf, *How Should One Read a Book?*, Vol. 5, pages 5–14

RICHARD BRINSLEY SHERIDAN, 1751–1816

The School for Scandal
Vol. 4, pages 85–159

SUGGESTED READINGS IN THE *Syntopicon*

CUSTOM AND CONVENTION, Vol. 2, pages 268–285, especially

Topic 5a: The conventional determination of moral judgments: the moral evaluation of conventions

OPINION, Vol. 3, pages 303–322, especially

Topic 6a: Good and evil as matters of opinion: moral standards as customs or conventions reflecting prevalent opinion

TRUTH, Vol. 3, pages 915–938, especially

Topic 8a: Prevarication and perjury: the injustice or lying or bearing false witness

VIRTUE AND VICE, Vol. 3, pages 975–1009, especially

Topic 2c: The appearances of virtue: imperfect or conditional virtues; the counterfeits of virtue; natural or temperamental dispositions which simulate virtue

RELATED AUTHORS AND WORKS IN *Great Books of the Western World*

Montaigne, Vol. 25, *Apology for Raimond de Sebonde*, pages 281–282

Shakespeare, Vol. 27, *Hamlet*, pages 29–72; *King Lear*, pages 244–283

Milton, Vol. 32, *Comus*, pages 33–56

Swift, Vol. 36, *Gulliver's Travels*, Part IV, Chaps. IV–XII, pages 146–184

Hegel, Vol. 46, *Philosophy of Right*, Second Part, pages 49–54

James, W., Vol. 53, *Principles of Psychology*, Chap. X, pages 190–191

RELATED AUTHORS AND WORKS IN *Gateway to the Great Books*

Bacon, *Of Discourse*, Vol. 5, pages 95–96; *Of Custom and Education*, Vol. 7, pages 18–19; *Of Followers and Friends*, pages 20–21; *Of Truth*, Vol. 10, pages 346–347; *Of Love*, pages 351–352

Bunin, *Gentleman from San Francisco*, Vol. 3, pages 102–123

Butler, "Customs and Opinions of the Erewhonians," Vol. 2, pages 483–506

Dickens, "Full and Faithful Report of the Memorable Trial of Bardell against Pickwick," Vol. 2, pages 391–448

Erskine, *Moral Obligation to Be Intelligent*, Vol. 10, pages 5–13

Galsworthy, *Apple-Tree*, Vol. 3, pages 323–367

La Bruyère, *Characters*, Vol. 6, pages 102–105

Molière, *Misanthrope*, pages 6–51; *Doctor in Spite of Himself*, Vol. 4, pages 52–81

Tolstoy, *What Men Live By*, Vol. 3, pages 707–727

Twain, *Man That Corrupted Hadleyburg*, Vol. 2, pages 346–386

ISAAC BASHEVIS SINGER, 1904–

The Spinoza of Market Street
Vol. 3, pages 466–480

SUGGESTED READINGS IN THE *Syntopicon*

DESIRE, Vol. 2, pages 323–344, especially
Topic 6a: The regulation of desire by reason: the discipline
of moral virtue or duty

EMOTION, Vol. 2, pages 413–436, especially
Topic 4a: The conflict between reason and emotion

HAPPINESS, Vol. 2, pages 684–710, especially
Topic 2b(5): The importance of friendship and love
for happiness
Topic 2b(7): The function of knowledge and wisdom
in the happy life: the place of speculative activity
and contemplation

PHILOSOPHY, Vol. 3, pages 342–362, especially
Topic 4b: Philosophy as a moral discipline: the consolation
of philosophy
Topic 6d: The philosopher as a man of theory or vision: neglect
of the practical; withdrawal from the affairs of men
and the market place

WISDOM, Vol. 3, pages 1102–1117, especially
Topic 4: The praise of folly: the wisdom of fools and innocents

RELATED AUTHORS AND WORKS IN *Great Books of the Western World*

Plato, Vol. 7, *Republic*, Bk. IV, pages 350–355
Cervantes, Vol. 29, *Don Quixote*, Second Part, Chap. 43,
pages 334–336
Spinoza, Vol. 31, *Ethics*, Part IV, Props. 44–73, pages 437–447
Pascal, Vol. 33, *Pensées*, Sect. VI, pages 242–243

RELATED AUTHORS AND WORKS IN *Gateway to the Great Books*

Adams, *Saint Thomas Aquinas*, Vol. 10, pages 422–450
Bacon, *Of Youth and Age*, Vol. 7, pages 3–4; *Of Love*, Vol. 10,
pages 351–352
Cicero, *On Old Age*, Vol. 10, pages 317–343
Eliot, T. S., *Tradition and the Individual Talent*, Vol. 5,
pages 404–411
Galileo, *Starry Messenger*, Vol. 8, pages 330–355
Gogol, *Overcoat*, Vol. 2, pages 452–478
Tolstoy, *What Men Live By*, Vol. 3, pages 707–727

ROBERT LOUIS STEVENSON, 1850–1894

The Strange Case of Dr. Jekyll and Mr. Hyde
Vol. 2, pages 288–341

SUGGESTED READINGS IN THE *Syntopicon*

GOOD AND EVIL, Vol. 2, pages 605–636, especially
Topic 6a: Knowledge, wisdom, and virtue: the relation of being good and knowing what is good
Topic 6b: The need for experience of evil
MEDICINE, Vol. 3, pages 113–132, especially
Topic 1: The profession of medicine, its aims and obligations: the relation of physician to patient; the place of the physician in society
Topic 6a: The distinction between sanity and insanity: the concept of mental health and the nature of madness
MIND, Vol. 3, pages 171–203, especially
Topic 7c: The conscious, pre-conscious and unconscious activities of mind
Topic 8: The pathology of mind: the loss or abeyance of reason
Topic 8b: The causes of mental pathology: organic and functional factors
Topic 8c: The abnormality peculiar to mind: systematic delusion

RELATED AUTHORS AND WORKS IN *Great Books of the Western World*

Sophocles, Vol. 5, *Ajax*, pages 143–155
Hippocrates, Vol. 10, *Oath*, page xiii; *Law*, page 144
Dostoevsky, Vol. 52, *Brothers Karamazov*, Part II, Bk. V, Chap. 4, pages 122–125; Part IV, Bk. XI, Chaps. 8–9, pages 329–346
James, W., Vol. 53, *Principles of Psychology*, Chap. VI, pages 108–115; Chap. VIII, pages 130–139; Chap. X, pages 240–258
Freud, Vol. 54, *Unconscious*, pages 428–443; *General Introduction to Psycho-Analysis*, Part III, Lecture 26, pages 620–621; *New Introductory Lectures*, Lecture 31, pages 830–831

RELATED AUTHORS AND WORKS IN *Gateway to the Great Books*

Butler, "Customs and Opinions of the Erewhonians," Vol. 2, pages 483–506
Eliot, G., *Lifted Veil*, Vol. 3, pages 157–193
Flaubert, *Legend of St. Julian the Hospitaller*, Vol. 3, pages 371–392
Hawthorne, *Rappaccini's Daughter*, Vol. 3, pages 128–152

STEVENSON, Dr. Jekyll and Mr. Hyde
continued

Lawrence, *Rocking-Horse Winner*, Vol. 3, pages 512–525
Mann, *Mario and the Magician*, Vol. 3, pages 573–610
O'Neill, *Emperor Jones*, Vol. 4, pages 357–382
Poe, *Tell-Tale Heart*, Vol. 2, pages 273–277
Pushkin, *Queen of Spades*, Vol. 3, pages 484–507

The Lantern-Bearers
Vol. 7, pages 112–121

SUGGESTED READINGS IN THE *Syntopicon*

ART, Vol. 2, pages 64–86, especially
    Topic 3: Art as imitation
    Topic 5: The sources of art in experience, imagination,
        and inspiration
MAN, Vol. 3, pages 1–41, especially
    Topic 13: The grandeur and misery of man
MEMORY AND IMAGINATION, Vol. 3, pages 133–157, especially
    Topic 7b: The fantastic and the realistic in poetry: the probable
        and the possible in poetry and history

RELATED AUTHORS AND WORKS IN *Great Books of the Western World*

Plato, Vol. 7, *Ion*, pages 142–148
Aristotle, Vol. 9, *On Poetics*, pages 681–699
Bacon, Vol. 30, *Advancement of Learning*, Second Book,
    pages 38–39
Pascal, Vol. 33, *Pensées*, Sect. II, pages 181–184, 195–204
Fielding, Vol. 37, *Tom Jones*, Bk. VIII, Chap. 1, pages 152–155;
    Bk. X, Chap. 1, pages 204–205
Kant, Vol. 42, *Critique of Judgement*, First Part, Sect. I,
    pages 525–532
Goethe, Vol. 47, *Faust*, First Part, pages 11–21, 37–44
Dostoevsky, Vol. 52, *Brothers Karamazov*, Part II, Bk. V, Chap. 5,
    pages 127–137

RELATED AUTHORS AND WORKS IN *Gateway to the Great Books*

Eliot, T. S., *Tradition and the Individual Talent*, Vol. 5,
    pages 404–411
Emerson, *Thoreau*, Vol. 6, pages 150–165
Mill, J. S., "Childhood and Youth," Vol. 6, pages 5–47
Ruskin, *Idealist's Arraignment of the Age*, Vol. 7, pages 126–136
Twain, "Learning the River," Vol. 6, pages 50–98
Whitman, *Death of Abraham Lincoln*, Vol. 6, pages 174–183

JONATHAN SWIFT, 1667–1745

Resolutions when I Come to Be Old
Vol. 7, page 32

A Meditation upon a Broomstick
Vol. 7, pages 40–41

SUGGESTED READINGS IN THE *Syntopicon*

MAN, Vol. 3, pages 1–41, especially
Topic 6c: The ages of man: infancy, youth, maturity,
senescence
Topic 12: Man as an object of laughter and ridicule: comedy
and satire

RELATED AUTHORS AND WORKS IN *Great Books of the Western World*

Aristophanes, Vol. 5, *Clouds*, pages 488–506; *Birds*, pages 542–563;
Frogs, pages 564–582
Montaigne, Vol. 25, *That Our Affections Carry Themselves
Beyond Us*, pages 6–10; *Apology for Raimond de Sebonde*,
pages 208–294
Shakespeare, Vol. 26, *As You Like It*, Act II, Scene VII,
pages 607–609
Pascal, Vol. 33, *Pensées*, Sect. II, pages 181–184; Sect. VI,
pages 233–234; Sect. VII, page 249
Sterne, Vol. 36, *Tristram Shandy*, pages 185–556
Goethe, Vol. 47, *Faust*, Part I, pages 44–48

RELATED AUTHORS AND WORKS IN *Gateway to the Great Books*

Bacon, *Of Youth and Age*, Vol. 7, pages 3–4
Cicero, *On Old Age*, Vol. 10, pages 317–343
Hazlitt, *On Swift*, Vol. 5, pages 280–283

An Essay on Modern Education
Vol. 7, pages 33–39

SUGGESTED READINGS IN THE *Syntopicon*

EDUCATION, Vol. 2, pages 376–399, especially
Topic 4b: The influence of the family in moral training
Topic 5d: The order of learning: the organization
of the curriculum
Topic 8: Education and the state

SWIFT, An Essay on Modern Education
continued

STATE, Vol. 3, pages 826–865, especially
Topic 5: The social structure or stratification of the state
Topic 7d: The educational task of the state: the trained
intelligence of the citizens

RELATED AUTHORS AND WORKS IN *Great Books of the Western World*

Plato, Vol. 7, *Laches*, pages 26–37; *Republic*, Bks. II–III,
pages 320–341
Aristotle, Vol. 9, *Politics*, Bk. VIII, pages 542–548
Rabelais, Vol. 24, *Gargantua and Pantagruel*, Bk. I, Chaps. 14–15,
pages 18–19; Chaps. 21–24, pages 24–30; Bk. II, Chap. 8,
pages 81–83
Montaigne, Vol. 25, *Of the Education of Children*, pages 62–80;
Of the Affection of Fathers to Their Children, pages 183–192
Fielding, Vol. 37, *Tom Jones*, Bk. III, Chaps. 2–10, pages 36–49
Smith, Vol. 39, *Wealth of Nations*, Bk. V, Chap. I, pages 334–343
Hamilton, Madison, Jay, Vol. 43, *Federalist*, No. 84, pages 252–256
Mill, J. S., Vol. 43, *Representative Government*, Chap. 2, pages
332–341, Chap. 8, pages 381–387
Dostoevsky, Vol. 52, *Brothers Karamazov*, Part IV, Bk. X, Chap. 5,
pages 290–292

RELATED AUTHORS AND WORKS IN *Gateway to the Great Books*

Bacon, *Of Custom and Education*, Vol. 7, pages 18–19
Faraday, *Observations on Mental Education*, Vol. 7, pages 208–232
Franklin, *Proposals Relating to the Education of Youth
in Pennsylvania*, Vol. 6, pages 536–542
Hazlitt, *On Swift*, Vol. 5, pages 280–283
Mill, J. S., "Childhood and Youth," Vol. 6, pages 5–47
Ruskin, *Idealist's Arraignment of the Age*, Vol. 7, pages 126–136
Schopenhauer, *On Education*, Vol. 7, pages 197–203

**A Modest Proposal for Preventing the Children
of Ireland from Being a Burden to Their Parents
or Country**
Vol. 7, pages 42–49

SUGGESTED READINGS IN THE *Syntopicon*

JUSTICE, Vol. 2, pages 850–879, especially
Topic 8: Economic justice: justice in production, distribution,
and exchange

NECESSITY AND CONTINGENCY, Vol. 3, pages 251–269,
especially
Topic 5d: The necessity or inevitability of slavery, poverty,
war, or crime
WEALTH, Vol. 3, pages 1038–1070, especially
Topic 8: The distribution of wealth: the problem of poverty
Topic 9g: Wealth and poverty in relation to crime and to war
between states

RELATED AUTHORS AND WORKS IN *Great Books of the Western World*

Aristotle, Vol. 9, *Politics*, Bk. I, Chaps. 3–11, pages 446–453; Bk. II,
Chaps. 5–7, pages 458–463
Montaigne, Vol. 25, *Of Cannibals*, pages 91–98
Locke, Vol. 35, *Concerning Civil Government*, Chap. V,
pages 30–36
Rousseau, Vol. 38, *Discourse on the Origin of Inequality*,
pages 323–366
Smith, Vol. 39, *Wealth of Nations*, Bk. I, Chaps. VI–X, pages 20–62
Marx, Vol. 50, *Capital*, Part VII, Chap. XXV, pages 345–353;
Part VIII, Chap. XXVIII, pages 364–366

RELATED AUTHORS AND WORKS IN *Gateway to the Great Books*

Epicurus, *Letter to Menoeceus*, Vol. 10, pages 230–233
Hazlitt, *On Swift*, Vol. 5, pages 280–283
Lincoln, *Address at Cooper Institute*, Vol. 6, pages 737–746
Long, *Power within Us*, Vol. 6, pages 246–261
Malthus, "Principle of Population," Vol. 7, pages 502–530
Prescott, "Land of Montezuma," Vol. 6, pages 231–243
Ruskin, *Idealist's Arraignment of the Age*, Vol. 7, pages 126–136
Tolstoy, *What Men Live By*, Vol. 3, pages 707–727
Voltaire, "English Men and Ideas: On Inoculation," Vol. 7,
pages 339–343

For Swift's *Gulliver's Travels* in *Great Books of the Western World*,
see Vol. 36, pages 3–184

JOHN MILLINGTON SYNGE, 1871–1909

Riders to the Sea
Vol. 4, pages 342–352

SUGGESTED READINGS IN THE *Syntopicon*

HAPPINESS, Vol. 2, pages 684–710, especially
Topic 4b: The attainability of happiness: the fear of death
and the tragic view of human life

SYNGE, *Riders to the Sea*
continued

LIFE AND DEATH, Vol. 2, pages 1013–1034, especially
    Topic 7: The causes and occurrence of death: the transition
        from life to death
    Topic 8*a*: The love of life: the instinct of self-preservation;
        the life instinct
PLEASURE AND PAIN, Vol. 3, pages 377–399, especially
    Topic 4*a*: The pleasant and unpleasant in the sphere
        of emotion: joy and sorrow, delight and grief

RELATED AUTHORS AND WORKS IN *Great Books of the Western World*

Homer, Vol. 4, *Iliad*, Bk. VI, pages 43–45
Euripides, Vol. 5, *Trojan Women*, pages 270–281
Montaigne, Vol. 25, *That the Relish of Good and Evil Depends
    in a Great Measure Upon the Opinion We Have of Them*,
    pages 115–119
Sterne, Vol. 36, *Tristram Shandy*, Bk. V, Chaps. 3–7, pages 388–395

RELATED AUTHORS AND WORKS IN *Gateway to the Great Books*

Bacon, *Of Parents and Children*, Vol. 7, pages 5–6; *Of Marriage
    and Single Life*, pages 7–8; *Of Death*, Vol. 10, pages 348–349;
    Of Adversity, page 350
Browne, "Immortality," Vol. 10, pages 575–580
Bunin, *Gentleman from San Francisco*, Vol. 3, pages 102–123
Crane, *Open Boat*, Vol. 3, pages 5–26
Dinesen, *Sorrow-Acre*, Vol. 3, pages 615–641
Gogol, *Overcoat*, Vol. 2, pages 452–478
Lincoln, *Meditation on the Divine Will*, Vol. 6, page 758
Long, *Power within Us*, Vol. 6, pages 246–261
Maupassant, *Two Friends*, Vol. 2, pages 159–164
Pater, "Art of Life," Vol. 10, pages 258–261
Poe, *Masque of the Red Death*, Vol. 2, pages 278–283
Scott, *Two Drovers*, Vol. 2, pages 182–205
Tolstoy, *Death of Ivan Ilyitch*, Vol. 3, pages 646–699; *What Men
    Live By*, pages 707–727

CORNELIUS TACITUS, c. 55–c. 120

The Life of Gnaeus Julius Agricola
Vol. 6, pages 274–298

SUGGESTED READINGS IN THE *Syntopicon*

HISTORY, Vol. 2, pages 711–727, especially
  Topic 4a(4): The role of the individual in history: the great
    man, hero, or leader
HONOR, Vol. 2, pages 728–748, especially
  Topic 3a: The reaction of the community to its good or great
    men
  Topic 5: Honor, fame, and the heroic
SLAVERY, Vol. 3, pages 774–790, especially
  Topic 6d: The imperialistic subjection or enslavement
    of conquered peoples or colonial dependencies
TYRANNY, Vol. 3, pages 939–956, especially
  Topic 1a: The lawlessness of tyrannical rule: might
    without right
  Topic 1b: The injustice of tyrannical government: rule
    for self-interest
  Topic 7: The ways of tyrants or despots to attain and maintain
    power
VIRTUE AND VICE, Vol. 3, pages 975–1009, especially
  Topic 7b: Civic virtue: the virtue of the good citizen compared
    with the virtue of the good man
WAR AND PEACE, Vol. 3, pages 1010–1037, especially
  Topic 6a: Conquest, empire, political expansion as ends of war
  Topic 10c: The military virtues: the qualities of the professional
    soldier; education for war

RELATED AUTHORS AND WORKS IN *Great Books of the Western World*

Plato, Vol. 7, *Apology*, pages 200–212; *Crito*, pages 213–219
Plutarch, Vol. 14, *Numa Pompilius*, pages 49–61; *Timoleon*,
  pages 195–213; *Caius Marius*, pages 344–354
Machiavelli, Vol. 23, *Prince*, pages 1–37
Shakespeare, Vol. 26, *Julius Caesar*, pages 568–596; Vol. 27,
  Coriolanus, pages 351–392
Swift, Vol. 36, *Gulliver's Travels*, Part I, pages 3–42
Gibbon, Vol. 40, *Decline and Fall of the Roman Empire*, Chap. I,
  pages 1–2; Chap. III, pages 24–33; Chap. IV, pages 35–39;
  Chap. XVI pages 213–215

T A C I T U S, *The Life of Gnaeus Julius Agricola*
continued

Hegel, Vol. 46, *Philosophy of History*, Introduction III,
pages 162–170

RELATED AUTHORS AND WORKS IN *Gateway to the Great Books*

Bacon, *Of Great Place*, Vol. 7, pages 9–11; *Of Seditions
and Troubles*, pages 12–17; *Of Adversity*, Vol. 10, page 350
Carlyle, *Hero as King*, Vol. 6, pages 110–145
Ibsen, *Enemy of the People*, Vol. 4, pages 164–246
James, W., *Great Men and Their Environment*, Vol. 7,
pages 171–194
Jefferson, "Biographical Sketches," Vol. 6, pages 522–528
Prescott, "Land of Montezuma," Vol. 6, pages 231–243
Shaw, *Man of Destiny*, Vol. 4, pages 300–338
Thoreau, *Civil Disobedience*, Vol. 6, pages 695–713
Whitman, *Death of Abraham Lincoln*, Vol. 6, pages 174–183
Woolf, *Art of Biography*, Vol. 6, pages 186–192

For other works by Tacitus in *Great Books of the Western World*,
see Vol. 15

HENRY DAVID THOREAU, 1817–1862

Civil Disobedience
Vol. 6, pages 695–713

SUGGESTED READINGS IN THE *Syntopicon*

DEMOCRACY, Vol. 2, pages 303–322, especially
Topic 5*b*(1): Majority rule and minority or proportional
representation
GOVERNMENT, Vol. 2, pages 637–664, especially
Topic 1*c*: The ends and limits of government: the criteria
of legitimacy and justice
Topic 1*f*: The abuses and corruptions to which government
is subject
JUSTICE, Vol. 2, pages 850–879, especially
Topic 10*b*: The legality of unjust laws: the extent of obedience
required of the just man in the unjust society

LAW, Vol. 2, pages 962–990, especially
Topic 6a: Obedience to the authority and force of law:
the sanctions of conscience and fear; the objective
and subjective sanctions of law; law, duty, and right

RELATED AUTHORS AND WORKS IN *Great Books of the Western World*

Aeschylus, Vol. 5, *Prometheus Bound*, pages 40–51
Sophocles, Vol. 5, *Antigone*, pages 131–142
Euripides, Vol. 5, *Medea*, pages 212–224
Aristophanes, Vol. 5, *Lysistrata*, pages 583–599
Plato, Vol. 7, *Apology*, pages 200–212; *Crito*, pages 213–219;
   Republic, Bk. VIII, pages 401–416
Aquinas, Vol. 20, *Summa Theologica*, Part I–II, Q 96, Art. 4,
   page 233; Part II–II, Q 42, pages 583–584
Hobbes, Vol. 23, *Leviathan*, Part II, Chap. 21, pages 112–117
Montaigne, Vol. 25, *Of Profit and Honesty*, pages 381–388
Shakespeare, Vol. 26, *King Richard III*, pages 105–148; *King
   Richard II*, pages 320–351; *King Henry IV*, First Part,
   pages 434–466; *King Henry IV*, Second Part, pages 467–502
Locke, Vol. 35, *Concerning Civil Government*, Chaps. XI–XII,
   pages 55–59
Swift, Vol. 36, *Gulliver's Travels*, Part I, pages 3–42
Mill, J. S., Vol. 43, *On Liberty*, pages 267–323

RELATED AUTHORS AND WORKS IN *Gateway to the Great Books*

Butler, "Customs and Opinions of the Erewhonians," Vol. 2,
   pages 241–256
Calhoun, "Concurrent Majority," Vol. 7, pages 276–290
Emerson, *Thoreau*, Vol. 6, pages 150–165
Great Documents, *Virginia Declaration of Rights*, Vol. 6,
   pages 415–417; *Declaration of Independence*, pages 418–421
Ibsen, *Enemy of the People*, Vol. 4, pages 164–246
Jefferson, "Virginia Constitution," Vol. 6, pages 502–517
Lincoln, *First Inaugural Address*, Vol. 6, pages 747–755
Paine, "Call to Patriots—December 23, 1776," Vol. 6, pages
   461–468
Tacitus, *Life of Gnaeus Julius Agricola*, Vol. 6, pages 274–298
Tocqueville, "Observations on American Life and Government,"
   Vol. 6, pages 564–690
Xenophon, "Character of Socrates," Vol. 6, pages 223–226

HENRY DAVID THOREAU
continued

A Plea for Captain John Brown
Vol. 6, pages 714–732

SUGGESTED READINGS IN THE *Syntopicon*

COURAGE, Vol. 2, pages 252–267, especially
Topic 7a: The courage required of citizens and statesmen:
the political recognition of courage
JUSTICE, Vol. 2, pages 850–879, especially
Topic 5: Justice and equality: the kinds of justice in relation
to the measure and modes of equality and inequality
Topic 6e: Justice and natural rights as the source of civil
liberty
REVOLUTION, Vol. 3, pages 626–644, especially
Topic 6a: The right of rebellion: the circumstances justifying
civil disobedience or violent insurrection
SLAVERY, Vol. 3, pages 774–790, especially
Topic 3c: The emancipation or manumission of slaves:
the rebellion of slaves

RELATED AUTHORS AND WORKS IN *Great Books of the Western World*

Sophocles, Vol. 5, *Antigone*, pages 131–142; *Ajax*, pages 143–155
Aristophanes, Vol. 5, *Peace*, pages 526–541
Aristotle, Vol. 9, *Politics*, Bk. III, Chaps. 12–13, pages 480–483
Aquinas, Vol. 20, *Summa Theologica*, Part I–II, Q 92, Art. 1,
Reply Obj. 4, page 214; Q 96, Art. 4, page 233; Part II–II,
Q 42, pages 583–584
Locke, Vol. 35, *Concerning Civil Government*, Chap. IV,
pages 29–30
Montesquieu, Vol. 38, *Spirit of Laws*, Bk. XV, Chaps. 9–18,
pages 111–115
Mill, J. S., Vol. 43, *Representative Government*, Chap. 7, pages
370–375

RELATED AUTHORS AND WORKS IN *Gateway to the Great Books*

Bacon, *Of Seditions and Troubles*, Vol. 7, pages 12–17
Emerson, *Thoreau*, Vol. 6, pages 150–165
Hawthorne, *Sketch of Abraham Lincoln*, Vol. 6, pages 168–171
Lincoln, *Address at Cooper Institute*, Vol. 6, pages 737–746;
First Inaugural Address, pages 747–755; *Second Inaugural
Address*, pages 760–761
Whitman, *Death of Abraham Lincoln*, Vol. 6, pages 174–183
Woolf, *Art of Biography*, Vol. 6, pages 186–192

ALEXIS DE TOCQUEVILLE, 1805–1859

"Observations on American Life and Government"
from *Democracy in America*
Vol. 6, pages 564–690

SUGGESTED READINGS IN THE *Syntopicon*

DEMOCRACY, Vol. 2, pages 303–322, especially
Topic 3c: Comparison of democracy, aristocracy, and monarchy
with respect to efficiency
Topic 4a(1): Universal suffrage: the abolition of privileged
classes
Topic 4b: The democratic realization of popular sovereignty:
the safeguarding of natural rights
Topic 4c: The infirmities of democracy in practice
and the reforms or remedies for these defects

GOVERNMENT, Vol. 2, pages 637–664, especially
Topic 1g(3): The sovereign people: the community
as the source of governmental sovereignty
Topic 2d: The influence of different forms of government
on the formation of human character

LIBERTY, Vol. 2, pages 991–1012, especially
Topic 1f: The freedom of equals under government:
the equality of citizenship
Topic 2c: Freedom in the sphere of economic enterprise: free
trade; freedom from governmental restrictions

MAN, Vol. 3, pages 1–41, especially
Topic 6b: The differences between men and women: their
equality or inequality

STATE, Vol. 3, pages 826–865, especially
Topic 2e: The political structure of the state: its determination
by the form of government

RELATED AUTHORS AND WORKS IN *Great Books of the Western World*

Plato, Vol. 7, *Republic*, Bk. VIII, pages 401–416
Aristotle, Vol. 9, *Politics*, Bk. III, Chaps. 8–13, pages 477–483;
Bk. IV, Chaps. 3–9, pages 488–494; Bk. V, pages 502–519
Locke, Vol. 35, *Concerning Civil Government*, Chap. XIX,
pages 73–81
Rousseau, Vol. 38, *Social Contract*, Bk. II, Chaps. 3–4,
pages 396–398
Kant, Vol. 42, *Science of Right*, Second Part, pages 436–437,
450–452

TOCQUEVILLE, "American Life and Government"
continued

Hamilton, Madison, Jay, Vol. 43, *Federalist*, No. 12, pages 56–58;
No. 39, pages 125–126; No. 62, pages 188–191; No. 73,
pages 218–221
Mill, J. S., Vol. 43, *Representative Government*, Chaps. 6–9,
pages 362–392
Hegel, Vol. 46, *Philosophy of Right*, Additions, pages 145–148;
Philosophy of History, Fourth Part, pages 348–369,
especially pages 360–369

RELATED AUTHORS AND WORKS IN *Gateway to the Great Books*

Adams, "United States in 1800," Vol. 6, pages 322–359
Calhoun, "Concurrent Majority," Vol. 7, pages 276–290
Crèvecoeur, "Making of Americans," Vol. 6, pages 546–559
Emerson, *Thoreau*, Vol. 6, pages 150–165; *Self-Reliance*, Vol. 10,
pages 525–545
Franklin, *Proposal for Promoting Useful Knowledge
among the British Plantations in America*, Vol. 6, pages 533–535;
Proposals Relating to the Education of Youth in Pennsylvania,
pages 536–542
Great Documents, *Declaration of Independence*, Vol. 6,
pages 418–421
Hawthorne, *Sketch of Abraham Lincoln*, Vol. 6, pages 168–171
Jefferson, *First Inaugural Address*, Vol. 6, pages 518–521
Lincoln, *Address at Cooper Institute*, Vol. 6, pages 737–746;
First Inaugural Address, pages 747–755; *Letter to Horace
Greeley*, pages 756–757; *Second Inaugural Address*, pages
760–761; *Last Public Address*, pages 762–765
Thoreau, *Civil Disobedience*, Vol. 6, pages 695–713
Washington, *Farewell Address*, Vol. 6, pages 484–497
Whitman, *Preface to Leaves of Grass*, Vol. 5, pages 247–259

LEO TOLSTOY, 1828–1910

The Death of Ivan Ilyitch
Vol. 3, pages 646–699

SUGGESTED READINGS IN THE *Syntopicon*

HAPPINESS, Vol. 2, pages 684–710, especially
Topic 2b(5): The importance of friendship and love
for happiness

Topic 4b: The attainability of happiness: the fear of death and the tragic view of human life

LIFE AND DEATH, Vol. 2, pages 1013–1034, especially

Topic 7: The causes and occurrence of death: the transition from life to death

Topic 8a: The love of life: the instinct of self-preservation; the life instinct

Topic 8c: The contemplation and fear of death: the attitude of the hero, the philosopher, the martyr

LOVE, Vol. 2, pages 1051–1082, especially

Topic 2b(2): Self-love in relation to the love of others

PLEASURE AND PAIN, Vol. 3, pages 377–399, especially

Topic 4e: The kinds of pain: the pain of sense and the pain of loss or deprivation

RELATED AUTHORS AND WORKS IN *Great Books of the Western World*

Euripides, Vol. 5, *Alcestis*, pages 237–247
Plato, Vol. 7, *Republic*, Bk. X, pages 434–436
Montaigne, Vol. 25, *Use Makes Perfect*, pages 176–180
Pascal, Vol. 33, *Pensées*, Sect. III, pages 211–212
Dostoevsky, Vol. 52, *Brothers Karamazov*, Bk. VI, Chap. 1, pages 148–150

RELATED AUTHORS AND WORKS IN *Gateway to the Great Books*

Bacon, *Of Death*, Vol. 10, pages 348–349
Browne, "Immortality," Vol. 10, pages 575–580
Cicero, *On Old Age*, Vol. 10, pages 317–343
De Quincey, *Literature of Knowledge and Literature of Power*, Vol. 5, pages 358–361
Dinesen, *Sorrow-Acre*, Vol. 3, pages 615–641
Gogol, *Overcoat*, Vol. 2, pages 452–478
Hemingway, *Killers*, Vol. 2, pages 169–177
Synge, *Riders to the Sea*, Vol. 4, pages 342–352
Whitman, *Death of Abraham Lincoln*, Vol. 6, pages 174–183

The Three Hermits
Vol. 3, pages 700–706

SUGGESTED READINGS IN THE *Syntopicon*

GOD, Vol. 2, pages 543–604, especially
Topic 7d: Grace
Topic 7e: Miracles

HAPPINESS, Vol. 2, pages 684–710, especially
Topic 7c(2): The joy of the blessed: the communion of saints

TOLSTOY, *The Three Hermits*
continued

RELIGION, Vol. 3, pages 588–625, especially
Topic 2*a*: Prayer and supplication: their efficacy
SIN, Vol. 3, pages 753–773, especially
Topic 7: Grace and good works in relation to salvation from sin

RELATED AUTHORS AND WORKS IN *Great Books of the Western World*

Augustine, Vol. 18, *City of God*, Bk. XXII, Chaps. 8–9,
pages 591–598
Aquinas, Vol. 20, *Summa Theologica*, Part I–II, Q 68,
pages 87–96; Q 109, Arts. 7–10, pages 344–347
Pascal, Vol. 33, *Pensées*, Sect. IV, pages 221–222; Sect. VII,
page 259
Dostoevsky, Vol. 52, *Brothers Karamazov*, Bk. II, Chap. 3,
pages 21–24

RELATED AUTHORS AND WORKS IN *Gateway to the Great Books*

Adams, *Saint Thomas Aquinas*, Vol. 10, pages 422–450
Bacon, *Of Discourse*, Vol. 5, pages 95–96; *Of Studies*, pages 97–98
Cicero, *On Old Age*, Vol. 10, pages 317–343
Long, *Power within Us*, Vol. 6, pages 246–261
Melville, *Billy Budd*, Vol. 3, pages 31–98
Plutarch, *Contentment*, Vol. 10, pages 264–281
Schiller, *On Simple and Sentimental Poetry*, Vol. 5, pages 155–211
Wilde, *Happy Prince*, Vol. 2, pages 261–268

What Men Live By
Vol. 3, pages 707–727

SUGGESTED READINGS IN THE *Syntopicon*

GOD, Vol. 2, pages 543–604, especially
Topic 5*h*: God's love: the diffusion of the divine goodness
GOOD AND EVIL, Vol. 2, pages 605–636, especially
Topic 2*a*: God's goodness as diffusive, causing the goodness
of things: God's love
LOVE, Vol. 2, pages 1051–1082, especially
Topic 3*a*: Friendship and love in relation to virtue
and happiness
Topic 3*d*: The heroism of friendship and the sacrifices of love
Topic 5*b*(1): The precepts of charity: the law of love

RELATED AUTHORS AND WORKS IN *Great Books of the Western World*

Augustine, Vol. 18, *On Christian Doctrine*, Bk. I, Chaps. 22–30, pages 629–633

Aquinas, Vol. 19, *Summa Theologica*, First Part, Q 20, pages 119–124

Chaucer, Vol. 22, *Canterbury Tales*, Tale of Melibeus, pages 426–432

Dostoevsky, Vol. 52, *Brothers Karamazov*, Bk. VI, Chap. 3, pages 167–168

RELATED AUTHORS AND WORKS IN *Gateway to the Great Books*

Arnold, *Sweetness and Light*, Vol. 5, pages 42–61
Bacon, *Sphinx*, Vol. 8, pages 2–4; *Of Love*, Vol. 10, pages 351–352
Bunin, *Gentleman from San Francisco*, Vol. 3, pages 102–123
Dinesen, *Sorrow-Acre*, Vol. 3, pages 615–641
Flaubert, *Legend of St. Julian the Hospitaller*, Vol. 3, pages 371–392
Long, *Power within Us*, Vol. 6, pages 246–261
Ruskin, *Idealist's Arraignment of the Age*, Vol. 7, pages 126–136
Sheridan, *School for Scandal*, Vol. 4, pages 85–159
Singer, *Spinoza of Market Street*, Vol. 3, pages 466–480
Synge, *Riders to the Sea*, Vol. 4, pages 342–352
Wilde, *Happy Prince*, Vol. 2, pages 261–268

For Tolstoy's *War and Peace* in *Great Books of the Western World*, see Vol. 51

IVAN TURGENEV, 1818–1883

First Love
Vol. 3, pages 217–271

SUGGESTED READINGS IN THE *Syntopicon*

FAMILY, Vol. 2, pages 486–514, especially
  Topic 6e: The initiation of children into adult life
  Topic 7a: Marriage and love: romantic, conjugal, and illicit love
  Topic 7d: The emotional impact of family life upon the child: the domestic triangle; the symbolic roles of father and mother

LOVE, Vol. 2, pages 1051–1082, especially
  Topic 1e: The intensity and power of love: its increase or decrease; its constructive or destructive force
  Topic 2a(1): The sexual instinct: its relation to other instincts

TURGENEV, *First Love*
continued

PLEASURE AND PAIN, Vol. 3, pages 377–399, especially
Topic 4a: The pleasant and unpleasant in the sphere
of emotion: joy and sorrow, delight and grief
Topic 7a: Pleasure and pain in relation to love and friendship

RELATED AUTHORS AND WORKS IN *Great Books of the Western World*

Euripides, Vol. 5, *Hippolytus,* pages 225–236
Dante, Vol. 21, *Divine Comedy,* Hell, Canto V, pages 7–8;
Paradise, Canto VIII, pages 116–118
Shakespeare, Vol. 26, *Taming of the Shrew,* Act I, Scene II–Act III,
pages 205–216; *Romeo and Juliet,* pages 285–319; Vol. 27,
Hamlet, pages 29–72
Fielding, Vol. 37, *Tom Jones,* Bk. IV, Chaps. 12–14, pages 67–73;
Bk. V, Chaps. 2–6, pages 75–86
Freud, Vol. 54, *General Introduction to Psycho-Analysis,* Part III,
Chap. 21, pages 581–584

RELATED AUTHORS AND WORKS IN *Gateway to the Great Books*

Anderson, *I'm a Fool,* Vol. 2, pages 511–520
Anonymous, *Aucassin and Nicolette,* Vol. 2, pages 523–551
Apuleius, "Cupid and Psyche," Vol. 3, pages 197–212
Bacon, *Of Youth and Age,* Vol. 7, pages 3–4; *Of Parents
and Children,* pages 5–6; *Of Love,* Vol. 10, pages 351–352
Chekhov, *Darling,* Vol. 3, pages 452–462
Conrad, *Youth,* Vol. 2, pages 210–236
Dostoevsky, *White Nights,* Vol. 3, pages 276–319
Galsworthy, *Apple-Tree,* Vol. 3, pages 323–367
Hawthorne, *Rappaccini's Daughter,* Vol. 3, pages 128–152
Pater, "Art of Life," Vol. 10, pages 258–261
Schopenhauer, *On Style,* Vol. 5, pages 124–136

MARK TWAIN (SAMUEL CLEMENS), 1835–1910

The Man That Corrupted Hadleyburg
Vol. 2, pages 346–386

SUGGESTED READINGS IN THE *Syntopicon*

HONOR, Vol. 2, pages 728–748, especially
Topic 3b: The conditions of honor or fame and the causes
of dishonor or infamy

PUNISHMENT, Vol. 3, pages 488–512, especially
  Topic 3c: Guilt, repentance, and the moral need for punishment
  Topic 5c: The pain of remorse and the torment of conscience:
    the atonement for sin
TRUTH, Vol. 3, pages 915–938, especially
  Topic 8a: Prevarication and perjury: the injustice of lying
    or bearing false witness
VIRTUE AND VICE, Vol. 3, pages 975–1009, especially
  Topic 2c: The appearances of virtue: imperfect or conditional
    virtues; the counterfeits of virtue; natural
    or temperamental dispositions which simulate virtue
  Topic 4e(3): Circumstances as affecting the morality of human
    acts
  Topic 9: The advance or decline of human morality

RELATED AUTHORS AND WORKS IN *Great Books of the Western World*

Sophocles, Vol. 5, *Philoctetes*, pages 182–195
Montaigne, Vol. 25, *Of Conscience*, pages 174–176
Shakespeare, Vol. 27, *Hamlet*, pages 29–72
Milton, Vol. 32, *Paradise Lost*, pages 93–333; *Areopagitica*,
  pages 379–412
Sterne, Vol. 36, *Tristram Shandy*, Bk. II, Chap. 17, pages 257–266
Kant, Vol. 42, *Critique of Practical Reason*, First Part, Bk. I,
  Chap. III, pages 325–327
Boswell, Vol. 44, *Life of Samuel Johnson*, pages 372–373
Goethe, Vol. 47, *Faust*, First Part, pages 11–114

RELATED AUTHORS AND WORKS IN *Gateway to the Great Books*

Bacon, *Of Riches*, Vol. 7, pages 25–27; *Of Truth*, Vol. 10,
  pages 346–347
Bunin, *Gentleman from San Francisco*, Vol. 3, pages 102–123
Butler, "Customs and Opinions of the Erewhonians," Vol. 2,
  pages 483–506
Fitzgerald, *Diamond as Big as the Ritz*, Vol. 3, pages 397–431
Hemingway, *Killers*, Vol. 2, pages 169–177
Ibsen, *Enemy of the People*, Vol. 4, pages 164–246
James, H., *Pupil*, Vol. 3, pages 530–568
Mann, *Mario and the Magician*, Vol. 3, pages 573–610
Molière, *Misanthrope*, Vol. 4, pages 6–51
O'Neill, *Emperor Jones*, Vol. 4, pages 357–382
Sheridan, *School for Scandal*, Vol. 4, pages 85–159

MARK TWAIN
continued

"Learning the River"
from *Life on the Mississippi*
Vol. 6, pages 50–98

SUGGESTED READINGS IN THE *Syntopicon*

EDUCATION, Vol. 2, pages 376–399, especially
Topic 5*f*: Learning apart from teachers and books: the role of experience
EXPERIENCE, Vol. 2, pages 468–485, especially
Topic 6*a*: Experience as indispensable to sound judgment and prudence
KNOWLEDGE, Vol. 2, pages 880–920, especially
Topic 6*b*(2): Memory as knowledge
Topic 8*b*(4): The possession or pursuit of knowledge as a good or satisfaction: its relation to pleasure and pain; its contribution to happiness
MEMORY AND IMAGINATION, Vol. 3, pages 133–157, especially
Topic 2*b*: Recollection: factors influencing ease and adequacy of recall
Topic 2*c*: The association of ideas: controlled and free association; reminiscence and reverie
Topic 3: Remembering as an act of knowledge and as a source of knowledge

RELATED AUTHORS AND WORKS IN *Great Books of the Western World*

Rabelais, Vol. 24, *Gargantua and Pantagruel*, Bk. I, pages 1–67, especially Chaps. 21–24, pages 24–30; Bk. II, pages 68–126
Montaigne, Vol. 25, *Of Three Commerces*, pages 395–398
Locke, Vol. 35, *Concerning Human Understanding*, Bk. II, Chaps. IX–X, pages 138–143
Sterne, Vol. 36, *Tristram Shandy*, Bk. II, Chap. 3, pages 236–238
Goethe, Vol. 47, *Faust*, First Part, pages 11–114
Melville, Vol. 48, *Moby Dick*, Chap. 24, pages 79–82
James, W., Vol. 53, *Principles of Psychology*, Chap. XVI, pages 424–427

RELATED AUTHORS AND WORKS IN *Gateway to the Great Books*

Bacon, *Of Custom and Education*, Vol. 7, pages 18–19
Conrad, *Youth*, Vol. 2, pages 210–236
Defoe, *Robinson Crusoe*, Vol. 2, pages 5–121
Emerson, *Self-Reliance*, Vol. 10, pages 525–545

JOHN TYNDALL, 1820–1893

"Michael Faraday"
from *Faraday as a Discoverer*
Vol. 8, pages 8–28

SUGGESTED READINGS IN THE *Syntopicon*

ELEMENT, Vol. 2, pages 400–412, especially
Topic 3: The theory of the elements in natural philosophy, physics, and chemistry
EXPERIENCE, Vol. 2, pages 468–485, especially
Topic 5: The theory of experimentation in scientific method
INDUCTION, Vol. 2, pages 805–815, especially
Topic 5: The role of induction in the development of science: the methods of experimental and enumerative induction
MAN, Vol. 3, pages 1–41, especially
Topic 2: Man's knowledge of man
MECHANICS, Vol. 3, pages 80–112, especially
Topic 6d: Force: its kinds and its effects
PHYSICS, Vol. 3, pages 363–376, especially
Topic 4: The experimental method in the study of nature
Topic 5: The utility of physics: the invention of machines; the techniques of engineering; the mastery of nature

RELATED AUTHORS AND WORKS IN *Great Books of the Western World*

Gilbert, Vol. 28, *On the Loadstone,* pages 1–121
Descartes, Vol. 31, *Discourse on Method,* Parts I–IV, pages 41–54
Newton, Vol. 34, *Mathematical Principles of Natural Philosophy,* pages 5–8, 11–14; Bk. I, pages 28–29, 37–38; Bk. III, pages 371–372

RELATED AUTHORS AND WORKS IN *Gateway to the Great Books*

Bacon, *Sphinx,* Vol. 8, pages 2–4
Curie, *Discovery of Radium,* Vol. 8, pages 32–42
Darwin, *Autobiography,* Vol. 8, pages 47–93

TYNDALL, "Michael Faraday"

continued

Einstein and Infeld, "Rise and Decline of Classical Physics,"
Vol. 8, pages 490–560
Eliot, T. S., *Tradition and the Individual Talent*, Vol. 5,
pages 404–411
Faraday, *Chemical History of a Candle*, Vol. 8, pages 368–439
Galton, "Classification of Human Ability," Vol. 8, pages 227–261
Helmholtz, *On the Conservation of Force*, Vol. 8, pages 451–484
Lamb, *Sanity of True Genius*, Vol. 5, pages 308–310
Poincaré, *Mathematical Creation*, Vol. 9, pages 294–304
Woolf, *Art of Biography*, Vol. 6, pages 186–192

For Faraday's *Experimental Researches in Electricity* in *Great Books of the Western World*, see Vol. 45, pages 261–866

VOLTAIRE, 1694–1778

Micromégas
Vol. 2, pages 241–256

SUGGESTED READINGS IN THE *Syntopicon*

ASTRONOMY, Vol. 2, pages 87–111, especially
Topic 5: Astronomy and cosmology: the theory of the world or universe as reflecting astronomical conceptions
Topic 9: The particular heavenly bodies
MAN, Vol. 3, pages 1–41, especially
Topic 10c: Man as an integral part of the universe: his station in the cosmos
Topic 10d: The finiteness and insufficiency of man: his sense of being dependent and ordered to something beyond himself
Topic 12: Man as an object of laughter and ridicule: comedy and satire
MATHEMATICS, Vol. 3, pages 42–62, especially
Topic 2: The objects of mathematics: number, figure, extension, relation, order
REASONING, Vol. 3, pages 546–568, especially
Topic 3c: Lack of truth in reasoning: sophistical arguments; material fallacies

SOUL, Vol. 3, pages 791–810, especially
Topic 1: Conceptions of soul
Topic 2c: The kinds of soul and the modes of life: vegetative,
sensitive, and rational souls and their special powers

RELATED AUTHORS AND WORKS IN *Great Books of the Western World*

Plato, Vol. 7, *Meno,* pages 180–183; *Republic,* Bk. VI, page 387;
Philebus, page 633
Nicomachus, Vol. 11, *Introduction to Arithmetic,* Bk. I,
pages 812–814
Newton, Vol. 34, *Mathematical Principles of Natural Philosophy,*
Definitions–Laws, pages 5–24; Bk. III, pages 269–372
Swift, Vol. 36, *Gulliver's Travels,* Part I, Chaps. I–VIII, pages 3–38

RELATED AUTHORS AND WORKS IN *Gateway to the Great Books*

Boeke, *Cosmic View,* Vol. 8, pages 600–644
Campbell, *Measurement,* Vol. 9, pages 204–221
Clifford, *Postulates of the Science of Space,* Vol. 9, pages 243–259
Eddington, *Running-Down of the Universe,* Vol. 8, pages 565–580
Epicurus, *Letter to Herodotus,* Vol. 10, pages 216–229
Galileo, *Starry Messenger,* Vol. 8, pages 330–355
Poincaré, *Space,* Vol. 9, pages 265–293
Singer, *Spinoza of Market Street,* Vol. 3, pages 466–480
Whitehead, "On Mathematical Method," Vol. 9, pages 51–67

"English Men and Ideas"
from *Letters on the English*
Vol. 7, pages 332–378
"On the Parliament," pages 332–334
"On the Government," pages 334–338
"On Trade," pages 338–339

SUGGESTED READINGS IN THE *Syntopicon*

LIBERTY, Vol. 2, pages 991–1012, especially
Topic 1h: Civil liberty under diverse forms of government
Topic 2: The issues of civil liberty
MONARCHY, Vol. 3, pages 204–224, especially
Topic 1b: Modifications of absolute monarchy:
other embodiments of the monarchical principle
STATE, Vol. 3, pages 826–865, especially
Topic 5: The social structure or stratification of the state
Topic 9a: Commerce and trade between states: commercial
rivalries and trade agreements; free trade and tariffs

VOLTAIRE, "English Men and Ideas"
continued

WAR AND PEACE, Vol. 3, pages 1010–1037, especially
Topic 2: The kinds of war

WEALTH, Vol. 3, pages 1038–1070, especially
Topic 4: The exchange of wealth or the circulation
of commodities: the processes of commerce or trade

RELATED AUTHORS AND WORKS IN *Great Books of the Western World*

Milton, Vol. 32, *Areopagitica*, pages 384–388
Locke, Vol. 35, *Letter Concerning Toleration*, pages 1–22;
Concerning Civil Government, Chap. V, pages 30–36;
Chap. VII, pages 44–46; Chaps. XII–XIV, pages 59–64;
Chap. XIX, pages 74–81
Smith, Vol. 39, *Wealth of Nations*, Bk. IV, Chap. I, pages 182–192;
Chaps. II–III, pages 197–204; Chap. III, 209–213; Chap. VII,
pages 256–266
Constitution of the United States of America, Vol. 43, pages 11–20
Mill, J. S., Vol. 43, *Representative Government*, Chap. 3,
pages 341–350

RELATED AUTHORS AND WORKS IN *Gateway to the Great Books*

Bacon, *Of Seditions and Troubles*, Vol. 7, pages 12–17; *Of Custom
and Education*, pages 18–19
Carlyle, *Hero as King*, Vol. 6, pages 110–145
Great Documents, *English Bill of Rights*, Vol. 6, pages 409–411;
Declaration of Independence, pages 418–421
Hume, *Of Refinement in the Arts*, Vol. 7, pages 52–61; *Of Money*,
pages 62–71; *Of the Balance of Trade*, pages 72–84; *Of Taxes*,
pages 85–88
Jefferson, *First Inaugural Address*, Vol. 6, pages 518–521
Lincoln, *Address at Cooper Institute*, Vol. 6, pages 737–746

"English Men and Ideas" (continued)

"On Inoculation," Vol. 7, pages 339–343

SUGGESTED READINGS IN THE *Syntopicon*

MEDICINE, Vol. 3, pages 113–132, especially
Topic 3d: The factors in prevention and therapy

RELATED AUTHORS AND WORKS IN *Great Books of the Western World*

Hippocrates, Vol. 10, *Regimen in Acute Diseases*, pages 26–44

"English Men and Ideas" (continued)

"English Men and Ideas" (continued)

VOLTAIRE, "English Men and Ideas"
continued

"On Infinities in Geometry, and Sir Isaac Newton's Chronology,"
Vol. 7, pages 366–371

SUGGESTED READINGS IN THE *Syntopicon*

MECHANICS, Vol. 3, pages 80–112, especially
  Topic 3*d*: Calculus: the measurement of irregular areas
    and variable motions
  Topic 6: Basic concepts of mechanics
SCIENCE, Vol. 3, pages 682–705, especially
  Topic 1*b*(1): The utility of science: the applications
    of experimental knowledge in the mastery
    of nature; machinery and inventions
  Topic 5: Scientific method

RELATED AUTHORS AND WORKS IN *Great Books of the Western World*

Descartes, Vol. 31, *Geometry*, pages 295–353
Newton, Vol. 34, *Mathematical Principles of Natural Philosophy*,
  Bk. I, Sect. I, pages 25–32, Sects. XI–XIII, pages 130–152;
  Bk. II, Sect. II, pages 168–170; Bk. III, pages 276–283,
  291–294; *Optics*, Bks. I–II, pages 379–506
Huygens, Vol. 34, *Treatise on Light*, Chaps. I–III, pages 533–575
Berkeley, Vol. 35, *Principles of Human Knowledge*, Sects. 123–132,
  pages 437–439

RELATED AUTHORS AND WORKS IN *Gateway to the Great Books*

Boeke, *Cosmic View*, Vol. 8, pages 600–644
Clifford, *Postulates of the Science of Space*, Vol. 9, pages 243–259
Eddington, *Running-Down of the Universe*, Vol. 8, pages 565–580
Einstein and Infeld, "Rise and Decline of Classical Physics,"
  Vol. 8, pages 490–560
Faraday, *Chemical History of a Candle*, Vol. 8, pages 368–439
Poincaré, *Space*, Vol. 9, pages 265–293

"English Men and Ideas" (continued)
  "On the Regard That Ought to be Shown to Men of Letters,"
    Vol. 7, pages 371–374
  "On the Royal Society and Other Academies," Vol. 7, pages 374–
    378

"The Philosophy of Common Sense"
from *Philosophical Dictionary*
Vol. 10, pages 453–474

VOLTAIRE, "The Philosophy of Common Sense"
continued

DEMOCRACY, Vol. 2, pages 303–322, especially
  Topic 3c: Comparison of democracy, aristocracy, and monarchy
    with respect to efficiency
DESIRE, Vol. 2, pages 323–344, especially
  Topic 2c: Desire as a cause of action: motivation or purpose;
    voluntariness
LAW, Vol. 2, pages 962–990, especially
  Topic 4e: The relation of natural law to natural rights
    and natural justice
  Topic 5e: The mutability or variability of positive law:
    the maintenance or change of laws
LOVE, Vol. 2, pages 1051–1082, especially
  Topic 2b: Friendly, tender, or altruistic love: fraternal love
  Topic 2b(2): Self-love in relation to the love of others
POETRY, Vol. 3, pages 400–419, especially
  Topic 5a: The aim of poetry to instruct as well as to delight:
    the pretensions or deceptions of the poet as teacher
STATE, Vol. 3, pages 826–865, especially
  Topic 3c: The condition of man in the state of nature
    and in the state of civil society: the state of war
    in relation to the state of nature
  Topic 5c: The classes or sub-groups arising from the division
    of labor or distinctions of birth: the social hierarchy
TRUTH, Vol. 3, pages 915–938, especially
  Topic 3b(3): Truth in reasoning: the truth of premises
    in relation to the truth of conclusions; logical
    validity and truth about reality
TYRANNY, Vol. 3, pages 939–956, especially
  Topic 3: The choice between tyranny or despotism and anarchy

RELATED AUTHORS AND WORKS IN *Great Books of the Western World*

Plato, Vol. 7, *Republic*, Bks. II–III, pages 320–339; *Statesman*,
  pages 598–604
Aristotle, Vol. 9, *Nicomachean Ethics*, Bks. VIII–IX, pages 406–426
Hobbes, Vol. 23, *Leviathan*, Part II, Chap. 19, pages 104–109
Locke, Vol. 35, *Concerning Civil Government*, Chaps. V–IX,
  pages 30–54
Rousseau, Vol. 38, *Discourse on the Origin of Inequality*,
  First Part, pages 338–340, 342–345
Kant, Vol. 42, *Critique of Pure Reason*, pages 211–218

Mill, J. S., Vol. 43, *Representative Government*, Chap. 4, pages 350–355
Marx, Vol. 50, *Capital*, Part IV, Chap. XIV, pages 164–180

RELATED AUTHORS AND WORKS IN *Gateway to the Great Books*

Bacon, *Of Discourse*, Vol. 5, pages 95–96; *Of Friendship*, Vol. 10, pages 353–358; *Of Truth*, pages 346–347
Cicero, *On Friendship*, Vol. 10, pages 286–316
Clifford, *Ethics of Belief*, Vol. 10, pages 16–36
Emerson, *Nature*, Vol. 10, pages 512–524
Erskine, *Moral Obligation to Be Intelligent*, Vol. 10, pages 5–13
Guizot, "Civilization," Vol. 6, pages 302–317
Mill, J. S., *Nature*, Vol. 10, pages 477–508
Sainte-Beuve, *Montaigne*, Vol. 5, pages 76–89
Shelley, *Defence of Poetry*, Vol. 5, pages 216–242

GEORGE WASHINGTON, 1732–1799

Circular Letter to the Governors of All the States on Disbanding the Army
Vol. 6, pages 474–483

SUGGESTED READINGS IN THE *Syntopicon*

DEMOCRACY, Vol. 2, pages 303–322, especially
Topic 7c: The challenge of war and peace: the citizen army
GOVERNMENT, Vol. 2, pages 637–664, especially
Topic 5d: Confederation and federal union: the division of jurisdiction between state and federal governments
WAR AND PEACE, Vol. 3, pages 1010–1037, especially
Topic 6b: Liberty, justice, honor, peace as ends of war

RELATED AUTHORS AND WORKS IN *Great Books of the Western World*

Plato, Vol. 7, *Laws*, Bk. VIII, pages 732–735
Shakespeare, Vol. 27, *King Lear*, Act II, pages 254–262
Locke, Vol. 35, *Concerning Civil Government*, Chap. XVI, pages 65–70; Chap. XIX, pages 76–81
Kant, Vol. 42, *Science of Right*, Second Part, pages 452–458
Articles of Confederation, Vol. 43, pages 5–9
Hamilton, Madison, Jay, Vol. 43, *Federalist*, Nos. 31–34, pages 103–111

WASHINGTON, *Circular Letter*
continued

RELATED AUTHORS AND WORKS IN *Gateway to the Great Books*

Adams, "United States in 1800," Vol. 6, pages 322–359
Bacon, *Of Seditions and Troubles*, Vol. 7, pages 12–17
Carlyle, *Hero as King*, Vol. 6, pages 110–145
Hawthorne, *Sketch of Abraham Lincoln*, Vol. 6, pages 168–171
Jefferson, "Biographical Sketches," Vol. 6, pages 522–528
Lincoln, *Second Inaugural Address*, Vol. 6, pages 760–761; *Last Public Address*, pages 762–765
Paine, "Call to Patriots—December 23, 1776," Vol. 6, pages 461–468

Farewell Address
Vol. 6, pages 484–497

SUGGESTED READINGS IN THE *Syntopicon*

DEMOCRACY, Vol. 2, pages 303–322, especially
　Topic 4c: The infirmities of democracy in practice and the reforms or remedies for these defects
DUTY, Vol. 2, pages 358–375, especially
　Topic 10: Political obligation: cares, functions, loyalties
GOVERNMENT, Vol. 2, pages 637–664, especially
　Topic 5a: Foreign policy: the making of treaties; the conduct of war and peace
STATE, Vol. 3, pages 826–865, especially
　Topic 3e: Love and justice as the bond of men in states: friendship and patriotism

RELATED AUTHORS AND WORKS IN *Great Books of the Western World*

Plato, Vol. 7, *Republic*, Bk. IV, pages 346–356
Shakespeare, Vol. 26, *King Richard II*, pages 320–351
Swift, Vol. 36, *Gulliver's Travels*, Part I, pages 3–42
Montesquieu, Vol. 38, *Spirit of Laws*, Bk. XII, Chaps. 19–22, pages 92–93
Hamilton, Madison, Jay, Vol. 43, *Federalist*, Nos. 49–50, pages 159–162
Mill, J. S., Vol. 43, *Representative Government*, Chaps. 17–18, pages 428–436

RELATED AUTHORS AND WORKS IN *Gateway to the Great Books*

Adams, "United States in 1800," Vol. 6, pages 322–359
Bacon, *Of Great Place*, Vol. 7, pages 9–11; *Of Seditions and Troubles*, pages 12–17

ALFRED NORTH WHITEHEAD, 1861–1947

"On Mathematical Method"
from *An Introduction to Mathematics*
Vol. 9, pages 51–67

WHITEHEAD, "On Mathematical Method"
continued

PHYSICS, Vol. 3, pages 363–376, especially

Topic 1*b*: The relation of the philosophy of nature
to mathematics: mathematical method
and mathematical principles in natural philosophy

Topic 3: The role of mathematics in the natural sciences:
observation and measurement in relation
to mathematical formulations

QUANTITY, Vol. 3, pages 527–545, especially

Topic 5*c*: The quantity of motion: momentum, velocity,
acceleration

Topic 5*d*: Mass: its relation to weight

Topic 5*e*: Force: its measure and the measure of its effect

UNIVERSAL AND PARTICULAR, Vol. 3, pages 957–974,
especially

Topic 4*c*: The abstraction of universal concepts
from the particulars of sense

RELATED AUTHORS AND WORKS IN *Great Books of the Western World*

Plato, Vol. 7, *Parmenides,* pages 486–511
Archimedes, Vol. 11, *On Floating Bodies,* pages 538–560
Plutarch, Vol. 14, *Marcellus,* pages 252–255
Galileo, Vol. 28, *Dialogues Concerning the Two New Sciences,*
Third Day, pages 197–237
Descartes, Vol. 31, *Geometry,* Second Book, pages 322–331
Newton, Vol. 34, *Mathematical Principles of Natural Philosophy,*
Bk. I, Sects. XI–XIII, pages 130–152; Bk. III, pages 276–282
Swift, Vol. 36, *Gulliver's Travels,* Part III, pages 91–131
Kant, Vol. 42, *Critique of Pure Reason,* Introduction, pages 15–20;
pages 29–33; pages 211–217
Faraday, Vol. 45, *Experimental Researches in Electricity,*
pages 298–301, 850–855

RELATED AUTHORS AND WORKS IN *Gateway to the Great Books*

Bernard, *Experimental Considerations Common to Living Things
and Inorganic Bodies,* Vol. 8, pages 266–290
Campbell, *Numerical Laws and the Use of Mathematics
in Science,* Vol. 9, pages 222–238
Einstein and Infeld, "Rise and Decline of Classical Physics,"
Vol. 8, pages 490–560
Euler, *Seven Bridges of Königsberg,* Vol. 9, pages 193–201
Forsyth, *Mathematics, in Life and Thought,* Vol. 9, pages 26–46

Hogben, *Mathematics, the Mirror of Civilization,* Vol. 9,
pages 3–23
Poincaré, *Mathematical Creation,* Vol. 9, pages 294–304
Russell, *Study of Mathematics,* Vol. 9, pages 84–94; *Mathematics
and the Metaphysicians,* pages 95–110

On the Nature of a Calculus
Vol. 9, pages 68–78

SUGGESTED READINGS IN THE *Syntopicon*

MATHEMATICS, Vol. 3, pages 42–62, especially
Topic 1*d*: The ideal of a universal mathesis: the unification
of arithmetic and geometry
Topic 3*d*: Symbols and formulae: the attainment of generality
Topic 4: Mathematical techniques

RELATED AUTHORS AND WORKS IN *Great Books of the Western World*

Descartes, Vol. 31, *Geometry,* pages 295–353
Newton, Vol. 34, *Mathematical Principles of Natural Philosophy,*
Bk. I, Sect. I, pages 25–32; Bk. II, Sect. II, pages 168–170

RELATED AUTHORS AND WORKS IN *Gateway to the Great Books*

Campbell, *Numerical Laws and the Use of Mathematics
in Science,* Vol. 9, pages 222–238
Dantzig, *Fingerprints,* Vol. 9, pages 165–177; *Empty Column,*
pages 178–189
Russell, *Mathematics and the Metaphysicians,* Vol. 9, pages 95–110

WALT WHITMAN, 1819–1892

Preface to Leaves of Grass
Vol. 5, pages 247–259

SUGGESTED READINGS IN THE *Syntopicon*

NATURE, Vol. 3, pages 225–250, especially
Topic 2*a*: Nature and art: the imitation of nature; co-operation
with nature
POETRY, Vol. 3, pages 400–419, especially
Topic 3: The inspiration or genius of the poet: the influence
of the poetic tradition
Topic 5*b*: Poetry contrasted with history and philosophy:
the dispraise and defense of the poet

WHITMAN, *Preface to Leaves of Grass*
continued

Topic 8b: Critical standards and artistic rules with respect
to the language of poetry: the distinction between
prose and verse; the measure of excellence in style

RELATED AUTHORS AND WORKS IN *Great Books of the Western World*

Plato, Vol. 7, *Republic*, Bks. II–III, pages 320–334
Aristotle, Vol. 9, *On Poetics*, pages 681–699
Cervantes, Vol. 29, *Don Quixote*, Preface, pages xi–xiii; Second
Part, Chap. 16, pages 251–252
Bacon, Vol. 30, *Advancement of Learning*, Second Book,
pages 32–39
Fielding, Vol. 37, *Tom Jones*, Bk. II, Chap. 1, pages 19–20; Bk. V,
Chap. 1, pages 73–75; Bk. VIII, Chap. 1, pages 152–155;
Bk. IX, Chap. 1, pages 189–191; Bk. XII, Chap. 1, pages 246–247;
Bk. XIII, Chap. 1, pages 273–274
Kant, Vol. 42, *Critique of Judgement*, First Part, Sect. I,
pages 521–528
Goethe, Vol. 47, *Faust*, Prelude on the Stage, pages 2–6
James, W., Vol. 53, *Principles of Psychology*, Chap. XXII,
pages 686–689

RELATED AUTHORS AND WORKS IN *Gateway to the Great Books*

Adams, "United States in 1800," Vol. 6, pages 322–359
Arnold, *Study of Poetry*, Vol. 5, pages 19–41; *Sweetness and Light*,
pages 42–61
Bacon, *Of Death*, Vol. 10, pages 348–349
Crèvecoeur, "Making of Americans," Vol. 6, pages 546–559
Eliot, T. S., *Tradition and the Individual Talent*, Vol. 5,
pages 404–411
Lamb, *Sanity of True Genius*, Vol. 5, pages 308–310
Schiller, *On Simple and Sentimental Poetry*, Vol. 5, pages 155–211
Shelley, *Defence of Poetry*, Vol. 5, pages 216–242
Tocqueville, "Observations on American Life and Government,"
Vol. 6, pages 564–690

Death of Abraham Lincoln
Vol. 6, pages 174–183

SUGGESTED READINGS IN THE *Syntopicon*

DEMOCRACY, Vol. 2, pages 303–322, especially
Topic 4: The praise of democracy: the ideal state

HISTORY, Vol. 2, pages 711–727, especially
Topic 4a(4): The role of the individual in history: the great man, hero, or leader
HONOR, Vol. 2, pages 728–748, especially
Topic 5d: The estimation of the role of the hero in history
LIFE AND DEATH, Vol. 2, pages 1013–1034, especially
Topic 7: The causes and occurrence of death: the transition from life to death
WAR AND PEACE, Vol. 3, pages 1010–1037, especially
Topic 4b: The factors responsible for civil strife

RELATED AUTHORS AND WORKS IN *Great Books of the Western World*

Plato, Vol. 7, *Phaedo*, pages 250–251
Plutarch, Vol. 14, *Caesar*, pages 577–604
Shakespeare, Vol. 27, *King Lear*, pages 244–283; *Antony and Cleopatra*, pages 311–350; *Coriolanus*, pages 351–392
Hamilton, Madison, Jay, Vol. 43, *Federalist*, Nos. 9–10, pages 47–53
Tolstoy, Vol. 51, *War and Peace*, Second Epilogue, pages 675–696

RELATED AUTHORS AND WORKS IN *Gateway to the Great Books*

Bacon, *Of Seditions and Troubles*, Vol. 7, pages 12–17; *Of Death*, Vol. 10, pages 348–349
Browne, "Immortality," Vol. 10, pages 575–580
Carlyle, *Hero as King*, Vol. 6, pages 110–145
Cicero, *On Old Age*, Vol. 10, pages 317–343
Hawthorne, *Sketch of Abraham Lincoln*, Vol. 6, pages 168–171
Lincoln, *Address at Cooper Institute*, Vol. 6, pages 737–746; *First Inaugural Address*, pages 747–755; *Letter to Horace Greeley*, pages 756–757; *Meditation on the Divine Will*, page 758; *Gettysburg Address*, page 759; *Second Inaugural Address*, pages 760–761; *Last Public Address*, pages 762–765
Tacitus, *Life of Gnaeus Julius Agricola*, Vol. 6, pages 274–298
Thoreau, *Plea for Captain John Brown*, Vol. 6, pages 714–732
Tolstoy, *Death of Ivan Ilyitch*, Vol. 3, pages 646–699
Woolf, *Art of Biography*, Vol. 6, pages 186–192

OSCAR WILDE, 1854–1900

The Happy Prince
Vol. 2, pages 261–268

SUGGESTED READINGS IN THE *Syntopicon*

LOVE, Vol. 2, pages 1051–1082, especially
   Topic 3d: The heroism of friendship and the sacrifices of love
   Topic 5b(1): The precepts of charity: the law of love
WEALTH, Vol. 3, pages 1038–1070, especially
   Topic 10e(1): Almsgiving to the needy and the impoverished

RELATED AUTHORS AND WORKS IN *Great Books of the Western World*

Homer, Vol. 4, *Iliad*, Bks. XXIII–XXIV, pages 161–179
Sophocles, Vol. 5, *Antigone*, pages 131–142
Euripides, Vol. 5, *Alcestis*, pages 237–247
Augustine, Vol. 18, *Confessions*, Bk. IX, pages 61–71
Aquinas, Vol. 20, *Summa Theologica*, Part II–II, Q 23,
   pages 482–489
Chaucer, Vol. 22, *Canterbury Tales*, Tale of Melibeus,
   pages 426–432
Montaigne, Vol. 25, *Of Three Good Women*, pages 358–362
Milton, Vol. 32, *Paradise Lost*, Bk. III, pages 135–151
Pascal, Vol. 33, *Pensées*, Sect. X, pages 294–295

RELATED AUTHORS AND WORKS IN *Gateway to the Great Books*

Bacon, *Of Love*, Vol. 10, pages 351–352; *Of Friendship*,
   pages 353–358
Balzac, *Passion in the Desert*, Vol. 3, pages 436–447
Bunin, *Gentleman from San Francisco*, Vol. 3, pages 102–123
Chekhov, *Darling*, Vol. 3, pages 452–462
Dinesen, *Sorrow-Acre*, Vol. 3, pages 615–641
Flaubert, *Legend of St. Julian the Hospitaller*, Vol. 3,
   pages 371–392
Gogol, *Overcoat*, Vol. 2, pages 452–478
Kipling, *Mowgli's Brothers*, Vol. 2, pages 126–141
Lamb, *Dream Children*, Vol. 5, pages 304–307
Lawrence, *Rocking-Horse Winner*, Vol. 3, pages 512–525
Tolstoy, *Three Hermits*, Vol. 3, pages 700–706; *What Men Live By*,
   pages 707–727

FRIEDRICH WÖHLER, 1800–1882

On the Artificial Production of Urea
Vol. 8, pages 312–314

SUGGESTED READINGS IN THE *Syntopicon*

ANIMAL, Vol. 2, pages 19–49, especially
Topic 1a: Characteristics of animal life: the animal soul
Topic 1e: The conception of the animal as a machine
or automaton

ELEMENT, Vol. 2, pages 400–412, especially
Topic 3c: The mutability of the elements: their transmutation
Topic 3d: Combinations of the elements: compounds
and mixtures

LIFE AND DEATH, Vol. 2, pages 1013–1034, especially
Topic 1: The nature and cause of life: the soul as the principle
of life in organic bodies
Topic 2: Continuity or discontinuity between living
and non-living things: comparison of vital powers
and activities with the potentialities and motions
of inert bodies

MECHANICS, Vol. 3, pages 80–112, especially
Topic 4b: The explanation of qualities and qualitative change
in terms of quantity and motion
Topic 4c: The mechanistic account of the phenomena of life

RELATED AUTHORS AND WORKS IN *Great Books of the Western World*

Aristotle, Vol. 8, *On the Soul*, Bk. II, pages 642–644
Lucretius, Vol. 12, *On the Nature of Things*, Bk. III, pages 31–41
Descartes, Vol. 31, *Discourse on Method*, Part V, pages 56–60
Lavoisier, Vol. 45, *Elements of Chemistry*, First Part, Chaps.
V–XVII, pages 22–52; Third Part, Chaps. VIII–IX, pages
117–128

RELATED AUTHORS AND WORKS IN *Gateway to the Great Books*

Bernard, *Experimental Considerations Common to Living Things
and Inorganic Bodies*, Vol. 8, pages 266–290
Curie, *Discovery of Radium*, Vol. 8, pages 32–42
Faraday, *Chemical History of a Candle*, Vol. 8, pages 368–439
Mendeleev, "Genesis of a Law of Nature," Vol. 8, pages 442–446

VIRGINIA WOOLF, 1882–1941

How Should One Read a Book?
Vol. 5, pages 5–14

SUGGESTED READINGS IN THE *Syntopicon*

ART, Vol. 2, pages 64–86, especially
    Topic 7a: Art as a source of pleasure or delight
    Topic 7b: The judgment of excellence in art
BEAUTY, Vol. 2, pages 112–125, especially
    Topic 5: Judgments of beauty: the objective and the subjective
        in aesthetic judgments or judgments of taste
MIND, Vol. 3, pages 171–203, especially
    Topic 1e(2): The relation of judgment to pleasure
        and displeasure: its application in the realm
        of art; aesthetic finality

RELATED AUTHORS AND WORKS IN *Great Books of the Western World*

   Plato, Vol. 7, *Phaedrus,* pages 130–141; *Republic,* Bks. II–III,
        pages 320–334
   Rabelais, Vol. 24, *Gargantua and Pantagruel,* Bk. I, Author's
        Prologue, pages 1–3
   Cervantes, Vol. 29, *Don Quixote,* First Part, Chap. 32, pages
        117–120; Chaps. 47–50, pages 184–192
   Pascal, Vol. 33, *Pensées,* Sect. I, page 176; Sect. VI, page 238
   Fielding, Vol. 37, *Tom Jones,* Bk. V, Chap. 1, pages 73–75; Bk. X,
        Chap. 1, pages 204–205; Bk. XI, Chap. 1, pages 223–225
   Kant, Vol. 42, *Critique of Judgement,* Introduction–First Part,
        pages 463–549

RELATED AUTHORS AND WORKS IN *Gateway to the Great Books*

   Arnold, *Study of Poetry,* Vol. 5, pages 19–41
   Bacon, *Of Beauty,* Vol. 5, page 94
   Eliot, T. S., *Dante,* Vol. 5, pages 371–403; *Tradition
        and the Individual Talent,* pages 404–411
   Hazlitt, *My First Acquaintance with Poets,* Vol. 5, pages 264–279
   Hume, *Of the Standard of Taste,* Vol. 5, pages 103–119;
        Of the Study of History, Vol. 7, pages 89–92
   Johnson, *Preface to Shakespeare,* Vol. 5, pages 316–353
   Lucian, *Way to Write History,* Vol. 6, pages 387–406
   Schopenhauer, *On the Comparative Place of Interest and Beauty
        in Works of Art,* Vol. 5, pages 143–150; *On Education,*
        Vol. 7, pages 197–203
   Shelley, *Defence of Poetry,* Vol. 5, pages 216–242

The Art of Biography
Vol. 6, pages 186–192

SUGGESTED READINGS IN THE *Syntopicon*

MEMORY AND IMAGINATION, Vol. 3, pages 133–157,
  especially
  Topic 5*a*: The distinction between reproductive and creative
    imagination: the representative image
    and the imaginative construct
TRUTH, Vol. 3, pages 915–938, especially
  Topic 4*b*: Truth in science and poetry: the truth of fact
    and the truth of fiction

RELATED AUTHORS AND WORKS IN *Great Books of the Western World*

Plutarch, Vol. 14, *Lives of the Noble Grecians and Romans*
Montaigne, Vol. 25, Author to the Reader, page 1; *Of Books,*
  pages 199–200; *Of Repentance,* pages 388–389
Bacon, Vol. 30, *Advancement of Learning,* Second Book,
  pages 34–36
Fielding, Vol. 37, *Tom Jones,* Bk. II, Chap. 1, pages 19–20; Bk. VII,
  Chap. 1, pages 121–123; Bk. VIII, Chap. 1, pages 152–155
Boswell, Vol. 44, *Life of Samuel Johnson,* pages 2–4

RELATED AUTHORS AND WORKS IN *Gateway to the Great Books*

Curie, *Discovery of Radium,* Vol. 8, pages 32–42
Darwin, *Autobiography,* Vol. 8, pages 47–93
De Quincey, *Literature of Knowledge and Literature of Power,*
  Vol. 5, pages 358–361
Emerson, *Thoreau,* Vol. 6, pages 150–165
Hawthorne, *Sketch of Abraham Lincoln,* Vol. 6, pages 168–171
Hazlitt, *On Swift,* Vol. 5, pages 280–283
Jefferson, "Biographical Sketches," Vol. 6, pages 522–528
Lucian, *Way to Write History,* Vol. 6, pages 387–406
Mill, J. S., "Childhood and Youth," Vol. 6, pages 5–47
Tacitus, *Life of Gnaeus Julius Agricola,* Vol. 6, pages 274–298
Tyndall, "Michael Faraday," Vol. 8, pages 8–28
Whitman, *Death of Abraham Lincoln,* Vol. 6, pages 174–183
Xenophon, "Character of Socrates," Vol. 6, pages 223–226

XENOPHON, *c.* 430–*c.* 355 B.C.

"The March to the Sea"
from *The Persian Expedition*
Vol. 6, pages 196–222

SUGGESTED READINGS IN THE *Syntopicon*

ART, Vol. 2, pages 64–86, especially
Topic 9c: The arts of war
COURAGE, Vol. 2, pages 252–267, especially
Topic 7c: Courage in war
WAR AND PEACE, Vol. 3, pages 1010–1037, especially
Topic 5a: The moral consequences of war: its effects
on the happiness and virtue of men
and on the welfare of women and children
Topic 10b: Different types of soldiery: mercenaries, volunteers,
conscripts, militia

RELATED AUTHORS AND WORKS IN *Great Books of the Western World*

Homer, Vol. 4, *Iliad*, Bk. XIII, pages 88–97
Herodotus, Vol. 6, *History*, Seventh–Eighth Books, pages 247–287
Thucydides, Vol. 6, *History of the Peloponnesian War*, Seventh
Book, pages 538–563
Plutarch, Vol. 14, *Pericles*, pages 135–140; *Agesilaus*, pages
480–499; *Artaxerxes*, pages 846–858
Shakespeare, Vol. 26, *King Henry V*, pages 532–567
Tolstoy, Vol. 51, *War and Peace*, Bks. 13–14, pages 563–613
Freud, Vol. 54, *Thoughts for the Times on War and Death*,
pages 755–766

RELATED AUTHORS AND WORKS IN *Gateway to the Great Books*

Bacon, *Of Adversity*, Vol. 10, page 350
Long, *Power within Us*, Vol. 6, pages 246–261
Prescott, "Land of Montezuma," Vol. 6, pages 231–243

"The Character of Socrates"
from *Memorabilia*
Vol. 6, pages 223–226

SUGGESTED READINGS IN THE *Syntopicon*

EDUCATION, Vol. 2, pages 376–399, especially
Topic 4a: The possibility and limits of moral education:
knowledge and virtue

Topic 5: The improvement of the mind by teaching
and learning
LIFE AND DEATH, Vol. 2, pages 1013–1034, especially
Topic 8c: The contemplation and fear of death: the attitude
of the hero, the philosopher, the martyr

RELATED AUTHORS AND WORKS IN *Great Books of the Western World*

Aristophanes, Vol. 5, *Clouds*, pages 488–506
Plato, Vol. 7, *Symposium*, pages 149–173; *Meno*, pages 174–190;
Apology, pages 200–212; *Crito*, pages 213–219; *Phaedo*, pages
220–251; *Gorgias*, pages 252–294, especially pages 291–292;
Republic, Bk. VII, pages 388–401
Aristotle, Vol. 9, *Nicomachean Ethics*, Bk. II, Chaps. 1–6, pages
348–352; Bk. III, Chaps. 6–9, pages 361–364; Bk. VI, Chap.
12–Bk. VII, Chap. 5, pages 393–399
Plutarch, Vol. 14, *Alcibiades*, pages 155–174
Montaigne, Vol. 25, *Of the Education of Children*, pages 63–75;
Apology for Raimond de Sebonde, pages 238, 243–244

RELATED AUTHORS AND WORKS IN *Gateway to the Great Books*

Emerson, *Montaigne; or, the Skeptic*, Vol. 10, pages 546–562
Epictetus, *Enchiridion*, Vol. 10, pages 236–254
Epicurus, *Letter to Menoeceus*, Vol. 10, pages 230–233
Erskine, *Moral Obligation to Be Intelligent*, Vol. 10, pages 5–13
Hawthorne, *Sketch of Abraham Lincoln*, Vol. 6, pages 168–171
Hazlitt, *Of Persons One Would Wish to Have Seen*, Vol. 5,
pages 284–295
Plutarch, *Contentment*, Vol. 10, pages 264–281
Thoreau, *Civil Disobedience*, Vol. 6, pages 695–713
Woolf, *Art of Biography*, Vol. 6, pages 186–192

Appendix I

A Plan of Graded Reading

It has been pointed out in the Introduction that the selections included in *Gateway to the Great Books* can serve younger as well as less experienced readers as an induction into the reading of the great books, because the works included in this set are much shorter than those included in *Great Books of the Western World* and are in other respects easier to read.

This does not mean, however, that it is necessary or even desirable to read entirely through the selections in *Gateway to the Great Books* before beginning to read some of the works included in *Great Books of the Western World*. The selections in *Gateway to the Great Books* are all worth reading in and for themselves, but they have additional value as a means of entry into the world of the great books, the great ideas, and the great conversation.

To guide younger or less experienced readers in a progressive course of readings which involves selections from both *Gateway to the Great Books* and *Great Books of the Western World*, the editors have prepared a plan of graded reading, set forth below. It is divided into four parts. Each of these parts consists of two lists: first, A, a list of selections from the Gateway set, and then, B, a list of selections from the Great Books set. The selections from the Gateway set are listed in the order in which they appear in the volumes of that set. The selections from the Great Books set are ordered in the same way by volumes.

The four parts of the plan of graded reading correspond to four levels of reading ability.

Part I recommends materials suitable for 7th- and 8th-grade readers (that is, for twelve- to fourteen-year-olds approximately), and for readers whose limited experience places them on this level of ability, whatever their chronological age. It will be seen that the list of selections from the Gateway set is much longer than the list of readings in the Great Books set. Though short, the latter is important; the reader who hopes to read extensively in the Great Books should start on them as soon as possible. The selections from the Gateway set which are here recommended consist mainly of stories, biographies, autobiographies, and short historical accounts. The list, however, does include at least one selection from each volume in the Gateway set.

Part II lists readings in the Gateway set and in the Great Books set for 9th- and 10th-grade readers. Here the selections from Great Books increase in number, and here we have the longest list of readings in the Gateway set. Though there are still many stories and plays in this list of Gateway readings, the number of nonfiction readings, especially biographical and historical writings, here increases.

In the list of suggested readings in Great Books for 9th- and 10th-grade readers, the following item will be noted: "Cervantes, *Don Quixote* (inspection)." What is intended by this can be explained as follows.

There are certain books of which some knowledge should be had early in one's reading career, but which probably cannot be read entire until one has attained a mature level of reading ability. *Don Quixote* is such a book. The 9th- and 10th-grade reader can read some of Cervantes' long, rambling novel. He can familiarize himself with Cervantes' style and with the general form and tone of the book. Indeed, he *may* read all of it. But it is not expected that he will choose to read all of it until he has attained junior-college reading ability. Thus *Don Quixote* appears in Part II with the notation "inspection," and it reappears in Part IV with no such notation.

The same approach applies to Apollonius' *Conics*, Pascal's *Pensées*, and Newton's *Mathematical Principles of Natural Philosophy*, in Part III, and to Aquinas' *Summa Theologica* and Marx's *Capital* in Part IV. In each case it is expected that the reader will gain some familiarity with the work at the indicated level. He should know what the book is like, what it tries to do, and how it does it. He can put off reading it all the way through until a later date.

The notation "inspection" in the various lists means, then, that the reader should do something like what he does when he "skims" a book. Skimming is an important kind of reading. The reader who skims a book holds it in his hand, hefts it, glances at the table of contents, perhaps reads the preface or introduction, runs quickly through the index, and spends some time reading the text more or less at random. In the process, he makes the acquaintance of the work. He has not read it thoroughly, of course. He does not know everything that is in it. But there are some serious mistakes that he cannot now make about it. Many grievous critical and other errors would be avoided if more readers—even very good ones —knew how to inspect a book intelligently.[1]

Part III lists readings, both in Gateway and in Great Books, for 11th- and 12th-grade readers. Here the A list and the B list are more nearly of the same length, though the Gateway list still predominates. At this level, the reader should have begun to make sizable inroads on the Great Books set. The selections from the Gateway set tend to be longer and somewhat more difficult. Here there are none from Volumes 2 and 4, and a mere scattering of stories from Volume 3. Most of the readings recommended here are taken from Volumes 5–10.

The reader who examines the Great Books list at this level will notice that several items appear on it for the second time. *The History* of Herodotus, for example, appears in Part I and reappears here.

The difference between the two listings is obvious. In the Part I list, it is suggested that the reader should be able to read Bks. I–II of *The History;* in Part III, it is suggested that the reader can, by now, read all of this work.

Similarly, selections from Thucydides' *History of the Peloponnesian War* are suggested in Part II, and the whole work is suggested in Part III. So, too, selections from Swift's *Gulliver's Travels* are suggested in Part I, and the whole in Part III. Many other works in the B lists are similarly treated.

Part IV lists selections for readers at the level of the first two years of college. It should be noted that the selections in the Gateway list are taken largely from Volumes 8 and 9 (Natural Science and Mathematics). It should also be noted that the Great Books list finally predominates, by a wide margin, over the Gateway list. At this level, the reader should be capable of reading major works in *Great Books of the Western World* with relative ease and facility.

The A lists in Parts I–IV all but exhaust the materials in the Gateway set. Nothing in the Gateway set is too difficult to be read with comprehension by college freshmen and sophomores or by readers of equivalent ability. But the B lists do not come anywhere near exhausting the materials in the Great Books set. By the time the reader has attained the level of ability corresponding to the difficulty of the selections in Part IV, he should be able to plan his own further reading or rereading of the works in *Great Books of the Western World;* or he may consult the Ten-Year Reading Plan which is described on pages 87–89 and is set forth on pages 112–131 of Volume I of the Great Books set.

Some young or inexperienced readers may at first be discouraged by what appears to be the formidable character of the lists which constitute

---

[1] The reader should note the difference between the inspection of a book and the first reading described on pp. 31–33.

this plan of graded reading. It is important to remind them, or their parents, that the general tendency in education is toward the reading of more and more difficult materials at younger and younger ages. Humanities courses have for some time been given in the freshman year at many colleges; these include a number of the works listed in Part IV. More recently, there has been a movement to upgrade the high school, to inject into its curriculum, both in the humanities and in the sciences, materials which were formerly considered appropriate only at the college level. In recent years, a cry has been raised against the paucity, even the vacuity, of high school curriculums. One response has been the development of the "junior great books movement" at the high school and even at the elementary school level.

The following plan of graded reading takes these tendencies into account. If it is not true now that a substantial number of the Gateway selections are required at the secondary-school level, it will probably be so within a decade. And there is no doubt that the reading of the great books is increasing both in college and after it. It may never happen that these books will be read by everybody. But it will become more and more widely recognized that a man is not educated unless he has read them.

PART I
Suggested Readings for the 7th and 8th Grades

A. *Gateway to the Great Books*

VOLUME 2 DEFOE, *Robinson Crusoe*, pages 5–121
HEMINGWAY, *The Killers*, pages 169–177
HUGO, "The Battle with the Cannon," pages 146–154
KIPLING, *Mowgli's Brothers*, pages 126–141
MAUPASSANT, *Two Friends*, pages 159–164
POE, *The Tell-Tale Heart*, pages 273–277; *The Masque of the Red Death*, pages 278–283
SCOTT, *The Two Drovers*, pages 182–205
STEVENSON, *The Strange Case of Dr. Jekyll and Mr. Hyde*, pages 288–341
TWAIN, *The Man That Corrupted Hadleyburg*, pages 346–386
WILDE, *The Happy Prince*, pages 261–268

VOLUME 3 CRANE, *The Open Boat*, pages 5–26
FLAUBERT, *The Legend of St. Julian the Hospitaller*, pages 371–392
LAWRENCE, *The Rocking-Horse Winner*, pages 512–525
MELVILLE, *Billy Budd*, pages 31–98

KASNER AND NEWMAN, *New Names for Old*, pages 121–136; *Beyond the Googol*, pages 137–162

VOLUME 10 ERSKINE, *The Moral Obligation to Be Intelligent*, pages 5–13

B. Great Books of the Western World

Bible, Genesis; Proverbs; Luke
HOMER, Vol. 4, *The Odyssey*, pages 183–322
HERODOTUS, Vol. 6, *History*, Bks. I–II, pages 1–88
PLATO, Vol. 7, *Meno*, pages 174–190; *Republic*, Bk. I, pages 295–310; Bks. VI–VII, pages 373–401
ARISTOTLE, Vol. 9, *Politics*, Bk. I, pages 445–455
EUCLID, Vol. 11, *Elements*, Bk. I, pages 1–29
VIRGIL, Vol. 13, *The Aeneid*, Bks. II–III, pages 124–166
SHAKESPEARE, Vol. 26, *The Taming of the Shrew*, pages 199–228; *Julius Caesar*, pages 568–596; Vol. 27, *The Tempest*, pages 524–548
SWIFT, Vol. 36, *Gulliver's Travels*, Parts I–II, pages 1–87
American State Papers, Vol. 43, pages 1–20

PART II
Suggested Readings for the 9th and 10th Grades

A. Gateway to the Great Books

VOLUME 2 ANDERSON, *I'm a Fool*, pages 511–520
ANONYMOUS, *Aucassin and Nicolette*, pages 523–551
BUTLER, "Customs and Opinions of the Erewhonians," pages 483–506
CONRAD, *Youth*, pages 210–236
DICKENS, "A Full and Faithful Report of the Memorable Trial of Bardell against Pickwick," pages 391–448
GOGOL, *The Overcoat*, pages 452–478
VOLTAIRE, *Micromégas*, pages 241–256

VOLUME 3 APULEIUS, "Cupid and Psyche," pages 197–212
BALZAC, *A Passion in the Desert*, pages 436–447
CHEKHOV, *The Darling*, pages 452–462
DOSTOEVSKY, *White Nights*, pages 276–319
ELIOT, G., *The Lifted Veil*, pages 157–193
GALSWORTHY, *The Apple-Tree*, pages 323–367

HAZLITT, *On the Feeling of Immortality in Youth,* pages 565–570

PATER, "The Art of Life," pages 258–261

B. *Great Books of the Western World*

Bible, Psalms; Ecclesiastes; Matthew; Acts

HOMER, Vol. 4, *The Iliad,* pages 1–179

SOPHOCLES, Vol. 5, *Antigone,* pages 131–142

EURIPIDES, Vol. 5, *Alcestis,* pages 237–247

ARISTOPHANES, Vol. 5, *The Clouds,* pages 488–506

THUCYDIDES, Vol. 6, *The History of the Peloponnesian War,* Bks. I–II, pages 349–416; Bk. V, pages 482–508

PLATO, Vol. 7, *Apology,* pages 200–212; *Crito,* pages 213–219; *Phaedo,* pages 220–251

ARISTOTLE, Vol. 9, *Nicomachean Ethics,* Bk. I, pages 339–348

HIPPOCRATES, Vol. 10, *The Oath,* page xiii

EUCLID, Vol. 11, *Elements,* Bks. II–V, pages 30–98

ARCHIMEDES, Vol. 11, *The Sand-Reckoner,* pages 520–526

VIRGIL, Vol. 13, *The Aeneid,* pages 103–379

PLUTARCH, Vol. 14, *Theseus,* pages 1–15; *Themistocles,* pages 88–102; *Pericles,* pages 121–141; *Alexander,* pages 540–576

DANTE, Vol. 21, *The Divine Comedy,* Hell, pages 1–52

CHAUCER, Vol. 22, *The Canterbury Tales,* Prologue, pages 159–174

MONTAIGNE, Vol. 25, *To the Reader,* page ix; *Of Idleness,* pages 14–15; *Of the Education of Children,* pages 62–80; *Of Cannibals,* pages 91–98; *Of Democritus and Heraclitus,* pages 145–147; *Of the Inconstancy of Our Actions,* pages 159–162; *Of Giving the Lie,* pages 322–324; *Of Repentance,* pages 388–395; *Of Experience,* pages 516–543

SHAKESPEARE, Vol. 26, *The Merchant of Venice,* pages 406–433; Vol. 27, *Hamlet,* pages 29–72; *Macbeth,* pages 284–310

CERVANTES, Vol. 29, *Don Quixote* (inspection)

BACON, Vol. 30, *New Atlantis,* pages 199–214

MILTON, Vol. 32, *Paradise Lost,* pages 93–333

LOCKE, Vol. 35, *Concerning Civil Government,* pages 25–81

FIELDING, Vol. 37, *Tom Jones*

SMITH, Vol. 39, *The Wealth of Nations,* Introduction and Bk. I, pages 1–116

The Federalist, Vol. 43, Nos. 1–10, pages 29–53; No. 15, pages 62–66; No. 31, pages 103–105; No. 47, pages 153–156; No. 51, pages 162–165; Nos. 68–71, pages 205–216

MELVILLE, Vol. 48, *Moby Dick*

PART III
Suggested Readings for the 11th and 12th Grades

A. *Gateway to the Great Books*

VOLUME 3 BUNIN, *The Gentleman from San Francisco,* pages 102–123
DINESEN, *Sorrow-Acre,* pages 615–641
FITZGERALD, *The Diamond as Big as the Ritz,* pages 397–431
JAMES, H., *The Pupil,* pages 530–568
MANN, *Mario and the Magician,* pages 573–610
SINGER, *The Spinoza of Market Street,* pages 466–480
TOLSTOY, *The Death of Ivan Ilyitch,* pages 646–699
TURGENEV, *First Love,* pages 217–271

VOLUME 5 ELIOT, T. S., *Tradition and the Individual Talent,* pages 404–411
HAZLITT, *On Swift,* pages 280–283
HUME, *Of the Standard of Taste,* pages 103–119
SAINTE-BEUVE, *Montaigne,* pages 76–89
SCHOPENHAUER, *On Style,* pages 124–136
SHELLEY, *A Defence of Poetry,* pages 216–242

VOLUME 6 BURY, *Herodotus,* pages 364–383
GUIZOT, "Civilization," pages 302–317
THOREAU, *Civil Disobedience,* pages 695–713
TOCQUEVILLE, "Observations on American Life and Government," pages 564–690

VOLUME 7 CALHOUN, "The Concurrent Majority," pages 276–290
HUME, *Of Refinement in the Arts,* pages 52–61; *Of Money,* pages 62–71; *Of the Balance of Trade,* pages 72–84; *Of Taxes,* pages 85–88
JAMES, W., *On a Certain Blindness in Human Beings,* pages 141–156
MACAULAY, *Machiavelli,* pages 295–329
MALTHUS, "The Principle of Population," pages 502–530
ROUSSEAU, *A Lasting Peace through the Federation of Europe,* pages 405–436
RUSKIN, *An Idealist's Arraignment of the Age,* pages 126–136
VOLTAIRE, "English Men and Ideas," pages 332–378

VOLUME 8 CAMPANELLA, "Arguments for and against Galileo," pages 359–364

B. Great Books of the Western World

PART IV
Suggested Readings for College Freshmen and Sophomores

A. *Gateway to the Great Books*

B. *Great Books of the Western World*

HUME, Vol. 35, *An Enquiry Concerning Human Understanding*, pages 450–509

ROUSSEAU, Vol. 38, *A Discourse on the Origin of Inequality Among Men*, pages 323–366; *The Social Contract*, pages 387–439

SMITH, Vol. 39, *The Wealth of Nations*

GIBBON, Vols. 40–41, *The Decline and Fall of the Roman Empire*

MILL, J. S., Vol. 43, *On Liberty*, pages 267–323

DARWIN, Vol. 49, *The Origin of Species*, pages 1–251; *The Descent of Man*, pages 253–600

MARX, Vol. 50, *Capital* (inspection)

TOLSTOY, Vol. 51, *War and Peace*

DOSTOEVSKY, Vol. 52, *The Brothers Karamazov*

FREUD, Vol. 54, *The Interpretation of Dreams*, pages 135–387

Appendix II

Recommended Novels

Gateway to the Great Books includes no complete novels, though it does contain excerpts from some, such as Robinson Crusoe and The Pickwick Papers. In a ten-volume set novels cannot be adequately accommodated; and if they were, other kinds of writing could not be. The decision to exclude novels does not mean, however, that it is the editors' opinion that novels should not be read. On the contrary, the editors believe that a good novel can not only be a rich experience but also constitutes an essential link in the tradition of Western thought. (Seven major novels are included in Great Books of the Western World: Cervantes' Don Quixote, Swift's Gulliver's Travels, Sterne's Tristram Shandy, Fielding's Tom Jones, Melville's Moby Dick, Tolstoy's War and Peace, and Dostoevsky's The Brothers Karamazov.) To the end that younger readers and readers of less than mature experience may make their way through the vast number of such books that are available, a list of some one hundred recommended novels follows.

The list might, of course, have been shorter or much longer. It is not claimed that all the novels on it are great works of the imagination, although all are good—excellent examples of their kind—and all can be learned from and enjoyed. A list of incontestably great novels (excluding those already in Great Books of the Western World) might be very short indeed. The list could have been much longer, too. It was the policy of the editors to include only one novel by each author (though a few authors are represented by more than one work). The list could have been doubled in length by adding other works of authors who already appear on it; and certain authors and works which seem to be quite inappropriate for younger readers do not appear and might have been included. In the end, any such list must be more or less arbitrary. It is believed, however, that the present one provides a good sampling of the available material.

The list includes novels appropriate for the different age levels for which Gateway was planned. There are novels that can be read with ease by readers in the 7th and 8th grade (see A Plan of Graded Reading, pp. 353–355), and novels that will demand the most careful attention of readers in the first two years of college. No attempt is made here to grade the novels or to indicate which novels should be read at what level. It will be evident, however, that certain works, like *Little Women, Alice in Wonderland, Huckleberry Finn, A Tale of Two Cities,* and *The Yearling,* can be enjoyed by younger readers, while certain others, such as Camus' *The Stranger,* Diderot's *Rameau's Nephew,* Joyce's *Dubliners,* Kafka's *The Trial* and *The Castle,* and Virginia Woolf's *To the Lighthouse,* are appropriate for more mature readers. Some of the novels in the latter group are, indeed, not often found in lists for readers of school age. However, good readers *can* read them, and all readers should know of their existence.

Included in the list are a few works which are ordinarily read only by specialists in the literatures of which they are leading examples. Among such novels might be mentioned Johnson's *Rasselas,* Mme. de Lafayette's *The Princess of Cleves,* and *The Saga of Burnt Njal.* These three are all fascinating books, however, if a little effort is made to accept and understand the special problems or intentions of the authors. The editors believe that Gateway readers, especially after they have become acquainted with the set, should be able to realize that the imaginative works of other ages and places can be as relevant to their own lives as the latest novel on the most familiar subject.

The list also includes some books which are not obviously in the novel form, such as *The Song of Roland* (originally a verse epic), *A Thousand and One Nights* (a collection of tales by numerous authors on many themes, gathered over hundreds of years), *Dubliners* (a collection of stories by one author and more or less on one theme), *Rasselas* (a philosophical tale), and *Hadrian's Memoirs* (the imaginary diary of a Roman emperor). The comprehensive and final definition of the word "novel" has not yet been given, and the editors make no apology for the inclusion of some rather surprising items.

Most, if not all, of the books on this list are in print, and many have been published in inexpensive, paper-bound editions. A good bookstore will usually be able to supply copies of any of these books, but if a good bookstore is not available (as is, unfortunately, too often true), the reader may consult the useful *Paperbound Books in Print.* This work, a new edition of which appears four times a year, may be consulted in a library or ordered directly from the publishers, R. R. Bowker & Co., 62 West 45th Street, New York 36, N.Y.

The novels are listed alphabetically by author, with the date of first publication after the title.

ALAIN-FOURNIER (real name Henri Alban Fournier), *The Wanderer*, 1913
ALCOTT, LOUISA MAY, *Little Women*, 1868
AMIS, KINGSLEY, *Lucky Jim*, 1954
ANONYMOUS, *The Arabian Nights*, 8th to 15th Century
———, *Burnt Njal*, tr. G. W. Dasent, 12th Century
———, *The Nibelungenlied*, c. 1200
———, *The Song of Roland*, tr. A. S. Way, c. 800
———, *The Romance of Tristan and Iseult*, tr. H. Belloc and P. Rosenfeld, 1210
AUSTEN, JANE, *Pride and Prejudice*, 1813
———, *Emma*, 1815
BAKER, DOROTHY, *Young Man with a Horn*, 1938
BALZAC, HONORÉ DE, *Eugénie Grandet*, 1833
———, *Old Goriot*, 1835
BELLAMY, EDWARD, *Looking Backward: 2000–1887*, 1888
BOWEN, ELIZABETH, *The Death of the Heart*, 1938
BRONTË, CHARLOTTE, *Jane Eyre*, 1847
BRONTË, EMILY, *Wuthering Heights*, 1847
BUCK, PEARL, *The Good Earth*, 1931
BUNYAN, JOHN, *The Pilgrim's Progress from This World to the Next*, 1678
BUTLER, SAMUEL, *The Way of All Flesh*, 1903
CAMUS, ALBERT, *The Stranger*, 1942
CARROLL, LEWIS, *Alice's Adventures in Wonderland*, 1865
———, *Through the Looking-Glass*, 1872
CATHER, WILLA, *My Antonia*, 1918
CLARK, WALTER VAN TILBURG, *The Ox-Bow Incident*, 1940
CLEMENS, SAMUEL LANGHORNE ("Mark Twain"), *The Adventures of Huckleberry Finn*, 1884
COLLINS, WILKIE, *The Woman in White*, 1860
CONRAD, JOSEPH, *Heart of Darkness*, 1902
CONSTANT, BENJAMIN, *Adolphe*, 1815
COZZENS, JAMES GOULD, *Guard of Honor*, 1948
CRANE, STEPHEN, *The Red Badge of Courage*, 1895
DICKENS, CHARLES, *David Copperfield*, 1850
———, *A Tale of Two Cities*, 1859
———, *Great Expectations*, 1861
DIDEROT, DENIS, *Rameau's Nephew*, 1785

DOSTOEVSKY, FYODOR, *Crime and Punishment*, 1866
DOYLE, ARTHUR CONAN, *The White Company*, 1891
DREISER, THEODORE, *An American Tragedy*, 1925
DUMAS, ALEXANDRE (père), *The Three Musketeers*, 1844
ELIOT, GEORGE, *Middlemarch*, 1872
FITZGERALD, F. SCOTT, *The Great Gatsby*, 1925
FLAUBERT, GUSTAVE, *Madame Bovary*, 1857
FORESTER, C. S., *Captain Horatio Hornblower*, 1939
FORSTER, E. M., *A Passage to India*, 1924
GALSWORTHY, JOHN, *The Man of Property*, 1906
GIDE, ANDRÉ, *The Counterfeiters*, 1925
GLASGOW, ELLEN, *Vein of Iron*, 1935
GOGOL, NIKOLAI, *Dead Souls*, 1842
GOODRICH, MARCUS, *Delilah*, 1941
GUTHRIE, JR., A. B., *The Big Sky*, 1947
HARDY, THOMAS, *The Return of the Native*, 1878
HASEK, JAROSLAV, *The Good Soldier, Schweik*, 1923
HAWTHORNE, NATHANIEL, *The Scarlet Letter*, 1850
HEMINGWAY, ERNEST, *The Old Man and the Sea*, 1952
HERSEY, JOHN, *A Bell for Adano*, 1944
HUDSON, W. H., *Green Mansions*, 1904
HUGHES, RICHARD, *The Innocent Voyage* (also published as *A High Wind in Jamaica*), 1929
HUGO, VICTOR, *Les Misérables*, 1862
HUXLEY, ALDOUS, *Brave New World*, 1932
JAMES, HENRY, *The American*, 1877
————, *The Portrait of a Lady*, 1881
JOHNSON, SAMUEL, *Rasselas Prince of Abyssinia*, 1759
JOYCE, JAMES, *Dubliners*, 1914
KAFKA, FRANZ, *The Trial*, 1925
————, *The Castle*, 1926
KIPLING, RUDYARD, *Kim*, 1901
LAFAYETTE, MME. DE, *The Princess of Cleves*, 1678
LAWRENCE, D. H., *Sons and Lovers*, 1913
LEWIS, SINCLAIR, *Babbitt*, 1922
LONDON, JACK, *The Sea-Wolf*, 1904
LONGUS, *Daphnis and Chloe*, 4th or 5th century
MCCULLERS, CARSON, *A Member of the Wedding*, 1946
MALORY, THOMAS, *Le Morte d'Arthur*, 1485
MANZONI, ALESSANDRO, *The Betrothed*, 1826
MAUGHAM, W. SOMERSET, *Of Human Bondage*, 1915
MEREDITH, GEORGE, *The Egoist*, 1879
MERIMÉE, PROSPER, *Carmen*, 1847
MITCHELL, MARGARET, *Gone with the Wind*, 1936
MUNTZ, HOPE, *The Golden Warrior*, 1948

ORWELL, GEORGE, *Animal Farm,* 1945
PATON, ALAN, *Cry, The Beloved Country,* 1948
PUSHKIN, ALEXANDER, *The Captain's Daughter,* 1836
RAWLINGS, MARJORIE KINNAN, *The Yearling,* 1938
RENAULT, MARY, *The Last of the Wine,* 1956
SALINGER, J. D., *The Catcher in the Rye,* 1951
SCOTT, WALTER, *The Heart of Midlothian,* 1818
———, *Ivanhoe,* 1820
SHELLEY, MARY WOLLSTONECRAFT, *Frankenstein,* 1818
SMOLLETT, TOBIAS, *The Expedition of Humphry Clinker,* 1770
SNOW, C. P., *The Masters,* 1951
STEINBECK, JOHN, *The Red Pony,* 1937
STENDHAL (Marie Henri Beyle), *The Red and the Black,* 1830
———, *The Charterhouse of Parma,* 1839
STEPHENS, JAMES, *The Crock of Gold,* 1912
STEVENSON, ROBERT LOUIS, *Treasure Island,* 1883
———, *Kidnapped,* 1886
THACKERAY, WILLIAM MAKEPEACE, *Vanity Fair,* 1847–48
TOLSTOY, LEO, *Anna Karenina,* 1875–77
TROLLOPE, ANTHONY, *Barchester Towers,* 1857
TURGENEV, IVAN, *Fathers and Sons,* 1862
VERGA, GIOVANNI, *The House by the Medlar Tree,* 1890
VITTORINI, ELIO, *In Sicily,* 1949
VOLTAIRE, FRANÇOIS MARIE AROUET DE, *Candide,* 1759
WELLS, H. G., *The Time Machine,* 1895
WOLFE, THOMAS, *Look Homeward, Angel,* 1929
WOOLF, VIRGINIA, *To the Lighthouse,* 1927
WOUK, HERMAN, *The Caine Mutiny,* 1951
YOURCENAR, MARGUERITE, *Memoirs of Hadrian,* 1954

Appendix III

Recommended Anthologies
of Poetry

Lyric poems, like novels, do not appear in *Gateway to the Great Books*. The editors felt that by devoting a volume or two to a collection of poems they could do little more than create another anthology, of which a great many are already in existence. However, as before, the decision to exclude poetry from the set does not mean that the editors believe that poetry should not be read. There follows, therefore, a list of representative poetry anthologies which, it is hoped, will be useful to Gateway readers.

This list of anthologies is by no means exhaustive. There are scores, if not hundreds, of anthologies of poetry, and many more might have been listed here. But the following selection is more than ample as an introduction to poetry.

The list is divided into four sections. The first includes anthologies of world poetry, most of which, for obvious reasons, appear in translation. The second includes anthologies mainly or wholly of English and American poetry. The third section includes anthologies of poetry in other languages. There are many more such collections. The fourth and final section includes a few anthologies that provide extensive editorial comment. For the reader with little experience in reading poetry, these might be consulted first.

The anthologies are listed, within groups, alphabetically by title, and where appropriate a short description or comment is added. Publishers are cited to aid the purchaser, but date of first publication is not given, as it is usually irrelevant. Where it is of special interest, it is given in a note.

Some of the anthologies are published both in hard-cover and in paper-bound editions; others, now in hard-cover editions only, will probably appear before long in paperback.

Anthologies of World Poetry

An Anthology of World Poetry, ed. Mark Van Doren. New York: Harcourt, Brace & World, Inc.

A Little Treasury of World Poetry, ed. Hubert Creekmore. New York: Charles Scribner's Sons

The World's Best Poems, ed. Mark Van Doren and Garibaldi M. Lapolla. Cleveland: World Publishing Co.

Anthologies Mainly or Wholly of English and American Poetry

An Anthology of Famous English and American Poetry, ed. William Rose Benet and Conrad Aiken. New York: Modern Library

A Concise Treasury of Great Poems, ed. Louis Untermeyer. New York: Permabooks, Inc.

Fifty Great Poets, ed. Milton Crane. New York: Bantam Books

The Golden Treasury of English Songs and Lyrics, ed. Francis Turner Palgrave. New York: Dolphin Books. This is a reprint of the original (1861) edition of this famous collection. The anthology, with additional selections, has been many times re-issued.

Immortal Poems of the English Language, ed. Oscar Williams. New York: Washington Square Press, Inc.

A Little Treasury of Modern Poetry, ed. Oscar Williams. New York: Charles Scribner's Sons. Williams has edited several other anthologies in the Little Treasury series, all published by Scribners.

Modern American Poetry and *Modern British Poetry*, ed. Louis Untermeyer. New York: Harcourt, Brace & World, Inc. This one-volume edition contains both of Untermeyer's famous anthologies.

The Oxford Book of American Verse, ed. F. O. Matthiessen. New York: Oxford University Press

The Oxford Book of English Verse, ed. Sir Arthur Quiller-Couch. New York: Oxford University Press. This anthology, first published in 1900, has been recently brought up to date by the addition of later poems.

The Pocket Book of Verse, ed. M. E. Speare. New York: Washington Square, Inc.

Six Centuries of Great Poetry, ed. Robert Penn Warren and Albert Erskine. New York: Dell—Laurel Poetry Series

The Viking Portable Poets of the English Language, ed. W. H. Auden and Norman Holmes Pearson, in five volumes: Vol. I, Medieval and Renaissance Poets; Vol. II, Elizabethan and Jacobean Poets; Vol. III, Restoration and Augustan Poets; Vol. IV, Romantic Poets; Vol. V, Victorian and Edwardian Poets. New York: Viking Press

Anthologies of Poetry in Other Languages

Greek Lyric Poetry, tr. Willis Barnstone. New York: Bantam Books

Poems from the Greek Anthology, tr. Dudley Fitts. New York: New Directions Paperbacks

The Latin Poets, ed. Francis R. B. Godolphin. New York: Modern Library

An Anthology of Spanish Poetry from Garciloso to Garcia Lorca, in English translation with Spanish originals, ed. Angel Flores. New York: Doubleday Anchor Books

An Anthology of French Poetry from Nerval to Valéry, in English translation with French originals, ed. Angel Flores. New York: Doubleday Anchor Books

An Anthology of Russian Verse, ed. Avrahm Yarmolinsky. New York: Doubleday Anchor Books

Anthologies with Extensive Editorial Comment

Exploring Poetry, ed. M. L. Rosenthal and A. J. M. Smith. New York: Macmillan Co. This is an introduction to poetry through the analysis of many individual poems.

Introduction to Poetry, ed. Mark Van Doren. New York: Holt, Rinehart & Winston, Inc. This work combines an anthology of English and American poetry with discussion of many poems.

The Poem Itself, ed. Stanley Burnshaw. Cleveland: Meridian Books. This is a collection of original poems in French, German, Spanish, Portuguese and Italian, with translations and extensive comment.

Understanding Poetry, ed. Cleanth Brooks and Robert Penn Warren. New York: Holt, Rinehart & Winston, Inc. This is an anthology of English and American poetry with critical interpretations.

3

GATEWAY TO THE GREAT BOOKS

VOLUME 7	VOLUME 8
BACON	BACON
SWIFT	TYNDALL
HUME	EVE CURIE
PLUTARCH	DARWIN
STEVENSON	FABRE
RUSKIN	EISELEY
WILLIAM JAMES	RACHEL CARSON
SCHOPENHAUER	HALDANE
FARADAY	HUXLEY
BURKE	GALTON
CALHOUN	BERNARD
MACAULAY	PAVLOV
VOLTAIRE	WÖHLER
DANTE	LYELL
ROUSSEAU	GALILEO
KANT	CAMPANELLA
CLAUSEWITZ	FARADAY
MALTHUS	MENDELEEV
❧	HELMHOLTZ